NEW CENTURY
COMMENT

General Editors

RONALD E. CLEMENTS
(Old Testament)

MATTHEW BLACK
(New Testament)

ISAIAH
40-66

THE NEW CENTURY BIBLE COMMENTARIES

EXODUS (J. P. Hyatt)
LEVITICUS AND NUMBERS (N. H. Snaith)*
DEUTERONOMY (A. D. H. Mayes)
JOSHUA, JUDGES, AND RUTH (John Gray)*
EZRA, NEHEMIAH, AND ESTHER (L. H. Brockington)*
JOB (H. H. Rowley)
PSALMS Volumes 1 and 2 (A. A. Anderson)
ISAIAH 1-39 (R. E. Clements)
ISAIAH 40-66 (R. N. Whybray)
EZEKIEL (John W. Wevers)*
THE GOSPEL OF MATTHEW (David Hill)
THE GOSPEL OF MARK (Hugh Anderson)
THE GOSPEL OF LUKE (E. Earle Ellis)
THE GOSPEL OF JOHN (Barnabas Lindars)
THE ACTS OF THE APOSTLES (William Neil)*
ROMANS (Matthew Black)*
1 and 2 CORINTHIANS (F. F. Bruce)
GALATIANS (Donald Guthrie)*
EPHESIANS (C. Leslie Mitton)*
PHILIPPIANS (Ralph P. Martin)
COLOSSIANS AND PHILEMON (Ralph P. Martin)*
1 PETER (Ernest Best)*
THE BOOK OF REVELATION (G. R. Beasley-Murray)

**Not yet available in paperback*
Other titles are in preparation

NEW CENTURY BIBLE COMMENTARY

Based on the Revised Standard Version

ISAIAH 40-66

R. N. WHYBRAY

WM. B. EERDMANS PUBL. CO., GRAND RAPIDS

MARSHALL, MORGAN & SCOTT PUBL. LTD., LONDON

First published 1975 by Marshall, Morgan & Scott, England
Softback edition published 1981

Printed in the United States of America
for
Wm. B. Eerdmans Publishing Company
255 Jefferson Ave. S.E., Grand Rapids, Mich. 49503
and
Marshall, Morgan & Scott
A Pentos company
1 Bath Street, London ECIV 9LB
ISBN 0 551 00896 2

Reprinted, November 1990

Library of Congress Cataloging in Publication Data
Whybray, Roger Norman.
Isaiah 40-66.
(New century Bible commentary)
Reprint of the 1978 ed. published by Oliphants, London.
1. Bible. O.T. Isaiah XL-LXVI — Commentaries.
I. Title. II. Series.
BS1520.W48 1981 224'.107 80-28892
ISBN 0-8028-1884-6 (pbk.)

CONTENTS

ABBREVIATIONS

BIBLICAL

OLD TESTAMENT (*OT*)

Gen.	Jg.	1 Chr.	Ps.	Lam.	Ob.	Hag.
Exod.	Ru.	2 Chr.	Prov.	Ezek.	Jon.	Zech.
Lev.	1 Sam.	Ezr.	Ec.	Dan.	Mic.	Mal.
Num.	2 Sam.	Neh.	Ca.	Hos.	Nah.	
Dt.	1 Kg.	Est.	Isa.	Jl	Hab.	
Jos.	2 Kg.	Job	Jer.	Am.	Zeph.	

APOCRYPHA (*Apoc.*)

1 Esd.	Tob.	Ad. Est.	Sir.	S 3 Ch.	Bel	1 Mac.
2 Esd.	Jdt.	Wis.	Bar.	Sus.	Man.	2 Mac.
			E. Jer.			

NEW TESTAMENT (*NT*)

Mt.	Ac.	Gal.	1 Th.	Tit.	1 Pet.	3 Jn
Mk	Rom.	Eph.	2 Th.	Phm.	2 Pet.	Jude
Lk.	1 C.	Phil.	1 Tim.	Heb.	1 Jn	Rev.
Jn	2 C.	Col.	2 Tim.	Jas.	2 Jn	

DEAD SEA SCROLLS (DSS)

1QIs^a	First Isaiah Scroll
1QIs^b	Second Isaiah Scroll

GENERAL

ANEP	*The Ancient Near East in Pictures Relating to the Old Testament*, edited by J. B. Pritchard, Princeton, 1954
ANET	*Ancient Near Eastern Texts Relating to the Old Testament*, edited by J. B. Pritchard, 2nd edn, Princeton, 1955
Arab.	Arabic
Aram.	Aramaic
AV	*Authorized Version* (King James Version) (1611)

BHS	*Biblia Hebraica Stuttgartensia*, edited by K. Elliger and W. Rudolph, 1968–
BJRL	*The Bulletin of the John Rylands Library*
BWANT	*Beiträge zur Wissenschaft vom Alten und Neuen Testament*
BZAW	*Beihefte zur Zeitschrift für die Alttestamentliche Wissenschaft*
CBQ	*The Catholic Biblical Quarterly*
Diss.	Dissertation
ET	English translation
ExpT	*Expository Times*
FRLANT	*Forschungen zur Religion und Literatur des Alten und Neuen Testaments*
G–K	*Gesenius' Hebrew Grammar as edited and enlarged by E. Kautzsch, revised by A. E. Cowley*, 2nd edn, London, 1910
Heb.	Hebrew
J	The Yahwistic source of the Pentateuch
JB	*The Jerusalem Bible* (1966)
JBL	*The Journal of Biblical Literature*
JNES	*The Journal of Near Eastern Studies*
JSS	*The Journal of Semitic Studies*
JTS	*The Journal of Theological Studies*
LXX	The Greek Septuagint Version
mg.	margin
MS, MSS	manuscript(s)
MT	The Massoretic Text of the Old Testament
NEB	*The New English Bible*
NF	Neue Folge
ns	new series; nouvelle série
P	The Priestly source of the Pentateuch
RB	*Revue Biblique*
RSV	*Revised Standard Version* (*NT*, 1946; *OT*, 1952)
RV	*Revised Version* (*NT*, 1880; *OT*, 1884)
Symm.	The Greek version of Symmachus
Syr.	The Syriac (Peshitta) Version
Targ.	Targum
TLZ	*Theologische Literaturzeitung*
VT	*Vetus Testamentum*
VT Suppl.	*Supplements to Vetus Testamentum*
Vulg.	The Vulgate Version
ZAW	*Zeitschrift für die Alttestamentliche Wissenschaft*

SELECT BIBLIOGRAPHY

Note: This selection of books and articles, though extensive, lists only a minute portion of the literature. In making the choice, emphasis has been placed on older works of abiding importance, commentaries consulted by the author, and recent studies. The wealth of articles dealing with specific points of interpretation remains unrecorded here, although a few of these studies are referred to in the commentary.

COMMENTARIES

A. *Chapters 40–66 (including commentaries on the entire book)*

P.-E. Bonnard, *Le Second Isaïe, son disciple et leurs éditeurs* (*Études Bibliques*), Paris, 1972.

T. K. Cheyne, *The Prophecies of Isaiah*, 5th edn, London, 1889.

F. Delitzsch, *Biblical Commentary on the Prophecies of Isaiah*, vol. 2, Edinburgh, 1890.

B. Duhm, *Das Buch Jesaia* (*Handkommentar zum Alten Testament*), 5th edn, Göttingen, 1968 (reprint of the 4th edn, 1922).

G. Fohrer, *Das Buch Jesaja*, vol. 3 (*Zürcher Bibelkommentare*), Zürich and Stuttgart, 1964.

E. J. Kissane, *The Book of Isaiah*, vol. 2, Dublin, 1943.

E. König, *Das Buch Jesaja*, Gütersloh, 1926.

K. Marti, *Das Buch Jesaja* (*Kurzer Hand-Commentar zum Alten Testament*), Tübingen, 1900.

J. Muilenburg, *Isaiah, Chapters 40–66* (*The Interpreter's Bible*, vol. 5, pp. 381–773), New York and Nashville, 1956.

C. von Orelli, *Der Prophet Jesaja* (*Kurzgefasster Kommentar zu den Heiligen Schriften Alten und Neuen Testamentes*), 3rd edn, Munich, 1904.

A. Schoors, *Jesaja II* (*De Boeken van het Oude Testament*), Roermond, 1973.

J. Skinner, *The Book of the Prophet Isaiah Chapters XL–LXVI* (*Cambridge Bible*), 2nd edn, Cambridge, 1917.

J. D. Smart, *History and Theology in Second Isaiah. A Commentary on Is. 35; 40–66*, London, 1967.

G. A. Smith, *The Book of Isaiah*, vol. 2, 2nd edn, London, 1927.

P. Volz, *Jesaja II* (*Kommentar zum Alten Testament*), Leipzig, 1932.

G. W. Wade, *The Book of the Prophet Isaiah* (*Westminster Commentaries*), London, 1911.

C. Westermann, *Isaiah 40–66* (*Old Testament Library*), London, 1969 (translated from the German edn in *Das Alte Testament Deutsch*, Göttingen, 1966).

B. *Chapters 40–55*

K. Elliger, *Jesaja II* (*Biblischer Kommentar*), Neukirchen-Vluyn, 1970– (complete only to 43:7).
H. Frey, *Das Buch der Weltpolitik Gottes. Kapitel 40–55 des Buches Jesaja* (*Die Botschaft des Alten Testaments*), 6th edn, Stuttgart, 1967.
G. A. F. Knight, *Deutero-Isaiah: A Theological Commentary on Isaiah 40–55*, New York and Nashville, 1965.
J. L. McKenzie, *Second Isaiah. Introduction, Translation and Notes* (*Anchor Bible*), New York, 1968.
C. R. North, *Isaiah 40–55* (*Torch Bible Commentaries*), London, 1952.
C. R. North, *The Second Isaiah*, Oxford, 1964.
L. G. Rignell, *A Study of Isaiah Ch. xl–lv*, Lund, 1956.
U. E. Simon, *A Theology of Salvation: A Commentary on Isaiah xl–lv*, London, 1953.

C. *Chapters 56–66*

D. R. Jones, *Isaiah 56–66 and Joel* (*Torch Bible Commentaries*), London, 1964.
W. Kessler, *Gott geht es um das Ganze. Jesaja lvi–lxvi und xxiv–xxvii* (*Die Botschaft des Alten Testaments*), 2nd edn, Stuttgart, 1967.

SPECIAL STUDIES

A. *Chapters 40–66*

S. H. Blank, *Prophetic Faith in Isaiah*, London, 1958.
L. Glahn and L. Köhler, *Der Prophet der Heimkehr* (*Jesaja xl–lxvi*), Copenhagen and Giessen, 1934.
S. Mowinckel, 'Neuere Forschungen zu Deuterojesaja, Tritojesaja und dem Äbäd-Jahwä-Problem', *Acta Orientalia* (Leiden) 16 (1938), pp. 1–40.
S. Porúbčan, *Il Patto Nuovo in Is. xl–lxvi* (*Analecta Biblica* 8), Rome, 1958.
N. H. Snaith, 'Isaiah 40–66. A Study of the Teaching of the Second Isaiah and its Consequences', *Studies on the Second Part of the Book of Isaiah* (*VT Suppl.* 14), Leiden, 1967, pp. 135–264.
C. C. Torrey, *The Second Isaiah: A New Interpretation*, Edinburgh, 1928.

B. *Chapters 40–55*

B. W. Anderson, 'Exodus Typology in Second Isaiah', *Israel's Prophetic Heritage. Essays in Honor of James Muilenburg*, ed. B. W. Anderson and W. Harrelson, London, 1962, pp. 177–95.
D. Baltzer, *Ezechiel und Deuterojesaja* (*BZAW* 121), Berlin, 1971.
J. Begrich, 'Das priesterliche Heilsorakel,' *ZAW* NF 11 (1934), pp. 81–92 = *Gesammelte Studien zum Alten Testament* (*Theologische Bücherei* 21), Munich, 1964, pp. 252–60.

J. Begrich, *Studien zu Deuterojesaja* (*BWANT* 77), 1938 = *Theologische Bücherei* 20, Munich, 1963.

A. Bentzen, 'On the Ideas of "the Old" and "the New" in Deutero-Isaiah', *Studia Theologica* 1 (1948–9), Lund and Aarhus, pp. 183–7.

P. A. H. de Boer, *Second Isaiah's Message* (*Oudtestamentische Studiën* 11), Leiden, 1956.

W. Caspari, *Lieder und Gottessprüche der Rückwanderer* (*Jesaja 40–55*) (*BZAW* 65), Giessen, 1934.

F. M. Cross, 'The Council of Yahweh in Second Isaiah', *JNES* 12 (1953), pp. 274–7.

K. Elliger, 'Der Begriff "Geschichte" bei Deuterojesaja', *Kleine Schriften zum Alten Testament* (*Theologische Bücherei* 32), Munich, 1966, pp. 199–210.

F. Feldmann, 'Das Frühere und das Neue', *Festschrift Eduard Sachau*, 1912, pp. 162–9.

H. Gressmann, 'Die literarische Analyse Deuterojesajas', *ZAW* 34 (1914), pp. 254–97.

L. Köhler, *Deuterojesaja* (*Jesaja xl–lv*) *stilkritisch untersucht* (*BZAW* 37), Giessen, 1923.

S. Mowinckel, 'Die Komposition des deuterojesajanischen Buches', *ZAW* 49 (1931), pp. 87–112, 242–60.

C. R. North, 'The "Former Things" and the "New Things" in Deutero-Isaiah', *Studies in Old Testament Prophecy Presented to T. H. Robinson*, ed. H. H. Rowley, Edinburgh, 1950, pp. 111–26.

G. von Rad, 'The Theological Problem of the Old Testament Doctrine of Creation', *The Problem of the Hexateuch*, Edinburgh and London, 1966, pp. 131–43 (translated from *BZAW* 66 (1936), pp. 138–47 = *Gesammelte Studien zum Alten Testament* (*Theologische Bücherei* 8), pp. 136–47).

G. von Rad, *The Theology of the Old Testament*, vol. 2, Edinburgh and London, 1965, pp. 248–70 (translated from the German edn of 1960).

A. Schoors, 'Les choses antérieures et les choses nouvelles dans les oracles deutéro-isaïens', *Ephemerides Theologicae Lovanienses* 40 (1964), pp. 19–47.

A. Schoors, *I am God Your Saviour. A Form-Critical Study of the Main Genres in Is. XL–LV* (*VT Suppl.* 24), Leiden, 1973.

S. Smith, *Isaiah Chapters xl–lv: Literary Criticism and History* (*Schweich Lectures*, 1940), London, 1944.

C. Stuhlmueller, *Creative Redemption in Deutero-Isaiah* (*Analecta Biblica* 43), Rome, 1970.

H.-E. von Waldow, *Anlass und Hintergrund der Verkündigung des Deuterojesaja* (Diss. Theol., Bonn), 1953.

H.-E. von Waldow, 'The Message of Deutero-Isaiah', *Interpretation* 22 (1968), pp. 259–87.

C. Westermann, 'Das Heilswort bei Deuterojesaja', *Evangelische Theologie* 24 (1964), pp. 355–73.

C. Westermann, 'Sprache und Struktur der Prophetie Deuterojesajas', *Forschung am Alten Testament* (*Theologische Bücherei* 24), Munich, 1964, pp. 92–170.

W. Zimmerli, 'Le nouvel "exode" dans le message des deux grands prophètes de l'exil', *Maqqel Shâqédh, La branche d'amandier, Hommage à W. Vischer*, Montpellier, 1960, pp. 216–27.

C. *The Ebed-Yahweh Problem*

K. Baltzer, 'Zur formgeschichtlichen Bestimmung der Texte vom Gottesknecht im Deutero-Jesaja-Buch', *Probleme Biblischer Theologie, Gerhard von Rad zum 70. Geburtstag*, ed. H. W. Wolff, Munich, 1971, pp. 27–43.

K. Budde, *Die sogenannten Ebed-Jahwe-Lieder*, Giessen, 1900.

H. S. Cazelles, 'Les poèmes du Serviteur', *Recherches de Science Religieuse* 43 (1955), pp. 5–55.

A. Condamin, 'Le serviteur de Yahvé. Un nouvel argument pour le sens individuel messianique', *RB* ns 5 (1908), pp. 162–81.

J. Coppens, 'Les origines littéraires des Poèmes du Serviteur de Yahvé', *Biblica* 40 (1959), pp. 248–58.

J. Coppens, 'Le serviteur de Yahvé et le fils de l'homme danïélique sont-ils des figures messianiques?', *Miscellanées Bibliques, Ephemerides Theologicae Lovanienses* 39 (1963), pp. 104–13.

J. Coppens, 'Le serviteur de Yahvé. Vers la solution d'un énigme', *Sacra Pagina 1, Bibliotheca Ephemeridum Theologicarum Lovaniensium* 12 (1959), pp. 434–54.

P.-E. Dion, 'Les chants du Serviteur de Yahweh et quelques passages apparentés d'Is 40–55', *Biblica* 51 (1970), pp. 17–38.

G. R. Driver, 'Isaiah 52, 13–53, 12: the Servant of the Lord', *In Memoriam Paul Kahle* (*BZAW* 103), 1968, pp. 90–105.

O. Eissfeldt, 'The Ebed-Yahwe in Isaiah xl–lv in the Light of the Israelite Conceptions of the Community and the Individual, the Ideal and the Real', *ExpT* 44 (1932–3), pp. 261–8 (translated from 'Der Gottesknecht bei Deuterojesaja', *Beiträge zur Religionsgeschichte des Altertums*, Heft 2, Halle, 1933).

O. Eissfeldt, 'Neue Forschung zum "Ebed-Jahwe-Problem" ', *TLZ 68* (1943), cols. 273–80.

F. Giesebrecht, *Der Knecht Jahwes des Deuterojesaia*, Königsberg, 1902.

H. Gressmann, *Der Messias* (*FRLANT* NF 26), Göttingen, 1929.

H. Haag, 'Ebed-Jahwe-Forschung 1948–1958', *Biblische Zeitschrift* NF 3 (1959), pp. 174–204.

O. Kaiser, *Der königliche Knecht* (*FRLANT* NF 52), Göttingen, 1959.
E. Kutsch, *Sein Leiden und Tod—unser Heil. Eine Auslegung von Jesaja 52,13–53,12* (*Biblische Studien* 52), Neukirchen-Vluyn, 1967.
J. Lindblom, *The Servant Songs in Deutero-Isaiah*, Lund, 1951.
S. Mowinckel, *He That Cometh*, Oxford, 1959.
A. Neubauer and S. R. Driver, *The Fifty-Third Chapter of Isaiah According to the Jewish Interpreters*, 2 vols., originally published 1877, reprinted New York, 1969.
C. R. North, 'The Suffering Servant: Current Scandinavian Discussions', *Scottish Journal of Theology* 3 (1950), pp. 363–79.
C. R. North, *The Suffering Servant in Deutero-Isaiah*, London, 1948.
H. M. Orlinsky, 'The So-Called "Servant of the Lord" and "Suffering Servant" in Second Isaiah', *Studies on the Second Part of the Book of Isaiah* (*VT Suppl.* 14), Leiden, 1967, pp. 1–133.
H. H. Rowley, 'The Servant of the Lord in the Light of Three Decades of Criticism', *The Servant of the Lord and Other Essays on the Old Testament*, London, 1952, pp. 1–57.
E. Sellin, *Der Knecht Gottes bei Deuterojesaja*, Leipzig, 1901.
E. Sellin, 'Die Lösung des deuterojesajanischen Gottesknechtsrätsels', *ZAW* 55 (1937), pp. 117–27.
E. Sellin, *Das Rätsel des deuterojesajanischen Buches*, Leipzig, 1908.
E. Sellin, 'Tritojesaja, Deuterojesaja und das Gottesknechtsproblem', *Neue Kirchliche Zeitschrift* 41 (1930), pp. 73–93, 145–73.
A. O. Swartzentruber, *The Servant Songs in Relation to their Context in Deutero-Isaiah* (Diss. Princeton), 1970.

A more extensive bibliography on this problem may be found in the works listed above, especially those by Eissfeldt, Haag, North, and Rowley.

D. *Chapters 56–66*

R. Abramowski, 'Zum literarischen Problem des Tritojesaja', *Theologische Studien und Kritiken* (Berlin), 96–7 (1925), pp. 90–143.
K. Elliger, *Deuterojesaja in seinem Verhältnis zu Tritojesaja* (*BWANT* 63), Stuttgart, 1933.
K. Elliger, *Die Einheit des Tritojesajas* (*BWANT* 45), Stuttgart, 1928.
K. Elliger, 'Der Prophet Tritojesaja', *ZAW* 49 (1931), pp. 112–41.
H. Gressmann, *Über die in Jes lvi–lxvi vorausgesetzten zeitgeschichtlichen Verhältnisse*, Göttingen, 1898.
D. R. Jones, 'The Cessation of Sacrifice After the Destruction of the Temple in 586 B.C.', *JTS* 14 (1963), pp. 12–31.
W. Kessler, 'Zur Auslegung von Jesaja lvi–lxvi', *TLZ* 81 (1956), cols 335–8.
W. Kessler, 'Studien zur religiösen Situation im ersten nachexilischen

Jahrhundert und zur Auslegung von Jes 56–66', *Wissenschaftliche Zeitschrift* (Halle) 6 (1956–7), pp. 41–74.

H.-J. Kraus, 'Die ausgebliebene Endtheophanie. Eine Studie zu Jes 56–66', *ZAW* 78 (1966), pp. 317–32.

D. Michel, 'Zur Eigenart Tritojesajas', *Theologia Viatorum* (Berlin) 10 (1966), pp. 213–30.

H. Odeberg, *Trito-Isaiah (Isaiah lvi–lxvi). A Literary and Linguistic Analysis*, Uppsala, 1931.

K. Pauritsch, *Die neue Gemeinde: Gott sammelt Ausgestossene und Arme* (*Analecta Biblica* 47), Rome, 1971.

E. Sehmsdorf, 'Studien zur Redaktionsgeschichte von Jesaja 56–66', *ZAW* 84 (1972), pp. 517–76.

G. Wallis, 'Gott und seine Gemeinde. Eine Betrachtung zum Trito-jesaja-Buch', *Theologische Zeitschrift* (Basel) 27 (1971), pp. 182–200.

A. Zillessen, ' "Tritojesaja" und Deuterojesaja', *ZAW* 26 (1906), pp. 231–76.

W. Zimmerli, 'Zur Sprache Tritojesajas', *Schweizerische Theologische Umschau* (Berne) 20 (1950), pp. 110–22 = *Gottes Offenbarung. Gesammelte Aufsätze zum Alten Testament* (*Theologische Bücherei* 19), Munich, 1963, pp. 217–33.

INTRODUCTION
to
Isaiah 40–66

A. THE DIVISIONS OF THE BOOK

All but the most conservative scholars now accept the hypothesis put forward by Doederlein in 1775, but already anticipated by Ibn Ezra in the twelfth century, that the prophecies contained in chapters 40–66 of the book of Isaiah are not the words of the eighth-century prophet Isaiah but come from a later time. The further hypothesis of B. Duhm (1892) that chapters 56–66 must equally be distinguished from chapters 40–55 has met with less unanimous agreement, but is nevertheless very widely accepted.

B. DEUTERO-ISAIAH

I. Date

These hypotheses both rest on very firm foundations. To express the matter briefly, chapters 40–66 are unintelligible if interpreted as a product of the eighth century BC, but yield excellent sense if seen against the background of later periods. In the case of chapters 40–55 the occurrences (44 : 28; 45 : 1) of the name Cyrus, which can only refer to the first Persian king of that name, the conqueror of Babylon in 539 BC (or, in theory, to one of his successors) are not, as was suggested quite arbitrarily by Torrey, later additions to the text, but rather pointers to the interpretation of these chapters as a whole; and their authenticity is confirmed by numerous other historical references, notably to Babylon or Chaldea (43 : 14; 47 : 1, 5; 48 : 14, 20) and to the Babylonian gods Bel (Marduk) and Nebo (46 : 1). The way in which the names Jerusalem and Zion are used points to the same historical situation. These words are used in two different senses. On the one hand they often designate not the city of Jerusalem itself but its former population, now exiled from its homeland. When on the other hand they refer to the physical city itself, they refer to it as lying in ruins, though soon to be rebuilt when its exiled citizens return home.

The historical situation indicated by the use of these proper names is confirmed by an abundance of other internal evidence. The remarkable consistency of the teaching and point of view of these chapters has led the majority of modern commentators to agree that they are substantially the work of a single prophet, addressed to a group of his fellow-exiles from Jerusalem who are bitterly complaining of their fate at the hands of the Babylonians who have conquered them and subsequently deported them to Babylonia. These exiles are disposed to reproach their God Yahweh for having abandoned them, and to doubt his willingness, or his ability, to intervene on their behalf and restore their fortunes. The prophet 'Deutero-Isaiah', whose real name is unknown to us, reproaches them for their lack of faith, and tells them that they have deserved their fate. Claiming the status of Yahweh's authorised spokesman, he announces to them something entirely new and unexpected: that they have now been sufficiently punished for their sins, and that the divine intervention of which they are so sceptical is about to take place, and on a dramatic scale. Yahweh has raised up the conqueror Cyrus to destroy the power of Babylon and to release its captives. The Jewish exiles will be miraculously led through the desert back to their homeland, Jerusalem will be built in a style more glorious than before, and the Jewish people will be restored to a position of political power and empire unequalled since the days of David, this time never to lose it again.

References to the religious situation of the times further confirm the date of these prophecies. In those passages in which Deutero-Isaiah seeks to convince his sceptical audience of Yahweh's supreme power over the universe which enables him to carry out this tremendous programme, he speaks of the Babylonian gods in ways which show that he possesses a not inconsiderable knowledge of Babylonian beliefs and practices. Again, his use of Israelite religious traditions and the similarity in some respects of his teaching to that of other Jewish religious works of the exilic period give a sure indication of his place in Israelite national and religious history.

All these lines of evidence, of which further details are to be found in the commentary, point to the conclusion that the book (that is, chapters 40–55) is substantially the work of a single anonymous prophet living amongst his fellow Jewish exiles in Babylonia during the sixth century BC. It is, moreover, possible to fix the date with somewhat greater precision. The first deportation of Jews to Babylonia took place in 597, and the second, after the destruction of Jerusalem, in 587. In 538 the Persian king Cyrus, having conquered Babylon, gave permission to the deported peoples to return to their homes. It is clear that the career of Deutero-Isaiah as a prophet belongs to the latter part of this period. There is nothing in the book to suggest that the horrors of the capture and destruction of Jerusalem and the subsequent deportation of the Jews were fresh in the minds of the prophet's audience. It is also significant that the only recent historical events to which there are clear allusions in the book are the conquests of Cyrus, who is always represented as having already established a reputation as an invincible conqueror and consequently become a potential menace to Babylon, but as having not yet attacked that city. There is good reason to suppose that those parts of the book in which there is no specific mention of these events should also be dated within the same relatively brief period. Attempts to arrange the various oracles in a chronological sequence covering a number of years (e.g. that of S. Smith) have failed to convince the majority of scholars. The remarkable degree of consistency in the prophet's teaching suggests strongly that it all proceeds from a divine call to proclaim a new message of salvation for God's people which was closely related to the achievements of Cyrus, the divinely appointed agent of the restoration of their fortunes.

II. Historical Background

The dates within which the prophecies were made can therefore be determined with some precision in relation to the career of Cyrus, which is well documented. The empire of the Medes, formerly the allies of the Babylonians in the conquest of the earlier Assyrian empire, had lain to the north and east of the Babylonian empire. Among its vassal kingdoms it had included the Persian kingdom of Anshan, in what had once been Elam. Cyrus I (550–529), the founder of the Persian empire which was to dominate the Near East for several centuries, began his career as king of Anshan; but soon after his accession he overthrew his Median overlord Astyages and so gained control of the whole Median empire. The series of lightning victories which then followed have established his reputation as one of the great conquerors of history. Although the Babylonians at first regarded him as an ally, his subjugation of northern Mesopotamia and

Asia Minor, including the powerful kingdom of Lydia (547–546), together with further extensive conquests in the east as far as India in the years which followed, soon transformed him into a grave menace to a Babylonian empire which had been becoming progressively weaker since the death of Nebuchadnezzar in 562 and was now, under Nabonidus (556–538) no longer really viable. In 538 Cyrus was able to occupy the city of Babylon without even a struggle. Since Deutero-Isaiah regards him as already a great conqueror, the prophet's career must fall within the years 550–538. Further precision, however, is hardly attainable. Deutero-Isaiah himself, in some of his oracles, regarded the capture of Babylon as imminent, but the actual event may have been delayed somewhat longer than he anticipated.

III. Deutero-Isaiah as Prophet

The Hebrew word *nāḇî'*, usually translated by 'prophet', does not occur in Deutero-Isaiah. Nevertheless he is undoubtedly to be reckoned among the company of those whom we call 'prophets'. The word *nāḇî'* itself, indeed, had on the whole been avoided or even repudiated (cf. Am. 7 : 14) by his predecessors, and therefore has no value as a criterion in this connexion. That Deutero-Isaiah was a true successor of those men of the two previous centuries whom we are accustomed to call 'the great prophets' (Amos, Hosea, Micah, Isaiah, Jeremiah, Ezekiel) is clear from the content of his message and also from the forms in which he expressed it. In his use of the divine oracle in the first person singular, often preceded or punctuated by the formulae 'Thus says Yahweh' (*kōh 'āmar yhwh*) and 'says Yahweh' (*ne'um-hywh*) he implicitly makes the characteristically prophetical claim to be God's mouthpiece, and in a number of passages (40 : 1–8; 42 : 1–4; 49 : 1–6; 50 : 4–9) he records, as did some of his predecessors, how God both has called him to this office and sustains him in its execution.

The content of Deutero-Isaiah's message may at first seem to be at variance with that proclaimed by his predecessors, especially those whose ministry lay entirely in the pre-exilic period. The message of Amos, Hosea, Isaiah, and Micah was primarily a sombre one: to denounce the people, whether of northern Israel or Judah, for their sins, and to announce that Yahweh had decreed the destruction of the nation. This is true also of many of the prophecies of Jeremiah and Ezekiel. There were indeed prophets before the Exile who, likewise in Yahweh's name, offered to the people an entirely opposite message, assuring them that all would be well: that Yahweh had no intention of destroying them, but would, on the contrary, protect them from their enemies. These prophets, who professed to give a divine assurance of 'peace' (*šālôm*, i.e. security, prosperity) were denounced by Jeremiah as wicked liars and false prophets (Jer. 8:10–12; 14:13–16; 23:16–17; 28:5–17).

In contrast to his predecessors, Deutero-Isaiah, on the basis of the same divine authority, offered to the exiled Jews a message of unalloyed happiness and prosperity which was about to begin and which would never again be disturbed. In other words, he offered precisely that *šālôm* which his genuine predecessors had declared to be the hallmark of false, rather than of true, prophecy. The explanation of this apparent contradiction lies in the basic nature of Hebrew prophecy and of the Israelite understanding of Yahweh's activity in history. Hebrew prophecy is in itself fundamentally neither a message of disaster nor one of hope. It is rather an announcement of Yahweh's reaction to his people's situation and of his intentions towards them at the precise moment when the prophecy is pronounced. The historical moment when Deutero-Isaiah prophesied was entirely different from that of the time before the exile, and Yahweh's intentions towards his people in this new situation were entirely different from his earlier intentions. Deutero-Isaiah understood this quite clearly. He refers frequently to the situation which had obtained before the exile, and in what he says about it he is entirely at one with his predecessors, the 'prophets of doom'. The latter had been as obedient to Yahweh's command in their day as he was in his. Their predictions had, indeed, come to pass: Yahweh had punished Judah for its sins, and taken its people into exile. But in Deutero-Isaiah's own day, a generation later, this same Yahweh, always in control of the events which took place in his world, now announced, through his prophet, his new plans for his people: an end to the punishment, forgiveness, and a new beginning. Deutero-Isaiah was as true a prophet for his own day as his predecessors had been for theirs. The joyful announcement of a new beginning was, moreover, not entirely unprecedented: even an eighth-century prophet such as Hosea had looked forward to the possibility of a new beginning after the expected disaster; and this element of hope, existing side by side with the prophecies of doom, is even more marked in the prophecies of Jeremiah and Ezekiel, whose prophetic careers spanned the fateful events of 587, and whose vision of a bright future is sometimes markedly similar to that of Deutero-Isaiah himself.

IV. Literary History and Structure of the Book

The interpretation of a prophetical book depends to a large extent on an understanding of its literary history. It is important to discover what are the limits of its component parts, and how these are related to one another: whether as elements in a single composition constructed from the outset as a literary whole by the prophet himself, or as separate poems or utterances originally distinct from one another and created for quite separate occasions and only subsequently gathered together into a single whole, either by the prophet himself or by a later editor. A solution to these questions may be sought through a study of the contents of a prophetical book and of its various parts—the actual substance of its teaching and the progression of its ideas—or of their literary form: the patterns formed by the arrangement and repetition of words and expressions which may provide a clue to their purpose and function. In fact these two approaches are inseparable and must be pursued simultaneously.

The form-critical method pioneered by Gunkel in *OT* studies, which, in spite of its name, does in fact combine these two approaches, has proved extremely fruitful in furthering the study of the prophetical books. In many cases it has succeeded in identifying 'basic forms of prophetic speech' (the title of a book by C. Westermann) and in tracing their development, and also in identifying other formal patterns of speech which originated outside prophetical circles, but which the prophets utilized and adapted to their purpose. In so doing it has thrown light on a number of matters of great importance for the understanding of the nature of prophecy as well as for the interpretation of particular prophetical books and passages: it has identified original units; it has increased our understanding of the prophets' own view of their authority and function, of the circumstances in which they worked and of their manner of operation; and it has enabled us to see them as men who were familiar with the various political, social and cultural currents of their time, and more especially to see how they made use of the various elements of Israel's religious traditions.

The application of the form-critical method to Deutero-Isaiah has been undertaken by a series of scholars, notably Gressmann, Begrich, Koehler, Westermann, and von Waldow, each of whom has utilized and refined the conclusions of his predecessors. It may justly be claimed that their studies are indispensable to the modern student of Deutero-Isaiah. At the same time it has become clear as a result of their work that Deutero-Isaiah presents peculiar problems to the form-critic, and that to apply the form-critical method to this book too exclusively and too insensitively may result in a distortion of its meaning.

First, Deutero-Isaiah impresses the reader with a massive religious and theological unity, due partly to his unusual capacity for logical and constructive thought which entitles him to be regarded as a theologian, and partly to the fact that his teaching is addressed to a single situation—in great contrast to that of Isaiah, who in the course of a long career was called upon to announce the divine message in a series of bewilderingly different situations. Thus although differences of emphasis can be found in different parts of the book, there is a remarkable theological unity here. A relatively small number of themes, all directly related to one simple message, constantly rearrange themselves in a variety of different patterns, and with a high degree of repetition of key words and expressions. This frequently makes it difficult to discern the limits between one section of the book and the next.

Secondly, Deutero-Isaiah is a master of double meanings, of subtle allusions, and of unexpected associations of ideas. To some extent these characteristics assist the reader in perceiving the literary pattern which he gives to his message; but they also frequently confuse him, in that he often cannot be sure, as might be the case in other prophetical books, whether the repetition of a word or phrase in consecutive verses, but in apparently quite different senses, is an indication of the juxtaposition of two passages of a purely external kind by a later editor, or whether it is an example of a brilliant literary twist of thought executed by Deutero-Isaiah himself within a single passage.

Thirdly, Deutero-Isaiah surpasses all his prophetic predecessors in his free adaptation of the traditional forms, both prophetic and non-prophetic, which he uses. Consequently the formal pattern often becomes blurred and the limits of a particular oracle difficult to determine. This is particularly true, as Westermann has pointed out, in the later chapters of the book.

In spite of these difficulties some account of the book's literary history may be attempted. It is difficult to see it as a single unitary literary work, with the prophet Deutero-Isaiah simply in the role of an author. As will be seen, many of the individual units identified by form-critical methods make a much more effective impact if they are interpreted in a literal manner as actual prophetical oracles spoken to a live audience rather than as artificial literary imitations invented to serve as components of a larger literary whole. The simpler explanation, that Deutero-Isaiah was a prophet much in the manner of his predecessors, is to be preferred to the more 'literary' one. Moreover, in spite of efforts to prove the contrary, the book as a whole does not possess a satisfactory structure suggestive of a coherent plan. The constant reiteration of the same themes in various combinations, though not unthinkable as a literary method in ancient Near Eastern literature, is here more easily accounted for by the theory of a multiplicity of short units later gathered into a comprehensive collection.

There is, it is true, evidence of thematic arrangement in some parts of the book; but this is not generally the case, and the *lack* of any such arrangement in the major part of the book is a piece of negative evidence of at least equal importance. It is difficult to discern any reason why Deutero-Isaiah, if he were himself the author of a coherently planned literary work, should have chosen to scatter numerous treatments of the same themes throughout the book in what appears to be such a haphazard way.

The evidence against the theory of a coherently organized single work and for a theory of a collection of short, independent pieces still leaves the question of the present arrangement of the book unanswered. There is, as has been suggested, some evidence of attempts at organization of the material. There are in some places traces of a thematic arrangement, and elsewhere evidence of the linking of one passage to the next by purely external means: a passage in which a particular word has a prominent place near the beginning has been placed immediately after another in which the same word occurs near the end, thus creating a purely artificial 'continuity'. But—in spite of Mowinckel's attempt to produce evidence of the latter of these methods throughout the work—neither of these principles of arrangement has been carried through consistently. Their existence, however, points to the existence of a collector of Deutero-Isaiah's oracles who made some attempt to be an editor. Probably it was he who incorporated into the book those relatively few passages which are not the work of Deutero-Isaiah.

The identity of this compiler remains unknown. In the absence of any precise evidence it is reasonable to assume that he was a disciple of Deutero-Isaiah, although the possibility that the prophet himself had some hand in the compilation of the collection cannot be excluded. Since parts of 'Trito-Isaiah' (chapters 56–66) are evidently the work of a person or persons who regarded Deutero-Isaiah as virtually a sacred text which, rightly interpreted, still held a message for a later generation (see Section C and the commentary on chapters 56–66, *passim*) it would seem likely that the editor and the interpreter(s) belonged at least to the same circle of disciples, although Elliger's theory that the editor of Deutero-Isaiah *was Trito-Isaiah* over-simplifies the issue.

Deutero-Isaiah was, like other Hebrew prophets, a poet: almost all his oracles are clothed in poetical form. Whether he was, as some commentators have urged, a *great* poet is of course a matter of opinion. In spite of much painstaking analysis in recent times of his poetical style, it is improbable that modern readers will ever succeed sufficiently in understanding the mental world of ancient Israel, or even in grasping the mechanics of ancient Hebrew poetry, to make a valid judgment on this question. It should also be remembered that, like other Hebrew poets, and perhaps even more than most, Deutero-Isaiah, in spite of his undoubted individuality in other respects, was heavily dependent on the forms and expressions of Israel's earlier religious poetry. The limitations of the competence of modern scholarship to assess the character of Deutero-Isaiah's poetry also have implications for the study of the literary structure of the book: thus Muilenburg, in his excellent commentary in which the analysis of style and poetical structure has been carried out more thoroughly than in any other work, has not proved convincing in his original attempt to show that Deutero-Isaiah's work consists of a small number of elaborately constructed long poems.

V. Deutero-Isaiah's Prophetic Ministry

Our knowledge of the manner of life of the Jewish exiles in Babylonia is extremely slight, being based mainly on inferences from scattered allusions. Since conditions may have varied considerably from time to time and from place to place, it is unwise to attempt to construct a picture simply by putting these scraps of information together. Nevertheless it is legitimate to make certain general inferences from a knowledge of the religious traditions and practices which the deported Jews must have taken with them, from the simple fact that their faith survived and even underwent substantial development during a half-century of exile, and from the very existence of the books of Ezekiel and Deutero-Isaiah. It is clear that the Jewish faith could only have survived for so long through the maintenance of some regularly instituted form of public worship, and it is reasonable to suppose that this would have consisted mainly of the traditional liturgical rites and ceremonies in as far as these were practicable and appropriate to the conditions of the Exile. There is no evidence that sacrifice was practised, and this is on the whole unlikely. But the traditional liturgical forms such as hymns, lamentations, thanksgivings, blessings, were available. There is no direct evidence of the form assumed by this kind of non-sacrificial worship: to say that it foreshadowed the liturgy of the later institution of the synagogue is mere guesswork. One can only make inferences from the literature of the period, of which the book of Deutero-Isaiah is itself a notable example. The book of Lamentations, which is a collection of liturgical lamentations over the destruction of the city and Temple of Jerusalem, and certain passages in other books (e.g. Zech. 7 : 1–7) suggest that among the population left by the Babylonians in Palestine the practice of lamentation and supplication, together with fasting, had become prominent in public worship during the exilic period. Deutero-Isaiah suggests that this was also the case, at least in some circles, among the exiles in Babylon. Begrich, Westermann, and others have pointed out how many of Deutero-Isaiah's attempts to persuade his audience, whether by argument or by simple prophetic proclamation, that the tide of their fortunes had really turned, incorporate quotations from, or references to, specific complaints on their part about their fate and about Yahweh's indifference to it, couched in the language and form of the traditional psalms of lamentation. (See e.g. on 41 : 8–13.) These observations make it probable that we should see some at least of Deutero-Isaiah's prophetic activity as having taken place in the context of an assembly of groups of exiles for public worship. This impression receives a measure of confirmation from other evidence that prophecy played an important part in the religious life of the exiles (e.g. Jer. 29; Ezek. 8 : 1; 14 : 1), whereas we have little evidence of what the role of the priests may have been. If this is so, it is reasonable to suppose that other characteristic types of Deutero-Isaiah's prophetic activity, especially the disputation (see on 40 : 12–17) and the so-called 'trial-speech' (*Gerichtsrede;* see on 41 : 1–5) also took place in the setting of public assemblies, whether specifically cultic or not. In the absence of more definite information it is impossible to be more specific than this. Unlike some other prophetical books Deutero-Isaiah lacks both narrative sections and editorial headings which might have given us a clearer picture of his life and work. (Further information about the forms of speech used by Deutero-Isaiah will be found in the body of the commentary.)

VI. Deutero-Isaiah's Message and Theology

As has already been stated, the message which Deutero-Isaiah believed himself to have been called by Yahweh to deliver to the Jewish exiles was essentially a simple one: the complete restoration of the Jewish nation to independence and prosperity in their own land and to a position of dominance over the other nations was about to begin. The exiles had served their sentence; now they were to be the recipients of every kind of good fortune, which Yahweh would unsparingly pour upon them; and nothing would ever again disturb this life of unalloyed happiness.

There has been considerable discussion of the question whether this message is properly to be described as 'eschatological'. Much of this discussion would have been unnecessary if there were agreement among scholars on the definition of the words 'eschatology, eschatological' in *OT* studies. There is certainly no eschatology in Deutero-Isaiah in the sense in which the word is used in the discussion of the apocalyptic literature and the *NT*, and in Christian dogmatic theology. There is no doctrine of the Two Ages, of this world and the world to come. The future which is promised to the Jews is presented in ideal terms, but it is quite definitely of this world. Deutero-Isaiah dwells hardly at all on the details: the life of the restored Jewish people will be ordinary life, though lived under ideal conditions; moreover there is no suggestion whatever of the individual's span of years being indefinitely prolonged. There is, indeed, to be an element of miraculous divine intervention in order to establish this new state of affairs; but this does not in principle go beyond the marvellous deeds already performed by God in the remote past within the bounds of human history: indeed, the whole sequence of future events—overthrow of the tyrant, release of the captives, march through the desert, miraculous food and drink provided on the way, expulsion of the inhabitants of the land, settlement and construction, dominance over the nations—is closely modelled on the tradition of Israel's earlier progress from exodus to empire. It is true that in some respects, in particular the creation of a highway through the desert involving the levelling of mountains and the filling in of valleys (40 : 3–4) and the turning of the desert into fertile land (55 : 13) the prophet has, under the inspiration of traditional mythical and poetical motifs, heightened the element of miracle in order to represent the future blessings as even more wonderful than those of the past; but this does not alter the entirely this-worldly character of the future which he foresees.

A second disputed point concerning Deutero-Isaiah's picture of the future concerns the part to be played by the nations of the world in this ideal life. The majority of commentators, following the traditional Christian interpretation of the book, believe that the prophet envisages the full participation of the nations in the salvation offered by Yahweh to Israel. Israel is frequently seen as a kind of missionary to the pagan world. It will be argued in the commentary that this is not so. The nations are depicted by the prophet in a number of somewhat different roles—as oppressors, as deluded worshippers of idols, as destined to become Israel's captives, suppliants and slaves; as seeing with astonishment Yahweh's marvellous acts on behalf of his people; as future vassals, recognizing the universal rule of the God of Israel. Their role should not be exaggerated: they are rarely in the forefront of Deutero-Isaiah's thought, which is centred entirely on what Yahweh will do for Israel. The rest of humanity, together with mountains, hills, and trees of the forest, remain on the sidelines, agape at Yahweh's irresistible power and love for his own people, and submitting themselves to his will. This is the only possible interpretation of the great majority of the references to them in the book. There remain a number of passages and texts (especially 42:1–4, 5–7; 45:6, 22–24; 49:6; 55:5) which, if they stood alone, might be interpreted as envisaging a free acceptance by the nations of the cult of Yahweh and their admittance to the same privileges as those enjoyed by Israel; but in no case is this the only possible interpretation; and the general context of Deutero-Isaiah's otherwise extremely consistent line of thought makes it most probable that nothing more than the submission of the nations to Yahweh's universal sovereignty is envisaged. Nor should the statements about Yahweh's special relationship with Cyrus be taken as implying a general conversion of the nations: nothing of the sort is mentioned in those passages (41:25; 44:28; 45:1; 46:11; 48:14) in which he is referred to in this way.

Most of Deutero-Isaiah's utterances show him struggling with the problem of how to convince his audience that his promises of unalloyed bliss due to begin at any moment could really be taken seriously. The attempt to persuade and convince is to be found not only in the disputations, in which the prophet argues with his opponents, and the trial-speeches, in which Yahweh is represented as disputing with the other gods, but even in the divine promises of salvation themselves. The attempt to persuade is sometimes direct, arguing from accepted truths to new propositions, and sometimes indirect, using traditional language and allusions to traditional themes to evoke and revive traditional faith. It is in the course of Deutero-Isaiah's attempts to persuade his audience, in which he uses every kind of method and argument available to him, that his individuality and originality as a theologian is most apparent.

It is clear from many passages in the book that some at least of the Jewish exiles in Babylon in Deutero-Isaiah's time had become disillusioned. They had lost faith in Yahweh in two respects: they no longer believed that he was *willing* to help them;

nor, even more serious, that he was *able* to do so. Deutero-Isaiah's task was to prove to them that neither of these doubts was justified. They must be ready for the great day of redemption when it came; they must be ready to accept what Yahweh offered them freely. Deutero-Isaiah also, like his predecessors, had another task which was in a sense basic to the others: to convince them that he himself, the one who was proclaiming the message of redemption, was a true prophet called by Yahweh, and that the message was itself God's word.

The willingness of Yahweh to help his people could hardly be proved by logical argument; but Deutero-Isaiah could and did muster arguments which were intended to counter the exiles' lack of faith by pointing out that they as a people had fully deserved their punishment. God's failure to intervene to save them during the years following their deportation was, therefore, due not to his bad faith or indifference, but was the result of a deliberate and entirely justified policy. This argument, however, carried with it the corollary that such punishment might not be without limit; and this in turn made plausible Deutero-Isaiah's assertion that that limit had in fact been reached. But plausibility was not enough. Deutero-Isaiah had to go further and convince his audience that the divine forgiveness and redemption was not only a possibility, but had actually been decided upon by God. Anything which he said on this subject depended for its credibility not on logical argument but on his ability to convince them that he was indeed a true prophet, and that the divine oracles which he pronounced were authentic. The letter of Jeremiah to the exiles (Jer. 29) shows that, at any rate in the earlier years of exile, other prophets had encouraged the community in Babylon with a message not unlike that of Deutero-Isaiah, and that their prophecies had proved to be false. Deutero-Isaiah could do no more than the genuine prophets of earlier times to prove the authenticity of his credentials: he reported his commissioning by God, his contacts with the heavenly divine council, and his subsequent dialogues with God, and he spoke confidently in God's name in the traditional prophetic style. Whether his authority was in fact accepted, other than by a small group of disciples, may be doubted. His career remains largely unknown to us; only a few passages, particularly the so-called Servant Songs (42:1–4; 49:1–6; 50:4–9; and especially chapter 53) provide some glimpses of the way in which this particular servant of Yahweh was treated both by his Jewish contemporaries and by the Babylonian authorities. The importance of the small group of disciples mentioned above cannot, however, be over-estimated. It was they who preserved his words for posterity; and, as chapters 56–66 bear witness (see Section C below) they were able to re-interpret his teaching to the needs of a new situation at a critical time when the exiles had returned to Palestine but found themselves facing new and unexpected problems.

Deutero-Isaiah also sought to persuade his audience of Yahweh's willingness to come to their aid by stressing his past faithfulness to his chosen people and his redemptive and forgiving nature. He made use of various incidents in past history—and even went back in the historical traditions as far as Noah—to show how Yahweh had in the past revealed himself as the God who had created Israel, called them to be his own people, guided them and rescued them from their enemies, given them their own land and made them into a great and powerful nation. The historical period to which he most frequently refers is that of the exodus from Egypt, for here he was able to point out the similarity of Israel's present plight to that of their ancestors in Egypt, and so to make more credible his assertion that there was now to be a new 'exodus', this time from Babylon. In order to evoke and revive the exiles' flagging faith, he expresses his confident predictions in the language and imagery of the liturgical hymns of praise in which Israel had traditionally expressed its thanks to God for his past mercies. In all these ways Deutero-Isaiah attempted to bridge the gap created by the apparent break in the relationship between Yahweh and Israel and to assert a continuity between the past and the present based upon Yahweh's unchanging love for his people.

The success of his attempt depended, however, entirely on his ability to deal with the even greater problem of the scepticism which had grown up among the exiles concerning Yahweh's *ability* to help his people. To the exiles it must have seemed that Israel's defeat by Babylon was due to the defeat of Yahweh by the Babylonian gods. Yahweh, whom Israel had regarded as its invincible protector, had been unable to withstand the attack of the Babylonians, and had so shown himself to be powerless before their gods. He was, in fact, discredited, and nothing more could be gained from serving him. Over the years of exile the Babylonian gods, worshipped with impressive pomp, still remained unchallenged, and the people who worshipped them remained, it seemed, the masters of the world.

In answer to this crisis of faith Deutero-Isaiah was able to point to signs in the international scene that the might of Babylon, though it had been real enough in the past, was now a mere sham. He pointed to the career of the Persian Cyrus and prophesied that Babylon would shortly fall into his hands. Here he had touched upon something tangible which his audience could appreciate, although his open proclamation of Babylon's imminent fall was extremely dangerous, and probably accounts for the harsh fate which befell him (50: 4–9; 53).

But to point to the imminent conquest of Babylon by Persia constituted in itself no proof of the power of Yahweh. On the contrary, the conclusion most naturally to be drawn from such an event would be that it was the gods of Persia who were the most powerful. Here, however, Deutero-Isaiah drew upon an interpretation of history which had earlier been adumbrated by his predecessors Isaiah and Jeremiah. According to this interpretation there lay behind the successes of the great world conquerors not the power of their own gods but the hidden power of Yahweh: the conquerors were merely tools in his hands. It was Yahweh who had permitted the Babylonians to conquer Israel as a punishment for Israel's disobedience to him. This had been the teaching of Jeremiah. But Deutero-Isaiah went further: if Yahweh could use foreign conquerors to punish Israel, he could also use them to save Israel. It was, then, Yahweh who had called Cyrus to destroy Israel's oppressors and to bring an end to her sufferings, which had now, in Yahweh's judgment, been sufficient.

But to make such an assertion to the disillusioned group of exiles, whose life daily reminded them of the utterly wretched and insignificant condition of Yahweh's people, was to invite total scepticism. It was incumbent upon Deutero-Isaiah to support his assertion by theological argument. A large proportion of his prophecies is consequently devoted to a comparison between Yahweh and the other gods, particularly those of Babylon. In the 'trial-speeches' the Babylonian gods are invited to participate in a contest with Yahweh, in which the claims of each party to control historical events are set out. The criterion by which these claims are to be judged is that of evidence of a divine purpose in history. Only if a god has announced beforehand that he will bring to pass a particular event can he rightly claim that it was he and not another god who was responsible for it. By this device Deutero-Isaiah was able to point to the evidential value of the phenomenon of Israelite prophecy: Yahweh had regularly announced his forthcoming actions by means of his prophets, and through the fulfilment of those prophecies had shown himself to be the controller of history. What he had once done he could and would do again. The Babylonian gods, Deutero-Isaiah argues, have no such record of prophecy and fulfilment. This shows them to be powerless, despite their great claims. A second line of argument is based upon the fact that Babylonian worship centred upon the statues of the gods, while the worship of Yahweh was distinguished by being imageless. Deutero-Isaiah—somewhat unfairly, as we know how, though plausibly enough—assumed that the Babylonians identified these statues with the gods whom they represented, and so was able to ridicule the idea that these man-made objects of wood, stone, and metal standing motionless on their pedestals or carried about by their worshippers could do anything at all, much less influence the course of history. These so-called gods were in fact made by men; it was the free and invisible Yahweh who, in contrast, was the one who had made men and, indeed, all the world, and who was therefore the supreme master of it all.

Deutero-Isaiah's doctrine of creation occurs in connexion with a number of themes; but the polemic against the Babylonian gods, which seems rarely to have been entirely absent from the prophet's thoughts, provided one of the main occasions for its introduction. The Babylonians also had their creation myths, and these probably occupied a prominent place not only in the official cult but also in popular religious beliefs. It was necessary for Deutero-Isaiah to convince his audience that the Israelite traditions according to which the world had been created by Yahweh were more credible than the Babylonian myths, and also revealed Yahweh's true character as unique and supreme God in contrast with Babylonian polytheism. There was less room for logical argument here than in the case of some of the other themes in Deutero-Isaiah's teaching, and much of what he says about Yahweh as Creator takes the form of a skilful evocation of the

Israelite creation traditions in an exalted style calculated to bring to life the flagging faith of his audience; but even here his polemical intention is often apparent, especially in his insistence on the act of creation as the unaided work of the one God (40: 13–14) and on the character of the heavenly bodies as simply creatures doing Yahweh's will rather than as gods (40: 26). In this connexion should also be mentioned his reference to the fact that in Israelite tradition Yahweh has no parentage, but was sole God from the very beginning (43: 10); in the Babylonian tradition the creator-god, Marduk, was a latecomer to power, an 'upstart' whose parents are named and who play a part in the myth. In passages such as this the basic question of the very nature of godhead is raised: in the 'family life' of polytheism there can be no 'God' in the absolute sense which is implicit in the Israelite traditions of creation. Thus Deutero-Isaiah reaches right back to the creation itself to find the basis for his message about the future: the God who is 'first' will also be 'last' (e.g. 44: 6), or 'with the last' (41: 4). In such phrases Deutero-Isaiah came as near to the concept of eternity as was possible within the limits of his theological world of thought.

The above sketch of some of the principal themes in the book has presented Deutero-Isaiah's thought in a systematic way which may be open to criticism as to some extent going beyond his own explicit statements; moreover, it would be possible to arrange the same themes in somewhat different ways and produce a somewhat different picture. Nevertheless a careful reading of the book suggests that there is in fact a structure of theological thought which should be taken seriously, and that therefore, although this is no academic theological thesis but a series of urgent messages addressed to a particular historical situation, Deutero-Isaiah deserves the title of theologian. It is this systematic aspect of his teaching which accounts for the great influence which the book has had upon subsequent theological development.

The fact of Deutero-Isaiah's significance for later theology necessitates one final comment. It is a paradox that this influence should have made itself felt despite the fact that in his basic prediction he was to a very large extent mistaken. Although Cyrus did capture Babylon and release the Jewish captives, and although they did return to their homes in Palestine and rebuild their national life and institutions there, Deutero-Isaiah's predictions of a future of unalloyed happiness and political power remained entirely unfulfilled. The period which immediately followed the Return was full of disappointments and frustrations, as the literature of that period, including Trito-Isaiah (chapters 56–66) amply testifies; moreover, never again, except for a very brief period several centuries later under the Hasmonean kings, did the Jews achieve political independence, much less imperial power. (The present secular state of Israel can hardly be considered to be a fulfilment of Deutero-Isaiah's prophecies.) It was because of this total lack of correspondence between the prediction and the reality that Torrey argued that the theory of a sixth-century 'Deutero-Isaiah' must be wholly mistaken: the debacle of the 'Return' would have totally discredited his claim to be a true prophet. To this argument a twofold reply may be given. First, neither Torrey nor any other commentator has succeeded in giving a convincing interpretation of the book against any other historical background than that of the Babylonian exile: everything points to the correctness of this view. Secondly, subsequent generations, from that in which Deutero-Isaiah's prophecies were collected and edited to the present day, have found in the book a wealth of religious and theological truth, despite the undoubted fact that the prophet's immediate expectations remained largely unfulfilled. Such a reputation cannot lightly be put aside; and to study the book anew is to discover that it is wholly justified.

C. TRITO-ISAIAH

No one reading chapters 56–66 could fail to recognize that in some parts they exhibit marked similarities to chapters 40–55. However, further study reveals equally great differences between the two bodies of literature: differences of style and form, of vocabulary, of the meanings given to certain key words common to both sections of the book, of the places of writing and historical backgrounds which they presuppose, of religious outlook and of theological emphasis. Analysis of these differences has confirmed Duhm's hypothesis that these final chapters are neither as a whole nor in part the work of the prophet whose teaching is recorded in chapters 40–55, and this view is now very generally accepted. At the same time the researches of Elliger, Zimmerli, and others have gone far to account for the equally undeniable similarities between the two bodies of literature, showing that there is evidence within chapters 56–66, more apparent in some chapters than in others, of a conscious re-interpretation of the themes and words of Deutero-Isaiah, and this on more than one level: in some cases it is simply a re-interpretation of individual key words and phrases, in others it amounts to something more like the composition of a sermon or a commentary on a 'sacred text'. There can be no doubt about the purpose of this interpretative activity: it was to draw lessons for the present from the words of an acknowledged religious leader of the past whose teaching had originally been given in a quite different situation—in other words, an early exercise in hermeneutics.

This realization must govern any attempt to understand these chapters in their original historical setting. A gap between the teaching of the earlier prophet and the needs of the later community, so great that it could only be bridged by methods such as these, can have been created only by a very considerable lapse of time or by some radical transformation of the situation of the Jews between one generation and the next. Of these two possibilities the latter is the more probable, since the remarkable persistence of Deutero-Isaiah's reputation and influence which this re-interpretative activity presupposes would be difficult to account for if more than one generation had elapsed since the end of his ministry.

The identity of the events in question is not far to seek. The capture of Babylon by Cyrus and the permission given to the Jewish exiles to return to their homes (538 BC) came soon—perhaps very soon—after Deutero-Isaiah had ceased to prophesy. It is not known how many took immediate advantage of this permission, but it is certain that some did so, and that this initial return was followed by others over a considerable period of years. To this extent, then, Deutero-Isaiah's prophecies had been fulfilled, and this fact alone would have been sufficient to revive general respect for him as a prophet, and to create the conditions in which his disciples could gain a hearing. Nevertheless very serious problems remained. Unfortunately the main biblical sources for this period—Ezr. 1–6; Hag.; Zech. 1–8—do not, for various reasons, provide us with a clear notion of either the exact sequence of events or the religious situation in Palestine. But it is clear that the returning exiles faced three major problems.

The first of these problems was that of the relationship of the newly returned exiles to the population already resident in Palestine. The land which was made available to them was far from embracing the whole of the territory of the empire of David and Solomon, or even the territory of the kingdom of Judah before the Exile. It consisted only of a few square miles of land with Jerusalem as its centre. It could therefore not be said that the exiles had been fully restored to their land. But in addition they had to share this territory with the descendants of the Jewish population which had not been deported in 587, together with an unknown number of foreigners who had moved in during the period of confusion which had followed the Babylonian military campaigns. It is probable that this population had to some extent continued to practise, whether side by side with a form of Yahwism or not, religions of Canaanite and perhaps also of foreign origin which had existed in pre-exilic times and had never been eliminated. The disordered conditions of the exilic period may have served even to foster these practices at the expense of Yahwism. It was natural that disputes of various kinds should arise between the former residents and the newcomers. The exact nature and history of these disputes is not clear from our sources. The situation was further complicated by the claims of an even more mixed population from the territory of Samaria further north to share the religious beliefs and practices of the Jews; and the returned exiles themselves were almost certainly not immune from internal disputes.

A second, and related, problem was that of the enormous gap between the realities of life in Palestine and the glorious promises made by Deutero-Isaiah and, probably, by other prophets. Not only had there (as yet) been no glorious march across the desert with the revelation of Yahweh's glory striking awe into the hearts of the surrounding nations but only a humble trickle homeward, a minor migration of a few people within the bounds of Persian imperial rule; but in addition life in Palestine, with Jerusalem and other towns still in ruins and pastoral life crippled, was as far as could be from a new marvellous life of prosperity and freedom. Life was a hard struggle. Only to a very limited extent could it be said that Deutero-Isaiah's prophecies had been fulfilled; and with the passing years there was no sign that their fulfilment was at hand. The period which followed the first return was therefore one of bitter disillusionment in which those who wished to remain faithful to Yahweh's promise found it as difficult to maintain that faith as they and their fathers had found it to be in Babylon. The questions Why? and When? continued to express themselves in disputation and lamentation.

Thirdly, it is evident from our sources that there were many disputes and difficulties over the rebuilding of the Temple in Jerusalem, which for some was first on the list of priorities, while for others it was an impractical, and perhaps even an unnecessary, undertaking. According to Ezr. 3:8–13 the foundations of the Temple were laid in 537 BC, the year following the first return; but all the sources agree that nothing more was done until 520 BC, when work was resumed and continued until the completion of the building in 516 BC.

While there is still no consensus of opinion concerning either the date(s) of composition of chapters 56–66 or their unity of authorship, many scholars including Elliger, Muilenburg, Westermann, Pauritsch, and Bonnard believe that the bulk of this material is directly concerned with the problems outlined above, and must therefore be dated within the first generation after the first return in 538 BC, a view which allows for the possibility of unity of authorship and also offers an explanation of the fact that while some passages seem to presuppose that the Temple has been rebuilt others equally presuppose either that it has not, or that it is only now in process of being rebuilt. This view does better justice to the evidence than either that of Duhm, who dates the whole composition in the middle of the fifth century on the grounds of supposed references to the controversy between Jews and Samaritans immediately before the arrival of Nehemiah in Jerusalem, or that of Volz, who believed it to be a collection of unrelated pieces ranging from the pre-exilic period to the Hellenistic.

The general background of a large proportion of the work is, then, one of a general mood of disappointment and disillusion and of divisions within the Jewish community in Palestine. The work in its various parts is concerned to encourage, strengthen and purify the faith of the faithful, to give them the assurance that Yahweh's promises will indeed be fulfilled, and, in some passages, to announce the divine condemnation of the faithless and apostates. The state of affairs which it presupposes may well have continued up to 444 BC, when Nehemiah brought about a great improvement in the community's fortunes.

The occasional references to the Temple might seem to offer the possibility of a more precise dating; but, while some of these clearly state that the Temple is in ruins and has not yet been rebuilt, and others probably—but not certainly—imply that it is once more in existence, only one (66 : 1–2) specifically narrows the field to the years 538–516 BC, when its rebuilding had been projected and perhaps begun but not yet completed. Whether the relatively precise dating of these two verses may be used to date the remainder of the chapters in question depends on the view which is taken of their homogeneity.

Some evidence on this question will be offered in the commentary. A comparison of the different units leads to the conclusion that their diversity is too great for them to be the work of one man. In this respect there is a striking contrast with chapters 40–55. There is what appears to be genuine prophetical material, including a genuine prophetical call-narrative (61 : 1–3) and a prophetical vision (63 : 1–6); but in other passages the prophetical form seems to hide some other function such as that of the preacher or the exegete, though the distinction between the genuinely prophetical and the 'quasi-prophetical' is not easy to make. Some material, moreover, is clearly not prophetical but liturgical (59 : 9–15*a*; 63 : 7–64 : 12). The precise situation presupposed also seems to be not always the same. There are a number of passages which are best explained as the result of a continuous process of interpretation, re-interpretation and expansion. There are passages in which there is evidence of substantial dependence on Deutero-Isaiah, and passages in which there is none. There is also considerable variation in theological standpoint.

But this diversity does not, for the most part, preclude the possibility that this is mainly a collection of material composed within a relatively short period of time. With the exception of a few passages there is no reason why the entire work cannot have been composed within a generation or two of the end of the Exile, though a later date (before 444 BC) cannot be absolutely excluded. These passages are 63 : 7–64 : 12, probably composed in Palestine during the exilic period and incorporated into the work perhaps at a fairly early stage; 65 : 17, 25; 66 : 6, 15–23, which give expression to an eschatology more developed than that of the rest of the book and were probably composed a century or two later than the main part, though certainly before the rise of the apocalyptic literature; and 66 : 24, which refers to a doctrine of eternal damnation and may be as late as the later third or early second century BC.

Apart from the obvious influence of Deutero-Isaiah shown in many passages, it is difficult to define precisely the circles in which the book took shape or the stages by which it reached its present form. The delineation of the original units is much more difficult even than in the case of chapters 40–55: the breakdown of sharply defined forms—e.g. in the cases of the oracles of salvation and of judgment—is well advanced, and some sections have so far defied all attempts at form-critical analysis. In some cases successive layers of accretions can be detected with some plausibility. In others, it seems that new techniques of biblical exegesis were being tried out. This was a period of transition, and the uncertainties and hesitations of the religious situation find their expression in its literary deposit. With regard to the structure of the work in its final form it is quite possible that additions were successively made to an original nucleus, though Westermann's theory of layers added symmetrically before and after a central core (chapter 61) is too schematic to carry conviction.

D. THE TEXT OF CHAPTERS 40–66

The Hebrew text of the book of Isaiah has been preserved with exceptional fidelity, as is shown by the evidence of the two Isaiah scrolls from Qumran, $1QIs^a$ and $1QIs^b$. Neither of these can well be later than the first century AD: that is to say, they are both at least 800 years older than any other extant Isaiah MS. $1QIs^b$, which is far from complete but nevertheless contains a substantial part of the book, is almost identical with MT. $1QIs^a$, whose variant readings are referred to frequently and occasionally adopted in this commentary, is also remarkably close to MT. The great majority of its variant readings are merely variations of spelling. Differences of substance are few, and only rarely does this MS offer a reading superior to that of MT. With regard to the much later MSS of post-Massoretic times, the likelihood of their having preserved an ancient reading different from that of MT is *a priori* very slight. In only one case (in 49 : 3) is it argued in the commentary that such a late MS (Kenn 96), in which the word 'Israel' is lacking, is superior to MT; but this might be simple coincidence, and the argument for the omission of 'Israel' here is not based solely on its evidence.

With regard to the ancient Versions, the Greek translation known as the Septuagint (LXX) has occasionally preserved a reading superior to that of MT; in a few other cases where both MT and LXX are corrupt LXX has preserved a trace of the original text and so a clue to the reconstruction of the true reading. In general, however, LXX is markedly inferior to MT. The contribution of the other Versions, especially Targum, Syriac, and Vulgate, is not entirely negligible but is nevertheless much less than that of LXX.

E. CONTENTS OF CHAPTERS 40–66

I. Deutero-Isaiah

40:1–8	The prophet's call and commission
40:9–11	The good news proclaimed
40:12–17	The Creator and Lord of history
40:18–26	Yahweh the incomparable
40:27–31	The source of strength
41:1–5	Cyrus Yahweh's instrument
41:6–7	How to make a god
41:8–13	Israel Yahweh's servant
41:14–16	Yahweh's threshing sledge
41:17–20	The flowering of the desert
41:21–29	The gods are nothing
42:1–4	The prophet's mission
42:5–9	The prisoners released
42:10–13	Yahweh the man of war
42:14–17	Yahweh leads the exiles home
42:18–25	The Exile a just punishment
43:1–7	The gathering of the dispersed
43:8–13	Israel as witness to Yahweh's power
43:14–15	The downfall of Babylon
43:16–21	The new overshadows the old
43:22–28	Yahweh defends his actions
44:1–5	Israel the envy of the world
44:6–8, 21–22	Israel's Redeemer the only God
44:9–20	The folly of idolatry

44:23	A short hymn of praise
44:24–45:7	Cyrus Yahweh's anointed one
45:8	A fragmentary prayer
45:9–13	Yahweh fashions his own tools
45:14–17	The nations prostrate at Israel's feet
45:18–19	Yahweh's open government
45:20–25	Yahweh's universal rule
46:1–4	Yahweh carries his people
46:5–8	The nations carry their gods
46:9–11	Cyrus carries out Yahweh's purpose
46:12–13	Deliverance is near
47:1–15	Babylon's fall
48:1–22	Yahweh's redemption; Israel's ingratitude
49:1–6	The disillusioned prophet encouraged
49:7–12	The land repopulated
49:13	A short hymn of praise
49:14–23	Zion rebuilt and repopulated
49:24–26	Yahweh to the rescue
50:1–3	Yahweh defends his actions
50:4–9	The prophet's confidence amidst suffering
50:10–11	The prophet avenged
51:1–8	The exiles encouraged
51:9–16	The Creator is also Redeemer
51:17–23	The cup of Yahweh's wrath
52:1–2	From slave-girl to queen
52:3–6	Yahweh freely redeems his people
52:7–10	The message of redemption
52:11–12	The command to depart
52:13–15	From humiliation to honour
53:1–12	The prophet's sufferings and release
54:1–10	Future expansion and prosperity
54:11–17	The new Jerusalem
55:1–5	The everlasting covenant
55:6–13	Yahweh's irresistible word

II. Trito-Isaiah

56:1–8	The true people of God
56:9–57:13	Unworthy leaders and idolaters
57:14–21	Comfort for the humble

58:1–14	God's true service
59:1–8	Alienation from God
59:9–15*a*	A confession of sin
59:15*b*–21	God redeems his loyal servants
60:1–22	Zion glorified
61:1–11	Prophetic call and message
62:1–12	Zion redeemed
63:1–6	Yahweh the avenger
63:7–64:12	Lamentation and prayer
65:1–25	Rewards and punishments
66:1–24	Judgment and salvation

Isaiah 40–66

CHAPTERS 40–55

THE PROPHET'S CALL AND COMMISSION

40 : 1–8

This poem consists of three sections: verses 1–2, 3–5, 6–8. The division is indicated by the introductory formula (**A voice . . .**) in verses 3 & 6 and by the clear structure of each section: imperative followed by statement in the indicative. The poem records the prophet's experience of his call and commission to be God's spokesman, and so corresponds to the 'call-narratives' of some earlier prophets (Isa. 6; Jer. 1; Ezek. 1–3; Am. 7 : 15), although its form is somewhat different.

The text does not directly indicate the identity of the speaker(s). In verses 1–2 it seems at first sight that the speaker is God. But the phrase **says your God** is not quite the same as the usual 'messenger-formula' ('Thus says the LORD') which frequently authenticates a prophetic word, and is probably part of the message itself (Elliger): the speaker is neither God nor the prophet but an unnamed spokesman telling others what God is saying (*yō'mar*).

In the case of the second and third sections it would appear that the 'voices' are those of heavenly beings conversing in God's heavenly council (H. W. Robinson, 'The Council of Yahweh', *JTS* 45 (1944), pp. 151–7; F. M. Cross, 'The Council of Yahweh in Second Isaiah', *JNES* 12 (1953) , pp. 274–8; for the concept see especially 1 Kg. 22 : 19–23; Job 1; 2). This suggests that the unnamed speaker in the first section is also a heavenly being.

But the persons addressed are not the same in each case: in sections one and two the imperatives are plural, whereas **Cry!** in verse 6 is singular. Here, as the words **And I said** show (see below), it is the prophet who is addressed. In the first two cases, however, the persons addressed can hardly be other than heavenly beings to whom one of their own number is speaking. The prophet is claiming to have been present at a meeting of God's heavenly council. (For this idea see Jer. 23 : 18, 22; Am. 3 : 7.) Unlike Micaiah (1 Kg. 22) and Isaiah (Isa. 6) in similar situations, he does not hear the voice of God himself; nevertheless it is God's authority which lies behind the voices.

In verses 1–2, then, one heavenly being informs others that God is commanding them to comfort the Jewish exiles with the news that the time of their suffering is at an end. In verses 3–5 one such being commands others to put in hand what is required for the imminent appearance of God's glory on the earth. Finally, in verses 6–8 comes the call to the prophet to proclaim the unalterable purpose of God which triumphs over all earthly power.

The poem has been appropriately placed at the beginning of Deutero-Isaiah's prophecies—either by the prophet himself or by an editor—partly because it describes the experience which made Deutero-Isaiah into a prophet, and partly because, like the inaugural vision of Isaiah (Isa. 6), it contains the essence of the message which is later expanded and elaborated: the astonishing announcement of God's forgiveness to the exiles and the end of their sufferings, and of the means by which this is to be achieved.

1. Comfort, comfort: the repetition adds force to the message. The verb is transitive, with **my people** as its object. The phrases **my people** and **your God** (although the latter is not strictly applied here to Israel) belong to the language of the covenant between Yahweh and Israel (cf. e.g. Jer. 7 : 23). The use of this language here indicates that in spite of all that has happened the old relationship has not been broken. This is Yahweh's answer to the self-pitying complaint of the Jews of this period, mournfully reiterated in Lam. 1, that 'There is none to comfort her (me)'.

2. Speak tenderly: literally, 'speak to the heart'. The meaning of this phrase here is perhaps 'persuade' or 'convince'. The prophet's most difficult task was to convince his despondent fellow-exiles of the truth of his message. **Jerusalem** (also 'Zion') is often used by Deutero-Isaiah to designate the exiles rather than the actual city. Such personification is not infrequent in the *OT*. That it should be used of a people no longer resident in their city shows the intensity of their identification with their home. **warfare:** *RSV* mg. has the better translation: 'time of service'. The military sense of *ṣāḇā'* is the more frequent, but here (as in Job 7 : 1; 14 : 14) it means misery and hardship, perhaps with the additional idea of a fixed term. **is ended:** the verb (*mālᵉ'āh*) is fem., whereas *ṣāḇā'* is almost always masc. But Marti's proposal to repoint the verb as *millᵉ'āh* (Piel), giving the meaning 'she has completed her period of service', is unnecessary. 1QIsª has a masc. verb. **her iniquity is pardoned:** Better, 'her penalty is discharged'. **double:** the word (*kiḇlayim*) is rare. 'Double punishment' may be a deliberate overstatement to drive home the point; but it has been suggested by G. von Rad (*ZAW* 79 (1967), pp. 80–2) that the word means 'equivalent', i.e. the right amount. **for all her sins:** Deutero-Isaiah, like the pre-exilic prophets, does not minimize Israel's guilt; the new element in his message is the announcement that it has been forgiven.

3. A voice cries (*ḳôl ḳôrē'*): better, 'Listen! someone is calling out.' For this use of *ḳôl* cf. 52 : 8; Gen. 4 : 10. **in the wilderness; in the desert:** the normal route from Babylon to Judah lay round rather than across the desert. But now the heavenly beings are to build a road across the desert for a miraculous journey. The prophet has in mind the earlier desert journey of the Israelites under God's guidance from Egypt to the Promised Land at the time of the Exodus. That the exiles' return from Babylon is to be an even more glorious Exodus is one of Deutero-Isaiah's constant themes. That he expected this command to be literally carried out is quite certain: for him, God's hand is not 'shortened, that it cannot redeem' (50 : 2)—in other words, the God who performed miracles in the past can and will perform them now. **prepare:** the word means 'clear of obstacles' (cf. Gen. 24 : 31). **make straight:** better, 'make smooth'.

a highway for our God: Babylonian parallels to this divine highway have been adduced (e.g. by F. Stummer, *JBL* 45 (1926), p. 172). But it is unlikely that Deutero-Isaiah would wish here to draw a parallel between Yahweh and other gods. It is more probable that he was thinking in general terms of the construction or repair of roads in preparation for the advance of conquering kings. The **highway** (*meṣillāh*) was literally a high way, raised up (*ṣll*) above the surrounding land.

4. rough places: the exact meaning of *reḵāsîm* is unknown.

5. the glory of the LORD: for Deutero-Isaiah this phrase probably had a more general sense than for the author of the Priestly Document: Yahweh will appear in awe-inspiring splendour. The prophet would be familiar with the earlier traditions represented by Exod. 33 : 18–23; Isa. 6 : 3, and may have been especially influenced by that of Ezek. 11 : 22–23, which describes the disappearance from the midst of Israel of that glory of Yahweh whose return is now envisaged. It is characteristic of Deutero-Isaiah that this glorious appearance of Yahweh will be witnessed by **all flesh**, that is, all mankind.

6. And I said: here *RSV*, following LXX, Vulg., and 1QIsª, correctly repoints MT's *w*ᵉ*'āmar*, 'And someone said', as *wā'ōmar* (or *w*ᵉ*'ōmar*) 'And I said'.
All flesh is grass: these words begin the message which answers the prophet's question. The reference is ostensibly to human nature as such; but the prophet especially has in mind the pretensions of the seemingly all-powerful Babylonian empire. **its beauty:** although this translation of *ḥasdô* has a long ancestry (LXX *doxa*) it cannot be justified. *ḥesed*, though a very common word in Hebrew, never has this meaning elsewhere. The normal meaning 'steadfastness, durability, reliability' is entirely satisfactory in the context (see N. H. Snaith, *ExpT* 52 (1940–1), pp. 394–6). The word has been chosen to make a contrast with verse 8, where although the word *ḥesed* is not used, the implication is that Yahweh alone has these qualities.

7. The imagery has been derived from the phenomenon of the sudden withering of the spring flowers (both in Palestine and Babylonia) when blown upon by the hot *sirocco*. The omission of this verse from LXX and some MSS (cf. its subsequent addition in IQIsª) is due to accident (homoioteleuton).

8. The grass . . . fades: repetitions for the sake of literary effectiveness are characteristic of the style of Deutero-Isaiah. **but the word of our God will stand for ever:** the final line makes the contrast and constitutes the climax. The phrase **word of God** (cf. the fuller exposition in 55 : 10f.) includes the idea of the prophetic word, but is not restricted to it. Deutero-Isaiah constantly had to struggle to convince his hearers that his message could be relied upon, and to this end frequently pointed to God's earlier fulfilment of his own promises made through the prophets (42 : 9; 44 : 6–8; 45 : 21; 46 : 8–11; 48 : 5). **stand** (*ḳûm*) is here used in the sense of 'endure, be established, succeed'.

THE GOOD NEWS PROCLAIMED

40 : 9–11

The prophet here addresses **Zion/Jerusalem** with a command to proclaim to the other **cities of Judah** the good news that God has won a decisive victory and is now on his way to them, bringing the exiles with him. The message is similar to that of verses 1–5, but is clothed in highly imaginative language. **Jerusalem** is pictured as God's messenger or **herald**, already aware of the victory and under orders to spread the news of it. The victory, believed by the prophet to be imminent, is pictured as already won. There is no reason to suppose that this passage is a continuation of verses 1–8 and that the speaker is yet another heavenly being.

9. Get you up: Zion/Jerusalem, like other cities, is addressed as a woman, and the imperatives in this verse are consequently fem. **to a high mountain:** the function of the **herald** is similar to that of the watchman stationed on an elevated place (normally a watchtower or city wall) to report the approach of troops (cf. 52 : 8) or of a military runner sent ahead to announce their arrival (cf. 1 Sam. 31 : 9; 2 Sam. 18 : 19–21), who might choose a high place from which to make his announcement. Possibly both ideas were in the prophet's mind: it is characteristic of him to oscillate between the two meanings of Zion/Jerusalem—the exiles who longed to return and the city itself.

O Zion, herald of good tidings: as *RSV* mg. indicates, it would be grammatically possible to translate this phrase by 'O herald of good tidings to Zion', and the parallel phrase similarly. But unless the person addressed is Zion it is difficult to account for the fem. imperatives and the fem. participle *meḇaśśereṯ* (**herald**). The verb *bśr* (Piel) denotes the function of the military runner who brings news of a victory.

Behold your God: for the significance of this announcement of God's imminent arrival see on verse 5 above.

10. with might: literally, 'as a mighty one' (*beḥāzāḳ*); see G–K §119 i.

and his arm rules for him: God's **arm**, the locus of his strength, is partially personified here. Such personifications of parts of the body are frequent in Hebrew. God's **arm** was especially associated with his deliverance of Israel at the time of the Exodus (e.g. Dt. 4 : 34).

his reward; **his recompense:** these words (*śāḵār, peʿullāh*) refer to the spoils of victory; but in this case the spoils are the rescued exiles, who are in a sense God's 'captives'.

11. But these captives are at the same time God's 'sheep', the **flock** whom he loves. The change of imagery is not as abrupt as it might seem, since a king in the ancient Near East was regarded as a **shepherd** of his people. The thought of God as shepherd is found frequently in the *OT* (e.g. Ps. 23 : 1; 95 : 7), and is speci-

fically associated with the gathering of the scattered exiles again in 49 : 9–11 and in Jer. 23 : 1ff.; 31 : 10; Ezek. 34 : 11ff.
he will gather . . . bosom: *BHS* divides the words of the Hebrew differently, giving 'he will gather them in his arms, he will carry the lambs in his bosom' (reading *beḥêḳô* for *ûḇeḥêḳô*). This would give a more regular metre, but is unnecessary.

THE CREATOR AND LORD OF HISTORY

40 : 12–17

These verses comprise the first of a series (verses 12–31) of 'disputations' (*Disputationswort* or *Streitgespräch*), a form of argument which proceeds, by means of rhetorical questions, from ground common to both sides to prove a disputed point. C. Westermann ('Sprache und Struktur der Prophetie Deuterojesajas', in *Forschung am Alten Testament*, 1964, pp. 92–188) has argued, on the grounds that the complaint voiced by Israel in verse 27 is the key to the whole, that these short disputations are integral parts of an original single composition. Nevertheless each is both complete and intelligible by itself.

The present editorial arrangement of this chapter is a logical one. It was not enough for Deutero-Isaiah to assert (verses 1–11) that Yahweh was about to intervene to rescue the exiles; he needed to marshal powerful arguments if he was to be believed.

12–14. The prophet begins by appealing, through a series of questions, to the common ground of the Israelite traditions of the creation of the world.

12. Whether this question expects a positive answer ('Yahweh') or a negative one ('no man'), the implication is that Yahweh alone has done all these things (cf. the questions put by God to Job in Job 38–39). He is depicted as a craftsman making the tiny universe at his bench: he needs only a handful of water and of dust carefully measured and weighed out.

13–14. The question of the type of reply expected is raised again here. But the questions gain the greatest significance if their purpose is to elicit the reply that Yahweh alone created the universe without assistance from other gods. Deutero-Isaiah is concerned to demonstrate the superiority of the monotheistic Israelite traditions of creation over those of other nations, especially those of Babylon, whose polytheistic traditions abounded in counsellor-gods, and who in *Enuma Eliš* (*ANET*, pp. 60–72) represented the creator-god Marduk as unable to create the world on his own, and needing the assistance of his father Ea.

The view of K. Elliger ('Der Begriff "Geschichte" bei Deuterojesaja', in *Kleine Schriften zum Alten Testament*, 1953, pp. 199–210) that verses 13–14 refer to Yahweh's work in history rather than in creation is based on too narrow an interpretation of certain words, especially *'ēṣāh* in the phrase *'îš 'aṣāṯô*, **his counsellor** (verse 13).

13. directed the Spirit: better, 'comprehended the mind'. On this and other problems of verses 13–14 see R. N. Whybray, *The Heavenly Counsellor in Isaiah xl 13–14*, 1971.

14. justice (*mišpāṭ*); **understanding** (*tᵉḇûnôṯ*): better, 'order'; 'creative skill'.

and taught him knowledge: these words are lacking in LXX and do not fit the metrical pattern. We should omit them, with most commentators.

15–17. Having established the nature of Israel's creation faith and its superiority, on which he and his audience are agreed, the prophet moves on from creation to history. If the universe itself is merely a tiny product of Yahweh's hands, this must also be true of the nations which inhabit it. The implication is that, in spite of outward appearances, Yahweh *can* save his people: the puny pretensions of Babylon are illusory and cannot oppose his will.

15. a drop from a bucket (*mar middᵉlî*): both words are of uncertain meaning. It has been suggested by D. W. Thomas (*In Memoriam Paul Kahle* (*BZAW* 103), 1968, pp. 214–21) that the true meaning may be 'dust of the balances', which provides a parallel with the following line.

he takes up (*yiṭṭôl*): read plur. *yiṭṭôlû* and translate 'the isles have only the weight of fine dust'. The meaning 'take up' for *nāṭal* is doubtful; in Syriac the root *nṭl* means 'weigh, turn the scales'.

16. Some commentators have regarded this verse as an irrelevant interpolation. But it would be rash to maintain that Deutero-Isaiah was incapable of a digression. **Lebanon** was famous as an abundant source of timber.

17. as less than nothing (*mē'eṗes*): this is a dubious interpretation of the Hebrew particle *min-*. It is probably best to read *kᵉ'eṗes* ('as nothing'), following 1QIs[a].

YAHWEH THE INCOMPARABLE

40 : 18–26

This is a second disputation along the same lines as the first. Some scholars (e.g. Begrich), noting the similarities between verses 18–24 and 25–26, hold that there are two independent disputations here, and von Waldow that there are three: verses 18–20, 21–24, 25–26. But verses 19–20 are rightly seen by most commentators as an interpolation; and, once these are removed, the remainder is probably best understood as a single piece.

18–21. That the prophet is engaged in an argument or disputation is very clear here. These questions make sense only if some of the prophet's audience had been thinking of Yahweh as simply one of a number of gods, and not the most powerful. He replies by appealing to the common ground of Israel's traditional faith.

18. then (Heb. *wᵉ*)**:** if original, this particle does not indicate a connexion with the previous verse, but with the (unrecorded) words of the prophet's opponents.
God: the prophet here uses neither the personal name Yahweh nor the more common *'ᵉlōhîm*, but *'ēl* (El), which apart from being a common Semitic word for 'god', was also the personal name of the king of the gods in the Canaanite religion. El had already been identified with Yahweh in the pre-exilic cult of Jerusalem (see O. Eissfeldt, 'El and Yahweh', *JSS* 1 (1956), pp. 25–37). Deutero-Isaiah uses the word in contexts (43 : 13 (MT 43 : 12); 45 : 14; 46 : 9) where he wishes to emphasize the absolute superiority of the one true God.

21. This verse originally followed directly upon verse 18. With these questions the prophet reproaches his audience. The character of God had been **known** to them from their religious tradition: they had **heard** and **been told** it **from the beginning** and **from the foundations of the earth** (reading *mîsūḏaṯ* for MT's *môsᵉḏôṯ*). The last two phrases probably mean simply 'from ancient times'. According to the Yahwist (Gen. 4 : 26) the worship of Yahweh reached back almost to the beginning of time.

19–20. These verses, which mock the manufacturers of images of gods and, by implication, their worshippers, belong to a group of passages (41 : 6–7; 44 : 9–20; 46 : 6–7) which are considered by many commentators to be the work of later interpreters of Deutero-Isaiah. Each must however be considered individually.

The mocking of idols is in itself not a theme foreign to Deutero-Isaiah's teaching (see e.g. 46 : 1–2). But these verses interrupt the sequence of thought and misunderstand the point of verse 18, which is concerned not with the folly of making idols but with the wrongness of comparing the true God with other gods.

19. This verse, of which 41 : 6–7 may be the original continuation, describes the manufacture of a gilt-metal image of a god. The Jewish exiles might well have been familiar with the process (for a Babylonian description of it see *ANET*, p. 331.) The authors of this and similar passages are wrong in their assumption that the Babylonians were incapable of distinguishing between a god and its image. Their contemptuous dismissal of this aspect of Babylonian religion was thus based on ignorance, though it shows a sound theological instinct. The implication is that the Babylonian gods are man-made and so *ipso facto* not gods at all. **casts for it silver chains**, if a correct translation, may be intended (cf. verse 20) to add a further point: the 'god' is held down by chains and unable to move. But **chains** (*r*ᵉ*ṯūqôṯ*) occurs only here and its meaning is doubtful, while **casts for it** involves an emendation (*ṣôrēp̄* to *yiṣrōp̄*) and is lacking in LXX.

20. Here the making of a second, wooden, idol is described. **that will not move** here certainly has a satirical implication. **He who is impoverished chooses for an offering** can hardly be a correct translation of the Heb. as it stands, which, in spite of many attempts to interpret or correct it, remains completely obscure.

22. The prophet now rehearses the traditions to which he has appealed in verse 21. **sits, stretches out, brings** (in verse 23) are expressed in the Heb. by participles; this is characteristic of the 'hymn' or song of praise in the Psalter (e.g. Ps. 104 : 2–4; 136), and shows that, as in many other passages, the prophet is appealing to the Israelite traditions contained in the pre-exilic psalms, which, in spite of the enforced cessation of the temple cult, must still have been in use among the exiles. Some of the expressions (e.g. **stretches out the heavens**; **like a tent**—cf. Ps. 104 : 2) are very similar to passages in the extant psalms; otherwise the prophet appears to be making use of similar psalms which have not survived.

the circle of the earth refers either to the circular horizon (the earth being thought of as a flat disc) or to the 'firmament' (Gen. 1 : 6) or solid hemisphere which God placed over the earth. The other passages where the word (*ḥûg*) occurs (Prov. 8 : 27; Job 22 : 14; possibly Job 26 : 10) do not provide clear evidence on this question.

23. The prophet now moves from the realm of creation to that of history. He has already pointed out in verse 22 (cf. verse 15) the implications of Yahweh's creatorship of the world: to him **its inhabitants are like grasshoppers** (for the simile cf. Num. 13 : 33), that is, puny creatures entirely at his mercy. The writer now applies this point more specifically to silence the doubters among his audience: **the rulers of the earth** (including the Babylonian powers) must consequently also be **as nothing**.

24. For the imagery here cf. verse 7. **stubble:** better, 'chaff'.

25–26. The prophet now returns, in conclusion, to the original question (verse 18) concerning Yahweh's incomparability.

25. Characteristically he repeats the question, but puts it into the mouth of God himself. The words attributed to God are not an independent oracle but a quotation by the prophet within the disputation: this, he says, is what God is indignantly demanding (imperfect *yō'mar*, 'is saying'). **the Holy One:** more frequently, 'the Holy One of Israel'. Holiness is the essential character of God as he reveals himself to man (cf. Isa. 6 : 3).

26. The reference (**these**) is to the heavenly bodies (sun, moon, planets, stars). Far from being an anticlimax, this verse is crucial to the whole argument. The Babylonian religion was an astral cult: the gods were identified with the heavenly bodies, and as such controlled the course of history. Deutero-Isaiah is at one with the teaching of the Priestly writer (Gen. 1 : 14–18) and possibly older traditions (cf. Ps. 147 : 4, whose date, however, is uncertain) in affirming that the heavenly bodies are part of the created order, to whom the creator assigns their proper and limited functions. **brings out their host by number, calling them all by name** suggests a general marshalling his troops and giving them their orders; **not one is missing** suggests that none dares fail to be 'on parade'.

But the crucial word is **created** (*bārā'*). This word is characteristic of Deutero-Isaiah, who uses it more frequently than any other *OT* author, followed closely by the Priestly writer. Before this time it seems not to have been in frequent use; to him, however, it was particularly appropriate for the expression of his uncompromising teaching about God as the sole Creator, since its use is entirely confined to the activity of Yahweh. Here therefore it marks the climax and conclusion of the disputation: Israel's own traditions, of which the prophet's audience have now been reminded, lead inevitably to the conclusion that Yahweh alone has absolute power over the whole universe.

and because he is strong in power: perhaps read 'and (by the) strength of (his) power' (reading *'ōmeṣ* for MT's *'ammîṣ*, following indications in some of the Versions, especially LXX, and—perhaps—1QIs[a]).

THE SOURCE OF STRENGTH

40 : 27–31

In this final disputation the prophet is no longer concerned with God's ability to help his people but with a complaint that he is unwilling to do so.

27. The complainants are now addressed as **Jacob/Israel**, since the basis of their complaint is that Yahweh by his inaction is ignoring their rightful claim to the fulfilment of the promises which he made to their ancestors the patriarchs (Gen. 12 : 2–3; 28 : 13–15). This time their words are quoted *verbatim*. They have the character of the 'communal lamentation' familiar from the Psalms and Lamentations (e.g. Ps. 44 : 24 (MT 25); Lam. 5 : 20), and are probably part of a psalm actually used in Deutero-Isaiah's time (cf. also 49 : 14; Ezek. 37 : 11).

My way is hid from the LORD: this does not mean that God is unable to see the fate (**way**) of the exiles, but that he has deliberately refused to do so: cf. Hos. 13 : 14: 'Compassion is hid from my eyes', and the frequent complaints in the lamentations in the Psalms that God has 'hidden his face'. Alternatively the meaning may be that God has concealed from his people their **way**, that is, he has confused them and made them 'lose their way' (cf. Job 3 : 23: 'a man whose way is hid, whom God has hedged in'). In either case it is God's good will which is questioned, not his competence. The parallel phrase **and my right is disregarded** has a similar meaning: Israel's **right** (*mišpāṭ*) is the right which the exiles are claiming on the basis of God's promises, and which entitles them to address him as **my God**.

28. The prophet begins his reply with the same questions as in verse 21, again appealing to the common ground of Israel's traditional faith. First, Yahweh is **the everlasting God** (*'elōhê 'ôlām*). No abstract idea of eternity is expressed here; the meaning is that Yahweh's controlling activity extends through time past, present and future. Second, as the **Creator of the ends of the earth** (and all that lies between them), God's power is equally unlimited in space. With the third affirmation, which is a conclusion drawn from the first two, the prophet begins his demonstration of the falseness of the complaint against God: is it possible to believe that such a God could **faint or grow weary** and so fail his people? In the fourth affirmation he goes further and puts forward a different explanation of God's apparent inactivity: **his understanding is unsearchable**—that is, the human mind is too small to comprehend God's mind or to judge his intentions: God will act, but only when he decides that the time is ripe.

29-31. The conclusion contains encouragement as well as argument. This God of unlimited power and unwearying vigilance whose mind no man can penetrate is not, as has been alleged, unmindful of his people or of their claims upon him.

29. Here the prophet reminds his audience indirectly but unmistakably of how God in the past (e.g. the Exodus) and in the lives of individual Israelites (cf. the 'songs of thanksgiving' in the Psalter) has come to the rescue of **the faint** and of **him who has no might**. The participle (*nōṯēn*, **gives**) indicates that such help is not sporadic but always characteristic of God.

30-31. A contrast is made between the frailty of unaided human strength and endurance at its best (**youths** and **young men**) and the **strength** which God gives and will give to those **who wait for the LORD**. The verb translated by **wait** (*ḳāwāh*) is not neutral like the English word, but means 'wait with confident expectation, trust', and occurs frequently in the lamentations and 'songs of confidence' in the Psalms. So those who trust God are promised new strength which will enable them to continue their 'way' (cf. verse 27) through life.

31. they shall mount up with wings like eagles: this translation is somewhat difficult, requiring **wings** (*'ēḇer*) to be taken as an adverbial accusative. The verb (*ya'alû*) can be taken either as Qal (as in *RSV*) or as Hiphil, and as Hiphil can mean either 'lift up' (so Targ.) or 'grow' in a transitive sense (so LXX, Vulg.). 'lift up wings' is not a very appropriate expression here, and 'grow wings' is probably the best translation, although the theory that here (and in Ps. 103 : 5) there is an allusion to a legend that the eagle grows new wings in old age (J. Achaj, *Beth Miqra* 11 (1965–6), pp. 144–7) is doubtful. The wings of an eagle are an obvious symbol of great strength.

CYRUS YAHWEH'S INSTRUMENT

41 : 1–5

This is the first of a number of examples of the 'trial-speech', in which Deutero-Isaiah presents his teaching in the form of a speech made by Yahweh, either as plaintiff or as defendant in a lawsuit. These are probably literary adaptations of types of speech made in connexion with pre-exilic court procedure (see L. Koehler, 'Judgment in the Gate', *Hebrew Man*, 1956, pp. 149–75). Earlier prophets (e.g. Isaiah, 1 : 18ff.) had already used this form of speech as a means of denouncing Israel's sins; but Deutero-Isaiah finds new uses for it.

1. This is not a criminal case, but a civil, 'fact-finding' one: the question at issue is the identity of the true God. No judge is mentioned: the court as a whole, which includes Yahweh's opponents, listens to the proceedings (**judgment**, *mišpāṭ*), and decides on the basis of the evidence presented. The court consists of the nations: **coastlands**, a vague term for distant lands along the Mediterranean coast, and **peoples**. Yahweh, as the appellant, calls the court to order. **let the peoples renew their strength** can hardly be right; possibly the original text had 'draw near and come', which now stands, slightly altered, in verse 5, while the present Heb. text is a repetition of part of 40 : 31.

2–4. As proof that it is he and not the gods of other nations who is in control of the events of history and so the true God, Yahweh cites the amazing career of Cyrus. The ancient view that the person referred to here is Abraham still has supporters (e.g. Kissane), and it may be that Abraham, who also was **stirred up . . . from the east** and who won a **victory** over the **kings** of four nations (Gen. 14) was not entirely absent from the prophet's mind: he frequently uses words and themes with a double significance. But the passage makes much better sense if it is taken as referring primarily to Cyrus, who elsewhere plays an important part in Deutero-Isaiah's teaching and is twice actually named by him (44 : 28; 45 : 1).

2. This verse describes the lightning career of Cyrus in the years preceding the fall of Babylon: a man **from the east**, winning a swift and apparently miraculous series of victories over the leading world powers. **whom victory meets at every step:** the syntax is disputed, but this is the most probable translation. **victory** (*ṣeḏeḳ*) **:** on the various meanings of this word (righteousness, divine rule, victory, etc.) see H. H. Schmid, *Gerechtigkeit als Weltordnung*, 1968. **tramples . . . under foot:** *RSV* reads *yārōḏ* for the anomalous *yard* of MT. But 1QIs[a] has *ywrd* = *yôrîḏ*, 'brings down'. **he makes them . . . sword:** the grammar is difficult, and it is probably best to read *yittᵉnēm* for MT's *yittēn*, rendering 'his sword makes them like dust'. (For masc. verb with fem. subject, see G–K, §145 o.) **his bow** will then be a second subject of the verb.

3. The subject is now Cyrus. **by paths his feet have not trod:** better, 'his feet do not touch the ground'. Various explanations have been given of this sentence; it is probably simply poetic hyperbole, suggesting the speed of Cyrus' movements.

4. Yahweh now repeats his question and answers it. **calling the generations:** better, 'he who calls the generations'. Only the God who, as Israel knows from its historical traditions, had always been behind the events of history, could have raised up Cyrus. **I, the LORD, the first:** probably better 'I, the LORD, am the first'. Yahweh was not only active **from the beginning** of history, but is also **first** in an absolute sense: unlike the Babylonian gods, who were themselves the children of older gods, Yahweh alone has no genealogy (cf. 43 : 10). Equally he is **with the last:** that is, he will be God when the last human generation comes to an end. The Babylonian and other Near Eastern religions could not match such a claim, which was inconceivable in a polytheistic religion. Even in Israelite belief this had never before been so clearly understood and expressed. **I am He**, as other passages (43 : 10, 13; 46 : 4; 48 : 12) show, is a characteristic expression used by Deutero-Isaiah to express the conviction that Yahweh is the only God.

In his speech Yahweh has challenged the implicit claims of the Babylonian gods to rule the world by pointing out that no such claim can stand which does not take account of the one man in contemporary history who is clearly the man of destiny: Cyrus. Only a god who has made possible Cyrus' victories has a right to make such a claim; the Babylonian gods and their supporters would hardly wish to do so, and so have no reply to make. Deutero-Isaiah does not even mention one rather obvious possibility, that Cyrus' victories were due to his own national gods. Instead he falls back on Israelite traditions which he sums up in the phrase **calling the generations from the beginning**. He invites his audience to remember how in the past many historical figures—the Egyptian Pharaoh, Assyrian kings, Nebuchadnezzar, and many others—had served Yahweh's purpose for his people, and had been raised up for that purpose. Cyrus falls into line as the latest in a series of such men who were the instruments of the God who is **the first, and with the last**.

5. The poem concludes with the reaction of the court of nations to Yahweh's speech. They have been invited to state their case (verse 1), but they have no case to state: they **have seen and are afraid. they have drawn near and come:** probably misplaced; see on verse 1.

HOW TO MAKE A GOD

41 : 6–7

These verses are sometimes interpreted as the reply of the nations to Yahweh's speech: the only answer which they can make is to refurbish their idols. But probably there is no connexion with what precedes: see on 40 : 19–20.

7. In the first half of this verse the details are not entirely clear. **smooths** (*maḥ^alîḳ*) is uncertain, and some of the Versions suggest an alternative reading meaning 'strike'. **anvil** (*pā῾am*) is also uncertain: it nowhere else has this meaning, and the Versions were uncertain how to render it. The image is probably made of base metal gilt: hence the suggestion that these verses may be connected with 40 : 19.

ISRAEL YAHWEH'S SERVANT

41 : 8–13

This passage is the first of a number of oracles which J. Begrich ('Das priesterliche Heilsorakel', *ZAW* 52 (1934), pp. 81–92) classified as 'oracles of salvation' (*Heilsorakel*). According to Begrich these are literary adaptations of a type of priestly oracle pronounced in pre-exilic times in answer to the complaint made by individuals who came to the sanctuary in distress: large numbers of such 'individual lamentations' are to be found in the Psalms. In spite of the fact that the evidence for the use of such oracles is only indirect, this theory has come to be widely accepted. More recently von Waldow (*Anlass und Hintergrund*, 1953, pp. 11–28) has argued that it was a prophet rather than a priest who had pronounced such oracles, and that the examples in Deutero-Isaiah are not literary imitations: the prophet was continuing an older prophetic practice, pronouncing them at meetings of the exiles for worship in answer to psalms of lamentation in which the worshippers lamented that Yahweh had deserted them.

8–9. Yahweh is the speaker throughout the oracle. Already in his opening words he seeks to reassure his people, addressing them with a series of epithets which reminds them of their special status as his chosen people and assures them that this has not changed. This assurance is already conveyed by the words **Israel/Jacob**, and is made more explicit by the phrases **my servant** and **whom I have chosen**. The word **servant** (*ʿeḇeḏ*) has a wide range of meanings; here the parallel phrase **whom I have chosen** shows that its purpose is to stress the protection which God has given and still gives to Israel. As elsewhere (51 : 2) the prophet looks back as far as **Abraham**, to whom the promise of a happy people dwelling in their own land had been given, as the recipient of God's initial act of grace. Fohrer's omission of the line in which Abraham is mentioned by name is not to be accepted: if the metrical pattern is in disorder, it is more probable that something has been accidentally omitted rather than that a line has been added.

8. But you: this indicates a connexion with something which has gone before, but not necessarily with the preceding section in the book as it is now arranged. Westermann sees it as related to the unrecorded lamentation to which this oracle is a reply. **my friend:** so also in 2 Chr. 20 : 7 and, later, in the Qur'an. There is no reason, with *BHS*, to repoint the active participle *ʾōhᵃḇî* as the passive *ʾᵃhûḇî*.

9. It is not clear in the Heb. whether **whom I took . . .** refers to Israel (so *RSV*) or to Abraham. In any case Abraham and his **offspring** are closely linked in the prophet's mind. **from the ends of the earth** could equally well refer to the call of Abraham, seen from the point of view of Palestine (where the prophet frequently places himself in imagination) or to the deliverance of Israel from Egypt. **You are my servant:** cf. on verse 8. Abraham is given this title in Gen. 26 : 24. **not cast you off:** the prophet's mind has already moved to the present situation, in which God was being accused of so doing (cf. 40 : 27; 49 : 14).

10. fear not: this phrase, which is characteristic of the oracle of salvation, also occurs in stories in which God appears ('theophany') to individuals to help them (e.g. Gen. 15 : 1; 21 : 17; Jos. 8 : 1). It is followed by an assurance of God's solidarity with the petitioner (**I am with you**; **I am your God**—cf. 43 : 5; 44 : 2) and then by a series of verbs—**strengthen**; **help**; **uphold**—which in Heb. are in the perfect tense, the so-called 'prophetic perfect' which indicates that help is both certain and imminent. **with my victorious right hand** (*bîmîn ṣiḏḵî*). On this meaning of *ṣeḏeḵ* see on verse 2 above.

11–12. The general promise of immediate help is now followed by a more specific assurance of the downfall of Israel's enemies. The tenses here are imperfect (i.e. future), indicating the concrete results which will follow God's determination to **help**.

11. all who are incensed (*hanneḥᵉrîm*): in view of the rarity of this verb (*ḥārāh*) in the Niphal, G.R. Driver (*JTS* 36 (1935), pp. 398f.) suggested that this word should be pointed *hannōḥᵉrîm* (Qal participle of a supposed verb *nāḥar*, 'snort with anger'; cf. Aram. *nᵉḥar*) and similarly in 45 : 24. But this is questionable.

11b–12. 1QIsᵃ has a shorter text: 'those who strive against you shall perish; and those who contend with you shall be as nothing, and those who war against you shall be as nothing at all.' This is accepted as original by Fohrer, but without sufficient reason.

13. This final verse serves to repeat and re-emphasize the assurance to the exiles that divine help is on its way. **hold your right hand:** cf. Ps. 73 : 23. The phrase expresses the idea of God's reassuring and protective presence.

YAHWEH'S THRESHING SLEDGE

41 : 14–16

Like 41 : 8–13 this is an oracle of salvation, though a shorter one. Its present position may be due to the fact that it begins by repeating the last words of verse 13: **Fear not . . . I will help you.** It consists characteristically of an address, together with the cry of encouragement **Fear not** and the general promise to help with verbs in the perfect tense (**will help**; **will make**) (verses 14, 15*a*) and finally a more precise statement of the consequences of this help (15*b*, 16).

14. Jacob/Israel: see on 41 : 8–9. **men of Israel** makes a feeble parallel for **worm Jacob**. Earlier commentators proposed to emend **men of** (*meṯê*) to *rimmaṯ*, 'maggot'; but G. R. Driver's suggestion (*JTS* 36 (1935), p. 399) that the word is related to the Accadian *mutu*, 'louse' has now been widely accepted. Both words of course are contemptuous, and are almost certainly used here because the exiles have so described themselves in a lamentation to which this oracle is the reply. The author of Ps. 22 (an individual lamentation) describes himself as a worm (verse 6; MT 7). **your Redeemer:** this word (*gōʾēl*) is used frequently by Deutero-Isaiah as an epithet of Yahweh. In secular use it designates the 'near kinsman' whose duty it was to help and protect a distressed relative in various circumstances (e.g. Lev. 25 : 47–49; Num. 35 : 19; Ru. 3 : 11–13). In using this word of Yahweh's relationship to Israel the prophet seeks to encourage the exiles in two ways: he suggests that Yahweh considers himself under an obligation to help them, an obligation which he will not break; and also, more startlingly, that Yahweh's relationship with them is so intimate that he can be described (even though metaphorically) as a 'near kinsman'. At the same time, in referring to God as the **Holy One of Israel**, an expression which he took over from the vocabulary of his predecessor, the eighth-century Isaiah, he emphasizes the amazing condescension of this utterly transcendent and mysterious God (cf. Isa. 6).

15. The metaphor is a curious one: Israel is to become a **threshing sledge** which will **thresh the mountains and crush them**. The **threshing sledge** was a board with nails affixed to it (**having teeth**) which was dragged round the threshing floor to separate the grain from the **chaff**. Here, however, it is the **mountains** and **hills** which are to be crushed. **mountains** and **hills** have been taken by many commentators to refer to Israel's enemies; but this would give to Israel an aggressive role not found elsewhere in Deutero-Isaiah; and the **mountains** probably stand for Israel's present difficulties, which will be swept away (cf. 40 : 4; Zech. 4 : 7). **sharp** (*ḥārûṣ*)**:** probably better understood as a noun meaning a threshing implement, added later as a gloss explaining the rare word *môrag* which it follows in the Heb.

16. In the process of threshing the useless chaff was blown away by the **wind**, leaving the grain. But here there is no grain: only dust, which is scattered, leaving nothing behind.

And you shall rejoice . . . glory: the final promise is that the exiles on their return home after the removal of all obstacles will sing a song of praise or thanksgiving. In the lamentations in the Psalms vows were sometimes made to do so if release from distress was obtained (cf. Ps. 71 : 14–16, 22–24, and Westermann's commentary), and these words may be an adaptation of such a vow made in the lamentation to which this oracle is a reply. This would account for the fact that God is referred to in the third person.

THE FLOWERING OF THE DESERT

41 : 17–20

This passage, like verses 8–13 and 14–16 above, is a promise of salvation made by Yahweh, but of a somewhat different kind. In particular the address and the cry of encouragement are missing. Westermann, (*Sprache und Struktur*, pp. 117–24) sees here a distinct type of oracle, which he calls the 'announcement of salvation' (*Heilsankündigung*), an imitation of an earlier type of *prophetic* oracle given in answer to the *communal* lamentation, whereas the 'oracle of salvation' (*Heilsorakel*) was originally a *priestly* oracle answering the *individual* lamentation. This distinction seems somewhat over-subtle, especially as the form of the 'announcement of salvation' is not very clearly defined. Probably both were used by Deutero-Isaiah in similar situations. In this commentary the distinction will be preserved, however, in that the *Heilsorakel* will be referred to as 'oracle of salvation', while all other divine promises will be designated simply 'promise of salvation'. It is necessary to bear in mind the unusual freedom with which Deutero-Isaiah treats traditional forms.

The oracle, however strange this may seem to the modern reader, is intended to be taken literally. It refers to the coming homeward march of the exiles through the desert, which has already been announced in 40 : 10–11, and which reappears in later oracles. We may presume that the exiles had complained that they were **poor and needy** and would not be able to endure the rigours of the journey. The prophet replies with a promise of miracles to come which are reminiscent of the divine help received by the Israelites long ago in their journey through the desert after their deliverance from Egypt.

17. poor: this word (Heb. *ʿānî*, plur. *ʿaniyyîm*) is regularly used in the lamentations in the Psalms by the petitioner as a description of himself. **needy** (*ʾeḇyôn*) is similarly used, though here it overloads the poetical line and may be a gloss. **answer:** a previous lamentation is presupposed.

18. open rivers on the bare heights: perhaps better, 'among the sand-dunes' (cf. also 35 : 6–7). This is a specific reference to Moses' action when he brought water out of the rock in the wilderness (Exod. 17 : 1–7; Num. 20 : 1–13). This time the action will be performed by Yahweh himself. **a pool of water** (*laʾagam-mayîm*)**:** emend, with most commentators, to 'pools' (*laʾaḡammîm*), which provides a better parallelism.

19. The identity of some of these seven trees is uncertain. **cedar** (*ʾerez*) is the cedar of Lebanon; **acacia** and **myrtle** offer no difficulty; the **olive** is the wild olive or oleander. **cypress** (*berôš*) is probably the Phoenician juniper. **plane** (*tiḏhār*) is uncertain, perhaps a kind of cypress; **pine** (*teaššûr*) is probably the box. None of these trees is a fruit tree; rather their purpose is to give shade, which travellers in the desert would, together with water, need most. We are to suppose that this great variety of trees will appear full-grown, providing a ready-made oasis. So great is God's loving care for his people. Behind the miracle lies the inexhaustible power of the Creator-God, put to Israel's service.

20. Yet the ultimate purpose of God's action lies, as Deutero-Isaiah constantly affirms, even beyond the salvation of Israel. **men** here (simply 'they' in the Heb.) is indefinite: not only Israel but all men will **see** and acknowledge Yahweh's supreme power (cf. 45 : 6; 49 : 26). The salvation of Israel is the means to this end.

THE GODS ARE NOTHING

41 : 21–29

This is a second 'trial-speech' (see on verses 1–5 above). Now Yahweh addresses the gods of the nations directly and challenges them to substantiate their claim to divinity. When they are unable to do so (their silence is implied in verse 24) Yahweh produces the **proofs** of his own claim to be God. The conclusion (verses 24, 29) is that the other gods are **nothing**. The purpose once more is to persuade the exiles that Yahweh's promises are not empty words.

21. The early episodes of the session are taken for granted. Evidently the gods have claimed that it is they who control history, and Yahweh invites them to produce evidence for this controversial claim (**case**; Heb. *rîḇ*). **proofs** (*ʿaṣūmōṯ*)**:** literally, 'powerful things', or possibly, 'arguments', Arab. *ʿasama*). **King of Jacob:** this title, which may seem inadequate in a context where it is Yahweh's universal power which is in question, is used by the prophet for the sake of his audience, to assure them that it is for their sake that Yahweh is battling.

22. The *RSV* translation and some minor textual corruptions have combined to obscure the meaning of this verse. **Let them bring them:** read *yiggešû* 'let them draw near' (a legal term for appearance in court), for *yaggîšû* (cf. LXX, Vulg., 1Q Isᵃ). **what is to happen:** the verb (*tiḳrénah*) should be taken not as future but in a general sense: 'what happens', i.e. 'the events of history'. **the former things:** this word—(*hā*)*ri'šōnôṯ*—occurs elsewhere in the book (42 : 9; 43 : 9, 18; 46 : 9; 48 : 3), and its meaning has been the subject of debate (see A. Schoors, 'Les choses antérieures et les choses nouvelles dans les oracles deutéro-isaïens', *Ephemerides Theologicae Lovanienses* 40 (1964), pp. 19–47). Each case must be decided on its own merits, and here the context requires a general meaning, 'past events', as distinct from future events (*habbā'ôṯ*, **the things to come**). **that we may know their outcome** should come at the end of the verse. Bearing all these points in mind we may translate the verse somewhat freely as follows: 'Let them draw near and explain to us the meaning of history. Explain to us the meaning of past events, and we shall consider it; or, alternatively, predict future events for us, so that we may note their fulfilment (*'aḥarîṯān*).' The point is that the real test of divinity is the ability to control history. This may be proved either by giving an account of past history which shows a complete mastery of it, or by a prediction of future events, which can be verified in the event.

23. The first two lines reiterate the request for predictions, and make explicit the purpose of the challenge: **that we may know that you are gods.**

do good or do harm: the meaning is, 'do anything at all': cf. Jer. 10 : 5; Zeph. 1 : 12. The tone is derisive: if the previous tasks are too much for the gods, any proof that they are really alive at all will be welcome! **terrified:** *RSV* correctly reads Qere *wᵉnīr'ā* rather than Kethib *wᵉnir'e* ('see').

24. nothing: probably read *'ayin* for *mē'ayin*: the *mem* is a repetition of the last letter of the previous word. **nought:** *RSV* correctly reads *(mē)'epes* for the meaningless *mē'āpaʿ*. Again the *mem* should probably be omitted.

an abomination is he who chooses you: a curious phrase, but the text is probably correct. The non-existent gods themselves can hardly give offence to Yahweh; it is their worshippers whom he abominates.

It needs to be said that in the foregoing verses the prophet makes no attempt to be fair to the heathen religions, whose adherents could certainly have produced arguments in defence of their gods. But as Duhm remarked, Deutero-Isaiah has 'not the slightest grain of self-criticism'.

25. Yahweh now produces his own case. He bases his claim to be God on his ability to predict historical events, which no one could know in advance except their creator. As an example he chooses the career of Cyrus. **I stirred up one from the north:** Cyrus in fact came from the east (**the rising of the sun**), but his conquest of the Median empire (550 BC) had made him master also of territories to Babylon's north.

he shall call on my name (*yiḳrā' bišᵉmî*)**:** this phrase undoubtedly states that Cyrus was or would become a worshipper of Yahweh: Dillmann's interpretation, that it means no more than that he would set forward the Jewish religion by his championship of the Jews, does not do justice to it. The difficulty is that not only did Cyrus not become a worshipper of Yahweh, but that Deutero-Isaiah himself says elsewhere (45 : 5) that he does not know Yahweh. If the text is correct, we can only suppose that at the moment when he composed this poem the prophet did expect that Cyrus would be converted. But the variety of different readings in 1QIsᵃ and the Versions suggests that the text may not be correct. In view of the fact that in 45 : 4 Yahweh is represented as saying to Cyrus '*I* call *you* by *your* name (*wā'eḳrā' lᵉkā bišᵉmekā*)', it has been proposed, not without plausibility, that something of the kind originally stood here. **trample:** *RSV*, following most commentators, emends *w^eyāḇō'* ('and he will come') to *w^eyāḇūs* or *wayyāḇos*. **rulers:** this word (*sāgān*) is a loan word from Accadian, where it means a provincial governor. Later it acquired a pejorative sense both in Accadian and in the *OT*. That this change of meaning has not yet taken place here is regarded by H. W. F. Saggs (*JTS* ns 10 (1959), pp. 84–7) as an argument against Torrey's and Simon's post-exilic dating for Deutero-Isaiah.

26. Yahweh now points out that none of the gods had foretold the rise of Cyrus. He is presumably referring to divinatory and other oracles.

27. The first half of this verse is unintelligible (see *RSV* mg.), and the unlikely variant in 1QIsª (*hnh hnwmh*) indicates that it was corrupt from an early date. Its reconstruction is now almost certainly impossible, though many attempts have been made. *RSV* emends to a verb, **I . . . have declared it** (possibly *higgadtîhā*). The context suggests that something of the kind is probable: Yahweh is claiming that he was the **first** to speak of Cyrus' rise, i.e. the only one to speak of it before it occurred. Although no such prophecies appear to have been preserved in the *OT* outside Deutero-Isaiah, it is evident that the prophet's audience knew of such. They may have been early prophecies by Deutero-Isaiah himself: it is to him that the phrase **herald of good tidings** most naturally refers.

28. But when I look: probably read *wā'ēre'* for the rather unusual *w^e'ēre'*. **among these:** there is insufficient reason to emend this word. **counsellor:** see on 40 : 13–14.

29. a delusion: the Heb. word (*'āwen*) can hardly have this meaning. Read *'ayin*, 'nothing', with 1QIsª (cf. also Targ.).

THE PROPHET'S MISSION

42 : 1–4

This is the first of the four passages (the others are 49 : 1–6; 50 : 4–9; 52 : 13–53 : 12) which were singled out by Duhm as forming a distinct group within the book, the 'Servant Songs'. But Duhm's further wholesale rejection of Deutero-Isaiah's authorship is justified neither by differences of style and language nor by contradictions of thought. The thought is admittedly in some ways distinctive, but expresses one aspect of the prophet's many-sided message.

These verses, as the demarcation in 1QIs[a] already shows, form a unit distinguished from its context by content, form, structure, and metre. Yahweh introduces his Servant as the person whom he has chosen for special service, describes his task, and gives an assurance of his success. Of the many theories concerning his identity—a question which, *pace* some modern commentators, must not be shirked—that which best accords with the evidence is that he is the prophet Deutero-Isaiah himself.

1. Behold (*hēn*): Yahweh is the speaker, and this is a formal presentation of the Servant which amounts to an act of appointment to, or confirmation in, an office. **my servant** (*ʿaḇdî*): the phrase *ʿeḇeḏ yhwh* or its equivalent is used in the *OT* of a number of persons who performed outstanding work in God's service (e.g. Abraham, Moses, David). In secular usage the 'servant of the king' was an important minister (2 Kg. 22 : 12). Elsewhere Deutero-Isaiah applies the title to Israel, but that meaning is improbable here: if it were so, it would doubtless be made explicit, as in 41 : 8; 44 : 2, 21; 45 : 4; 48 : 20. It is not unusual for Deutero-Isaiah to use a word in more than one sense. The fact that Israel's role as Servant is always passive, while here the Servant is emphatically given an active role, is a decisive argument against this identification here.

No explicit indication is given of the circumstances in which Yahweh's presentation of his Servant takes place. In this respect the passage is reminiscent of 40 : 1–8; and it is probable that here as there the setting is that of the heavenly council. Yahweh presents his prophet to the heavenly beings. Elliger's suggestion that the occasion is not the prophet's original appointment but is subsequent to it is probably correct: he has already experienced difficulties and opposition, and now Yahweh reaffirms his confidence in him. (See further on 49 : 1–6.) Whether the prophet recounted this experience publicly to the exiles in order to strengthen his authority, or whether the passage was originally intended only as a private record (cf. the 'confessions' of Jeremiah) cannot be determined.

my chosen: this word, like **my servant**, is elsewhere applied by Deutero-Isaiah to Israel. LXX adds 'Jacob' after **servant** and 'Israel' after **chosen**. Although some commentators hold that this is a correct interpretation, it is universally agreed that this is not the original text. **I have put my Spirit upon him:** earlier Israelite leaders also had received the special gift of God's spirit to empower them to perform special tasks. The pre-exilic canonical prophets avoided this form of expression, but it was used of earlier prophets (e.g. 1 Sam. 10 :10) and came into use again with Ezekiel and subsequent prophets.

he will bring forth justice (*mišpāṭ . . . yôṣî'*) **to the nations:** the phrase **bring forth justice** is used again in verse 3, and a similar phrase **established justice** (*yāśîm . . . mišpāṭ*) in verse 4. **bring forth** here means 'publish, proclaim'. *mišpāṭ* is a word of many meanings, but it may probably be assumed that it has the same meaning in all three places. In determining the meaning of this crucial word account must be taken of the fact that in verse 4 it stands in parallelism with **his law** (*tôrāṯô*); but *tôrāh* also has more than one meaning (see below on verse 4). The context in which *mišpāṭ* is used here implies that it is something which the exiles will welcome (verse 3), but which will be applied to all nations. The narrow sense of 'judgment' therefore appears to be excluded. On the other hand vague renderings like 'revelation' and 'true religion' are hardly justified. The most probable meaning is Yahweh's sovereign universal rule or order (cf. 40 : 14), which will mean salvation for Israel but submission for the other nations.

2. This is a difficult verse. **cry** (*ṣā'aḳ*), often in association with **lift up** one's **voice** (i.e. 'shout'), frequently refers to cries of distress, and this line has been interpreted as describing the uncomplaining suffering of the Servant. But this does not explain the second line, **or make it heard in the street**; moreover we should expect here a description not of the Servant's character but of his work and methods. The verse is probably best understood in the light of verse 3, where the Servant's positive function is described. The three negative clauses suggest a contrast between the Servant's functions and those of someone else; and those commentators (Volz, Fohrer, Elliger) are probably right who see here a reference to the earlier prophets of doom. In contrast to their work, which was a public and impassioned announcement of God's condemnation of Israel, that of the present Servant will be the quiet proclamation of God's universal rule, which brings comfort to the exiles. This interpretation involves the unusual interpretation of *ṣā'aḳ* (Qal) as 'shout aloud'; this may be defended on the grounds that the passive (Niphal) of this verb regularly means 'to be summoned (by public proclamation)'.

3. This verse confirms the above interpretation of verse 2. In contrast to the work of destruction of the earlier prophets, Deutero-Isaiah's work will be to handle the **bruised reed** with great care and to keep the **dimly burning wick** from going out: that is, to nurture the remains of faith and hope among the exiles, by announcing the imminent arrival of Yahweh's universal rule. **faithfully** (*le'ᵉmeṯ*): better, 'undoubtedly'.

4. fail; **be discouraged:** Deutero-Isaiah's love of play upon words has led him to use somewhat unusual expressions here. **fail** (*kāhāh*) means literally 'grow dim', and corresponds to the adjective **dimly burning** in verse 3. The word translated **be discouraged** (*yārûṣ*) normally means 'run', which cannot be right. Most commentators repoint it as *yērôṣ*, Niphal of *rāṣaṣ*, 'crush'. It may be possible to retain the pointing by taking it as the Qal either of *rāṣaṣ* with—unusually—an intransitive meaning 'be crushed', or of another verb *rûṣ* with that meaning. In any case it is used here as an echo of *rāṣûṣ*, **bruised**, in verse 3. The exiles are **discouraged**, but the Servant, in spite of difficulties, will never be. **established justice** (*yāśîm . . . mišpāṭ*): better, 'proclaimed God's universal rule'. As Elliger points out, *śîm* (usually 'put, give, make', etc.) has in Deutero-Isaiah a very general and flexible range of meanings. The closest parallel to its use here is 42 : 12, where *yāśîmû . . . kāḇôḏ*, 'let them give glory', is parallel with *ûṯᵉhillāṯô . . . yaggîḏû*, 'and let them declare his praise'. There is therefore no difference in meaning between *yāśîm* here and *yôṣî'* in verse 1: the reference is to the proclamation of a prophetic message. For the meaning of *mišpāṭ* (**justice**) here see on verse 1 above.

coastlands: see on 41 : 1. **wait** (*yᵉyaḥēlû*): the word does not necessarily imply a pleasurable expectation. **his law** (*tôrāṯô*): not the 'Law' in the Deuteronomic or later legal sense, but the will of the sovereign God announced by the prophet (cf. 8 : 16).

THE PRISONERS RELEASED

42 : 5–9

Interpretations of this passage differ greatly, and none yet offered can claim more than probability. Some commentators regard it as the continuation of verses 1–4; but the opening words suggest independence. It has been argued that it is the work of an interpolator whose purpose was to modify the teaching of verses 1–4; if so, the interpolator deliberately imitated the prophet's style and phraseology. There is however no reason to deny these verses to Deutero-Isaiah if it is recognized that these are quite separate pieces whose verbal similarities account for their present editorial juxtaposition. The crucial question is the identity of the person referred to in verse 6, in the sing., as **you**. Is he the Servant of verses 1–4?

5. The opening verse, which states the doctrine of creation in a series of participial clauses drawn from the style of the hymn of praise (cf. 40 : 22), provides no answer to the above question. The purpose of these clauses is to establish Yahweh's claim to control the events of history by reminding the hearers of their own traditions about his creation of the world. **spread forth** (*rōḳaʿ*)**:** literally, 'beat out'—a metaphor drawn from the work of the goldsmith (cf. 40 : 19). **people:** the word *ʿam*, which normally means a people or nation, is here most unusually used of mankind as a whole. **spirit** (*rûaḥ*)**:** here simply the breath of life.

6. Yahweh now speaks and addresses an unnamed individual. Three proposed identifications of this person deserve consideration: Israel, Cyrus, and the Servant (understood as an individual). All three are said elsewhere in the book to have been **called** by Yahweh, and the other expressions used in verse 6 are used elsewhere in connexion with one or more of them. **in righteousness** (*beṣeḏeḳ*)**:** better, 'in accordance with my purpose': see on 41 : 2. **and kept you** (*weʾeṣṣoreḵā*)**:** *RSV* takes this as a form of the verb *nāṣar*. It should rather be taken as the verb *yāṣar*, 'form, make', and read with the following line. **I have given you as a covenant to the people:** these words occur again in 49 : 8 (on which see the commentary), where however they are an interpolation. That a person should become a **covenant** (*berîṯ*) seems strange, but such bold metaphors are not unusual in biblical Hebrew. However, the phrase (*berîṯ ʿām*) is extremely difficult. Commentators are divided on the question whether **people** (*ʿam*) refers to Israel or to mankind. Two facts speak in favour of the latter interpretation. First, the phrase **a covenant to the people** is parallel with **a light to the nations**; and although it might be argued that two separate spheres of work are here referred to, one with regard to Israel and the other with regard to the nations, there is no other indication of this, and it is therefore more probable that both phrases refer to one and the same work. Secondly, although 'mankind' is a most unusual translation of *ʿam*, the word is used in the previous verse in this very sense (see on verse 5). But how can a man (or Israel) become a **covenant** to mankind? The difficulty of this problem has led some commentators to resort to emendation, others to the linguistically dubious translation 'covenant-people' (referring to the restoration of Israel's status), and others again to philological arguments giving *bᵉrîṯ* a totally different meaning from that which it has elsewhere. The difficulty probably lies in the translation of *bᵉrîṯ* (here and elsewhere in the *OT*) as 'covenant'. It has recently been convincingly argued (by E. Kutsch, *ZAW* 79 (1967), pp. 18–35) that its proper meaning is not a mutual relationship but an obligation, imposed by a person either upon himself or upon others. The person addressed here, then, is to 'become an obligation' to the nations of the world: that is, he is to be the agent who imposes Yahweh's obligations upon them.

This interpretation is confirmed by the phrase **a light to the nations.** Most commentators see here a commission to convert the nations to the worship of Yahweh. But in 51 : 4, where the similar phrase 'a light to the peoples' occurs, it is associated with God's expressed will (*tôrāh*) and universal rule (*mišpāṭ*). The two lines therefore probably mean that the nations of the world will be obliged to accept Yahweh's sovereignty, of which they will now become aware for the first time (hence **a light**), and will thus be forced to accept the obligation (*bᵉrîṯ*) which he imposes upon them.

7. A further aspect of the task imposed by Yahweh is now described in concrete terms. The first line, **to open the eyes that are blind**, must clearly be taken metaphorically; but the remainder, which speaks of the release of **prisoners**, may be interpreted either metaphorically, of *spiritual* captivity and darkness, or more concretely, of an actual liberation of peoples deprived of their freedom. Two other passages suggest that the latter interpretation is correct. According to 47 : 5 it is to be the fate of Babylon, Israel's oppressor, to 'sit in silence, and go into darkness'; in 49 : 9 the Jewish exiles are called 'the prisoners' and 'those who are in darkness'. It is, then, from such 'imprisonment' (that is, exile) that Babylon's 'captives' are now to be released. Here we have the most definite clue to the identity of the person addressed in this oracle. While the rather generalized language of verse 6 might apply either to the prophet Isaiah or to Cyrus, the action of the release of the peoples held in exile by the Babylonians is *par excellence* the work of Cyrus, and it is therefore most probable that it is he to whom this oracle is addressed.

It is now possible to form some notion of the purpose and character of verses 5–9 as a whole. Elliger is probably right in seeing the passage as a disputation which makes use of a variety of literary types. Its purpose is to persuade the exiles that the victories of Cyrus are part of Yahweh's plan for their deliverance. He begins (verse 5) with the common ground of Yahweh's supreme power over the world and human history. He then (verses 6f.) argues that it can only be he who has raised up Cyrus. This part of the argument is presented, for dramatic effect (cf. Yahweh's speeches in 41 : 1ff. and elsewhere) in the form of a solemn speech of appointment.

8–9. These verses are not, as some commentators have maintained, an independent piece but the culmination of the argument.

8. Yahweh now addresses the exiles, giving a reason for his action. As in some other passages (e.g. 48 : 9–11) this is not primarily his love for his people Israel, but his **glory**. The phrase **I am the LORD** (echoing verse 6) uses the word LORD (i.e. Yahweh) in an absolute sense: as in verse 5, he is God absolutely (*hā'ēl*), and will not tolerate the blasphemous pretensions of the Babylonian gods; he has therefore raised up Cyrus to destroy their **graven images**.

9. Now comes the final proof that it is indeed Yahweh who is behind these events. **the former things** here (cf. 41 : 22) are probably primarily the events of Cyrus' career which preceded the composition of this passage. Yahweh claims to have foretold these (presumably through Deutero-Isaiah himself or through other prophets), and may therefore be believed when he now foretells their climax: the overthrow of Babylon and the release of the captives (verse 7). **you** here is plural, indicating that it is the exiles who are addressed.

YAHWEH THE MAN OF WAR

42 : 10–13

The commentators are divided over the extent of this section. Many (McKenzie, Wade, Auvray, Fohrer, North) regard the whole of verses 10–17 as a single unit; others (Duhm, Marti, Westermann) restrict the unit to verses 10–13 and a few (Skinner, Kissane) to verses 10–12. Three distinct elements are present: a summons to praise (verses 10–12), a statement about Yahweh as a warrior (verse 13), and a speech by Yahweh himself (14–17). The first of these clearly corresponds in form, content, and phraseology to the introductory section of the hymns of praise in the Psalter, which is normally followed by a statement about Yahweh's past deeds or about his gracious character. Verse 13 fits the description of this second section. But the hymn of praise does not normally include a divine oracle comparable with verses 14–17, and it is probable that verses 10–13 are an independent poem. However, the hymn of praise in Deutero-Isaiah is of a special kind peculiar to this prophet (Westermann, *Sprache und Struktur*, pp. 157–63): the '*eschatological* song of praise'. The action of Yahweh in verse 13 is not a past event but one which lies in the immediate future: the prophet's intention is to elicit from his audience an act of faith expressed through praise of God for something which has not yet occurred but is confidently expected. (The word 'eschatological' is not really satisfactory, however: see the Introduction, pp. 30–31.)

10–12. The introductory call to praise consists of an imperative and a series of jussives. As in some corresponding passages in the Psalter the whole world, including its most remote parts, is drawn into the act of praise.

10. The singing of a **new song** is mentioned in a number of Psalms (Ps. 33 : 3; 40 : 3 (MT 4); 96 : 1; 98 : 1; 144 : 9), some of which have other features which closely resemble these verses. Such 'songs' were **new** in that they reflected a renewed realisation of God's grace towards the worshippers. The phrase **new song** acquires an even deeper meaning here through Deutero-Isaiah's radical distinction between **the former things** and the **new things** (verse 9). In its present position the song forms an appropriate conclusion to the previous section. **Let the sea roar and all that fills it:** the Heb. has 'those who go down to the sea and all that fills it' (*yôrᵉḏê hayyām ûmᵉlō'ô*). *yôrᵉḏê hayyām* occurs in Ps. 107 : 23, but here it makes poor sense. The emendation (*yirʿam* for *yôrᵉḏê*) followed by *RSV* was first proposed by Lowth and has since been widely accepted. It is supported by Ps. 96 : 11*b*; 98 : 7*a*, which are identical with the emended line. This emendation is probably preferable to the others which have been proposed (see e.g. *BHS*). For a suggestion about the way in which the corruption may have taken place, see L. C. Allen, *JTS* ns 22 (1971), pp. 146f.

11. The **cities** of the **desert** and their **villages** are oases, some of which supported large populations. **lift up their voice:** literally, 'lift up'. The word **their voice** is understood: no emendation is necessary. **Kedar:** a tribe of the Syro-Arabian desert. **Sela:** the word means 'rock'. This may be a reference to the Edomite city later known as Petra.

13. Yahweh's decisive action is presented in military terms, following an ancient tradition that Yahweh led the Israelite tribes to victory. In view of Deutero-Isaiah's frequent portrayal of the coming deliverance as a new Exodus, it is significant that the statement that Yahweh is (like) a **man of war** is also found in Exod. 15 : 3 in connexion with the first Exodus. This verse does not contradict the assertion made elsewhere in the book that it is Cyrus whose victories will save the exiles: Cyrus always acts under Yahweh's orders.

YAHWEH LEADS THE EXILES HOME

42 : 14–17

A promise of salvation similar to 41 : 17–20, which it closely resembles in form. Yahweh is again the speaker throughout.

14. held my peace refers not merely to God's silence but also to his inaction, which he himself admits: **For a long time**, that is, since the Babylonian conquest of Judah or even earlier. These words are clearly the answer to a lamentation in which the exiles had reproached him with inactivity in similar terms—cf. 64 : 12; Ps. 89 : 46 (MT 47) and other corporate lamentations in the Psalter. But now he promises drastic action against Israel's enemies. The simile of the **woman in travail**, which is reinforced in the Hebrew by a breathless and convulsive style which seems ugly to modern western taste, is intended to convey not only a sudden burst of noise and commotion but also the idea that something new is about to be born—these are the 'birthpangs of God' (Muilenburg).

15. The turning of fertile **mountains and hills** into arid deserts symbolises the destruction of Israel's enemies. The contrast with the promise to Israel in 41 : 18 is obvious. The drying up of **rivers** is reminiscent also of the drying up of the Red Sea (Exod. 14 : 16–29; cf. Ps. 66 : 6; 107 : 33–35) which meant salvation for Israel but destruction for her enemies. **islands** does not make good sense, and the majority of commentators favour the emendation of *'iyyîm* to *ṣiyyā* or *ṣiyyôṯ*, 'waterless (land)'.

16. In contrast with the fate of the Babylonians, the happy return home of the exiles is now described. **blind** refers to their present hopeless state (cf. 42 : 7) and their total dependence on Yahweh. **that they know not** (identical in the Hebrew with **that they have not known**) spoils the metre and is an erroneous repetition. The turning of **darkness . . . into light** recalls the pillar of fire which had given light to the Israelites after the Exodus (Exod. 13 : 21–22). Like the rest of the verse, it is probably to be taken literally. **the rough places into level ground:** cf. 40 : 4. **forsake them:** better, 'leave them undone'. The reference is not to the exiles but to the things which Yahweh is promising to do. Both this verb and **I will do** are in the perfect tense, indicating certainty.

17. The reference to the fate of idolaters may seem an anticlimax. But for Deutero-Isaiah God's gracious actions towards his people are always intended to assert his right to be recognized as the only God.

THE EXILE A JUST PUNISHMENT

42 : 18–25

It is generally recognized that it is not possible to make sense of this passage as it stands owing to later expansions; but there is no consensus of opinion about the extent of these. Westermann's solution is the most probable: he regards verses 18, 19*a*, 20, 22–23, 24*a* (to **robbers**), 25 as the original poem and interprets it as a disputation. Traces of the lamentation to which it is a reply can be seen in verses 24*a*, 25, and also in verse 18: the exiles have reproached Yahweh with being **deaf** and **blind** to their fate (cf. 40 : 27 and lamentations in the Psalter), but he turns the reproach against them. *They* are **deaf** and **blind** in that they have failed to understand the cause of their present miserable situation, which has come about not in spite of Yahweh but because he himself has willed it. The implied conclusion is that the present misery is no reason for doubting the bright future announced elsewhere by the prophet: both are the work of the same God who is actively in control of events.

18. The passage has probably been placed here because of the occurrence of **blind** in verse 16; but the word is used here in a quite different sense. Yahweh now addresses the dissatisfied exiles as **deaf** and **blind** (both plurals).

19. Yahweh points out how paradoxical is the situation: he is served by a **blind servant** and a **deaf messenger**! **my messenger whom I send** refers to the function which Israel is intended to perform as a witness of Yahweh's power to the nations of the world.

The last two lines are repetitious. The threefold repetition of **blind** is extremely ugly by the canons of Hebrew poetic style, and their reduction to two by reading 'deaf' for **blind**, on the evidence of two MSS and Symm., in the final line does not improve the situation. The reason for the interpolation of these two lines is not clear. It may have been intended to identify the **servant** Israel here with the Servant of the Servant Songs.

dedicated one: the interpretation of the Hebrew word (*mᵉšullām*) is so difficult that one modern commentator (Westermann) abandoned the attempt to translate it. Other proposed interpretations include 'perfect', 'friend', 'partner in a covenant of peace', 'one who has received his due', 'forgiven'. Elsewhere in the *OT* (e.g. 2 Kg. 22 : 3) the word is a personal name, Meshullam, and it has been suggested that it was the name of Deutero-Isaiah himself. The difficulty is that the root *šlm* is capable of a variety of different nuances, especially if the usage of other Semitic languages (cf. Arab. *muslim*, 'submissive') is thought to be relevant. (See W. Eisenbeis, *Die Wurzel* שלם *im Alten Testament*, *BZAW* 113, 1969.) In view of the difficulties an emendation to *mᵉšullāḥî*, 'the one sent by me', has been proposed. LXX, which has 'servants' for **servant** (twice), appears to have read *mōšᵉlêhem*, 'their rulers', and this was accepted by Duhm. None of these proposals can be unreservedly commended.

20. The verbal forms are inconsistent here: for **He sees** the consonantal text has 'you see' (sing.); **does not observe** is second pers. sing. in the Heb. (*RSV* has emended to third pers.): **does not hear** is third pers. We should probably read second pers. sing. verbs throughout.

21. This reference to God's **law** interrupts the thought. The idea of the **law** as a wonderful and glorious thing is characteristic of a certain type of post-exilic piety (cf. Ps. 19 : 7–14 (MT 8–15); 119). The verse is a gloss, perhaps intended to increase the emphasis on the folly of God's people, who had had every opportunity to understand his will, but had chosen to ignore it.

22. But this is a people: better, 'Yet they are a people'. Yahweh takes up the highly coloured language of the lamentations. The exiles are indeed in a wretched state, and yet do not understand why. **trapped** (*hāp̱ēaḥ*)**:** literally, 'a trapping' (infinitive absolute Hiphil). This construction is not impossible, though the frequently proposed emendation to *hūp̱aḥû*, 'they are trapped', may be right.

23. Here the prophet takes up the argument, enquiring whether there are not among this deaf people some who will **listen. for the time to come** (*leʾāḥôr*) probably means 'from now on' ('hereafter' in 41 : 23).

24. The questions in the first two lines express the main point of the whole disputation, which is made more explicit in verse 25: it was Yahweh himself who allowed the Babylonians to afflict his people. **the spoiler:** this follows the consonantal text, which should be pointed *mešôseh* (Poel participle of *šāsāh*). Qere and 1QIsa have *mešissāh*, 'spoil', a word which has already occurred in verse 22. **spoiler** is probably correct.

against whom we have sinned: the collective confession at this point is strange. Probably this line is a later addition intended to make explicit the meaning of the questions. The remainder of the verse, which reverts once more to the third pers. (**they**) is a further pious addition whose phraseology betrays Deuteronomic influence.

25. That **he** means Yahweh is taken for granted. The metaphorical language is once more probably taken from the lamentation. The disputation ends with a further expression of astonishment at the inability of the exiles to understand the cause of their troubles. **heat:** for MT's abs. *ḥēmāh* read the construct *ḥamaṯ* with 1QIsa.

THE GATHERING OF THE DISPERSED

43 : 1–7

These verses have all the characteristics of an oracle of salvation (cf. 41 : 8–13, 14–16), but the structure is complex. Westermann sees here a double structure (verses 1–4, 5–7) within a single oracle. But it may be better, with H.-E. von Waldow (*Biblische Studien* 29, 1960) to treat the passage as two quite separate salvation oracles: (*a*) verses 1–3*a*; (*b*) verses 5*a*, 3*b*–7.

1–3a. This forms a complete oracle of salvation: address (verse 1*a*), **Fear not** followed by a brief statement of reassurance (verse 1*b*), promise of immediate help (verse 2), and motivation (verse 3*a*).

1. But now refers back not to the previous passage but to an unrecorded lamentation to which this oracle is a reply (cf. 49 : 5). **created you** (*bōra'ᵃḵā*); **formed you** (*yōṣerᵉḵā*): the reference is to Yahweh's 'creation' of the nation Israel and probably includes the whole series of events from the call of Abraham to Israel's occupation of Canaan. In using in this way verbs which were normally reserved for statements about the creation of the world, Deutero-Isaiah was asserting that Israel has a unique place in the divine order of things. At the same time, by speaking of what were normally thought of as *redemptive* acts in terms of creation, he was making it possible for the *new* redemptive acts of which he was about to speak to be regarded as nothing less than a new creation. **have redeemed**; **have called:** as in 41 : 10 the perfect tenses refer not to what Yahweh had done in the past but to what he was about to do. **redeemed:** the verb (*gā'al*) denotes the function of the *gō'ēl*) or 'near kinsman': see on 41 : 14. **called you by name:** there is no need to emend the text to 'by *my* name'. The meaning of the phrase is the same as in 45 : 3, 4, where it is used of Yahweh's singling out of Cyrus from the rest of humanity to serve him; here, however, Israel is singled out to be redeemed. **you are mine** completes the list of expressions of reassurance. Only Yahweh has power over Israel, and that power is now to be used for Israel's good.

2. Walking **through the waters** and **through fire** are quite general metaphors for danger: cf. Ps. 66 : 12. A similar passage in Ps. 91 : 7–13 suggests that such metaphorical language may have been quite familiar to an Israelite audience. In addition to the general reference there may, however, be an allusion to the journey through the desert which the exiles are shortly to undertake. **I will be with you:** this form of reassurance of the divine presence and help is already found in much older *OT* literature, e.g. Jg. 6: 16. It also has parallels in the religious literature of other peoples of the ancient Near East.

5a (to **with you**), **3b–4**, **5b–7.** This second oracle of salvation is longer than the first, although it lacks the initial address. It consists of **Fear not, for I am with you** as in 41 : 10 (the very slightly different wording is probably without significance) in verse 5*a*, followed by promises of help (verses 3*b*, 4*b*, 5*b*–6), interwoven with statements of motivation (verses 4*a*, 7). Two things are promised here: the ransoming of the Israelites and their repatriation to their homeland.

3b and **4b** are parallel statements (*we'ettēn* in verse 4*b* should perhaps be repointed *wā'ettēn*). It is presupposed that Cyrus' conquests will not stop short of **Egypt, Ethiopia and Seba**, names which together comprise the whole of Africa which was then known. In fact it was not Cyrus but his successor Cambyses who conquered Egypt, but Deutero-Isaiah's assumption was a natural one. But the real ruler of all these lands, as of the whole world, is Yahweh, and as such he is able to offer their temporal rule to Cyrus in return for the freedom of the Jews. The concept is a highly poetical one intended to express the extreme lengths to which Yahweh will go for the sake of his people Israel. It would be wrong to subject it to a strict logical scrutiny. In verse 4*b* there is no need, with Duhm and later commentators, to emend *'āḏām*, **men**, to *'adāmōṯ*, 'territories'.

4a. The motive clause does not fit very satisfactorily between the two promises, and it may be that the two halves of this verse have been copied at some stage in the wrong order.

5b–6. The implication that the Israelites have been dispersed to the four points of the compass is probably to be understood as poetical hyperbole, although it is not far from the literal truth. It is the poetical style which accounts for the otherwise strange omission of a specific reference to Babylon. The **offspring** of Jacob/Israel are the individual Israelites, whom Yahweh then also designates **my sons** and **my daughters**. The idea of Yahweh as the father of Israel was not new (cf., e.g. Hos. 11 : 1); but here, and even more explicitly in verse 7, there is a more personal note: each Israelite is Yahweh's own son or daughter. This has already been suggested in verse 4*a* with its strong assertion of Yahweh's love.

7. called by my name: see on verse 1. But the phrase, like the other expressions in the verse, is now applied to each individual Israelite. **for my glory:** see on 40 : 5; 42 : 8. This expresses the other aspect of Yahweh's motivation: he acts out of love for his people, but the very existence of that people as his own special creation serves the even higher and overriding purpose of his glorification as universal God.

ISRAEL AS WITNESS TO YAHWEH'S POWER

43 : 8–13

This is another trial-speech (see on 41 : 1–5) whose theme is the same as that of those already discussed: the identity of the true God. But here a new feature is introduced: the Israelites are summoned as witnesses to testify on Yahweh's behalf. After a summons to the hearing (verses 8–9*a*) the subject of the debate is announced (verse 9*b*). Yahweh then confirms the status of his own witnesses (verse 10*a*), and delivers his speech in his own cause (verses 10*b*–13). As in the other similar scenes, the witnesses on the other side remain silent, their silence implying that they have no convincing answer to give.

8. Bring forth: if the Heb. word (*hôṣî'*) is intended to be an imperative, the form is somewhat anomalous. Whether it is explained as an irregular form or emended, the sense intended is almost certainly imperative. 1QIs^a has the plural imperative *hwṣy'w*. The verb denotes the requirement to appear in court, and the **blind** and **deaf**, as in 42 : 18, are the exiles. In spite of their inability to understand much of what Yahweh has done and is doing, they at least **have eyes** and **have ears** sufficiently acute to enable them to act as his witnesses.

9. Let all the nations gather together: in Heb. the verb (*niḳbeṣû*) is perfect, whereas **let the peoples assemble** is jussive. The view that the perfect sometimes has a jussive sense is dubious, and perhaps the most likely solution is to give both verbs a perfect sense by pointing the second (*weyē'āsepû*) as a *waw* consecutive. In that case these lines are a statement that the court has assembled. **among them** refers to the heathen gods, not to the peoples. For the meaning of **declare this, and show us the former things**, see on 41 : 22. **this** is given no explanation in the text, but presumably refers to contemporary events, in particular the career of Cyrus. None of the gods had been able to predict events either past or present. **show us** is in the plural in the Heb., whereas **Who?** demands a singular verb. Read *yašmîʿēnû* for *yašmîʿûnû*. **justify:** *RSV* rightly reads *yaṣdîḳû* for *yiṣdāḳû*, 'be in the right'.

10. my servant (*ʿaḇdî*)**:** some commentators repoint this as the plural *ʿᵃḇāḏay*, 'my servants'; but this does not appear to be necessary, as Israel is elsewhere called Yahweh's servant. **that you may know and believe me and understand:** the usual function of a witness is to enlighten others rather than himself. Nevertheless there is no justification for altering these verbs to the third person. It is necessary to remember that these trial scenes are fictitious, and that Deutero-Isaiah is a poet. In defiance of contextual appropriateness he here states what is the real aim of this oracle and indeed of his whole work, that the *exiles*, his audience, should be convinced of Yahweh's unique power. **I am He:** see on 41 : 4. **Before me no god was formed:** the prophet does not intend to suggest that Yahweh was 'formed', that is, created or born. He is attempting to make two related points in a single sentence: that Yahweh, unlike the gods of other nations, is uncreated; and that, again unlike them, he exists from the beginning. There is here a clear allusion to the Babylonian gods, who stood in a genealogical succession. The statement **nor shall there be any after me** extends the same thought into the future.

11. I, I am the LORD: on the origin and history of this formula (here given in an emphatic form) see W. Zimmerli, 'Ich bin Yahwe', *Geschichte und Altes Testament* (Alt *Festschrift*), 1953, pp. 179–209. Here it serves a double purpose: on the one hand it is the equivalent of 'I am He' in verse 10, and so gives to the personal name Yahweh the absolute sense of 'sole and universal God'; on the other hand it recalls the specifically Israelite religious tradition according to which Israel had been the recipient of unique privileges. The two thoughts are closely related, since for Israel the apprehension of God's true nature was mediated precisely through their realization of what Yahweh had done for them in the past. This thought is further expressed by the words **and besides me there is no saviour**.

12. This verse is the counterpart of verse 9. There the heathen gods were characterized as unable to 'declare' or 'show', that is, predict, events past or future, and their worshippers, summoned as their witnesses, had been silent. Now in emphatic contrast Yahweh asserts **I** (*ʾānōḵî*) **declared . . . and proclaimed** (the verbs are the same as those used in verse 9), and confidently calls on Israel to be *his* witness. (The word **saved**, which has no parallel in verse 9, and which stands awkwardly between two verbs of speaking, is probably an erroneous interpolation.) The reference is to Yahweh's prophecies in the past, which, as Israel can testify, have been fulfilled. **when there was no strange god among you:** literally, 'and there was no stranger (*zār*) among you'. The point is that Israel had never known any other god who might in consequence claim to have brought about the events in question. If such a claim is to be made, it is only Yahweh who can make it.

13. I am God: in MT these words belong to verse 12, but they are best taken with the present verse. Yahweh now draws the final conclusion: as he has been in the past, so also he can and will be in the future; there is no other god who can prevent him from carrying out his good intentions towards his people. After **I am God** LXX adds 'from of old' (*ap' archēs*), which brings out the contrast with **also henceforth**. It is possible, though not certain, that a phrase such as *mēʿôlām* has fallen out from the Hebrew text. The metre is somewhat uncertain at this point. **I am He:** see on 41 : 4.

THE DOWNFALL OF BABYLON

43 : 14–15

These verses consist of a characteristic introduction and conclusion embracing a central section so brief that it is difficult to believe that it is a complete oracle. Its character is that of the divine promise of help in the oracles of salvation, and despite the obscurity of its language it is clearly a promise of the downfall of the Babylonians. It may be a fragment of a more extensive oracle. Westermann has suggested the possibility that the central section may have originally been part of verses 1–7, but it could hardly be inserted there in such a way as to preserve the smoothness of that oracle

14. On the epithets applied to Yahweh, see on 41 : 14.
I will send to Babylon: it is natural to think of Cyrus as the one who is sent. But the omission of the object is surprising, and in the context (**I will send . . . and break down**) the first verb (*šillaḥtî*) probably has an auxiliary function: 'I will give orders

for (the bars) to be broken down' (so frequently with *šalaḥ* in the Qal; cf. *G–K* §120d).

break down: the Heb. has 'bring down'. **all the bars:** Heb. has 'the fugitives, all of them'. *RSV*, in common with many commentators, has followed Vulg. (*vectes*) in repointing MT's *bārîḥîm*, a rare word which probably means 'fugitives', as *b^e^rîḥîm*, 'bars'. **and the shouting of the Chaldeans will be turned to lamentations:** Heb. has 'and (as for) the Chaldeans, in ships is their cry'. Here again *RSV* follows a common opinion in repointing *bo'^o^niyyôṯ*, 'in ships', as *ba'^a^niyyôṯ*, 'in lamentations'. The verse as it stands in MT is not entirely unintelligible if it is understood as a description of an attempt of the Babylonians, during the destruction of their city by Cyrus, to escape in ships down the Euphrates. The alternative rendering of the verse (as in *RSV*) as a promise that the bolts and bars which now imprison the exiles will be broken and the Babylonians discomfited is itself not entirely free from difficulties as a translation. Of the many emendations proposed, the most plausible is perhaps *b^e^rîḥê kil'^a^ḵem*, 'the bars of your prison', for *bārîḥîm kullām*. Corruptions undoubtedly exist in the text, and no satisfactory solution has yet been found. The entire last line has been suspected as a gloss (see e.g. G. R. Driver, *L'Ancien Testament et l'Orient, Orientalia et Biblica Lovaniensia* I, 1957, p. 128). **Chaldeans:** here and frequently used as the equivalent of 'Babylonians': it was the Chaldeans, a people settled in lower Mesopotamia, who had founded the Neo-Babylonian dynasty.

15. the Creator of Israel: see on verse 1 above. **your King:** see on 41 : 21.

THE NEW OVERSHADOWS THE OLD

43 : 16–21

This is a promise of salvation somewhat similar to 41 : 17–20 and 42 : 14–17, although the allusion to a specific communal lamentation to which it might be a reply is less clear. Westermann's suggestion that such a lamentation may be reflected in the Exodus allusions (verses 16–17), since such allusions sometimes occur in corporate lamentations (e.g. 63 : 11–14) is not entirely convincing, since their primary background is not the lamentation but the song of praise.

The oracle consists of an introductory 'messenger-formula' which the prophet has characteristically expanded by introducing a hymn-like passage (verses 16–17), followed by the words of Yahweh himself in which he contrasts his former actions with the things which he is now about to do for Israel (verses 18–19*a*), describes the latter (verses 19*b*–20), and gives his reason for them (verse 21).

16–17. The sequence of events corresponds closely to the traditional account of the crossing of the Red Sea—cf. Exod. 14. The use of tenses in the Hebrew is particularly effective: the change from participles to imperfect and then to perfect tenses emphasizes the completeness of the destruction of the Egyptian army. *RSV* has for some reason omitted the word 'together', which stands in the Hebrew after **army and warrior** and contributes to the poetical effect.

17. brings forth: this is the same word as in 40 : 26. It is used in the military sense of marshalling an army and leading it into battle. Since Yahweh is the subject, the prophet intends the audience to understand that it was not only the destruction of the Egyptians which was Yahweh's work; even the decision of Pharaoh to pursue the Israelites was in fact inspired by Yahweh, who led them out so that they might be destroyed. The same idea is found in Ezek. 38 : 4.

18. the former things (*rī'šōnôṯ*)**:** not, as in 42 : 9, the earlier career of Cyrus, but Yahweh's earlier acts of deliverance of his people (cf. 41 : 22; 43 : 9), in particular the events described in verses 16–17. They are thus also described as **the things of old** (*ḳaḏmōniyyôṯ*)—Israel's ancient history. **Remember not . . . nor consider** is to be taken in a rhetorical sense. Deutero-Isaiah was in fact constantly *reminding* his audience of these things, and in 46 : 9 specifically admonishes them to remember them. Here he means simply that even they will pale into insignificance beside the far greater wonders which are about to be performed. Cf. Jer. 23 : 7–8.

19. a new thing: in 42 : 9 Yahweh's **new thing** was contrasted with more recent past events. The meaning of the phrase is nevertheless the same. But in 42 : 9 the **new thing** had not yet begun. Here the promise is expressed more dramatically: **now it springs forth**. This does not mean that this oracle has to be dated later than 42 : 5–9: the difference is in the expression, not in chronology.

do you not perceive it?: if original, this phrase also must be taken rhetorically. But it has been suggested by G. R. Driver (*L'Ancien Testament et l'Orient*, p. 157) that it is a gloss added by a reader for the benefit of his own contemporaries. The **way in the wilderness** is the highway of 40 : 3 which is to be constructed at Yahweh's command for the returning exiles. It corresponds partly to the **way in the sea** of verse 16: the new Exodus (implied but not specifically referred to here) will be followed, like the old, by a miraculous journey through the desert. The themes of Exodus, crossing of the Red Sea, and consequent journeying through the desert formed part of the same complex in Israel's traditions, and Deutero-Isaiah, here and elsewhere, is able to compare and contrast the former acts and the new acts of Yahweh simply by picking out details here and there without needing to specify every one. **rivers:** 1QIs[a], probably correctly, has 'paths', which makes a better parallelism. The reference to water comes later (verse 20).

20. The wild beasts will honour me: that the whole creation will give glory to its creator as a result of Yahweh's deliverance and restoration of his people is a constant theme of Deutero-Isaiah. But the specific reference to the taming of the **wild beasts** expresses a concept found elsewhere in the *OT* as a feature of the ideal age to come (e.g. 11 : 6–9). **water in the wilderness:** for the reference to Israel's earlier journey through the desert see on 41 : 18.

21. A characteristic conclusion. Cf. 41 : 16*b*; 43 : 7.

YAHWEH DEFENDS HIS ACTIONS

43 : 22–28

At first sight these verses may seem to have no unifying structure: a promise of unconditional forgiveness (verse 25) is apparently incongruously sandwiched between two sombre passages condemning Israel's sins (verses 22–24, 26–28). The apparent inconsequentiality disappears, however, once it is recognized that this is a bold and startling adaptation of the trial-speech: one in which Yahweh summons, not the heathen gods and their worshippers, but his own people, to defend himself against their claim that their punishment has been undeserved. His defence takes the form of counter-accusations, similar to the indictments of the pre-exilic prophets: Israel's sins have been so heinous that they deserve to be punished. But the purpose of the indictment is not, as in the earlier prophets, to justify a *future* punishment: the punishment has already been inflicted. Its purpose is rather to shake the exiles out of their complacency about their spiritual condition, which is preventing them from accepting the new promise of salvation which is being offered to them. Consequently there is no announcement of judgment such as usually follows the indictment. In its place there follows in verse 25 a totally unexpected declaration of forgiveness and renewal. Verse 25 is not, however, the climax of the oracle, but functions as a further element in Yahweh's defence. He shows himself not only to be guiltless of the charge of inflicting an unjust punishment, but also to be willing now, without imposing any conditions, to reply to the exiles' unrepented sin with love and grace. In the verses which follow he offers to listen to their counter-argument (verse 26); but since none is forthcoming he concludes by summarizing his main defence (verses 27–28): the misfortunes which befell Israel were the proper and inevitable consequence of their sin.

22–24. The argument is not easy to interpret. Only verse 24 (from **But you have burdened me**) is relatively free from difficulty: Yahweh replies to the exiles' accusation with a blunt denial: their punishment was indeed deserved. The difficulty lies in the references to sacrificial worship (verses 23, 24*a*). There are two problems here. The first is that of Deutero-Isaiah's attitude towards sacrifice: does he, in contrast to the great pre-exilic prophets (Isa. 1: 11ff.; Mic. 6: 6ff.; Am. 5: 21ff.) regard the importance of sacrifice so highly that he can make Israel's neglect of it the main indictment against the nation? The second concerns the identity of those accused, the **you** of the indictment. If these are the present generation of exiles, Yahweh could hardly be justified in accusing them of not offering sacrifice, since they had no opportunity to do so. In that case, if Yahweh is really accusing Israel of sin in not offering sacrifice, he must include former generations in the term **you**.

The clue to these problems is to be found in verse 23*b*, which must be read in conjunction with verse 24*b*. Here Yahweh appears to deny that he has imposed the burden of sacrifice on Israel; the use of the same verbs in verse 24*b* implies, moreover, that such a burden would have been intolerable and unjustifiable. The reference, then, is primarily to pre-exilic Israel, of which such a demand might have been made. Deutero-Isaiah's attitude, then, is similar to that of his pre-exilic predecessors. But what is the meaning of verses 23*a*, 24*a*? The answer lies in the phrase with which the series of negative statements begins (verse 22*a*): in the Heb. the first line of this verse places a strong emphasis on the object of the verb: 'But it was not *me* (*wᵉlōʾ–ʾōṯî*) whom you called.' The force of this emphasis is retained, by implication, through the whole series of negative statements about Israel's shortcomings. Yahweh is not accusing Israel of not offering sacrifice, but claims that it was not to him that it was offered. We must assume that the exiles had protested that the disaster of the exile had occurred in spite of Israel's diligence in offering to Yahweh all the sacrifices which he had demanded. Yahweh replies in terms similar to those used by his prophetic predecessors (cf. Isa. 1 : 11, 'What *to me* is the multitude of your sacrifices?'; cf. also Jer. 6 : 20) that these sacrifices had not been offered *to him*: that is, their worship had never reached him, because it had been offered by a people incapable, through its sinfulness, of acceptable worship.

We may conclude that these verses are an indictment of Israel as a whole for its **sins** and **iniquities** (verse 24) for which no amount of sacrifice had been able to atone. As elsewhere (e.g. 40 : 2) the present generation of exiles, in view of its corporate identity as Israel, shared in the guilt, which only Yahweh's unconditional forgiveness could set aside.

22. Yet: Heb. has simply 'and' (*wᵉ*), which, with the negative particle, has the effect of an emphatic denial, presumably of the claim, unexpressed here, of Israel that true worship had been duly offered. **you did not call upon me:** literally, 'it was not me whom you called'. *ḳārāʾ* with the direct accusative can mean either 'invite, summon' or 'call on, pray to' (as in 55 : 6). It is not clear whether Yahweh means that Israel did not invite him to participate in their feasts or that they did not offer true prayer to him. If the latter, the accusation might be intended to apply, as the references to sacrifice do not, to the present generation of exiles as well as to their ancestors. **but you have been weary of me:** LXX, whose text differs in other respects also from the Hebrew, has a negative verb. *yāgaʿ* (*yāgēaʿ*) *bᵉ* means both 'weary of' and 'labour for'. Consequently if the LXX reading were accepted and *welō'*, 'and . . . not', substituted for *kî*, 'but', the second line could be translated 'nor did you take trouble on my account'. But there is no reason to suspect the Heb. text.

23–24. The effectiveness of these verses is enhanced by their careful structure. Verses 23*a* and 24*a* are strictly parallel to one another; 23*b* and 24*b* bring out the contrast between Yahweh's indulgence and Israel's ingratitude both by their respective relationship to the lines which precede them and by their partial parallelism with one another, which extends as far as the use of identical vocabulary (**burdened . . . with**; **wearied . . . with**). These two repeated verbs are crucial to the argument: the true meaning of **burdened** (*he'ebîḏ*) is 'enslaved, made to labour like a slave'. Yahweh has not treated Israel like a slave, as he had a right to do; yet in return Israel has actually treated him like a slave, weighing him down with the burden of its sins. Again, Israel, unreasonably tiring (*yāga'*, verse 22) of its obligations to Yahweh even though they were not onerous (*lō' hôga'tîḵā*, **I have not wearied you**), has exhausted him (*hôga'tanî*, **you have wearied me**) with its iniquities (verse 24).

23. Yahweh lists some of the sacrifices which had been offered in the past. **burnt offerings** and **sacrifices** (the word is *zeḇāḥîm*, equivalent to the *šelāmîm* or 'peace-offerings') were the two basic offerings in pre-exilic times. **offerings** (*minḥāh*): literally, 'gifts'; but in view of its association with **frankincense** here the word probably already has the technical sense of 'grain-offering' as in the Priestly Code. **frankincense** was a fragrant resin used for making incense (Exod. 30 : 34–37) but also used, together with oil, for mixing with the *minḥāh* (Lev. 2 : 2).

24. sweet cane: used as an ingredient in making holy oil (Exod. 30 : 23). It is mentioned together with frankincense in Jer. 6 : 20, where the use of both in the cult is condemned as an unnecessary and meaningless extravagance. Both were imported from abroad, and were probably relatively recent innovations in the cult. There is a play on words here between *ḳāneh*, **sweet cane**, and **bought** (*ḳānîṯā*).

25. for my own sake: elsewhere (48 : 11) Deutero-Isaiah uses this phrase to emphasize that Yahweh's motive for redeeming Israel is the maintenance of his own reputation and glory; and a similar phrase is used by Ezekiel in the same sense (e.g. Ezek. 20 : 14). But here there appears to be no such implication; rather the meaning is that Yahweh's readiness to forgive proceeds from his own nature.

26. Put me in remembrance (*hazkîrēnî*)**:** like the other verbs in this verse, this is a technical term of the law-court. It means 'State your case against me!' Similarly **argue together** means 'argue our respective cases'.

27. Your first father sinned: this verse shows how completely Deutero-Isaiah stands in the tradition of his predecessors the great prophets of the pre-exilic period. He sweepingly denounces Israel's record of sin from the very beginning of its history. The **first father** is probably Jacob. Deutero-Isaiah appears to be following a tradition recorded also in Hos. 12 : 2–4, where also Jacob is singled out as a notorious sinner. **your mediators:** the reference is not clear. It probably refers mainly to prophets, although priests and even kings are perhaps included. All these persons in various ways stood between God and the people, and could be described as **mediators**.

28. This verse refers to the destruction of the kingdoms of Israel and Judah. The two verbs (*wa'ᵃḥallēl* and *wᵉ'ettᵉnāh*) have a future sense as pointed by the Massoretes, but should certainly be pointed as waw consecutives, giving them a past sense. **I profaned the princes of the sanctuary:** the phrase **princes of the sanctuary** occurs in 1 Chr. 24 : 5, where it denotes the leaders of the Jerusalem priesthood. The word **profaned** (*ḥillēl*) is used in a similar context in Lam. 2 : 2, where it is said that Yahweh 'profaned the kingdom and its rulers': that is, that he took away from them the status of a people especially consecrated to his service, with the privileges consequent upon it. There is therefore really no difficulty in the interpretation of the Hebrew text, and no sufficient reason to adopt the reading of LXX, 'the princes have profaned my holy things'. The alternative rendering of the verb as 'pierced, wounded' is also improbable in the context. The only problem is the meaning of **princes of the sanctuary.** Some commentators have urged that the meaning which it has in 1 Chr. 24 : 5 is improbable before the post-exilic period since it assigns a very high importance to the priesthood. It may be best to take it as meaning 'princes of holiness', i.e. 'holy, consecrated rulers': in other words, the kings of Israel.

ISRAEL THE ENVY OF THE WORLD

44 : 1–5

This is an oracle of salvation belonging to the same general type as 41 : 8–13, characterized by the formula **Fear not!** But as is frequently the case with Deutero-Isaiah, there are some variations in the form. The first part (verses 1–2) consists basically of a command to **hear**, the messenger-formula **Thus says the LORD** and the formula of encouragement **Fear not**. The combination of these three phrases confers on the oracle a strong note of authority intended to arouse in the audience the needed conviction that they are listening to the authentic voice of God. This effect is further strengthened by the characteristic clauses added to each formula reminding the exiles of the longstanding and still operative relationship between Yahweh and Israel. The contents of the promise (verses 3–5) differ somewhat from those of earlier oracles of salvation in that they refer mainly to a more remote future.

1. But now: see on 43 : 1.

2. formed you from the womb: the metaphor is based on the belief that Yahweh was at work in the development of the human embryo, a belief most fully expressed in Job 10 : 10–11. Its application to Israel indicates that Yahweh's care for his people reaches back to a time even before the latter's appearance on the stage of history; consequently there is good reason to believe him when he promises to **help** Israel in its present distress. **Jeshurun:** another name for Israel occurring only here and in Dt. 32 : 15; 33 : 5, 26 (and in some MSS of Sir. 37 : 25). It is generally supposed to be related to *yāšār*, 'upright'; but the contexts in which it occurs give no clue to its particular nuance.

3. There is a general agreement among the commentators that unlike other passages (e.g. 41 : 18) which use similar language, these promises of abundant rain do not refer to miracles which will occur during the promised journey through the desert but are metaphorical, denoting the conferring of a blessing. **thirsty land:** Heb. has simply the masc. adjective 'thirsty (one)'.

Spirit, here parallel with **blessing**, refers to the renewal of God's lifegiving strength which creates fertility and prosperity, without the deeper spiritual significance attached to it in, e.g., 42 : 1. The emphasis is on future generations, but this does not exclude the present one. A numerous offspring was an essential mark of God's blessing (cf. Gen. 12 : 2).

4. Luxurious vegetation was a common symbol for prosperity: cf. Ps. 1 : 3. **like grass amid waters:** *RSV* follows LXX here. But the sense is still not entirely satisfactory. The Heb. has no reference to water, but is simply *beḇên ḥāṣîr*, of which the first word, translated by *RSV* mg. as 'in among', is a dubious form, while the second means 'grass'. It is possible that *bên* is in fact the name of a tree, the ben-tree, a kind of poplar (see North for details). This would provide a parallel for **willows**, and is perhaps supported by the reading *keḇên* (*ke* 'as') attested by ten MSS and 1QIsa. The line could then be translated 'they shall spring up like the green poplar'. *BHS* emends *ḥāṣîr* to *ḥāṣôr*: presumably the phrase would then be rendered 'like the poplar of Hazor'.

5. This one . . . another . . . another (*zeh . . . weżeh . . . weżeh*): the reference is to individuals who, seeing Israel's prosperity, will eagerly seek to become members of God's people. Although this is not specifically stated, these can hardly be other than foreigners: those later to be known as 'proselytes'. See on 56 : 3, 6–8. **will call himself by:** Heb. has 'will call upon'; but a passive (reflexive) verb is needed. **will write on his hand, 'The LORD's':** literally, 'will write his hand to Yahweh'. There is no agreement about the meaning of this phrase. The two main possibilities are that such a person will inscribe the words 'property of Yahweh' on his hand (perhaps by tattooing) or that he will write the words on a document *with* his hand. But it is doubtful whether *yāḏō*, 'his hand', can be taken adverbially; and although some of the Versions have been supposed to have read *beyāḏô*, 'with his hand', this is quite uncertain: the ancient translators may well have been faced with the same problem as modern commentators and have made the best they could of a difficult text. Moreover 'with his hand' would in any case be superfluous in a text which speaks of writing. The view that the text refers to inscribing words *on* a hand is therefore the more probable, though the material on which words are written is only rarely (e.g. Jer. 36 : 6) expressed in the accusative. The reference may be to the practice of marking slaves with the names of their masters (cf. also Ezek. 9 : 4), but it is not to be taken literally. **surname himself:** *RSV* follows the common opinion of commentators in repointing the active (Piel) verb *yeḵanneh* as the Pual *yeḵunneh*.

ISRAEL'S REDEEMER THE ONLY GOD

44 : 6–8, 21–22

There are good grounds for following Duhm and many more recent commentators in regarding these verses as constituting a single unit which has been broken into two by the interpolation of verses 9–20. This conclusion holds good irrespective of any conclusions which may be reached concerning the authorship and literary form (poetry or prose) of verses 9–20, on which see below. The interpolated verses, which are concerned with the absurdity of idolatry, are not entirely irrelevant to the preceding assertions concerning Yahweh's uniqueness, but the connexion, though sufficient to account for the interpolation, is not strong enough to outweigh the arguments against its originality, while the connexion between verses 20 and 21 is extremely tenuous: **these things** in verse 21 by no means necessarily refers to what immediately precedes, and could at least equally well be a reference to verse 8. On the other side, the length of verses 9–20 is wholly disproportionate to the present context and distorts its form. There is no other example in Deutero-Isaiah either of such an excessively long digression or of such an abrupt change of style.

Verses 6–8, 21–22, on the other hand, constitute an example of the trial-speech. As such they have certain peculiarities, but these are no greater than is to be expected from Deutero-Isaiah. The setting of the scene is lacking, as in 43 : 22–28, and the messenger-formula is used. The second part of the poem (verses 8, 21–22) makes use, again as in 43 : 22–28, of elements from the oracle of salvation: the formula **Fear not** (verse 8) and a declaration of forgiveness (verse 22). A further peculiarity is the call to repentance (verse 22*b*); on this see below.

6. The messenger-formula is expanded by three epithets which show that, although in the main the form is that of a trial-scene between Yahweh and the heathen gods, the intention of the poem is to reassure the prophet's real audience, Israel: **King of Israel** (cf. 41 : 21); **Redeemer** (cf. 41 : 14) and **LORD of Hosts**, an ancient title expressing the majesty of Yahweh's power. **the LORD** on its first occurrence should probably be omitted. **the first . . . the last:** cf. on 41 : 4. **besides me there is no god:** an even clearer assertion of Yahweh's uniqueness than 43 : 10–11.

7. Let him proclaim it: LXX has a longer text, which suggests that Heb. may originally have read 'Let him stand up and (*ya'ᵃmōḏwᵉ*) proclaim it'. Although this makes the line rather long, it also makes the sense clearer. 'Stand up' in this sense is a technical term for preparing to make a statement in court: cf. 50 : 8. **and set it forth:** the verb (*'āraḵ*) is another forensic term for the presentation of a case or argument. Once more Yahweh is challenging the heathen gods to meet his claims.

The second half of the verse hardly makes sense in the Heb. (see *RSV* mg.). *RSV* follows the majority of commentators in making two emendations (**Who has announced from of old the things to come?** and **us**). The former is obtained mainly by a rearrangement of the consonants in MT on the supposition that some disarrangement had previously occurred; the second (*lānû* for *lāmô*) is suggested by Targ.

8. Yahweh now turns to his **witnesses**, that is, to the exiles, assuring them that their own knowledge of his fulfilled predictions of past events should be sufficient to relieve them of all fear. **nor be afraid** (*wᵉ'al tirᵉhû*): this verb is unattested elsewhere in Hebrew. It is best to follow 1QIsᵃ's *w'l tyr'w*. It is this verb *yārē'*, 'to fear', which is found elsewhere in the formula 'Fear not'. The verb translated **Fear not** by *RSV* here is another verb, *pāḥaḏ*. **There is no Rock:** it has been suggested that *'ên*, 'there is not', should be repointed as *'în*, an Aram. interrogative particle supposedly found occasionally in the Hebrew OT (G. R. Driver, 'Notes on Isaiah', *BZAW* 77 (1958) p. 47; cf. also *BHS*). But this is hardly necessary. **Rock:** this epithet of Yahweh occurs elsewhere in contexts which stress his protective role. **I know not any:** although it has seemed to some commentators that this phrase is improbable in a speech by Yahweh, we are not sufficiently familiar with ancient Hebrew idiom to be justified either in emending it or in rejecting it as a gloss.

21. Remember these things: the reference is probably to the reminder given by Yahweh in verse 8 that he had in the past showed himself to be the true God by predicting future events. **for you are my servant:** Yahweh now gives the reason why it is important for Israel to remember these things: in view of their special status in Yahweh's purpose, they may now be confident that they will **not be forgotten** by him in the future. **you will not be forgotten by me** (*lō' ṯinnāšēnî*): the construction (verbal suffix after a passive verb instead of the usual *lᵉ* + suffix) is unique, but may perhaps be explicable on the analogy of a similar construction with intransitive verbs (cf. H. Bauer and P. Leander, *Historische Grammatik der Hebräischen Sprache des Alten Testaments*, 1922, §48 h''). The Versions have an active verb, e.g. LXX 'Do not forget me'; they may have read the same text as 1QIsª, *lw' tš'ny*. But the passive sense is more satisfactory, in spite of the **Remember** at the beginning of the verse. If MT may be accepted it strikes the same note of assurance as 49 : 15.

22. like a cloud . . . like mist: the simile denotes that which is ephemeral: cf. Hos. 6 : 4; Job 30 : 15. **return to me:** not, as Westermann supposes, a warning note inserted after verses 21–22 became separated from verses 6–8. Deutero-Isaiah has boldly taken an admonitory phrase from his predecessors, the prophets of doom, and turned it into one of encouragement: God's grace has not waited for Israel's repentance, but has created a situation in which Israel may now return to him not out of fear but in confident trust.

THE FOLLY OF IDOLATRY

44 : 9–20

On the relationship of this passage to its present context, see on verses 6–8, 21–22, above. The commentators differ on the question whether it is prose or poetry. Much of it has poetical characteristics, especially that of parallelism, but a metrical pattern is sometimes hard to find. Whether it is prose or poetry, its style and treatment are quite different from Deutero-Isaiah's authentic oracles. The theme is admittedly the same as that of other passages in the book, although some of these (40 : 19–20; 41 : 6–7; 45 : 16–17) may well also be interpolations. Some phrases are reminiscent of Deutero-Isaiah, but the style is clumsy, and the irony, although effective, more laboured and less subtle than his. Another significant feature is that, although the contrast between the idols and the true God is strongly implied, Yahweh is not mentioned at all, and Deutero-Isaiah's characteristic note of praise of his glory is consequently entirely lacking. It is probably best to regard the passage, with von Rad, as a satirical tract of a type which flourished for many centuries from the time of the Exile, when Israel first encountered the heathen world at close quarters (see G. von Rad, *Weisheit in Israel*, 1970, pp. 229–39;

ET *Wisdom in Israel*, 1972, pp. 177–85). Whether von Rad and Fohrer are correct in attributing the passage to a 'wisdom teacher' on account of its didactic tone is another matter. Israel's intellectual activity was not the exclusive preserve of 'wisdom schools'. On the validity of the type of polemic represented here see on 40 : 19.

The passage falls into three parts: a general statement of the theme (verses 9–11); a satirical description of idol-making, in which the satire is implicit rather than explicit (verses 12–17); and a sententious conclusion (verses 18–20). The author has been led into a good deal of inelegant repetition through his desire to make his point clearly.

9. their witnesses: the idols have their 'witnesses', that is, their worshippers and defenders, as Yahweh has his. The word has probably been chosen to make an explicit link with verse 8. There is no justification for emending, with some commentators, to 'their worshippers' (*ʿaḇᵉḏêhem* for *ʿēḏêhem*). **neither see nor know:** the perception of the worshipper cannot be greater than that of the idol whom he serves. **that they may be put to shame:** the purpose is, of course, Yahweh's, not their own. **put to shame:** better, 'shown up as fools' (so also in verse 11).

10. It is probably better to translate this verse as follows, following Duhm: 'Whoever fashions a god has cast an image which is profitable for nothing.' On the construction see G–K §143d.

11. all his fellows . . . but men: there are two difficulties here which suggest a corruption of the text: it is not clear who **his fellows** are, and why they are mentioned; and **but men** is a dubious translation of *mēʾāḏām*. Of the suggestions for a solution that of Duhm remains perhaps the most probable: by repointing *ḥᵃḇērâw*, 'fellows' as *ḥᵃḇārâw*, 'incantations' and *ḥārāšîm*, 'craftsmen', as *ḥᵃrāšîm*, 'spells', he obtains the translation: 'all his incantations will be put to shame, and the spells, which originate from men.' The point will then be that the magical powers which are believed to belong to the idol are in fact non-existent and the magical rites merely human inventions, which are therefore worthless. **let them all assemble . . . put to shame together:** the wording strongly resembles the words of Yahweh when he summons the gods and their worshippers in the trial-scenes. Here they seem hardly to fit the context, and this remains the case even if, with some commentators, we read the jussives (**let them . . .**) as imperfects ('they assemble, they stand forth'). Fohrer omits these lines as a later interpolation. We should perhaps rather retain them and explain them as rather poor writing by an author who was trying to imitate Deutero-Isaiah.

12. The casting of an iron statue is described in order to point out the absurdity of the idea that an object made by men subject to human weakness can nevertheless itself possess supernatural power. **The ironsmith . . . coals:** the Hebrew is impossible to translate: 'The ironsmith an axe and works it . . .' *RSV* has substituted **fashions** for 'axe', but there is no support for this emendation in the MSS or Versions. The problem remains unsolved. The two most widely supported proposals for emendation are (*1*) to omit 'axe' as a gloss and change **and works** to 'works', giving the single sentence 'The ironsmith works over the coals'; (*2*) to add *yāḥēḏ*, 'sharpens', at the beginning of the verse: 'The ironsmith sharpens an axe and. . .' It may be objected against the first proposal that no sufficient explanation has been found for the existence of the gloss. The second proposal is derived from LXX, which has 'sharpens'; but if *yḥd* stood in the Hebrew text used by LXX, it was probably not original but an accidental repetition of the last three consonants of verse 11.

13. Next the shaping of a wooden idol is described. The description is unduly repetitive; this is probably due to the incorporation of variant readings into the Hebrew text. **planes:** the word occurs only here; probably some kind of scraping instrument is meant.

14–17. The author now—if the present order of the verses is original—goes back in time to trace the way in which a particular piece of wood came to be selected for making an idol. The satire speaks for itself.

14. He cuts down: the verb has the form of an infinitive. The older commentaries emend either by substituting the perfect or by prefixing an additional verb such as 'he goes'. But McKenzie takes *lkrt* here as the perfect tense (*kāraṯ*) prefixed by an emphatic *lamedh*. Whether such a construction, attested in some other Semitic languages, existed in biblical Hebrew is a matter for debate. **holm tree:** the Heb. word occurs only here, and its precise meaning is unknown. **lets it grow strong:** probably better, 'selects it'. **a cedar:** *RSV* has emended the otherwise unknown *'ōren* to *'erez*, 'cedar', a reading found in a few MSS. If *'ōren* is original, it may be a kind of laurel.

15. The Latin poet Horace makes a similar satirical point (*Satires* I. i. 8ff.). **before it:** Heb. has 'before them'.

16. over the half: that is, the second half. But in that case there would be no **rest of it** (verse 17). Possibly the author is using **half** loosely in the sense of 'part'; but 1QIs[a], although its text is somewhat different in other respects, contains the expression 'on the coals' (cf. verse 19). Since LXX (Vaticanus) and Syr. also give some support to this reading, we should probably read 'over the coals' in place of **over the half. eats . . . roasts:** the order should be reversed as in some of the Versions. **I have seen:** better, 'I have felt'. The verb *rā'āh* is not confined in its meaning to visual perception.

18. This verse is probably a later addition by a reader commenting sententiously on the situation depicted in the previous verses. In fact it merely repeats the sentiments of verse 19*a*. Its plural verbs betray the fact that it is an intrusion. **he has shut their eyes:** better, 'their eyes are blinded'. *ṭaḥ* is best taken as the Qal of *ṭḥḥ* with an intransitive meaning: literally, 'be smeared over'. There is no need to emend to the plural form: verbs which precede their subject as here do not necessarily agree with it in number.

19. No one considers: literally, 'And he does not consider'. The translation of *RSV* is intended to smooth the transition from the plural verbs of verse 18. But if verse 18 is a gloss, 'he' refers to the idol maker of verses 14–17.

20. He feeds . . . led him astray: both the meaning and the interpretation of these words is disputed. Duhm's rendering is probably the best: 'As for him who herds ashes, a deluded mind has led him astray.' The verb *rā'āh* is a term of pastoral life often used metaphorically. It may be used intransitively of cattle feeding or grazing, but also transitively of the work of the herdsman in herding or tending his cattle. That the latter (in a metaphorical sense) is the meaning here is suggested by a similar expression in Hos. 12 : 1 (MT 2): 'Ephraim herds the wind.' Both expressions refer to hopeless, and therefore absurd, undertakings. 'Herding ashes' may be a proverbial expression. **a lie:** that is, a sham.

A SHORT HYMN OF PRAISE

44 : 23

Like 42 : 10–13 this is a hymn of praise structurally identical with those in the Psalter: a summons to praise followed by a statement about Yahweh's redemptive work introduced by the particle **for** (*kî*). Its formal perfection suggests that it was originally a completely independent utterance of Deutero-Isaiah. Its extreme brevity is no argument against this view: Ps. 117 is equally brief. Its position in its present context is probably due to the phrase **For the LORD has redeemed Jacob**, which echoes **for I have redeemed you** in verse 22. Like 42 : 10–13 it is to be understood as a so-called 'eschatological hymn of praise': the prophet has substituted a statement about Israel's future redemption for the usual statement about his mighty deeds in the past. It is also characteristic of Deutero-Isaiah in that the whole universe—heavens, underworld, and the earth with its contents—are drawn into the singing of Yahweh's praises (cf. 42 : 10–12; 43 : 20; 49 : 13; 55 : 12). **has redeemed:** the perfect tense is used to indicate that the imminent redemption can be counted on as a certainty. That it does not refer to a past event is proved by the use of the imperfect immediately afterwards (**will be glorified**).

CYRUS YAHWEH'S ANOINTED ONE

44 : 24–45 : 7

Westermann's insistence that these verses form an independent unit must, in spite of all the difficulties, be accepted. Verses 24–28 taken by themselves are a mere torso consisting entirely, after the expanded messenger-formula in verse 24*a*, of the statement **I am the LORD**, expanded by a long series of subordinate clauses, almost entirely participial. The repetition of the messenger-formula in 45 : 1 must therefore be understood as intended to resume the main thread of discourse, and the change at this point from an address to Israel to an address to Cyrus must be attributed to the fact that, as in some other passages, the real audience is the exilic community throughout: the supposed address to Cyrus is a literary fiction similar to the speeches made by Yahweh to the heathen gods and their worshippers in the trial scenes.

Of all the oracles concerning Cyrus this is the most explicit and the one most calculated to astonish the exiles and to impress on them, not by its logical argument but by its very audacity, that Yahweh is a God of infinite resource who is prepared to set aside all accepted traditions in his determination to come to his people's aid. Since Israel has no leader of its own, he has chosen a heathen king not only to be his agent like the Assyrian kings and Nebuchadnezzar in the past, but to be **his anointed** one (45 : 1), that is, to fulfil the role previously reserved for the native Judaean kings.

24–28. Formally these verses are introductory to the main oracle, but they partly anticipate the promises which follow. The participial form in which the statements about Yahweh are expressed is characteristic of the hymn of praise, but here it is Yahweh who is speaking about himself. It has been suggested, above all by H.-M. Dion, 'Le genre littéraire sumérien de l' "hymne à soi-même" et quelques passages du Deutéro-Isaïe', *RB* 74 (1967), pp. 215–34, that this literary form is modelled on a type of hymn current in Mesopotamia in which deities praised themselves; but this is improbable both because most of the extant examples are from a much earlier period and because such borrowing from a polytheistic tradition would hardly have served Deutero-Isaiah's purpose. See the discussionin R. N. Whybray, *The Heavenly Counsellor in Isaiah xl 13–14*, 1971, pp. 66–8.

24. On the various characteristic expressions employed in this verse see on 40 : 22; 41 : 14; 42 : 5; 44 : 2. **Who was with me?:** *RSV* has followed the Kethib (*mî 'ittî*), which is supported by some Versions and MSS and 1QIs[a] and is probably to be preferred to Qere's *mē'ittî*, literally 'from with me', usually taken to mean 'by myself'. For the thought see on 40 : 13–14.

25–26. From creation the thought moves to Yahweh's control of history, both negative (verse 25) and positive (verse 26).

25. The reference is primarily to the Babylonians' attempts to predict the future by either supernatural or rational means. **liars** (*baddîm*): this translation is not wholly satisfactory, and the proposal of P. Haupt (*JBL* 19 (1900), p. 57) to see here an otherwise unattested word *bārîm* based on the Accadian *bārû*, 'diviner' is attractive and has been widely adopted.

26. his servant: if the text is correct, this could refer either to Israel, which is elsewhere so called, or to the Servant of the Servant Songs, whose identity is disputed. But the fact that the word is parallel with the plural **his messengers** suggests that those Versions which have the plural 'servants' may have had the true text. If this is so, the choice is between Israel and Israel's prophets of the past, whose prophecies have been fulfilled. Their **counsel** is Yahweh's counsel or plan which they were commissioned to announce, just as their **word** is also Yahweh's word.

26b–28. There are some duplications here, and it is probably impossible to restore the original text. **their ruins:** Heb. has 'her ruins', which may be an indication that **and of the cities . . . built**, which make the line unusually long, is an addition.

27. There is no agreement among the commentators about the meaning of this verse. It could refer to the creation, to the Exodus, or even to the unimpeded progress of Cyrus during his campaigns. The last of these three is the least probable; but if it refers to creation or Exodus the present order of the verses can hardly be original.

28. The reference to **Cyrus** (mentioned by name only here and in 45 : 1) is clearly the climax of these introductory verses, but the climax is spoiled in the present text by the anticipation in verse 26*b*. **my shepherd:** a title commonly used of kings in the ancient Near East and within the *OT* itself.

The second half of the verse (from **saying of Jerusalem**) has been rejected by some commentators, probably rightly. Deutero-Isaiah elsewhere shows no interest in the Temple. On the other hand the context (especially **he shall fulfil all my purpose** in verse 27) seems to imply that Cyrus was expected himself to rebuild Jerusalem and lay the foundation of the Temple. Since he did not in fact do so, the interpolation, if it is such, cannot have been inserted more than a few years after the composition of the prophecy.

45 : 1–7. The core of the oracle is contained in verses 1–4. It resembles the promise of salvation to the extent that in it Yahweh makes promises and states his reasons (verses 3*b*, 4*a*; cf. 43 : 3*a*, 4*a*, 7, 21). But it is unique in that it is addressed not to the exilic community but to an individual, the Persian king Cyrus. Westermann is correct in classifying it as a 'royal oracle': that is, an oracle addressed by a god to a king at his accession, confirming his appointment. In the *OT* 2 Sam. 7 and 1 Kg. 3 : 10–14 have something of this character, and some psalms, especially Pss. 2 and 110, reflect a ceremony of the same kind. As has frequently been pointed out, the inscription known as the Cyrus Cylinder, in which Cyrus claims to have been chosen and appointed by Marduk as king of Babylon (*ANET*, pp. 315–16; D. W. Thomas (ed.), *Documents From Old Testament Times*, 1958, pp. 92–4) contains similar material, some of which is expressed in language superficially very close to that of Deutero-Isaiah; but in spite of the almost exact contemporaneity of the two, there is no question of any direct connexion: the Cyrus Cylinder must be slightly later than Deutero-Isaiah's oracles, and the possibility of its dependence on them is extremely remote. Moreover the similarity of language is much less close than has been supposed by some writers, including Westermann (see Whybray, *The Heavenly Counsellor*, pp. 65–6).

1. *RSV* regards this verse as introductory, and begins Yahweh's address with verse 2. This leaves the two verbs in the first person (**I have grasped** and **open** (literally, 'I will open')) unexplained. North is probably right in beginning Yahweh's words with **to his anointed**, the initial address in the third person being an honorific, formal expression, comparable with the formal address at the beginning of a letter. **his anointed:** the act of anointing denoted appointment to an office, but in the *OT* the expression 'anointed one' is reserved mainly, though not exclusively, for Israelite kings (cf. Ps. 2 : 2). There is little doubt that Deutero-Isaiah's audience would take it in this sense here. Even though there was some precedent for such a bold transference of Israelite royal titles to foreign kings in that Nebuchadnezzar had been designated Yahweh's servant in Jer. 27 : 6, the use of the phrase **his anointed** here will have administered a fully calculated shock to those who first heard it. **whose right hand I have grasped:** attempts to relate this expression to a supposedly similar phrase about Marduk and Cyrus in the Cyrus Cylinder are misconceived. The Accadian does not have this meaning. On the Hebrew phrase see on 41 : 13. **ungird the loins:** that is, disarm. The **doors** and **gates** are the gates of the cities captured by Cyrus.

2. mountains: *RSV* here follows LXX. The Hebrew word, which occurs only here, is of uncertain meaning. Another possible emendation is 'paths'. **doors of bronze:** Babylon had one hundred such gates, according to the Greek writer Herodotus.

3. treasures of darkness: that is, treasures hidden away. Some commentators have seen here a reference to the fabulous wealth of the city of Sardis, captured by Cyrus in 546. **that you may know:** some commentators, following Duhm, propose the omission of these words on various grounds: it is urged that Cyrus could hardly derive such knowledge from his military successes, that his conversion did not in fact take place, and that the words are inelegant stylistically and metrically. That the prophecy should have gone unfulfilled is no argument against its genuineness, but each of the other arguments has some force. Nevertheless the omission has no support from any Version or any extant MS and is hardly justified. **call you by your name:** see on 43 : 1.

4. From this point onwards the oracle stresses that Cyrus' task, in spite of the titles of honour accorded to him (**surname you**), is a strictly limited one. He is merely Yahweh's instrument in carrying out a task whose real purpose is the liberation of Israel and the universal honouring of God's name. Verses (3)4–7 are not, as Fohrer maintains, a separate oracle but are formally an expanded form of the part of the salvation-oracle which states the reasons for Yahweh's gracious actions. **though you do not know me:** Cyrus, like the rest of humanity, would eventually recognize that Yahweh was the one who shaped his career, but not initially. Yahweh's purpose was at first a hidden one.

6. from the west: the form *maʿarāḇāh* is otherwise unattested. Probably read 'from its setting' (inserting a mappiq in the last consonant).

7. I form light and create darkness: that this is a reference to Zoroastrian dualism is most unlikely. It is not certain that Cyrus, who is supposedly addressed here, was an adherent of that religion. The assertion is entirely in line with Hebrew thought: cf. Am. 3 : 6.

A FRAGMENTARY PRAYER

45 : 8

It is difficult to understand why Westermann (*Sprache und Struktur*, pp. 157ff.) includes this verse among the 'eschatological hymns of praise'. In fact it is not a hymn of praise at all. The imperatives and jussives do not correspond in content to the call to praise, nor can the words **I the LORD have created it** be regarded as the central affirmation of a hymn of praise. The verse is a torso, and is probably the work of a later disciple or editor (so Fohrer), possibly intended to mark the end of a section of the book (cf. 44:23). The final phrase was probably originally unconnected with the rest: the Hebrew has not 'created it' but 'created *him*' (*berā'tîw*). There are grammatical peculiarities in the rest of the verse: **open** (Qal of *pātaḥ*) is a transitive verb which requires, but here lacks, an object; **sprout forth** (*yiperû*) is unaccountably plural; **cause . . . to spring up** (*taṣmîaḥ*) is awkward. These difficulties can be, and frequently have been, smoothed out by emendations; but they may simply be the marks of inferior composition.

The idea that such divine gifts as **righteousness** and **salvation** may be conferred on men by means of the reproductive processes of nature is found also in Ps. 85:9–13 (MT 10–14) and in Ps. 72:1–7, where as elsewhere in the ancient Near East both the fertility of the ground and the maintenance of the national and social order are linked with the person of the king. Like the two psalm passages, this fragment, considered apart from the final phrase, has the form of a liturgical prayer rather than of a divine command.

YAHWEH FASHIONS HIS OWN TOOLS

45:9–13

Westermann, following Elliger, finds such serious inconsistencies in this passage that he postulates for it a complicated redactional history. For Muilenburg, at the other extreme, it is a 'beautifully constructed' literary unity. The sequence of thought is less strained than Westermann supposes: the purpose is to meet objections raised against Deutero-Isaiah's prophecies of deliverance through Cyrus by showing that it is meaningless and blasphemous for the creature to doubt and criticize the purpose, power, or skill of the creator. The passage is basically a disputation, although other forms of speech are pressed into service. Probably the objections raised by the exiles are twofold: they have questioned the likelihood of the fulfilment of the prophecies, and they have objected to Yahweh's choice of a foreigner, Cyrus, as the instrument of his acts of salvation of his chosen people.

9–10. The argument begins with a series of three examples of the folly and presumption of the creature's criticism of his maker. Of these the first and third are preceded by the particle **Woe**

(*hôy*), but the second has the form of a rhetorical question to which a negative reply is expected. The first word of this sentence (*h^a^yō'mar*, **Does** (it) **say?**) is somewhat similar to the *hôy* of the other two, and it is tempting to follow 1QIs^a^ in reading *hôy* here also, although MT is quite acceptable as it stands. The contrary suggestion that in all three cases the original text consisted entirely of questions rather than woes (Duhm, *BHS*) has little to commend it. The woe-formula, the origin of which is disputed, had already been adopted into prophetic speech (e.g. Isa. 5 : 8ff.). It expresses the strongest possible condemnation; this is its only occurrence in Deutero-Isaiah.

9. The thought and language here closely resemble Isa. 29 : 16, a passage which Deutero-Isaiah probably had in mind. The theme was also developed by Jeremiah (18; 19). **an earthen vessel with the potter:** MT has 'a potsherd with the earthen potsherds'. This involves a somewhat unusual meaning for *'eṯ* ('with' = 'among'), but the correction is probably unnecessary. **Your work has no handles:** it is doubtful whether *yāḏayim*, literally, 'hands', can mean 'handles'. A more probable meaning is 'skill'. No emendation is necessary here.

10. The speaker here can hardly be the child himself. This is not because of the incongruity of the thought, which would not be impossible for Deutero-Isaiah, but because of the word **a father,** where '*his* father' would be expected. Nevertheless the point made here is not as far removed from that of verse 9 as some commentators have maintained, though the standpoint is somewhat different. Deutero-Isaiah may be using proverbial material here. The point is that a parent, like the creator, is responsible for his own actions and not to be questioned by others in the very act of procreation.

11. It is only now that the point of the disputation begins to become clear. The prophet moves from the common ground of agreement on his general propositions to accuse the exiles of doing the very thing which they have tacitly acknowledged to be wrong. This verse is further linked with the preceding verses by the word **Maker** (*yōṣēr*), already used in verse 9 both in this sense and in the sense of 'potter, one who shapes something'. Yahweh is Israel's 'potter'. **Will you question me . . . ?:** MT has 'Ask me of things to come'; but the slight emendation adopted by *RSV* (*h'ty tš'lwny* for *h'tywt š'lwny*) is probably right. **my chil-**

dren and **the work of my hands** refer back to the preceding verses.

12–13. The point is now made absolutely clear. The prophet applies the general proposition that the ways of the creator are not to be questioned to the case in dispute: it is Yahweh who is the creator of the world, and his use of Cyrus as his instrument needs no justification.

13. him: this can only refer to Cyrus. The curious omission of his name may perhaps imply a specific context of which we are ignorant. **in righteousness:** see on 42 : 6. **he shall build my city:** an example of an unfulfilled prophecy. **my exiles:** there is no reason to follow LXX here and emend to 'the captivity of my people'. **not for price or reward:** there is no real contradiction with those passages (43 : 3f. and possibly 45 : 14) which speak of the rewards which Cyrus will receive. Here it is Cyrus' motive rather than the actual results of his actions which is under discussion.

THE NATIONS PROSTRATE AT ISRAEL'S FEET

45 : 14–17

Westermann finds in these verses nothing but a series of fragments. More probably there are two independent pieces here: verses 14–15 and 16–17. Between these two it is difficult to find any continuity of thought.

14–15. This is a short promise of salvation addressed to Israel (presumably under the figure of Zion-Jerusalem) in the fem. sing. The proposal of some commentators to repoint these particles as masc. and to take the passage as addressed to Cyrus is misconceived. There is no real contradiction with 43 : 3–4, where these same three African peoples are promised to Cyrus as a ransom for Israel. The only difference is one of imagery. Here these peoples, conquered by Cyrus, will be handed over to Israel to make a direct confession of the superiority of Israel's God, a confession which they will in any case share with all other peoples.

14. wealth, merchandise: literally, 'toil', 'profits'. These abstract nouns are probably to be taken as representing the peoples themselves: 'the toilers of Egypt'; 'the traders of Ethiopia'. **shall come over:** this verb occurs twice in this verse. It should perhaps be omitted at its second occurrence.

15. As the text stands this verse is addressed to God and has no connexion with verse 14. But a slight emendation (*'ittāḵ*, 'with you' for *'attāh*, **thou**) would make it a continuation of the speech of the conquered peoples to Israel: 'Truly, with you is a God who hides himself, the God of Israel, the Saviour'. Westermann's argument that this cannot be part of the speech of the peoples because they have encountered God as a God who *reveals* himself is not valid. It is the sudden revelation of God which has made them realize how thoroughly he had previously hidden himself.

16–17. The sudden reference to idol-makers is incongruous and suggests that these verses are unconnected with what precedes. The contrast between the fates of these idolaters and of Israel which is **saved by the LORD** is reminiscent of trial speeches and polemics against idolatry earlier in the book.

16. All of them: we should expect a more concrete phrase here parallel with **the makers of idols.** But LXX's 'all that are opposed to him' hardly seems appropriate.

17. you shall not be put to shame: the change from third to second person here is strange, but not unique in Deutero-Isaiah.

YAHWEH'S OPEN GOVERNMENT

45 : 18–19

Despite the connecting particle **For,** which must be regarded as editorial, this passage is an independent, though perhaps fragmentary, piece, placed here because it has similarities of theme with those which precede and follow it. It has the function, if not precisely the form, of a disputation. The argument is contained partly in the elaborate cluster of epithets attached to the name **the LORD** in verse 18 and partly in the words of Yahweh himself in verse 19; but it is in the latter that its central point is to be found. The matter at issue is the character and reliability of the prophetic word. What Yahweh speaks to his people is **the truth** and **what is right**. We may therefore infer that the disputation is a reply to doubts expressed by the exiles concerning the authenticity of Deutero-Isaiah's message.

18. The disputation begins with a reassertion of the undisputed propositions that Yahweh is sole God and sole creator, and then proceeds to speak of the *purpose* of his act of creation. The word

chaos (*tōhû*) is the same as that used in Gen. 1 : 2, where it is translated in *RSV* as 'without form'. Whether Deutero-Isaiah was familiar with an account of creation—perhaps a forerunner of Gen. 1—in which this word occurred, it is impossible to say. But its meaning here should be understood in terms of its context and of its meaning elsewhere in Deutero-Isaiah, where it designates that which is utterly ineffectual. The creation of the world was not due simply to a divine whim but directed towards a clear and purposeful end: he formed it **to be inhabited** by the human race.

19. We now see where the argument of verse 18 is leading. What is true of the creation as a whole must also be true of God's communication with men, in particular with his own people. The phrases **in secret** and **in a land of darkness** are probably allusions to the mysterious and ambiguous divinatory and oracular practices of the ancient world, and of the Babylonians in particular. **land of darkness** probably alludes to the practice of conjuring up messages from the underworld, known also in Israel (e.g. 1 Sam. 28 : 6–19). The recurrence of the word **chaos** links the argument with the previous verse: it is not by such ineffectual means that Israel is to learn the will of God. Yahweh has always spoken out clearly and openly, with a definite and reliable purpose no less effective than the purpose which he showed in creation. **in chaos:** Heb. has simply 'chaos'. Either the particle *b*^{e} ('in') has dropped out or the noun without the particle is to be understood adverbially.

YAHWEH'S UNIVERSAL RULE

45 : 20–25

This is the last of the full trial-speeches (see on 41 : 1–5). It differs from the others in that the prophet has placed himself in imagination in the time following the capture of Babylon by Cyrus. After his world-wide conquests it is only the **survivors of the nations** who remain to be summoned to the dispute with Yahweh.

Almost all commentators, following an ancient Christian tradition, see in this passage an offer of 'salvation' to all mankind. This would be a most significant doctrinal innovation; but this view cannot be sustained. (See especially N. H. Snaith, 'The Servant of the Lord in Deutero-Isaiah' (in *Studies in Old Testament*

Prophecy, ed. H. H. Rowley, 1950, pp. 196f.); *Studies on the Second Part of the Book of Isaiah* (with H. M. Orlinsky) (*VT* Suppl. 14), 1967, pp. 160, 185f.; P. A. H. de Boer, *Second-Isaiah's Message*, (Oudtestamentische Studiën XI), 1956, pp. 89f.; R. Martin-Achard, *Israël et les Nations*, 1959, pp. 20f.) Like the other trial-speeches in Deutero-Isaiah, this passage is concerned to encourage the Jewish exiles and them alone. This is quite clear from verse 25, which marks its climax, where the **triumph and glory** is reserved for **all the offspring of Israel.** Only verse 22 is susceptible of an universalist interpretation. Yet even here there is no clear reference to the nations of the world. Nowhere does Deutero-Isaiah use the phrase **the ends of the earth** (*’ap̱^{e}sê/ḳ^{e}ṣôṯ ’ereṣ/hā’āreṣ*) unequivocally in this sense. It is more probable that the whole created world is addressed here, not only its human inhabitants. Yahweh's 'salvation' is cosmic in the sense that it will be recognized by the whole creation (cf. 42 : 4, 6; 52 : 10); but **be saved** in Hebrew does not have the soteriological connotations of Christian theology. It means simply that the whole world will acknowledge Yahweh's triumphant vindication of his people Israel.

20. together: 1QIs^{a} has 'and come', which makes a better parallelism. The second half of the verse (from **They have**) interrupts the thought and may be a later addition.

21. your case: missing in Heb. It is not clear whether a word has fallen out or whether the object of the verbs is intended to be understood. **Who told this long ago?: this** is the triumph of Cyrus, probably especially his conquest of Babylon. The reference is to earlier prophecies of Israel's restoration such as those of Jeremiah. Yahweh reminds the defeated nations that he has **long ago** predicted the events which have just occurred. **righteous:** probably better, 'victorious'.

22. On this verse see the general introduction to this section. **all the ends of the earth:** Snaith, de Boer, and Martin-Achard interpret this expression (and also **survivors of the nations** in verse 20) as referring to the scattered Israelites. This is improbable; but it does not affect the general proposition that there is no universalism in these verses.

23. By myself I have sworn: Yahweh confirms his promise with a solemn oath: compare his earlier oaths to the patriarchs, e.g. Gen. 22 : 16. He calls himself to witness, since there is no higher authority. **has gone forth in righteousness:** or possibly, 'righteousness has gone forth'. But the meaning of **righteousness** (*ṣᵉdāḳāh*) here is not clear: it may mean either 'truth' or 'justice', hardly 'victory'. **swear:** that is, an oath of obedience.

24. it shall be said of me (*lî 'āmar*)**:** the Heb. expression is odd, and *RSV* appears to have emended the verb from a perfect tense to an imperfect. 1QIsᵃ has a passive (Niphal). Of the emendations proposed, that based on LXX (to read *lē'mōr*, 'saying', and place it at the beginning of the verse) is perhaps the most probable. In that case the first part of the verse (to **strength**) contains the words of the oath referred to in verse 23; the remainder of the verse and verse 25, which can hardly be Yahweh's own words, must be a final comment by the prophet. **righteousness:** the plur. form (*ṣᵉdāḳôt*) and the context show that the meaning here is 'victory'. **shall come:** read the plural *yābô'û* for MT's *yābô'*, with 1QIsᵃ and a number of MSS and Versions.

YAHWEH CARRIES HIS PEOPLE

46 : 1–4

At first sight chapter 46 seems to possess a kind of literary unity: an initial statement about the fate of the Babylonian gods (verses 1–2) is followed by sections each beginning with a plur. imperative—**Hearken to me** (verse 3); **Remember** (verse 8); **Hearken to me** (verse 12). Moreover, all the references to Yahweh are in the first person, and it might be argued that he is the speaker throughout. But there is no corresponding unity of theme, and it must be concluded that the unity is editorial and not original.

Verses 1–4 form one of the best constructed and most effective passages in Deutero-Isaiah. By means of a number of keywords used with reference both to the Babylonian gods and to Yahweh —carry, bear, load, burden, save—the prophet draws a devastating contrast which demonstrates the utter futility of the former. He takes for granted the view that the Babylonians believed their gods to be actually embodied by their images (cf. 45 : 20, and see on 40 : 19), and describes in imagination what will happen to them when Cyrus attacks Babylon: their worshippers will strap them ignominiously on the backs of pack-animals and carry them with them in their flight. So it is the Babylonians who have to **carry** their useless gods who **cannot save** them and are in fact

burdens to them (verses 1–2). In contrast (verses 3–4) it is Israel which is a burden to Yahweh: it is he who has always 'carried' them and saved them.

1–2. The style is descriptive, but the mood of the poetry, with its short lines, is one of excitement. That the Babylonians might have taken their 'gods' with them in anticipation of the city's fall is not improbable: Merodach-baladan did precisely that when Sennacherib approached the city with his army. But this is a further example of a prophecy which was not fulfilled: in the event Cyrus proclaimed himself a follower of Marduk and actively promoted the worship of Babylon's gods. It has been suggested that this picture of a 'procession' of defeated gods is a mocking allusion to the triumphant festival processions of the days of Babylon's glory; but this is probably to read too much into it.

1. Bel was another name of Marduk, the city-god of Babylon and the head of the Babylonian pantheon. **Nebo** (properly Nabu) was also most important in Babylonia at this period: city-god of Borsippa, son of Marduk, god of writing and wisdom, keeper of the Tablets of Destiny and, as can be seen from such royal names as Nebuchadnezzar and Nabonidus, especially honoured by the reigning dynasty. **these things you carry:** this is clearly wrong; probably read *-hem*, 'their', for *-ḵem*, 'your': 'these things *they* carry'. The whole verse from **their idols** is somewhat clumsy, but no emendation yet proposed is wholly satisfactory.

2. they cannot save: if, as is probable, the subject is the gods, Deutero-Isaiah appears here somewhat inconsistently to make a distinction between the gods and their images which he did not make in verse 1.

3–4. Yahweh now speaks and addresses Israel in a short promise of salvation grounded in his previous acts of kindness towards his people.

3. house of Jacob: it is unlikely though not impossible that this designation refers specifically to the descendants of the inhabitants of the old northern kingdom of Israel. **who have been borne . . . from the womb:** the concepts of Israel as a child cared for by Yahweh, and of his 'bearing' or 'carrying' Israel are found elsewhere in the *OT*: Dt. 1 : 31; Exod. 19 : 4; Ps. 28 : 9; Hos. 11 : 3. Cf. also Isa. 40 : 11.

4. even to your old age: the figure of Israel as a man is continued here, in the form of a promise that Yahweh's care will never cease. The expression is poetical and does not imply that Israel's 'life' is of limited duration. **I am He:** here this characteristic phrase comes close to meaning 'I am the same'. **I have made:** the meaning is not clear. Possibly another verb originally stood here. In view of the piling up in this verse of verbs meaning 'carry', it has been suggested that this was *ʿāmastî*, but this is very uncertain.

THE NATIONS CARRY THEIR GODS

46 : 5–8

This passage can hardly be the continuation of verses 1–4, which are complete in themselves and not improved by the addition of the themes of Yahweh's incomparability (verse 5) and of the folly of idolatry (verse 6–7). The picking up in verse 7 of the keywords **lift** and **carry** from the preceding section is no proof of an original continuity. It is either an example of an editorial use of keywords as an artificial means of providing continuity, or possibly an indication that verses 6–7 at least were deliberately composed by a later author as an extension of verses 1–4.

It is by no means certain that verses 5–8 themselves are a literary unit. Verse 5 strongly resembles 40 : 18, 25, and is in the style of Deutero-Isaiah, though the possibility of a later imitation should be borne in mind. Like 40 : 18, this verse serves to introduce a passage about the making of an idol. Another possibility is that verse 5 is a genuine Deutero-Isaianic verse which was originally followed by verse 9, verses 6–8 being an interpolation. The vocabulary of verses 6–7 is similar to that of 44 : 9–20, which is not the work of Deutero-Isaiah. Verse 8 presents a further problem: it is not clear whether **this** refers to what precedes or what follows. The use of the unusual phrase *hāšîḇ ʿal-lēḇ* (**recall it to mind**) both here and in 44: 19 perhaps suggests that the verse comes from the same hand as verses 6–7.

6–7. Like 44 : 9–20, these verses are somewhat lacking in metrical regularity. For the thought see also 40 : 19–20; 41 : 6–7.

6. lavish: the exact sense of this verb is uncertain. **scales:** this word (*ḳāneh*) normally means a reed or rod. Here it must mean **scales**—perhaps originally the beam from which the scale-pans are suspended. **makes it into a god** (*wᵉyaʿaśēhû ʾēl*): 1QIs^{a} has simply 'and makes a god' (*wyʿśh ʾl*).

8. and consider (*wᵉhiṯʾōšāšû*)**:** the meaning of this word has never been satisfactorily elucidated. *RSV* seems to have followed the suggestion of Volz and Duhm that it may be derived from the same root as *tûšiyyāh*, which means something like 'wisdom', a suggestion which receives some support from Syr. Other suggested emendations are conjectural. *BHS* follows G. R. Driver (*JTS* 36 (1935), p. 400) in deriving it from a Semitic root meaning 'be founded, firmly planted', emends it to (*wᵉ*)*yiṯʾōšaš* and transfers it to verse 7 before **and it stands there**, where its meaning would be '(and) it is firmly planted', referring to the idol. This seems an unnecessarily complicated proposal in view of the lack of support from either MSS or Versions. **transgressors:** better, 'rebels'.

CYRUS CARRIES OUT YAHWEH'S PURPOSE

46 : 9–11

It is best to regard this passage as a disputation (see on 40 : 12–17), in which Yahweh is the speaker. The argument, however, resembles that of the trial-speeches, especially in the appeal to **the former things** (cf. 41 : 22; 43 : 9), the call to **remember** (cf. 44 : 21) and the theme of Cyrus. The passage ends in a promise (verse 11*b*), an element also found elsewhere in disputations (cf. 40 : 31). The purpose of the disputation is to convince the exiles of the truth of the prophet's assertions, which they have questioned, that Cyrus has been sent by God to deliver Israel. The argument moves from the claim, with which the audience may be expected to agree, that Yahweh has proved himself by his former fulfilment of his own prophecies to be the sole God (verses 9*b*–10*a*), to the conclusion that his will cannot be frustrated (verse 10*b*), and thence to the further specific conclusion that the promise which he is now making about his use of Cyrus must likewise receive its fulfilment.

9. As has already been remarked (see on 46 : 5–8) this verse may originally have followed verse 5; but this is not certain. **remember the former things of old:** this line lacks a parallel, and it is possible that some words have fallen out. **former things** here, as in 41 : 22; 43 : 18, refers to Israel's past history in general. **for** (*kî*)**:** this word would be better translated by 'that'.

10–11. The hymn-like participles in these verses are characteristic of Deutero-Isaiah's style, and to some extent carry the argument. What appears to be a series of parallel statements made by Yahweh about himself is really an argument moving from premiss to conclusion.

10. declaring the end from the beginning: that is, announcing the future before it began to take shape. **counsel:** see on 44 : 26. **stand:** see on 40 : 8.

11. This verse marks the conclusion of the argument. **bird of prey** (*'ayiṭ*)**:** the Heb. term is generic and does not denote any particular species. The reference is to Cyrus, and is appropriately used, like 'eagle' in Jer. 49 : 22; Ezek. 17 : 3, of swift military conquest. **from the east:** cf. 41 : 2. **the man of my counsel: counsel** (*'ēṣāh*) is used in the same sense as in verse 10: the meaning is not that Cyrus gave advice to Yahweh (in which sense the phrase is used in 40 : 13), but that he is the man called to carry out Yahweh's plan. The last line (from **I have spoken**) is very emphatic, three of the clauses being preceded in the Heb. by the emphatic participle *'ap̱*. **purposed:** literally, 'formed' (*yāṣartî*).

DELIVERANCE IS NEAR

46 : 12–13

This passage might be a continuation of verses 9–11 but is more probably an independent piece. The point is somewhat different: the emphasis is not simply on the certainty of deliverance but on its imminence. Some of the exiles may have accepted in principle that Yahweh had not totally abandoned his people, but questioned the prophet's insistence that his intervention was imminent. The reply to these sceptics is given not in the form of a disputation but simply as a straightforward divine promise of immediate salvation. If these verses were originally independent, their position here may be accounted for by the similarity of the opening words to those of verses 3 and 9, by the occurrence of the keyword **far** (*merḥāḳ*, verse 11; *hārᵉḥôḳîm*, verse 12; *tirḥâḳ*, verse 13) and by the general similarity of theme.

12. stubborn of heart: such an appellation seems out of place in view of the parallel **far from deliverance**, i.e. unable to believe that deliverance is coming. Most commentators, following a clue from LXX, rightly emend *'abbîrê lēḇ* to *'ōbᵉḏê lēḇ*, '(you who have) lost heart' (for the expression cf. Jer. 4 : 9). **deliverance:**

the Heb. word *ṣᵉḏāḳāh* could mean 'righteousness', which would make sense if **stubborn of heart** were retained. But since *ṣᵉḏāḳāh* occurs again in verse 13 where it can only mean something like 'deliverance', that is likely to be the meaning here also.

13. This verse is the main section of the promise of salvation, consisting of the general promise followed by a more concrete statement of its consequences. **I bring near my deliverance:** 1QIsᵃ has 'my deliverance is near'. There is little to choose between the two readings. **not far off:** there is a play on the two meanings of **far**, here and in verse 12. **for Israel my glory:** an alternative translation would be 'in Israel my glory', 'my glory' being a second object of the verb **I will put. glory:** not *kāḇôḏ* but *tip̄'ereṯ*, meaning 'splendour'. Yahweh will restore and beautify the now wretched Israel so that it reflects and witnesses to his own splendour.

BABYLON'S FALL

47 : 1–15

This chapter is the only example in Deutero-Isaiah of a type of oracle represented in a number of the other prophetical books: the oracle directed against, and predicting the fall of, a foreign nation or city. Like many of the other examples in the prophetical books (the largest collections are found in Isa. 13–23; Jer. 46–51; Ezek. 25–32) this oracle makes use of elements taken over from two originally distinct forms of speech: the mocking-song or taunt-song and the funeral-song or dirge over the dead. The purpose of the mocking-song was to expose a people (or an individual) to ridicule and contempt and so to sap its power and correspondingly to strengthen that of the mocker or his people. The funeral-song, as used by the prophets, underwent two changes: it was used no longer to express genuine grief over the dead or over the downfall of the people concerned, but in mockery of them; and it was used in an anticipatory way, referring to the expected downfall as if it had already occurred. This gave it the effect of prophecy, involving the notion that the utterance of the song was itself a factor in bringing about the events of which it spoke.

The total devastation of Babylon envisaged in this song did not in fact occur when Cyrus took the city, and there can therefore be no doubt that it was composed before that event. The prevailing metre is the so-called *ḳînāh*-metre (three beats before the caesura and two after it) characteristic of dirges. The poem is divided into six stanzas of somewhat unequal length. If a few later interpolations are set aside, it is seen to be a poem of consummate literary skill.

It is not clear who is the speaker. The **I** of verses 3*b* and 6 is clearly Yahweh, while in verse 4 this is equally clearly not the case. But verse 3*b* might be a quotation within a poem spoken by another person, and verse 4 (see below) an acknowledgement of that fact, while verse 6 has been regarded by some commentators as an interpolation. On the other hand, verse 4 might be regarded as an interpolation or gloss inserted into a poem spoken by Yahweh. The question is perhaps not one of great importance: if the prophet is the speaker he is unlikely to have spoken such a weighty condemnation of Babylon simply in his own name.

1–4. The first stanza. Babylon, the queen of the nations, is brusquely commanded to descend from her throne and to join the ranks of the lowest class of slave. This passage makes a striking contrast with those other passages, especially 52 : 1–2, in which Zion/Jerusalem, now a slave, is to become a queen. Although there is no positive proof that these passages were spoken at one and the same time, we must suppose that their contrasting images belong to the same strand of Deutero-Isaiah's thought.

1. virgin daughter of Babylon: the representation of a city (or people) by the figure of a woman is part of the regular poetical imagery of the *OT*: cf. Zion/Jerusalem. **virgin:** that is, 'inviolate' in the sense of never having been conquered. This was not historically true, though it was correct as far as the contemporary Babylonian dynasty was concerned. **without a throne:** this phrase is omitted by LXX, but is necessary for the metre. **Chaldeans:** see on 43 : 14.

2. The grinding of corn was a characteristic occupation of female slaves in the ancient Near East. **veil:** or, possibly, 'tresses'. **robe** (*šôḇel*)**:** this word occurs only here. Another possible translation is 'skirt'. 1QIs[a] has *šwlyk*, 'your skirts'. **uncover your legs:** in order to be free to perform heavy manual labour, as illustrated in Egyptian pictorial scenes. **pass through the rivers:** the meaning is not clear. It may refer either to the necessity to cross small streams in the course of outdoor labour, or to the possibility of having to undertake long journeys in the course of transportation to distant places.

3. The reference in the first half of the verse is to sexual intercourse. Probably the implication is that as a young female slave Babylon will be subjected to the final humiliation of being forced to accept the casual sexual attentions of any man who happens to want her. **and I will spare no man** (*wᵉlōʾ ʾepgaʿ ʾāḏām*)**:** this is an extremely difficult phrase. It might perhaps be translated by 'and I will meet no one'; but this would make no sense. The secondary meanings of the verb *pāgaʿ*, 'attack', 'entreat', are equally out of the question. Of the emendations of the consonantal text which have been proposed, the alteration of *ʾepgaʿ* to the third pers. *yipgaʿ*, giving 'and no one will attack (i.e. resist) me', which receives support from Vulg. & Symm., is perhaps the most likely because the least substantial. But it is more probable that a repointing of the consonantal text to give *ʾeppāgaʿ* (Duhm) is all that is needed: 'I will not be entreated'—that is, will not allow anyone to intercede for Babylon. Even with this change, *ʾāḏām*, '(any) man', still causes some grammatical difficulty. Here, with some support from some MSS of LXX, we may perhaps accept Duhm's proposal to amend *ʾāḏām* to *ʾāmar*, 'says', while also transferring **Our Redeemer** from verse 4 to follow it. This gives the translation 'says our Redeemer'. It also improves the metre.

4. If the above proposal is accepted, this verse is a continuation of verse 3: 'whose name is the LORD of hosts, the Holy One of Israel'. If, however, *ʾāḏām* is retained in verse 3 and if the whole poem is regarded as a speech by Yahweh, verse 4 must be regarded as a gloss.

5–7. The second stanza. The sentence passed on Babylon is now repeated briefly in different imagery (verse 5*a*) and the indictment follows. There are two charges: cruelty and arrogance.

5. darkness: the same imagery is used in connexion with the Jewish exiles in 42 : 7. Now Babylon is to suffer the same fate. This does not necessarily mean that the prophet specifically envisaged captivity or exile for the Babylonians, though he may have done so. **darkness,** whether of the prison—as here—or in general simply indicates a state of misery: cf. Lam. 3 : 2. **the mistress of kingdoms:** that is, the imperial city.

6. Here it is clearly Yahweh who speaks. There are no sufficient grounds for regarding this verse as a gloss, and its omission would seriously weaken the stanza. **I profaned my heritage** (*ḥillaltî naḥ^alāṯî*): on the meaning of **profaned** see on 43 : 28. **heritage** (*naḥ^alā*), like **people** (*ʿam*), refers, as often in the *OT*, to the people of Israel as Yahweh's special 'possession'. Yahweh does not hold Babylon responsible for the defeat and captivity of his people but admits, **I gave them into your hand** in order to punish them for their sins. But he accuses her of treating them with unnecessary harshness: **you showed them no mercy.** Unlike some of his predecessors Deutero-Isaiah taught that Yahweh intended the punishment to be strictly limited in scope (cf. 40 : 2; 54 : 7–8). Babylon, admittedly, was not to know this; but the cruel treatment of prisoners, such as making **the aged** do forced labour, was regarded even outside Israel as a crime. The accusation of cruelty is not incompatible with the impression gained from other texts that the conditions of exile were not, in general, unduly harsh: there were no doubt exceptions, and Deutero-Isaiah and his audience were evidently familiar with some of these.

7. The second accusation is one of arrogance amounting to blasphemy. As in other prophetic denunciations of powerful cities (e.g. Tyre, Ezek. 28), Babylon is accused of arrogating quasi-divine attributes to herself. **so that** (*ʿaḏ*): the Massoretic punctuation treats this word as a conjunction. This is not an impossible construction, but the consensus of commentators is probably correct in treating *ʿaḏ* as a noun denoting an indefinite period of time, and **mistress** (*g^eḇāreṯ*) as a construct. Babylon's words would then be, 'for ever shall I be queen in perpetuity'. 1QIs[a] has *ʾwd*, 'still'. **remember:** the verb *zāḵar* does not refer only to things past. 'bear in mind' or 'consider' would be a better translation. **end:** that is, 'consequences'.

8–9. The third stanza. Babylon's arrogance is now described more fully, and its false basis disclosed. Her overthrow will come when least expected.

8. Now therefore hear this: this is the language of the formal prophetic announcement of doom. **lover of pleasures:** in condemning excessive luxury Deutero-Isaiah stands in the classical prophetic tradition. **securely:** that is, self-confidently. **in your heart:** the Massoretic pointing would necessitate the translation 'in *her* heart'. But many MSS lack the dot (*mappiq*) in the final consonant, giving *bil^eḇāḇāh*, 'in *the* (i.e. 'your') heart'. **besides me:** the final *yodh* in *'ap̱sî* can hardly be the suffix 'me, my', and is probably an ancient case-ending which no longer has any significance (so G–K §90 l). **who say . . . besides me:** this phrase is identical with words attributed to Nineveh in a similar passage in Zeph. 2:15. The theme appears in a number of prophetical oracles against foreign cities, and it would seem that there was a common stock of phrases which could be drawn upon. Here in Deutero-Isaiah, however, the phrase has additional significance, because the claim made by Babylon is almost identical with that attributed frequently by this prophet to Yahweh himself (e.g. 45:5, 6, 18, 22; 46:9). Viewed in this context of thought it becomes more than self-confidence (as in verse 7): it is a blasphemous claim to absolute divine status and so a direct challenge to Yahweh. **widow, loss of children:** the imagery has changed: Babylon is now no longer seen as a **virgin** (verse 1) but as a wife and mother. The **children** may be more or less equated with the inhabitants of the city; but it would be pedantic to enquire who was Babylon's husband. The point is that widowhood and loss of children were the two greatest calamities which could happen to a woman in the ancient Near East, especially if they happened together: she would be deprived of any means of support except as a slave. As in the case of the imagery in verse 1, there can be no doubt that the prophet has in mind an exchange of roles between Babylon and Zion/Jerusalem: cf. 49:21–23; 54:1–6.

9. in one day: that is, the day when Cyrus captures the city. **in full measure:** this translation of *k^eṯummām* is just possible. LXX and Syr. have 'suddenly', which makes a better parallel with **in one day**, and might be a translation of Heb. *piṯ'ōm*. However, emendation may not be necessary to obtain an appropriate sense. A similar expression in 2 Sam. 15:11; 1 Kg. 22:34 appears to have the sense of guilelessness or lack of suspicion; thus here we may perhaps translate by 'unexpectedly' (see G. R. Driver, *Von Ugarit nach Qumran*, *BZAW* 77 (1958), p. 47). **shall come:** perhaps read imperf. *yāḇō'û* for perf. *bā'û*. **sorceries, enchantments:** the Babylonians were well known for the importance which they attached to magic. Deutero-Isaiah appears to assume that their religion consisted of nothing else. **great power:** ironical, unless, following the analogy of the cognate adjective *ʿāṣûm*, we may take the noun *ʿoṣmāh* to have the additional sense of 'large number'.

10–11. The fourth stanza. The thought is similar to that of the preceding stanza, but the reference to Babylon's **sorceries** and **enchantments** is further developed.

10. in your wickedness (*beraʿāṯēḵ*)**:** 1QIsa differs by one consonant, reading *bdʿtk*, i.e. 'in your knowledge'. **wickedness** seems rather weak, but 'knowledge' is perhaps unlikely because the word occurs again in the next line. Moreover *rāʿāṯēḵ*, if correct, permits a characteristic play on meanings: Babylon's **wickedness** (*rāʿāh*) will lead to her misfortune (*rāʿāh*, **evil**, verse 11). **sees me:** the pointing (*rō'ānî*) is unusual, but not on that account necessarily to be 'corrected'. The thought that **no one sees me** is a consequence of Babylon's conviction that she has divine status, and is not quite the same as that attributed to wicked or idolatrous Israelites in Ps. 94: 7 and Ezek. 8: 12 concerning Yahweh's inability to see their evil deeds. But the thought of God's all-seeing eye, a commonplace of the literature of the ancient Near East as well as of Israel, lies in the background as an encouragement to the Jewish exiles: Yahweh may appear to be oblivious of their wrongs, but events will soon show that he has missed nothing. **wisdom; knowledge:** the reference is to the Babylonians' skill in sorcery and divination (cf. the 'wise men of Babylon' in Dan. 2; 5). **I am . . . besides me:** the same phrase as in verse 8.

11. Babylon is now to learn by bitter experience that Yahweh has seen and noted her wicked deeds. **evil; disaster; ruin:** the alliteration (*rāʿāh, hōwāh, šō'āh*) conveys a sense of completeness and irrevocability. On **evil** see on verse 10. **shall come:** there is no need to emend the masc. verb *bā'* to a fem., since a verb preceding its subject does not necessarily agree with it in gender. 1QIsa has the fem.; but this is an alternative rather than a superior reading. **atone:** perhaps better 'charm away'. The emendation of *šaḥrāh* to *šaḥadāh*, 'bribe away', though tempting in view of the parallelism of *kpr* and *šḥd* in Prov. 6: 35, is unjustified since the Heb. text is quite satisfactory. **expiate:** *kippēr* is here used not in the technical sense of atonement for sin, as in the laws of the *OT*, but has the wider meaning of 'avert', as in Prov. 16: 14. Both 'charm away' and 'avert' refer to the Babylonians' misplaced confidence in their magical spells. **of which you know nothing:** the same phrase occurs earlier in the verse in the sense of **cannot**, and in parallelism also with **will not be able to** (*lōʾ tûkᵉlî*). This suggests that here also *lōʾ tēḏāʿî* means 'cannot', and that a third infinitive has fallen out.

12–13. The fifth stanza. Here the style of the mocking-song is evident. Like Elijah on Mount Carmel (1 Kg. 18 : 27) Deutero-Isaiah mockingly encourages Babylon to believe that her magical rites will be able to save her from her fate.

12. Stand fast (*ʿimᵉḏî-nāʾ*)**:** the enclitic particle *nāʾ*, which properly signifies entreaty, here has the effect of mockery, as in Job 40 : 10. **with which . . . youth:** these words are unmetrical and partly repeat a phrase in verse 15. That there is some corruption here is indicated by 1QIsᵃ, which follows MT up to **from your youth**, adds 'and until today', and omits the last part of the verse and the first word of verse 13 altogether. It has been suggested with some plausibility that **with which . . . youth** is a misplaced alternative reading from verse 15. **inspire terror:** the object is not indicated. It may be the evil forces which the magical rites are intended to neutralize.

13. This verse is directed against the Babylonian astrologers. The science of astronomy was highly developed by the Babylonians, but was used for astrological purposes to discern the future. **You are wearied:** better, 'You have exhausted yourself (to no purpose)'. **your . . . counsels** (*ʿᵃṣāṯāyiḵ*)**:** the plural suffix with a singular noun is anomalous, but the Massoretic pointing may indicate a double reading, that is, an alternative text. In view of this the proposal of some commentators to emend to *yôʿᵃṣāyiḵ*, 'your counsellors', may be justified. The 'counsellors' here would be the astrologers referred to in the subsequent lines. **those who divide the heavens:** Kethib has the perfect (*hāḇᵉrû šāmayîm*); but the Qere *hôḇᵉrê* (participle) is to be preferred. The verb *hāḇar* occurs only here. It has generally been taken to be cognate with an Arab. root meaning 'cut', and so to refer to the Babylonian division of the heavens into segments in order to study the movements of the heavenly bodies across the sky and from these to predict earthly events. It is from this that the present zodiacal 'map' is derived; but it appears to be uncertain whether Babylonian astrology had reached this point of development at the time of Deutero-Isaiah. Further, it has been argued by J. Blau (*VT* 7 (1957), pp. 183–4) that this derivation of *hāḇar* is unlikely; he associates the verb with a Ugaritic root meaning 'worship'.

This interpretation does not conflict with the following phrase **who gaze at the stars**, which does not necessarily presuppose such a highly developed art. The **stars** were worshipped by the Babylonians as deities who controlled human destiny. **at the new moons:** better, 'month by month'. **what:** Heb. has *mē'ᵃšer* where one would expect *'ᵃšer*. The exact sense of *min* (*mē*) here is uncertain. Some commentators regard it as partitive: 'something of what . . .'. But this is hardly appropriate in the context, and those commentators may be right who omit it as an intrusion due to dittography. **befall:** MT has the plur. *yāḇō'û*; probably read sing. *yāḇō'* with 1QIsᵃ.

14–15. The final stanza. Babylon's last chance has gone: the mocking encouragement of the previous stanza gives way to an uncompromising declaration that the magical experts on whose skill she has staked everything will perish with her. The certainty and imminence of her fall is emphasized by the series of verbs in the perfect tense (*RSV* **are**; **consumes**; **are**; **wander about**).

14. Behold (*hinnēh*)**:** this word frequently introduces a prophetic announcement of doom. **themselves:** that is, not even themselves. **No coal . . . sit before:** the irony resembles that of 44 : 9–20, and the line may be a gloss added by a reader who had 44 : 16 in mind. **for warming oneself:** the form (*laḥmām*) is probably a pausal form of the infinitive Qal of *ḥāmam* (see G–K §28b, 67cc), and no emendation or repointing is necessary.

15. with whom: two MSS have *ba'ᵃšer* for MT's *'ᵃšer*, but the latter is not necessarily wrong. In prose it would have been necessary to write *'ᵃšer bāhem*; but ellipses of this kind are not unusual in poetry. **laboured:** cf. verse 12. **who have trafficked with you** (*sōḥᵃrayiḵ*)**:** *RSV* retains the traditional interpretation of this word as referring to the foreign merchants who traded with Babylon. Somewhat similar references are made in oracles directed against Nineveh (Nah. 3 : 16) and Tyre (Isa. 23 : 1–8, 17–18); but here a sudden change of reference from native astrologers and diviners to foreign traders is highly unlikely. Although 'trader' is the normal meaning of *sôḥēr*, in this instance the word is probably cognate with Accadian *saḫāru* and Arab. *sāḥirun* and means 'practitioners of magic arts' (G. R. Driver, *JTS* 36 (1935), p. 401). **they wander about . . . direction:** in other words they will be confused and terrified like the other inhabitants of the city when the blow falls.

YAHWEH'S REDEMPTION; ISRAEL'S INGRATITUDE

48 : 1–22

There are many uncertainties about the interpretation of this chapter. In particular the question whether it should be treated as a single unit or as several (e.g. verses 1–11, 12–16, 17–19, 20–22) is inextricably related to the more fundamental problem of authorship, which is encountered in almost every section. It can hardly be denied that two quite different moods alternate. On the one hand the themes of Israel's status before God (verses 1*a*, 12*a*), of the contrast between the **former things** and the **new things** (verses 3, 5*a*, 6, 7*a*), of Yahweh as the only God and as creator (verses 12, 13), of the mission of Cyrus (verses 14–16), of the imminent release of the Jewish exiles (verse 20) and of the Exodus (verse 21) are themes associated elsewhere in the book with the proclamation of salvation and the giving of encouragement to the exiles. On the other hand, interspersed throughout the chapter, are a number of extremely harsh words addressed to an 'Israel' which certainly includes the contemporary Israelites as a group, and is condemned for insincere profession of faith (verse 1*b*), obstinate lack of faith (verse 4), overt idolatry (verse 5*b*), arrogance, treachery and rebellion (verses 7*b*, 8, 18, 19). Equally harsh is the mood of verses 9–11, where Yahweh is represented as deferring punishment for these things, but for his own sake rather than that of his people.

The accusations, especially that of idolatry, are more thoroughgoing than in any other part of Deutero-Isaiah. But it is not this which constitutes the greatest difficulty for the interpreter: it is rather the abrupt alternations of mood which make a consistent interpretation of the chapter, whether as a whole or in its constituent parts, extremely difficult. Consequently the view, held by a large number of commentators, that two quite different kinds of material have been interwoven here appears inevitable; and if so it is reasonable to take the further step of regarding the denunciatory material as having been composed by someone other than Deutero-Isaiah and added at various points to his work.

To have reached this conclusion is not, however, to have solved all the problems. Several important questions remain. First, it is one thing to recognize the two types of material, another to determine precisely the points of division between the two.

There are important differences of opinion between the commentators on this matter. Secondly, while it is not difficult to define in general terms the character of most of the secondary material (see C. Westermann, 'Jesaja 48 und die "Bezeugung gegen Israel" ', *Studia Biblica et Semitica*, Vriezen *Festschrift*, 1966, pp. 356–66), both the occasion of its interpolation and the reason for it remain to a large extent obscure. Thirdly, there remain the questions of the unity of Deutero-Isaiah's original material and of its form and character. All these questions will be considered in the course of the detailed exegesis.

1–2. The chapter begins with an address to Israel, who is then characterized in true Deutero-Isaian style by a series of epithets. But the verbs in verse 2 are in the third person, suggesting that this verse is a comment by a later hand. The sense of both elements is improved if the last line of verse 1 (**but not in truth or right**) is taken with verse 2: 'It is not in truth or right that (*kî; RSV* **For**) they call themselves . . .'. The re-application of Deutero-Isaiah's words thus begins here, with the denial by the secondary author of the sincerity of the worship offered by Israel.

1. Jacob/Israel, Judah: the prophet apparently wishes to make it clear that the whole of the former nation of Israel and not merely the Judaeans is involved in what he has to say. **loins:** *RSV* rightly accepts the emendation of the meaningless 'waters' (*mê*) of the Heb. to **loins** (*meʿê*). **swear by**; **confess:** the reference is probably to liturgical professions of faith.

2. Nowhere else does Deutero-Isaiah say that the exiles **call themselves after the holy city**, although the phrase **holy city** meaning Jerusalem occurs again in 52 : 1. It occurs frequently in later Jewish literature. It has been suggested that the phrase as a whole would come more naturally to Jews after the Exile, when Jerusalem had been restored and repopulated.

3–5. In verses 3, 5*a* we have an echo of earlier passages concerning the **former things**; and a comparison with 46 : 9–11 suggests that there is a connexion between these verses and verse 6, where the announcement of **new things** may be seen as deriving its credibility from the argument from past history. This is the normal sequence of Deutero-Isaiah's arguments; but verses 3–5 as they stand make a quite different kind of argument: Yahweh's announcement of the **former things** before he brought them to pass is now explained as necessitated by Israel's refusal, without such proof, to believe that it was he who brought them about. This argument does not appear elsewhere in Deutero-Isaiah. Moreover verses 4 and 5*b* (from **lest**) are subordinate clauses which may be detached from the remainder without damage to the syntax or sequence of thought, and perhaps indeed with some improvement to both. There is therefore good reason to regard these as subsequent interpolations intended to alter radically the meaning of the original.

3. The former things: not the previous career of Cyrus, as in 42 : 9; 43 : 9, but Yahweh's past deeds in general, as in 41 : 22; 43 : 18; 46 : 9. The argument of C. R. North, *Studies in Old Testament Prophecy*, Robinson *Festschrift*, 1950, p. 123, that *mē'āz* (**of old**) might refer to more recent events here is unconvincing. **and I made them known:** Heb. has 'that I might make them known'. *RSV* may be right in changing a vowel point here to give a past sense. LXX understood the word in this way.

4. The language in this verse is characteristic of Ezekiel rather than of Deutero-Isaiah.

5. The second half of the verse (from **lest**) accuses Israel of practising a thoroughgoing idolatry which regarded idols rather than Yahweh as the controllers of the events of history. This view is quite different from that of Deutero-Isaiah, who in 43 : 12 asserts exactly the opposite, basing an argument on the generally accepted fact that no other god had played a significant role in Israel. **My idol:** this word, *'ōṣeḇ*, occurs only here in the *OT*. We should perhaps read *'aṣabbî*, with the same meaning. On the **graven image** see 40 : 19, 20.

6–8. As has been suggested above, verses 6, 7*a* (to **of them**), 8*a* appear to be the continuation of 3, 5*a*, while verses 7*b*, 8*b* (from **For I knew**) are interpolations of the same kind as verses 4, 5*b*.

6. now see all this (*ḥazēh kullāh*, literally 'see it all'): the meaning is not clear. Of the various proposals for emendation the most likely is perhaps the correction of *ḥazēh* to *ḥāzîṯā*, 'you have seen', following Syr. **and will you not declare it?:** the sudden and momentary change from a sing. to a plur. form of address (*'attem*, **you**; *taggîḏû*, **declare it**) is strange, even for Deutero-Isaiah. The emphatic *'attem*, **you**, is also strange since no emphasis seems to be required. The plural ending of the verb (*w* in the consonantal text) perhaps ought to be attached to the next word, where it would mean 'and'. Instead of *we'attem* Duhm suggested *re'īṯem*, 'you have seen'; but if a sing. is required *rā'īṯā* would be necessary. This verb would be parallel with **You have heard. new things:** cf. 42 : 9; 43 : 19. The reference is probably to the entire chain of events which is expected to begin with Cyrus' conquest of Babylon. If this chapter, apart from the later interpolations, was originally a single unit, the prophet goes on to speak specifically of the fall of Babylon (verse 14) and the release of the exiles (verse 20); but see below. All these things the exiles are now to **declare** (*taggîḏ*). Elsewhere Deutero-Isaiah calls on them to *witness* to Yahweh's past actions and the prophecies which foretold them, rather than to declare or make them known to others: hence some commentators wish to emend the verb to *tā'îḏ(û)*. But this seems rather arbitrary.

7. before today: the Hebrew expression *lip̄enê-yôm* is unusual, but emendation—e.g. to *lep̄ānayim*—is probably unnecessary.

8. your ear has not been opened: MT has an active verb (*pitteḥāh*) of which **your ear** must be the subject: 'your ear did not open'—but this makes no sense, and there is no object. *RSV*'s passive rendering is based on either a repointing of the Piel verb as Pual (*putteḥāh*) or its emendation to Niphal *nip̄teḥāh*, both of which have been proposed in the commentaries. 1QIs[a] has *lw' ptḥt*, probably 'you have not opened (Qal) (your ear)'. But perhaps the best solution is to emend, with some of the older commentators, to *pāṯaḥtî*, giving 'I have not opened your ear', following LXX. The idea that Israel was rebellious from the very beginning of its history, expressed in the second half of the verse, is characteristic of Ezekiel rather than of Deutero-Isaiah.

9–11. Verse 11 refers to the **new things** of verses 6, 7*a*, 8*a*, expressing the thought that the ultimate ground for Yahweh's redemption of Israel is the maintenance of his own reputation and glory. The same thought, also found in Ezekiel, is expressed in 42 : 8; 43 : 25 in similar contexts and similar language. Verses 9–10, however, refer to a different situation altogether: like verses 4, 5*b*, 7*b*, 8*b*, they speak of an Israel which has deserved in the past, and still deserves, to be **cut off**, that is, annihilated. Once again the interpolations alter the whole tenor of the passage.

9. The argument in this verse is precisely that of Ezekiel, especially Ezek. 20 : 8–9; 36 : 21–23, where Yahweh explains why he refrained from exterminating his people both during their wandering in the wilderness after the Exodus, and again at the time of the Babylonian exile. In both of those passages the phrase 'for the sake of my (holy) name' occurs. At the same time this verse has verbal affinities with verse 11. Duhm may be right when he suggests that verses 9–10 have been misplaced: they originally occurred *after* verse 11: cf. the earlier interpolations in this chapter. **I defer my anger** (*a' ᵃrîḵ 'appî*): the English phrase suggests that God's anger will still take effect, though not yet. The Hebrew phrase refers rather to God's patience: even now he still withholds his anger. This is not quite the same thing. **for the sake of:** this word (*lᵉma'an*) occurs only once in the verse, but is clearly intended to govern both **my name** and **my praise**. **restrain:** the meaning of this verb (*ḥāṭam*) is obscure, but some such meaning as **restrain** may be presumed.

10. This verse appears to mean that Yahweh has in the past tried to bring Israel back to obedience by means of disciplinary punishments, but to no avail. The thought is frequent in the pre-exilic prophets. Here a post-exilic situation is the most probable: Israel has not profited from the punishment of the Exile. **but not like silver:** this phrase (*wᵉlō' bᵉḵāsep̱*) has defeated all commentators up to the present. 'Not for money', 'without producing silver', and 'not as silver is refined', may all be possible translations, but none offers a really satisfactory meaning. **I have tried you:** MT has *bᵉḥartîḵā*, which normally means 'I have chosen you', but this is clearly not the meaning. We should probably read *bᵉḥantîḵā*, 'I have tested you', with 1QIsᵃ (though see G. R. Driver, *JTS* 36 (1935), p. 401).

11. for how should my name be profaned?: 'my name' is lacking in Heb. *RSV* has supplied it from LXX, probably correctly. The metre is improved by its insertion. The profaning of the name of Yahweh is a concept found in Ezekiel (20 : 9, 14, 22), and this line may be an interpolation of the same type as those found in the earlier verses of the chapter.

12–16. These verses contain no such interpolations, but are substantially the work of Deutero-Isaiah. The problem remains, however, of their relationship to the original Deutero-Isaian core of verses 1–11. At first sight the theme of Cyrus (verses 14–15) may seem to follow naturally from the announcement of the new things in verses 6, 7*a*, 8*a*, 11; but a number of considerations make it probable that verses 12–16 are an independent piece: the unexplained introduction of the theme of creation (verse 12); the new introductory address (verse 12*a*); and the change from singular to plural verbs in addressing Jacob/Israel (verses 14, 16). Seen as a separate section these verses have rather the character of a disputation in which Yahweh, as the speaker, seeks to overcome the exiles' doubts about the mission of Cyrus by arguing from the common ground of his limitless power and purpose already demonstrated in the creation of the world and the call of Israel (cf. 45: 9–13 and the trial-speech addressed to Israel in 44 : 24–45 : 7).

12. The similarity of the address to Jacob/Israel to that in verse 1 may partially account for the editorial placing of this section here.

12b–13. These expressions are almost all characteristic of Deutero-Isaiah: see especially on 40 : 22, 26; 41 : 4. **when I call to them:** cf. 40 : 26. Creation is by the Word, as in the near-contemporary Gen. 1 (P). **stand forth together:** this is the idea of 'being on parade', as in 40: 26 'not one is missing').

14. This verse is difficult, and appears to have suffered both textual corruption and interpolation. **Assemble:** it is not clear who is addressed, nor, if this is still Israel, why such a call is necessary at this point. The first two lines of the verse (to **these things?**) strongly resemble 43 : 9 and 45 : 20–21, where it is the nations who are summoned, and may be a gloss referring to those passages. There remains the inconsistency of **all of you** and **among them.** A number of MSS have 'among you'; but this may be an early attempt to correct a difficult text. Consistency is not, it may be noted, always a characteristic of glosses. The remainder of the verse refers to Cyrus, who is frequently introduced in an oblique fashion (cf. 41 : 2, 25; 45 : 13). Possibly too obvious a reference to him may have been dangerous at some points in Deutero-Isaiah's ministry, while at others this was not the case (44 : 28; 45 : 1). **The LORD loves him:** the sudden reference to Yahweh in the third person can hardly be right. Among the proposals for emendation, Duhm's suggestion, partly based on LXX, to omit 'Yahweh' and to read *ʾōh^{a}ḇî* for *ʾ^{a}hēḇô*, giving 'my friend shall perform his purpose . . .', is plausible; but the text cannot be restored with any certainty. **his arm shall be against the Chaldeans:** literally, 'and his arm the Chaldeans', which cannot yield the sense given to it by *RSV*. We should perhaps read 'and (against) the seed of the Chaldeans', substituting *wᵉzeraʿ*, which seems to have been the reading of LXX, for *ûzᵉrōʿô*.

15. he will prosper in his way: it is unnecessary to emend to 'I have prospered him in his way', as is done by some commentators, following some of the Versions.

16. Another difficult verse. **Draw near . . . this:** it is not clear why this additional call to assemble is necessary, but although these words are metrically somewhat unusual in that they form an isolated half-line, there are insufficient grounds for omitting them. The middle section (from **from the beginning** to **have been there**) is presumably intended to strengthen the argument concerning the reality of Cyrus' mission by referring, as in 45 : 19, where the same phrase **I have not spoken in secret** is used, to Yahweh's earlier record of prophecy and fulfilment— an argument characteristic of this prophet. Yahweh's announcement of what he intended to do has always been openly and plainly made **from the beginning**, that is throughout Israel's history. The next words are somewhat obscure. **it** in **from the time it came to be** has no antecedent, but must refer to the former prophecies mentioned in the previous line, which then **came to be**, that is, were fulfilled. But **I have been there** (*šām ʾānî*) is puzzling. Perhaps it means that Yahweh never failed to be present in the midst of the events to bring them to pass. But this means reading a great deal into **there**. The final line (**And now . . . Spirit**), obviously the words of some new speaker, has no original connexion with what precedes. If it is a genuine word of Deutero-Isaiah it must be an isolated or fragmentary word spoken by the prophet about himself. It is reminiscent of 61 :1, and may have been added in the same mood, but with the intention of bringing the person of the prophet into greater prominence at this point in the prophecy. **Spirit** is a second object of **has sent**, not a second subject. The connexion of the **Spirit** of Yahweh with prophecy, rare in the pre-exilic classical prophets, is more characteristic of later prophecy: see, in addition to Isa. 61 : 1, Zech. 7 : 12.

17–19. Several features show that these verses are not the work of Deutero-Isaiah, in spite of the style of the opening words. The tone is one of divine grief and regret over Israel's refusal to obey Yahweh's commandments, which has brought the nation close to annihilation (verse 19*b*). There is perhaps a hint that all may yet be well if Israel experiences a change of heart, but the picture is a sombre one, with the triumphant expectation, characteristic of Deutero-Isaiah, of the imminent redemption of Israel entirely lacking. We are reminded of passages in the earlier prophets (e.g. Isa. 30 : 15–18; Hos. 6 : 4–6; Jer. 2 : 29–32), but also of Trito-Isaiah (Isa. 65 : 1–7). The background is early post-exilic Palestine: the ideal of the perennially flowing river (*nāhār*, verse 18) reflects the harsh reality of the life of the Palestinian farmer with his inadequate and uncertain water supply, and the reference to underpopulation (verse 19) also reflects the reality of early post-exilic Palestine in contrast with the massive repopulation prophesied by Deutero-Isaiah in such passages as 49 : 18–21; 51 : 2; 54 : 1–3. These are also the concerns of Trito-Isaiah. C. Westermann ('Jesaja 48 und die "Bezeugung gegen Israel" ', Vriezen *Festschrift*, pp. 356–66) points out the resemblance between these verses and Ps. 81 : 13–16 (MT 14–17) and concludes that they have the character of a liturgical sermon preaching repentance. This may well be so, although his further argument that the whole chapter in its present form belongs to that literary category is more doubtful.

17. In contrast with verses 12–16, Israel in this section is addressed in the sing. **teaches you to profit:** the concept of Yahweh as teacher is mainly restricted in the *OT* to the later books.

18. There is no reference elsewhere in Deutero-Isaiah to Yahweh's commandments. **peace** (*šālôm*)**:** better, well-being, prosperity. **river:** see the introduction to this section.

19. like the sand: a clear reference to the promise to the patriarchs (Gen. 22 : 17; 32 : 12). According to Deutero-Isaiah's own teaching these promises still hold good and will shortly be fulfilled. **and your descendants:** literally, 'and the offspring of your loins' (*wᵉṣeʾᵉṣāʾê mēʿeḵā*). 1QIsª has simply 'and your offspring', which may be the better text. **their name:** probably read 'your name' with LXX.

20–21. These verses are composed of two elements: the first line (**Go forth from Babylon, flee from Chaldea**) has the form of a military order commanding the withdrawal of troops: cf. 'To your tents, O Israel', 1 Kg. 12 : 16. The remainder closely resembles the communal thanksgiving, which sometimes (Ps. 66; 118) begins with an introduction similar to that of the hymn of praise (here **declare this . . . earth**) followed by a short statement of what Yahweh has done (**The LORD . . . Jacob**) and then a narrative section (verse 21) in which the community or its spokesman describes Yahweh's act of deliverance in more detail. The combination of the two elements, one military and one cultic, is unique, and is the work of Deutero-Isaiah himself. It is conceivable, but improbable, that the section is the continuation and climax of verses 12–16. The prophet's purpose is still to persuade his audience of the genuineness of his message, but no longer by means of a disputation: rather, as in 40: 9–11; 44 : 23; 46 : 1–4, his method is psychological: he brings the future vividly into the present (cf. Westermann's 'eschatological hymn of praise'), causing his audience in imagination to live proleptically through the moment when they will hear the call to leave the stricken city, and also the subsequent moment when they will again gather in their homeland and sing their song of thanksgiving for the completion of their redemption.

20. In suddenly and unexpectedly pronouncing this 'command' to depart from Babylon the prophet was deliberately evoking in the minds of his hearers a comparison with the equally unexpected and miraculous moment when, according to their most fundamental traditions, their remote ancestors in Egypt had received a similar call. What could happen in the past, he implies, can—and will—happen now. **flee:** elsewhere (52 : 12) Deutero-Isaiah *contrasts* the old and the new Exodus, asserting that this time there will be no hasty flight. But the verb *bāraḥ* (not used in 52 : 12), though it implies haste, does not necessarily imply fear or confusion. **this** refers to the statement that **The LORD has redeemed his servant Jacob. redeemed** (*gā'al*)**:** see on 41 : 14. **his servant:** see on 41 : 8.

21. Here the events of the old and new Exodus are made so closely parallel that this song of the returned Babylonian exiles might in another context have been sung by their ancestors who had escaped from Egypt: cf. Ps. 105 : 41. The thought is modelled on the events narrated in Exod. 17 : 1–7; Num. 20 : 2–11. Cf. also 41 : 17–20; 43 : 16–21.

22. This verse is virtually identical with 57 : 21. Here it is clearly an interpolation unrelated to the context, perhaps added by an editor as a marker: its double occurrence divides Isa. 40–66 into three roughly equal parts.

It is not possible to offer definite conclusions about either the structure or the character of this difficult chapter, but some concluding observations may now tentatively be made. It is probable that three blocks of Deutero-Isaianic material underlie the chapter in its present form, and that these are to be found in verses 1–11, 12–16, and 20–21. Their character is difficult to define. Verses 1–11 use the techniques of the disputation and the trial-speech to defend what is basically a promise of salvation. Verses 12–16 are also primarily a disputation. Verses 20–21 cannot be defined in terms of any traditional literary form. They attempt to defend the prophet's message by psychological means.

To the original material has subsequently been added the following: verses 1*b* (from **but not in truth . . .**), 2, 4, 5*b* (from **lest you should say . . .**), 7*b* (from **lest you should say . . .**), 8*b* from (**For I knew . . .**), 9, 10, part of 11 (**for how should my name be profaned?**), 14*a* (**Assemble . . . these things?**), 16*b* (from **And now . . .**), 17–19, 22. The interpolations in verses 1–11 together with verses 17–19 may all have been added by the same hand, since they have the same purpose of adapting soteriological material to make a kind of admonitory sermon suited to a post-exilic situation in which the future of the Jewish community was threatened by further serious outbreaks of sin. If this is so, they must have been added during or after the main editorial process which brought the present book of Deutero-Isaiah together. There are some resemblances between this material and parts of Trito-Isaiah. (On the relationship between Deutero- and Trito-Isaiah see the Introduction, pp. 38–43).

THE DISILLUSIONED PROPHET ENCOURAGED

49: 1–6

This is the second of the so-called 'Servant Songs'. The speaker, who claims that Yahweh appointed him to be **his servant** (verses 5, 6) is identical with the person whom Yahweh calls **my servant** in the first 'Song' (42: 1–4): that is, he is Deutero-Isaiah himself. In view of the fact that in the prophetical books generally the subject of speeches in the first person singular, when it is not Yahweh and not otherwise indicated, is normally the prophet himself, it is remarkable that this identification should have been contested in this case by so many commentators. The task assigned in both 'Songs' is substantially the same. But here the Servant describes his disillusionment at his apparent lack of success since his original call (40 : 1–8), and how Yahweh then spoke to him directly, giving him a fuller explanation of the importance of his task.

The main alternative view, that this 'servant' is only a figure of speech standing in some sense for the people of Israel, is excluded by a number of considerations. The vividness of the detail of the presentation of the servant as an individual is extremely marked, and goes beyond the possibilities of metaphor. For example, although the figure of being **called . . . from the womb** (verse 1) is used elsewhere (44 : 2, 24) of Israel, the phrase **the body of my mother** could hardly be used in that connexion. Nor is it clear what could be meant by Yahweh's 'hiding' Israel in verse 2. Even more difficult for a corporate view of the servant is verse 5, where the servant is given the task of bringing Israel back to Yahweh: the servant here must clearly be distinct from the nation. Further, the reference to his earlier disappointments (verse 4) corresponds exactly to the impression conveyed in Deutero-Isaiah's other oracles, that the prophet had to face indifference and incredulity in the carrying out of his task. These experiences were very similar to those of another prophet, his predecessor Jeremiah: cf. Jer. 1 : 5, 9, 19; 10 : 19; 20 : 7.

There is, however, one word in this passage which, if it belongs to the original text, would make this interpretation impossible: the word **Israel** in verse 3. This undoubtedly identifies the servant with Israel. But there are reasons for supposing it to be a gloss. See further on verse 3.

The literary form of the passage cannot be defined precisely. It has something of the character of the individual thanksgiving, but the giving of thanks is not its real purpose. It belongs to the general category of the prophetic call narrative (see on 40 : 1–8) in which a prophet seeks to authenticate his claim to speak on God's behalf—cf. especially Am. 7 : 14–15, where it can be seen how a prophet could be driven by opposition to make such a statement. But the passage is not a duplicate of 40 : 1–8; rather it describes a subsequent experience. Unlike the first, this second call has come not indirectly through subordinate heavenly beings but in a direct word from Yahweh himself, after the prophet has already experienced a sense of disappointment in carrying out his initial task. A further difference from 40 : 1–8 is that this narrative is addressed to the nations of the world (verse 1*a*). The nations are not directly mentioned in 40 : 1–8, although their dependence on Yahweh's sovereignty is certainly implied there. In this passage we see how the full implications of this, which are apparent in many passages in the book, were directly revealed to the prophet through this second call. 49 : 1–6 is thus closely related to 42 : 1–4, which probably also belongs to this second stage in the prophet's apprehension of his task.

1. On the address to **coastlands** and **peoples** see the introduction to this section. **The LORD called me:** in the Hebrew this phrase is very emphatic. In the second part of this verse and in verse 2 the prophet sums up his understanding of Yahweh's purpose for him which he has gained as a result of his two calls. Much of the language in this verse is identical with or similar to language used elsewhere in the book with reference to Israel, Cyrus, and Abraham. It is thus characteristic of Deutero-Isaiah; and comparison with these other passages cannot therefore be used in arguments concerning the identity of the servant. On the other hand the parallel with Jer. 1 : 5 is striking. **named my name:** see on 43 : 1; 45 : 3, where similar expressions are used about Israel and Cyrus.

2. Here the prophet speaks of his function as the mouthpiece of Yahweh. His weapon is the word of Yahweh which he speaks: it is the **sharp sword** and the **polished arrow**, both of which are the more effective because they are hidden until the time comes for their use.

3. This verse is not an account of the prophet's first call, (40 : 1–8), which was not a direct word from Yahweh but an indirect message conveyed through heavenly beings. It is the continuation of the prophet's summary of what he now understands to be his mission, and does not describe an experience chronologically prior to that related in verses 5–6. **Israel:** apart from one late MS (Kenn 96) there is no evidence either in the MSS or the Versions for the rejection of this word, nor is it metrically redundant. Yet many commentators since Michaelis (1779) have argued that it is not part of the original text. Its presence makes a clumsy sentence and gives the impression that it has been added as an afterthought (Duhm). Its natural place would have been at the beginning of the passage. The evidence of Kenn 96 should not, perhaps, be allowed to carry much weight; however, as has been pointed out by H. M. Orlinsky (*Studies on the Second Part of the Book of Isaiah, VT* Suppl. 14, 1967, pp. 83f.), that MS has never been scientifically evaluated. The foregoing facts are sufficient collectively to render the word doubtful; but the case against retention is made overwhelmingly probable by the impossibility of reconciling it with the servant's mission *to* Israel in verse 5. The possibility of its being an early interpretative gloss is further strengthened by the fact that in the first 'Song' (42 : 1) LXX contains two glosses ('Jacob' and 'Israel') which have exactly the same purpose, but which did not find their way into the textual traditions represented by MT and 1QIs[a].

4. **But I said** (*wa'ᵃnî 'āmartî*): better, 'But I thought (to myself)'. The prophet now describes his thoughts before his second call. **yet surely . . . my God:** in spite of his sense of failure, he had not despaired, but remained confident that God would accept his efforts and not forget him.

5. **And now:** better, 'But now'. The prophet now describes his second call. **to bring Jacob back to him:** here and in verse 6 (**to raise up . . . Israel**) Deutero-Isaiah's mission as Servant is described as the restoration of the scattered nation. On a different level this is also the task of Cyrus (cf. 42 : 7; 44 : 28; 45 : 13). The tasks of the two men, though entirely different in the methods which they employed, were identical in their divine origin (Yahweh's call) and in their aim. They were complementary; and because of this the prophet uses similar language to describe his own mission and that of Cyrus. This is one of the chief causes of the difficulties in the interpretation of a number of passages. Cyrus is to restore Israel by means of a military operation which will enable the exiles to return home; but these events can only be set in motion through the word of Yahweh (cf. 55 : 10–11) which it is Deutero-Isaiah's function to proclaim (cf. 42 : 1, 4; 49 : 2).

The task of the Servant as described in these verses makes his identification with Israel impossible. Even if, as some commentators have argued, the subject of the three infinitives **bring . . . back** (verse 5); **raise up**; **restore** (verse 6) is Yahweh and not the Servant—and this would be syntactically clumsy, if not impossible—it would still be true that the Servant is involved in the task, and therefore cannot himself be Israel. **and that Israel**

might be gathered to him: *RSV*, probably rightly, follows Qere, which is supported by 1QIs^a and some MSS and Versions, in preference to Kethib, which has not *lô* ('to him') but *lō'* ('not'). If Kethib is correct the verb *'āsap̱* must mean not 'gather' but 'sweep away': 'that Israel might not be swept away'. The general sense is not affected. **for I am honoured . . . my strength:** many commentators, probably correctly, believe these lines to have been misplaced from an original position at the end of verse 3, where they fit the context better.

6. he says: this word is not strictly needed. It was probably added after the accidental insertion of the last part of verse 5, which impaired the sequence of thought. The new word of Yahweh to his prophet is intended to encourage him, not by lightening his task, but by assuring him that it is even more significant than he had previously thought: not merely the restoration of the scattered Israelites to their homeland and the rebuilding of the nation, but the establishment of Yahweh's rule throughout the world. As in the first 'Song' (42 : 1–4), which belongs to the same stage in Yahweh's revelation of his purpose to the prophet, there is no suggestion here of a 'preaching mission' to the nations, or of their inclusion in a worldwide community of faith. **a light to the nations:** this phrase is also used of Cyrus (42 : 6). It is equally applicable to the prophet: each man in his own way is to act as Yahweh's instrument to bring about the nations' recognition of Yahweh's universal sovereignty. This interpretation is confirmed by the parallel phrase **my salvation** (*yᵉšûʿāṯî*)**:** the word *yᵉšûʿāh* generally in Deutero-Isaiah denotes not spiritual blessings but Yahweh's coming victory over Babylon: it is this which will convince the other nations that submission is their only possible course of action. The best commentary on this line is 52 : 10, where in a context which can only be interpreted as a triumphant cry of victory it is said that 'all the ends of the earth shall see the salvation (*yᵉšûʿāh*) of our God'. **It is too light a thing . . . servant:** the sentence is clumsy and the idiom (*nāḳēl mihᵉyôṯᵉḵā lî*) strange, although a similar expression occurs in Ezek. 8 : 17. **that you should be my servant** is perhaps a gloss: its omission would relieve the difficulties. **raise up; restore:** see on verse 5. **preserved:** this appears to be the meaning of both Kethib (*nᵉṣîrê*) and Qere (*nᵉṣûrē*); but the sense is not good. Probably read *niṣᵉrê*, 'offshoots, descendants'.

THE LAND REPOPULATED

49 : 7–12

The repetition of the messenger-formula in verse 8 at first seems to suggest that verse 7 is an independent, though fragmentary, oracle. According to Westermann, however, this impression is caused by the misplacement of some lines which, if replaced in their original position, reveal verses 7–12 as a single salvation-oracle addressed to Israel. According to him, verse 7*b* (from **Kings**) originally stood at the end of the oracle, after verse 12, appropriately setting out the consequences of the restoration promised in verses 8–12. The phrase **Thus says the LORD** in verse 8 is not original, but was added after the misplacement of the lines because it was now necessary to emphasize that Yahweh's words begin at this point: **Kings . . . chosen you** in verse 7*b* refer to Yahweh in the third person. This theory has a high degree of probability. The whole passage was originally addressed to Israel and was entirely unconnected with verses 1–6; but it has been placed here by an editor who believed that it refers—or ought to be made to refer—to the Servant (cf. the similar treatment of 42 : 5–9). Either he or another glossator has, as the majority of the commentators agree, added the words **I have kept you . . . the people** in verse 8. These words have been taken, exactly as they stand, from 42 : 6, where also, although they originally referred to Cyrus, they were thought to refer to the Servant. There can be no doubt that they are original in 42 : 6 and not in 49 : 8. They fit their context in 42 : 6, but not here. If **a covenant to the people** (*b^erîṯ ʿām*) means '(one who imposes) an obligation on the nations' (see on 42 : 6), this is quite irrelevant to the main tenor of this oracle, which in this central section is wholly concerned with the restoration of Israel.

7. Like other promises and oracles of salvation in the book (e.g. 41 : 14, 17; 42 : 14) the oracle begins with a reference to the situation of which the exiles have been complaining in their lamentations (cf. Lam. 1 : 1–11; 3 : 45; 5 : 1). On the meaning and function of **Redeemer** and **Holy One** see on 41 : 14. **deeply despised:** MT has *b^ezōh-nep̱eš*, literally, 'a despising of *nep̱eš*', which can hardly be right. Some commentators, following LXX, repoint *b^ezōh* as the active participle *bōzēh*: 'one who despises (himself)'; but the true reading is probably that of 1QIs^a, which has the pass. participle 'despised' (*bᵉzûy*); this is supported by a number of Versions. *nepeš* in that case is used to express the intensity of the contempt which the **nations** felt for the defeated Israelites (cf. 2 Sam. 5 : 8, and see A. R. Johnson, *The Vitality of the Individual in the Thought of Ancient Israel*, 1949). **abhorred by the nations:** this participle is pointed in MT as active, but there can be little doubt that the passive was intended (*mᵉṯōʿāḇ* for *mᵉṯāʿēḇ*); it was so understood by LXX, Targ., and Vulg. **nations:** if the singular *gôy* is the correct reading, it must be interpreted collectively as in 55 : 5 (compare the use of *ʿām* in 42 : 5). The second half of the verse (from **Kings**) will be considered after verse 12 (see the introduction to this section).

8. Thus says the LORD: see the introduction to this section. Yahweh now responds to the exiles' complaints with a word of promise and assurance. The perfect tenses **I have answered you** and **I have helped you**, and the phrases **time of favour** (cf. 61 : 2) and **day of salvation** indicate the certainty of the events which are about to take place. **I have kept you . . . to the people:** see the introduction to this section. **to establish**; **to apportion:** the subject of these infinitives is Yahweh himself rather than the exiles. Yahweh promises to repopulate and restore the land of Palestine which has been left **desolate** as a result of the Exile. **the land:** the metre suggests that a word has been accidentally dropped—perhaps *ṣiyyāh*, 'dry'.

9. After this brief glimpse of the ultimate result of Yahweh's plan for the exiles, a more detailed picture is now given of the stages by which it is to be carried out: first, the release of the exiles from Babylon (cf. 42 : 7); then the miraculous journey through the desert from Babylon to Palestine (cf. 40 : 11; 41 : 18). **saying:** Yahweh is still the subject. **They shall feed:** the returning exiles are depicted in this verse and verse 10 as flocks of sheep guided by Yahweh. **the ways:** perhaps better, 'all the ways' (so LXX). **bare heights:** see on 41 : 18.

10. There is an implied comparison here with the miraculous feeding of the Israelites in their earlier desert wanderings at the time of the Exodus: cf. 48 : 21. **scorching wind:** or possibly 'burning sand' as in 35 : 7. **he who has pity:** Yahweh is here speaking of himself.

11. On the theme of the **way** to be constructed through the desert see on 40 : 3. **my mountains** (*hāray*): probably a mistake for 'mountains' (*hārîm*). Similarly for **my highways** read 'highways'. **raised up:** that is, built up above the level of the desert.

12. Yahweh now promises the return home not only of the exiles from Babylon, but of all the dispersed Israelites. **these . . . these . . . these:** better, 'some . . . others . . . others'. **north; west:** Israelites were in fact scattered over a wide area at this period. **the land of Syene:** Heb. has *sînîm*. The reading of 1QIs[a], *swnyym*, has put an end to a long controversy about this geographical location. The true reading is certainly *s^e^wēnîm*, meaning the inhabitants of the territory known to Ezekiel (29 : 10; 30 : 6) as *s^e^wēnēh*, to the Greeks as Syene and to the modern Egyptians as Assouan, i.e. a district on the southern frontier of ancient Egypt. Jer. 44 : 1 refers to Jews living in this region ('the land of Pathros'), and the Elephantine Papyri, where it is called *swn*, provide direct evidence of the existence of a Jewish colony there founded before the Persian conquest in 525 BC. Deutero-Isaiah uses the term here to denote the extreme south.

7b. See the introduction to this section. The oracle concludes with a statement of the effects of Israel's restoration on the nations, and a final word of encouragement based on Yahweh's faithfulness and the fact of Israel's election. The first of these themes is paralleled in 52 : 15. **shall see:** the reference is to the events of verses 9–12. **arise:** to show respect for a superior. Cf. Job 29 : 8.

A SHORT HYMN OF PRAISE

49: 13

This short hymn of praise closely resembles 44 : 23 in form, content and function. **break forth:** *RSV* follows Qere and 1QIs[a]. Kethib has 'let the mountains break forth'.

ZION REBUILT AND REPOPULATED

49: 14–23

There is considerable divergence of opinion among the commentators over the division of verses 14–26 into their component units. Westermann pointed out that in three places (verses 14, 21, 24) Zion is represented as putting forward an assertion or a question which is then countered or answered by Yahweh, and divides the section into three parts on this basis. However, Zion's three speeches are not all of the same kind. Whereas in verses 14 and 24 she expresses her lack of confidence in Yahweh's willingness or ability to save her, in verse 21 she is represented as joyfully bewildered at the *results* of his intervention. It is therefore probable that there are only two oracles here: verses 14–23 and 24–26. This is confirmed by the phrases **Then you will know . . .** (verse 23) and **Then all flesh shall know . . .** (verse 26), which respectively round off the two oracles.

In spite of its complexity, the sequence of thought in the first oracle (verses 14–23) is clear. Zion's complaint (verse 14) is countered by a divine word of reassurance (verse 15), and this is followed by a detailed account of the form which Zion's restoration will take: the rebuilding of the city (verses 16–17), its repopulation (verse 18), and the abundant numbers of those who will return (verses 19–20). This last arouses the astonishment of the mother-city (verse 21), and an explanation is then given of the way in which the exiles will be gathered together and brought home (verses 22–23*a*). Finally the ultimate aim of these redemptive acts is stated (verse 23*b*). This is a promise of salvation given in answer to a lamentation, but containing elements of the disputation (verse 15).

14. But: this particle does not necessarily imply a connexion with the previous words. **Zion:** as in 40 : 9–11 there is an oscillation of thought between Zion as the Jewish exiles and Zion as the actual city of Jerusalem; but in this oracle it is the latter which predominates. The words attributed to 'Zion' in this verse, like the similar words in 40 : 27, may be presumed to be the actual words of a cultic lamentation used by the exiles. They strongly resemble the sentiments of the Jews living in the vicinity of Jerusalem during the exilic period recorded in Lamentations, especially Lam. 5 : 20–22.

15. Yahweh begins his reply to Zion's complaint with an unprecedented affirmation of the depth and constancy of his love for his people, which exceeds that of a mother for her baby. This statement is less an argument than a passionate declaration. **that she should have no compassion** (*mēraḥēm*)**:** the construction is possible, but the sense is perhaps improved if the word is pointed as a participle, *m*ᵉ*raḥēm*, 'one who loves', i.e. a loving mother, and treated as a second subject of **forget:** 'or a loving mother the son of her womb'. Grammar does not require a feminine form in such cases (see G–K §122a). **these:** parallelism with **a woman** leads the reader to expect a singular pronoun here. However, the variant 'these shall not be forgotten' is not an improvement, while the proposal to treat **forget** as an unusual singular form with **these** as its object (see *BHS*) involves a somewhat speculative grammatical theory. It is probably best to retain MT.

16. Yahweh now presents himself as the architect of a new city of Jerusalem, whose building-plan (**you**; **your walls**) he has inscribed on his hands to be a constant reminder of his undertaking. For a similar metaphor, cf. Exod. 13 : 16; Dt. 6 : 8; 11 : 18. There is a remarkable parallel in an extant statue of Gudea, Sumerian ruler of Lagash c. 2100 BC, holding in his lap the plan of a city of which he was presumably reckoned to be the architect (*ANEP*, illustration 749). This verse sheds no light on the obscure practice referred to in 44 : 5, nor does the prohibition of making marks on the flesh (Lev. 19 : 28) appear to be relevant, as some commentators have maintained.

17. The rebuilding of the city is now described as if it were already taking place. **Your builders . . . destroyers:** MT has 'Your sons make haste; your destroyers and those who laid you waste . . .'. *RSV*, in agreement with many commentators and following some Versions and 1QIsª (*bwnyk*), has repointed MT's *bānayiḵ*, 'sons', as *bōnayiḵ*, 'builders'. This makes a better contrast with **destroyers** and is probably correct, although it is likely that Deutero-Isaiah intended a play on the two meanings: Zion's 'sons' will also be her **builders**. Secondly, *RSV* has again followed 1QIsª and a clue from LXX in repointing MT's *meₕāreₛayiḵ* (Piel participle), 'your destroyers', as *mēhōreₛayiḵ* (Qal participle preceded by *min*-), 'from/than your destroyers'. Thus in place of 'Your sons make haste; your destroyers . . .' *RSV* achieves the translation **Your builders outstrip** (literally, 'make more haste than') **your destroyers.** This gives a more satisfactory metrical balance, and is probably right. If so, the rebuilding is portrayed as miraculous: the city will be rebuilt in even less time than it took the Babylonians to burn it (2 Kg. 25 : 8–10)! In fact it was not rebuilt until the time of Nehemiah a century later, and without the aid of miracle. The second half of the verse presumably refers to the ignominious departure of a Babylonian garrison.

18. Zion is now urged to view the astonishing sight of a host of her 'sons' marching home to populate the rebuilt city. Some commentators have pointed out the lack of orderly sequence of the images in these verses (17–19). This is partly due to textual corruption; but it should be borne in mind that the whole oracle is in an extremely passionate style, in which the images tumble over one another without regard for logic. **Lift up your eyes . . . come to you:** cf. 60 : 4, where these words are repeated. **As I live, says the LORD** may be an interpolation. In the second half of the verse Zion's returning 'sons' are to become her jewels, which will raise her to a position of glittering splendour. For the imagery compare the claim of the mother of the Gracchi that her two sons were her most precious jewels.

19–21 express Zion's astonishment at the number of her new-found 'sons', and her bewilderment at their sudden appearance.

19. Surely . . . devastated land: three subjects without a verb. LXX seems to have lacked the word **land**; and Torrey ingeniously pointed out that the remainder could be repointed as verbs: 'I devastated you, laid you waste, and razed you to the ground'. But this reference to the afflictions of the past is inappropriate, and it is more probable that some words have fallen out. In the second half of the verse (from **surely**) the bustling, teeming life of the restored city is contrasted with the departure of its former conquerors into oblivion.

20. The children . . . bereavement: literally, 'the children of your bereavement'. *RSV* gives the correct sense. **bereavement** here means loss of children rather than of a husband. The imagery of the mother bereft of her children, who now sees them unexpectedly alive and well, is inadequate to express what the prophet wants to say. The population of the city will be greater than ever before, because the returning Israelites will include not only the descendants of the Babylonian exiles but the descendants of dispersed Israelites of all kinds, gathered from many countries (verse 12). These are now all Zion's sons; yet, in terms of the imagery, she was not present at their birth! Part of the cause of the breakdown of the imagery is the fact that 'Zion' for Deutero-Isaiah is both the city and the whole nation: the rightful occupants of the whole land, not only of one city. We should note that a numerous population, which fulfils the ancient promises to the Patriarchs, is regarded as in itself an absolute blessing: the quarrels which the 'mother' overhears, caused by a shortage of living-space, are regarded as an indication that all is well, not as a cause for alarm. It should also be noted that there is a contrast here, probably intentional, with the fate of Babylon expressed in chapter 47, especially verses 8–9.

21. Judged by prosaic standards the imagery of mother and sons here reaches the point of absurdity. Although the verb translated **has borne** (*yālaḏ*) is masc., and might therefore refer to the generative act of the male, it is probable that Zion is enquiring about the identity of the *mother* of her own children! The absurdity of this situation could be mitigated by supposing that the 'host countries' of the Israelites are regarded as 'handmaids' to Zion who have borne sons for her, as Hagar bore sons for Sarah (Gen. 16 : 1–3), but it is probably best not to press the details of the imagery. **I was bereaved and barren; I was left alone:** these words have probably been taken directly from actual lamentations used by the exiles (the Heb. can also be translated 'I *am* bereaved . . .', 'I *have been* left alone') in order to emphasize the change of fortune which, in exact contrast to the fate of Babylon (47 : 9), they are about to experience. **exiled and put away:** these words give the literal meaning of the foregoing metaphors and are a gloss.

22–23. The answer given to Zion's incredulous questions is that the miraculous is about to occur. The Israelites dispersed all over the world will be gathered and will return home, with their former oppressors attending them as their slaves. No interest is shown in the fate of the heathen nations except as a foil to the triumph of Zion.

22. Thus says the Lord GOD: the purpose of the messenger formula, whether it is original or an editorial addition, is to draw attention to a further divine promise. **Lord GOD:** literally, 'the Lord Yahweh' (*'ᵃḏōnāy yhwh*): 1QIsᵃ and LXX have the more usual form, which lacks *'ᵃḏōnāy*. Yahweh himself will give the sign for the operation to begin. **bosom:** better, 'lap'. Two ways of carrying small children are mentioned. Mother Zion will now see the arrival in state of the recently born children of whose existence (verse 21) she had been unaware.

23. your foster fathers (*'ōmᵉnayiḵ*)**:** the word *'ōmēn* can mean a true foster-father, as in Est. 2 : 7 (where it is translated 'brought up'), but here it means rather 'tutor' or 'attendant', as in 2 Kg. 10 : 1, 5 (where it is translated 'guardian'). The former **Kings**

and **queens** of the now subject nations will be reduced to the status of slave-attendants on Zion's children. **lick the dust of your feet:** see *ANEP*, illustration 355, where Jehu, king of Israel, is depicted in this posture before Shalmaneser III, king of Assyria. **wait:** see on 40 : 31.

YAHWEH TO THE RESCUE

49 : 24–26

On the independence of this section see on 49 : 14–23. Its present position is no doubt due to the fact that the theme is similar to that of the section which precedes. Whereas verses 14–23 answered the exiles' lament (verse 14) that Yahweh had abandoned them and was not *willing* to save them, and also the subsidiary question (verse 21) by what means or in what manner the restoration of the nation could take place, verses 24–26 answer the question whether Yahweh is *able* to save them from the power of Babylon. The form of the passage is a quotation from a lamentation (verse 24) followed by its answer in the form of a short promise of salvation.

24. This is a cry of despair springing from a lack of faith. The exiles feel that nothing can possibly induce Babylon to disgorge its prey, that is, the conquered nations. **tyrant:** MT has *ṣaddîḳ*, 'righteous one', and many older commentators took this to refer to Yahweh, who would snatch back the exiles from Babylon, brooking no interference. But 1QIs[a] has now confirmed the view, based on LXX, Vulg., Syr. and a comparison with verse 25, that *ṣaddîḳ* is a scribal error for *ʿārîṣ*, 'tyrant'.

25. The exiles' rhetorical questions, calling for a negative answer, are firmly answered by Yahweh in the affirmative: the miraculous *can* happen. (Note the transposition, for reasons of style, of the order of **prey** and **captives**.) Yahweh then justifies this assertion by pointing out that the rescue will be his own personal doing: note the emphatic **I** (*'ānōḵî*) before both **contend** and **save**. When the tyrant's adversary is not man but the true God, the issue is not in doubt. **I will contend:** better, 'I will fight'. **with those who contend with you:** *RSV* follows those MSS and Versions which have the plur. *yᵉrîḇayiḵ*; MT has the sing. *yᵉrîbēḵ* .But LXX, Vulg., and Targ. have *rîbēḵ*, '(for) your cause', while 1QIs[a] appears to offer both readings as alternatives. The same problem arises in Ps. 35 : 1. Whatever the solution, it should be noted that the wording of the promise made by Yahweh corresponds to that of appeals actually made to him in extant individual lamentations (Ps. 35 : 1; 43 : 1; 74 : 22).

26. eat their own flesh: probably not the flesh of their own bodies, but of their own kin or fellow-countrymen (cf. English 'one's flesh and blood'). Such cannibalism was not unknown to the ancient Near East, nor even to the Israelites (cf. Dt. 28 : 53–57; 2 Kg. 6 : 24–31); but it was an exceptional horror, due only to extreme famine. There is no mention of famine here, and the expression, together with **be drunk with their own blood**, is to be taken as metaphorical, signifying self-destructive internecine strife: cf. Isa. 9 : 20; Zech. 11 : 9. But the tone is extremely harsh, and is hardly, as some commentators maintain, mitigated by the last half of the verse. That **all flesh shall know** the power of Yahweh as manifested on behalf of Israel goes no further than similar statements in such passages as 40 : 5; 45 : 6, 23; 49 : 7. **the Mighty One of Jacob:** this name, occurring as the final phrase of the passage, well expresses the tone of the whole, which speaks of redemption for Israel alone. It was one of the traditional epithets of Yahweh (cf. Gen. 49 : 24).

YAHWEH DEFENDS HIS ACTIONS

50 : 1–3

This short passage, which ends abruptly and may be incomplete, resembles 42 : 18–25 and 43 : 22–28 in that Yahweh is represented, whether in a trial-speech or in a disputation, as defending himself against accusations made by the exiles. These are the same as in 40 : 12–31—that he is unwilling (verse 1) and also unable (verse 2*b*) to help his people.

1. Probably the wording of the rhetorical questions with which Yahweh begins his reply to the first accusation is based on that of actual lamentations—cf. Ps. 44 : 12 (MT 13). He is accused of severing his ancient ties with his people irrevocably and without sufficient cause. These ties are symbolically represented in terms of the relationship of a husband and father with his family, a symbolism already employed by Hosea, Jeremiah, and Ezekiel. The 'children' of the erring 'mother' are addressed in the plur.; but there is an oscillation, not unusual in Hebrew poetry, between children and mother in the assignment of blame. The **bill** or certificate **of divorce** in the first figure is the document which a husband must by law give to a wife whom he divorced (Dt. 24 : 1–4; Jer. 3 : 1, 8); and, assuming that she subsequently remarried, it was forbidden for him ever to take her back again. In the second figure Yahweh is seen in the role of a husband who, finding himself in financial difficulties, sells his family into slavery to pay his debts (cf. Exod. 21 : 7; 2 Kg. 4 : 1; Neh. 5 : 5). In this case also he has no right, even if he has the power, to insist on buying them back again: they have passed out of his control. Yahweh refutes these charges in their own terms, an exercise which some commentators have characterized, not entirely unreasonably, as sophistry. He does not deny that there has been a separation between himself and his 'wife', or that his 'children' have been handed over to others—the Babylonians. But he defends himself on two grounds. First, as in 42 : 24f.; 43 : 22–28, he places the entire responsibility for this upon Israel itself. Secondly, he denies that the alienation is permanent and irrevocable. Here he appears to play upon the double meanings of certain words. The verb **put away** (*šillaḥ*, literally 'let go, send away') would normally, in the context of married life, have the meaning 'divorce'; but Yahweh claims that in this case this is not so: if it were, there would be a formal certificate (*sēp̄er kᵉrîṯûṯ*, **bill of divorce**) to prove it. Since no such document exists, there is no divorce (contrast Jer. 3 : 8, with regard to northern Israel), but only an informal separation or 'sending away', and consequently no hindrance to subsequent resumption of the marriage. In the second figure there may be a play on two meanings of *māḵar*. This verb usually means 'sell'; but it has been argued (Z. W. Falk, 'Hebrew Legal Terms: II', *JSS* 12 (1967), pp. 242f.) that it sometimes has the less specific meaning of 'transfer, hand over'. In this case the idea of a sale is absurd: Yahweh cannot have incurred debts (**which of my creditors** is ironical); no money can have changed hands, and there was therefore no 'sale' but only a transfer of the custodianship of Israel from Yahweh to the Babylonians, an arrangement which was not necessarily permanent. **sold**, therefore, on its second occurrence in this verse, should perhaps be translated 'handed over'.

2a. The first two of these questions are usually taken to be a counter-charge made by Yahweh in which he accuses his opponents of failing to respond to him when he **came** and **called**

to them in the persons of his prophets such as Deutero-Isaiah. But this seems somewhat inappropriate in the context, and the questions may refer to the immediate circumstances of a trial-speech. Yahweh, summoned to defend himself, **came** and made his defence (**called**); but, like the heathen gods and their worshippers in other trial-speeches (41 : 5, 24; 43 : 13), the accusers have been overwhelmed by his arguments and are unable to reply to his defence. **Is my hand . . . deliver?:** following his earlier argument that he has not given up his rights over his people, Yahweh now, with an oblique reference to his earlier great deeds at the time of the Exodus (cf. Num. 11 : 23), asserts the all-sufficiency of his power. (**shortened,**) **that it cannot redeem** (*mippᵉḏûṯ*)**:** literally, '(too short) for redemption'. The proposal to change the noun 'redemption' into the infinitive 'redeem' (*pᵉḏôṯ*) by changing one of the vowels of MT is unnecessary.

2b (**Behold . . .**)**–3.** It is not clear whether these verses refer to the creation of the world, the historical past (Exodus) or Yahweh's power over nature. A multiple reference would be characteristic of this prophet. If so, Yahweh now uses every possible argument to demonstrate that he is not only willing, but overwhelmingly able, to redeem his people. **die of thirst:** the line is unexpectedly short, and the sequence of events surprising: the fish would presumably **die** first and **stink** later. Possibly a second subject has fallen out and the line originally read 'and their cattle (*bᵉhemtâm*, meaning the great marine creatures) die of thirst'. The passage ends somewhat abruptly.

THE PROPHET'S CONFIDENCE AMIDST SUFFERING

50 : 4–9

This is the third of the 'Servant Songs'. Although the word 'servant' (*'eḇeḏ*) is not used, the similarity of this passage with the second 'Song', together with the use of the first person sing., leaves no doubt that it belongs to the same series. There are, however, some important developments which show that this poem comes from a somewhat later stage in the prophet's life. To the temptation to despair of the success of his mission (49 : 4*a*) there have now been added the pain and humiliation of actual persecution (verse 6). There is no reason to doubt that this verse describes insults which were actually inflicted upon the prophet. No direct indication is given of the circumstances, but verse 8 suggests that he had been arrested by the Babylonian authorities and put on trial. In view of his public predictions that Babylon would shortly fall to the Persians, it is not surprising that he should have been regarded as a danger to the state. The situation of the prophet and his reaction to it in some respects strongly resemble those of Jeremiah as revealed in that prophet's 'confessions', especially Jer. 11:18–20; 15:15–18; 18:19–23; 20:7–12, though there are significant differences: unlike Jeremiah, Deutero-Isaiah accepts his sufferings willingly, does not complain about them, and does not call on Yahweh for vengeance against his persecutors. He is confident that Yahweh is on his side, and that he will vindicate him. Appropriately the form of the passage is strongly influenced by the 'songs of confidence' of the individual in the Psalter (e.g. Ps. 22).

4–5. The prophet begins by referring once more to his prophetic call and mission. Like his prophetic predecessors, he speaks **a word** which is not his own: it is Yahweh who has given him **the tongue**, or ability to speak, and the **word**, with which he is to **sustain** the **weary** exiles; and, as a true prophet (cf. e.g. Jer. 1:9; 15:16) he has faithfully performed his task.

4. the tongue of those who are taught: the word translated **those who are taught** (*limmûḏîm*) occurs twice in this verse. It is used in Isa. 8:16 of the pupils or disciples of the prophet Isaiah; but the phrase 'the tongue of pupils' is rather strange. It has been suggested by G. R. Driver (*JTS* 36 (1935), p. 406) that in the two occurrences of *limmûḏîm* there is a characteristic play on words: in the first case it means 'teaching(s)', and the phrase means something like 'an expert tongue'; in the second it means 'pupils'. In any case the prophet here refers to himself as Yahweh's pupil rather than, as elsewhere, as his servant, no doubt in order to emphasize that his words are not his own but those of his divine 'teacher'. **sustain:** the meaning of the Hebrew word is uncertain and it occurs only here; but this is not sufficient justification for emending it. The context shows that it must have a meaning similar to that given it by *RSV*. **Morning . . . my ear:** there is some repetition here. The first **he wakens** (*yāʿîr*), which was regarded with suspicion by the Massoretic editors, should be omitted. For **Morning by morning** (*babbōḵer babbōḵer*) some Versions seem to have read simply 'in the morning', but MT may be correct. The prophet describes his reception of Yahweh's messages in terms reminiscent of the classroom.

5. The Lord GOD has opened my ear: this line simply repeats two phrases from verse 4 and is probably an accidental repetition.

6. The humiliations described here could have been inflicted in the course of the prophet's ordinary life, by hostile Jews; but in view of verse 8 it is more likely that they came from his guards after his arrest: cf. Mt. 26 : 67 and parallels.

7–9. The prophet is confident that Yahweh will help him, but how this will come about is not stated. It is possible that he believes that Yahweh will intervene directly at his trial and secure his acquittal and release; but it is also possible that he is thinking of an eventual vindication, whatever his personal fate may be, through the fulfilment of his prophecies of the destruction of Babylon and the release of the exiles. A less probable interpretation is that he regards his sufferings themselves as in some way contributing to this result (see on chapter 53).

7. I have not been confounded (*lō' niklāmtî*)**:** this verb is related to the noun translated in verse 6 by **shame** (*kᵉlimmôt*), and it is this which gives point to the prophet's assertion. The humiliation was real enough, but it failed in its purpose: the persecuted prophet knew that in reality he was the victor. **I have set my face like a flint:** cf. Jer. 1 : 18; Ezek. 3 : 8–9.

8–9a. The language in these verses is that of the lawcourt. This terminology is characteristic of Deutero-Isaiah.

9b. The similes of the **garment** which will **wear out** and which will be ruined by **the moth**, found elsewhere in Deutero-Isaiah (51 : 6, 8) and elsewhere in the *OT* (Job 13 : 28; Ps. 39 : 11 (MT12); 102 : 26 (MT 27)) with reference to the created world and to man, do not denote sudden destruction but rather point to what is ephemeral. The prophet is not demanding vengeance on his adversaries but expressing confidence that God's purposes will outlast mere human malice.

THE PROPHET AVENGED

50 : 10–11

These verses are unusually difficult. The two main problems are the identity of **you** both in verse 10 and in verse 11, and the syntax of verse 10. The two **yous** are contrasted: in verse 10 it is the faithful exiles who are addressed and exhorted to find their salvation in obedience to Yahweh's Servant, that is, the prophet; in verse 11 those addressed are the Servant's persecutors. In verse 10 the speaker is the prophet, while verse 11 is a divine announcement of judgment. The contrast between the two groups addressed binds the two verses into a unity. In the sense that **servant** here has the same meaning as in the other 'Servant Songs', this passage must be regarded as belonging to the same group; indeed, it is possible that it is a continuation of verses 4–9, though the difference of style and tone makes this improbable.

10. The syntactical relationships between the six verbal and quasi-verbal clauses (*RSV* **fears**; **obeys**; **walks**; **has**; **trusts**; **relies**) can be understood in a number of ways. All the main English versions (*AV*, *RV*, *RSV*, *JB*, *NEB*) have in fact understood them differently; and these do not exhaust the possibilities. The most important problem for the exegete is to decide the extent of the question with which the verse begins. If—as in *RSV*—it extends to the end of the verse, the last two lines (from **who walks**) refer to the Servant. But if the question ends with the words **his servant**, the remainder can be translated as referring to the persons addressed, as in *RV*: 'He that walketh in darkness, and hath no light, let him trust in the name of the LORD, and stay upon his God.' Fohrer, who thinks of the passage as speaking about the Servant after his death, translates these lines in the past tense: the Servant 'walked . . . and had no light . . . although he trusted . . . and relied . . .'. Probably the best solution is that of *RV*. Those among the exiles who are faithful to Yahweh and obedient to his prophet and yet **walk in darkness**, that is, can see no end to their misfortunes, are assured that their trust in God will not be disappointed. **his servant:** the prophet refers to himself in the third person out of humility: 'obeys my voice' would be arrogant. Cf. the use of 'your servant', meaning 'I', used in addressing a superior.

11. This fierce oracle of judgment is unique in Deutero-Isaiah, but cf. Am. 7:11; Jer. 20:4–6. It should be remembered that these people are not simply the enemies of the prophet but have attempted to frustrate Yahweh's purpose for his people; moreover this is not the prophet's own word but that of Yahweh spoken through him. Their activities are not described literally but metaphorically, and we can only surmise that it is their persecution of the prophet which is meant. The point of the metaphor is that they will in some way themselves fall into the trap which they have laid. **set brands alight:** *RSV*, probably rightly and following Syr., accepts the emendation of MT's *me'azzerê* to *me'îrê*. *RSV* mg. supposes an unusual sense for the Piel. **Walk by the light:** this translation assumes a repointing of MT's *'ûr*, 'flame', to *'ôr*, 'light'. But MT is correct: those who have started the fire will be caught by it and will find themselves unable to escape its flames. **you shall lie down in torment:** the verb *šāḵaḇ*, 'lie down', is sometimes used of death, but this is probably not the meaning here. The phrase continues the metaphor of the **fire:** unable to escape from it, the arsonists will writhe in agony on the ground.

THE EXILES ENCOURAGED

51 : 1–8

The threefold exhortation, **Hearken to me** (verse 1); **Listen to me** (verse 4); **Hearken to me** (verse 7), has led some commentators to conclude that this is a single poem in three stanzas. The three sections are similar in that they are all addressed to the nation, begin with solemn exhortations and conclude with messages of comfort; but in other respects they differ from one another, and their juxtaposition here is probably editorial. They belong to the same general type as 46 : 12–13, which would no doubt have been hailed as a fourth stanza if the editor had seen fit to include it in the series.

1–3. This oracle is addressed to those among the exiles who have remained faithful to Yahweh but are nevertheless discouraged. The cause of their discouragement may be inferred from the reply which is given to them: they are concerned about the smallness of their numbers and fear that, even if they are able to return to their homeland, they will be unequal to the task of restoration. From the point of view of form the passage does not fit precisely into any category. At some points Yahweh is clearly the speaker, while at others he is referred to in the third person. But this anomaly does not justify Westermann's radical rearrangement of these verses.

1. deliverance: the word *ṣeḏeḳ* here must mean 'righteousness' rather than 'deliverance' or 'salvation': this is proved by the use of the verb **pursue** and by the parallel phrase **seek the LORD**, which, although originally it denoted cultic observance, here has the sense of desiring to know and do the righteous will of God (cf. 45 : 19; Prov. 28 : 5). The metaphors of the **rock** and the **quarry** are given their interpretation in verse 2. **quarry:** this word (*maḳḳeḇeṯ*) is followed in the Heb. by the more prosaic word 'pit' (*bôr*); but this is a gloss.

2. Unlike John the Baptist (Mt. 3 : 9; Lk. 3 : 8), the prophet finds in the exiles' descent from Abraham and Sarah a proof that they may confidently expect to enjoy Yahweh's favour once more. The argument is based on the promises made to Abraham (Gen. 12 : 2–3; 15 : 5; 18 : 18; 22 : 17–18) that his descendants would become a great nation, and on the fulfilment of those promises in the past. Yahweh does not go back on his word, nor, as history shows, can anything hinder him from carrying out what he has promised. **and I blessed him and made him many:** these are clearly intended to be past tenses, although MT has not pointed them as such.

3. What Yahweh once did for the solitary Abraham, he will now do once more for the handful of exiles in Babylon: their small number will not matter, since he himself will build them into a prosperous nation in Palestine with flourishing cities and a fertile countryside. **For:** better, 'Surely'. The perfect tenses in the Heb. indicate the certainty of the outcome. **Eden; the garden of the LORD:** the expressions are equivalent. The wonderful garden which God had once given to man to inhabit (Gen. 2 : 8–9) has become in the *OT* a symbol of the ideal pastoral or agricultural existence (cf. Gen. 13 : 10; Ezek. 31 : 8–9; Jl 2 : 3). Here, however, and also in Ezek. 36 : 35, we have the additional idea of 'Paradise Regained': the promise of the return of a Golden Age. Deutero-Isaiah was probably familiar with the Eden story in the form in which it appears in Gen. 2–3, although he may also have known other versions of the myth (e.g. Ezek. 28 : 13ff.).

4–6. In this passage Yahweh is the speaker throughout. The exiles are addressed as **my people** and **my nation** (on the text see below on verse 4). No specific complaint on their part is alluded to, but it is clearly the intention of the oracle to assert that the promised deliverance is imminent (verses 4–5) and that nothing can resist it (verse 6). The similarity of this passage to the first 'Servant Song' (42 : 1–4) has often been remarked: the universal rule of Yahweh (*mišpāṭ*, *RSV* **justice**) and his **law** (*tôrāh*) which it is the Servant's task according to 42 : 1–4 to 'bring forth' to the nations will, according to 51 : 4–6, go forth directly from Yahweh. According to both passages the **coastlands** will **wait** for Yahweh or for his law. The Servant is not mentioned in 51 : 4–6. There is, however, no contradiction between the two passages: there is merely a difference of emphasis. In 51 : 4–6 the emphasis is on the *certainty* of the promised manifestation of Yahweh's universal power; in 42 : 1–4 it was the credentials and adequacy of the *human agent*, the Servant-prophet, which needed to be clearly stated. For an interpretation of the vocabulary which the two passages have in common see on 42 : 1–4.

4. my people, my nation: although the latter expression (*leʾummî*) is not used of Israel elsewhere in the *OT*, there is no justification for following Syr. and emending these two words to 'peoples' (*ʿammîm*) and 'nations' (*leʾummîm*). The message concerns the Jewish exiles no less than the nations. **a light to the peoples:** see on 'a light to the nations' in 42:6.

5. My deliverance: the word (*ṣeḏeḵ*) is the same as that translated 'deliverance' in verse 1. There, as has already been said, 'righteousness' is the correct translation. Here, however, as the parallel word **salvation** (*yēšaʿ*) shows, *RSV*'s translation is correct: the event which is described as 'drawing near speedily' and, by anticipation, as having already **gone forth**, is the act by which Yahweh will both save Israel and establish his sovereignty over the whole world. **speedily:** the interpretation of this word (*ʾargîaʿ*) is notoriously difficult. It stands between verses 4 and 5, and MT takes it as the last word of verse 4. If this is correct it is probably a verb governing *mišpāṭî*: 'I will flash' (or perhaps 'cause to rest') 'my justice (rule) . . .'. On the whole it is more probable that it is to be taken with verse 5 and treated as a kind of adverb: **speedily** (so LXX). **has gone forth:** LXX adds 'like the light', perhaps correctly: both metre and parallelism are thereby improved.

6. In so far as there is argument here and not merely assertion, the point seems to be that the purpose of the Creator, who is eternal, cannot be overturned by his creatures, who are necessarily ephemeral. **will vanish**; **will wear out**; **will die:** these are not so much assertions as suppositions: even though these events will take place, Yahweh's purpose endures for ever. The similes of

smoke and **garment** come from a common poetical stock: see on 50 : 9, and cf. Ps. 68 : 2 (MT 3); 102 : 26 (MT 27); Hos. 13 : 3. **vanish:** the meaning of this verb (*mālaḥ*) is not clear. It may mean either 'be torn to shreds' or 'become murky'. **like gnats** (*k*ᵉ*mô-ḵēn*): *RSV* mg.'s 'in like manner' is improbable. *kēn* as a noun does not occur elsewhere in the *OT*, but the word may be connected with *kinnīm* or *kinnām*, a word which occurs in the account of the plague of 'gnats', Exod. 8 : 16ff. An alternative suggestion, perhaps supported by 1QIs[b], where the consonants are written as a single unhyphenated word, is that *môḵēn* is an otherwise unattested word related to Arabic *makin*, '(swarm of) locusts'.

7–8. This oracle is addressed to those exiles who are suffering some kind of humiliation at the hands of Babylonians, or perhaps even of fellow-Jews. The language in verse 7*b* is strongly reminiscent of the last two Servant Songs, especially 50 : 6; 53 : 3–5, and it is possible that this is a small group of Deutero-Isaiah's intimate disciples who are being persecuted because of their association with him. The same assurance is given them as in 50 : 9 and 51 : 6.

7. you who know righteousness: this phrase does not, as some commentators have stated, imply a deeper faith than 'you who pursue deliverance' in verse 1. Both phrases denote a wholehearted devotion to the moral demands of God. The word here correctly translated righteousness (*ṣeḏeḳ*) is the same as that translated by 'deliverance' in verse 1. **in whose heart is my law** has a similar meaning; cf. Jer. 31 : 33, which Deutero-Isaiah may have had in mind.

8. The close similarity between this verse and verse 6 is not to be regarded as evidence that the two passages originally formed a literary unity, though it helps to account for their editorial juxtaposition. The use in different contexts of almost but not precisely identical phraseology is characteristic of Deutero-Isaiah. On the use of these similes see on 50:9. **the worm** (*sās*): this is the only occurrence of this word in the *OT*, but its meaning is clear both from the context and from its Semitic cognates. **will eat them like wool:** the verb (*yō'ḵ*ᵉ*lēm*) is the same as that translated **eat them up** earlier in the verse. Since the parallelism of Hebrew poetry normally requires the use of pairs of *different* words with similar meanings, it is possible that, as in a similar phrase in Jer. 10 : 25, this second member of the pair was originally *vᵉkallēm*, 'destroy them'. The similar appearance and sound of the two words would account for the corruption.

THE CREATOR IS ALSO REDEEMER

51 : 9–16

This section and the two which follow it (verses 17–23; 52: 1–3) all begin with double imperatives. The first of these (**Awake, awake,** verse 9) is addressed to Yahweh (literally, to his **arm**), the second and third (**Rouse yourself, rouse yourself,** verse 17; **Awake, awake,** 52 :1) to Jerusalem/Zion. The three passages have little in common apart from their opening words, and, as in 51 : 1–8, their present grouping is due to an editor. 51 : 9–16 is basically a promise of salvation and resembles other oracles of this type in Deutero-Isaiah except for one important feature: the lamentation to which the promise of salvation is a reply is not merely alluded to but quoted at some length (verses 9–10) before the oracle itself begins.

9–10. The appeal to Yahweh for help supported by a reminder of his former mighty deeds is characteristic of the corporate lamentation (see especially Ps. 44 : 1–3, 23 (MT 2–4, 24); 80 : 2, 8–11 (MT 3, 9–12), where the same verb *'ûr*, **Awake,** is used). But by far the closest parallel to these verses is found in another corporate lamentation, Ps. 74, which may be from the same period as Deutero-Isaiah.

9. Awake: compare the allegation that Yahweh has forgotten his people (49 : 14). **put on strength, O arm of the LORD:** metaphorical expressions of this kind are part of the stuff of Hebrew poetry and reflect the Hebrew way of thinking. In addressing Yahweh's **arm** the worshippers are addressing Yahweh himself in his capacity as warrior. Similarly he is thought of as clothing himself with **strength**, the attribute above all needed by a warrior (cf. Ps. 93 : 1). The list of Yahweh's mighty deeds begins with an allusion to a mythological battle in which he slew a sea-monster variously known as **Rahab** and **the dragon** (*tannîn*). Myths of this type were widespread in the ancient Near East. According to a Babylonian text such a battle was the preliminary to the creation of heaven and earth by the god Marduk (*ANET*, p. 67); but the myth alluded to here probably comes from nearer home, from Canaan. A Ugaritic myth—not, however, specifically connected with the creation of the world in the texts which have been preserved—tells how the god Baal slew a similar adversary who is referred to by precisely the same word (*tannîn*) as Yahweh's adversary here (*ANET*, pp. 130–1). But Deutero-Isaiah is alluding to a specifically Israelite form of the myth with Yahweh as the warrior-god, which is also referred to elsewhere in the *OT*, especially Ps. 74 : 13–14; Isa. 27 : 1. The reference is probably to the creation of the world, although this is not specifically stated. The highly mythological language appears surprising in view of Deutero-Isaiah's otherwise monotheistic theology; but this is the traditional language of the cult. **cut . . . in pieces:** 1QIs^a has a variant reading, but MT is perfectly satisfactory. **Rahab:** unlike *tannîn*, this name for Yahweh's adversary is, as far as it is possible to tell, peculiar to the Israelite version of the myth. In some contexts in the *OT* it appears to refer to Egypt, a fact which has not so far been satisfactorily explained.

10. didst dry up the sea: the thought has clearly moved from the mythological to the historical: this is a reference to the Exodus. Yet *yām*, **sea**, and **great deep**, *t^{e}hôm rabbāh*, still have mythological overtones: Yam is the name of the adversary killed by Baal in the Ugaritic myth, and **great deep** elsewhere denotes the primaeval ocean (Gen. 7: 11; Am. 7: 4; Ps. 36: 6 (MT 7)) and is hardly appropriate to the 'sea' crossed by the Israelites at the Exodus. A similar fusion of the mythological and the historical is made in the cultic context of Ps. 74 : 13–14. The second half of the verse, however, refers wholly to the Exodus: there is no doubt about the meaning of **a way for the redeemed to pass over**.

11. This verse is virtually identical with 35 : 10, where it is clearly at home. Here it is a gloss: it interrupts the sequence of lamentation and promise of salvation. The glossator saw in the resemblance between **redeemed** (*g^e'ûlîm*) in verse 10 and **ransomed of the LORD** (*p^{e}ḏûyê yhwh*) in 35 : 10 an opportunity to make the point that what Yahweh did in the past he will do again. **ransomed:** MT is preferable to 1QIs^a's *p^{e}zûrê*, 'scattered'. **they shall obtain joy . . . :** or perhaps 'joy . . . shall overtake them'.

12–16. Yahweh now replies to the lamentation of verses 9–10. The opinions of the commentators on these verses differ so widely, from unqualified admiration of their artistic perfection (Torrey) to their dismissal as a series of unrelated fragments of doubtful authorship (Duhm), that the lack of agreed criteria in such matters becomes painfully obvious. Here it will be argued that, though the passage has suffered from subsequent manipulation, it makes sense as substantially the work of Deutero-Isaiah.

12–13. The double imperative of verse 9 is answered by the equally emphatic *'ānōḵî 'ānōḵî* (**I, I**) with which Yahweh indignantly refutes the charge of inactivity. Here, as in 40 : 1, 'comfort' is not just a matter of speaking soothing words, but of bringing the nation's suffering to an end. The remainder of these two verses goes to the root of the exiles' despairing cry of verses 9–10: they have failed to understand the true meaning of their own traditional faith. For them the activity of Yahweh has been confined to the past; yet it ought to be obvious to them that his creation of the world implies an unchallenged and continuing mastery over the universe beside which **man who dies** and **who is made like grass** is of no account at all. Fear of **the fury of the oppressor** consequently shows a lack of faith. So Yahweh turns the tables: it is not he who has **forgotten** his people (cf. 49 : 14), but they who have **forgotten** him: to fear men is to forget God.

In these verses the exiles are addressed in a variety of ways: the **you** of **comforts you** is second pers. masc.; but **you** in the remainder of verse 12 is fem. sing., while in verse 13 masc. sing. forms are used. Different readings in some of the Versions and in 1QIs[a] show that the problem was recognized from an early date. The original readings are probably irrecoverable, and no purpose is served by the creation of an artificial consistency by means of arbitrary emendation. Variations of this kind are in any case insufficient grounds for questioning unity of authorship.

12. who are you (*mî-'att*) **that you . . . ?:** perhaps better, 'how is it that you . . . ?'. Compare Am. 7 : 2, 5; Ru. 3 : 16, where also the usual translation of *mî* by 'Who?' seems inappropriate.

13. who stretched out . . . the earth: see on 40 : 22, and cf. Ps. 104 : 2, 5. **And where . . . oppressor?:** this phrase may be a gloss, laboriously underlining a point which was already clear.

14. It is difficult to understand why Skinner (and others) should have considered this verse to be 'hopelessly unintelligible'. It is, as Westermann recognized, the central affirmation of the oracle. *ṣōʿeh*, **He who is bowed down**, is an unusual word, but the occurrences of this verb elsewhere (Jer. 2 : 20; 48 : 12) make it probable that *RSV* is correct. It is used here of the captive exiles. They will **speedily be released**, and so freed from fear of violent death and starvation. **die and go down to the Pit:** literally, 'die to the Pit'. Such elliptical expressions are not uncommon in Hebrew poetry: cf. Ps. 74 : 7. **the Pit** (*šaḥaṯ*)**:** i.e. the grave. **his bread** (*laḥmô*)**:** there is insufficient reason to alter this, whether by emendation (*lēḥô*) or by repointing (*lēḥāmô*) to 'his vigour'. Although in general the exiles were perhaps not illtreated by the Babylonians, our knowledge of their condition is insufficient to permit the judgment that they could not have lacked food. Cf. 47 : 6; 51 : 23.

15–16. The oracle concludes with a return to the argument from creation. But this has been interrupted by the interpolation into verse 16 of **And I have put . . . my hand**, on which see below.

15. who stirs up . . . his name: these words are almost identical with part of Jer. 31 : 35; but there they are certainly an interpolation. Here—assuming the interpolation of the first two lines of verse 16—they are essential to the context, although they may be a quotation made by the prophet from elsewhere. This would account for **his name** instead of 'my name'. **stirs up** (*rōgaʿ*) **the sea:** the meaning of this verb is not clear, and it has been suggested that it is an error for *gōʿēr*, 'rebukes'. But this is not certain.

16. The first two lines (to **my hand**) clearly do not fit the context. The second line has a close verbal resemblance to part of 49 : 2, and the thought of the first line is found in 50 : 4. This suggests that these lines are addressed to the Servant, that is to Deutero-Isaiah; but whether they are a fragment of another 'Servant Song' or a gloss by a later hand cannot be determined. The last two lines resume verse 15; but it is the final line which contains the climax of the whole oracle. Yahweh's assurance to 'Zion' that she is his people is made the concluding member of a series of clauses asserting his creation of the world. No clearer answer could be given to those who had complained that he was no longer interested in their fate: his creation of the world and his special relationship with Israel are equally important to him, and both are equally enduring. **stretching out:** Heb. has 'planting' (*linṭōaʿ*); but this would be an unusual metaphor, and is almost certainly a mistake for the more usual *linṭōṯ*, **stretching out**, the verb which is employed in verse 13 and other creation passages.

THE CUP OF YAHWEH'S WRATH

51 : 17–23

In this passage the prophet's call to the nation (**Jerusalem**) to rouse itself from the state of hopelessness into which its sufferings have cast it (verses 17–20) is made to prepare it (**Therefore hear this**, verse 21) for Yahweh's promise (verses 22–23) that he is about to bring those sufferings to an end and inflict them instead on the nation's oppressors.

17–20. Although these verses are in the form of an appeal by the prophet to the exiles rather than of a complaint made by them to Yahweh, the substance of what is said is derived mainly from actual lamentations, as the strong verbal resemblances to the contemporary book of Lamentations, especially chapters 1 and 2, clearly show. They thus perform a somewhat similar function to verses 9–11 in introducing an oracle of salvation. The prophet takes up the complaints of the exiles and admits their truth. The thought of the whole passage is thus the same as that of 40 : 1–2: the suffering is admitted; but it was a well-merited suffering which is now sufficient; and it is to be brought to an end immediately.

17. Rouse yourself, rouse yourself: there is perhaps a deliberate contrast here with 47 : 1. **Jerusalem:** as elsewhere in Deutero-Isaiah the thought oscillates between the community of the exiles and the city itself. The metaphor of **the cup of . . . wrath** which Yahweh gives to Israel or to other nations to drink, and which makes them drunk and causes them to stagger, appears frequently in the *OT* literature of this period (e.g. Jer. 25 : 15–27; Ezek. 23 : 31–34). A particularly interesting example is Lam. 4 : 21–22, where as here the cup drunk by Jerusalem is to be taken from her and given to her enemy. **drunk to the dregs:** almost the same expression is used in Ezek. 23 : 34. **the bowl of staggering: bowl** here represents two Heb. words—*ḳubbaʿaṯ kôs*, of which the second is the same as that translated **cup** earlier in the verse. Here it is a gloss, explaining the meaning of the rare word *ḳubbaʿaṯ*.

18. The change from second to third pers. in speaking of Jerusalem, reversed again in verse 19, is surprising, but does not justify the excision of the verse by some commentators as a later addition. Jerusalem is now pictured as a mother staggering under the influence of drink: she thus personifies the nation, yet at the same time the nation is represented by her **sons**: a characteristically complex image. The 'sons' cannot help her because (verse 20) they have fallen at the hands of the Babylonians. For the image of the son who is expected to assist a drunken parent, cf. the Ugaritic *Tale of Aqhat*, where a son is promised who, among other regular duties towards his father, 'takes him by the hand when he's drunk, carries him when he's sated with wine' (*ANET*, p. 150).

19. The **two things** (cf. 47 : 9) are the destruction of Jerusalem and its surroundings and the decimation of its population; but each is expressed by a pair of words to give an impression of the completeness of the disaster. The thought of Jerusalem as a city now predominates over that of Jerusalem as a symbol of the Babylonian exiles. The lack of anyone to **comfort** her is a recurring theme in Lam. 1. **who will comfort you?**: in MT the verb is first pers. sing. (*'ᵃnaḥᵃmēḵ*). This can only be translated on the assumption that *mî* here means 'how?' rather than 'who?' (cf. on verse 12). But 1QIsᵃ has the third pers. (*ynḥmk*), which provides a better parallelism with the third pers. **will condole**, and this is probably correct. (So also the Versions, though without other support their evidence would not be conclusive, since they might have attempted to correct a difficult text.)

20. at the head of every street: these words hardly agree with the next line, and may be a gloss introduced from Lam. 2 : 19. Their omission would improve the metre.

21. Therefore (*lāḵēn*): in the pre-exilic prophets this word frequently introduces a divine threat of punishment following the prophet's denunciation of the nation's sins which are the cause of the punishment. Here the opposite is announced: a divine promise to bring the punishment to an end follows the prophet's demonstration that it has been amply sufficient. **drunk, but not with wine:** cf. 29 : 9, with which Deutero-Isaiah may have been familiar.

22. the LORD (*yhwh*): this word may be a later addition. **pleads the cause of his people** (*yārîḇ 'ammô*): that the verb *rîḇ* sometimes denotes action more robust than legal argument is shown by Ps. 35 : 1. The word is employed here probably because it had been used in the exiles' lamentations to which this oracle is a reply. **Behold** (*hinnēh*)**:** this word regularly calls attention to some new action. **I have taken:** the use of the perf. indicates certainty and imminence. **bowl:** the unusual word *ḳubbaʿaṯ* is again glossed by *kôs*, 'cup', as in verse 17.

23. and I will put . . . tormentors: the line is metrically too short. 1QIs[a] adds *wmʿnyk* = *ûmeʿannayiḵ*, 'and your oppressors', and LXX has a similar addition. The original reading may have been *ûḇeyaḏ meʿannayiḵ*, 'and into the hand of your oppressors'. **Bow down, that we may pass over:** the barbaric practice of a conquering army driving over the prostrate bodies of the conquered is well attested in ancient literature.

FROM SLAVE-GIRL TO QUEEN

52 : 1–2

This is a stirring call by the prophet to Zion/Jerusalem, once again conceived of simultaneously as city and as exiled community, to prepare itself for its imminent restoration to honour and strength. But the poem appears to be incomplete. The expected divine oracle promising Yahweh's immediate action is lacking: verses 3–6, which are in prose, can hardly be the continuation of verses 1–2. Once again there is a deliberate contrast with the fate of Babylon foretold in 47 : 1ff. Queen and slave-girl are to exchange roles.

1. Awake, awake: the imperatives are the same as in 51 : 9. As Duhm pointed out, this fact confirms the view that 51 : 9–52 : 3 is not a single, long poem, since it is unlikely that the prophet would have addressed Yahweh and Zion in the same way in the same poem. **the holy city:** this phrase, found also in 48 : 2, is used here to emphasize that Jerusalem will be fully restored to its former status as the place of Yahweh's especial favour. The **uncircumcised and the unclean**, that is, the Babylonians who have defiled it by their very presence (cf. Ps. 79 : 1; Lam. 1 : 10) will not only be expelled (cf. 49 : 17), but the promise is made that such defilement will never again take place. Deutero-Isaiah here expresses the same concern as Ezekiel (Ezek. 44 : 9) for the inviolable holiness of the new community which was to be established in and around the restored Jerusalem.

2. This verse is the counterpart to 47 : 1. **O captive Jerusalem:** *RSV* here is based on a conjectural emendation (*šeḇiyyāh*). Heb., which is supported by the Versions, has 'Sit down (*šeḇî*), O Jerusalem!' There is no reason to reject the Heb. Jerusalem is told first to **arise** from the dust and then to take her seat on a throne. The word *šeḇiyyāh*, 'captive', already occurs once in the verse, and a repetition of it is unlikely. **loose the bonds:** here *RSV* rightly follows Qere and the Versions. Kethib has 'the bonds are loosed'. The proposal to render 'loose yourself from the bonds', which involves the emendation of *môserê* to *mimmôserê*, is probably not necessary.

YAHWEH FREELY REDEEMS HIS PEOPLE

52 : 3–6

In spite of the initial word **For**, these verses cannot be regarded as the continuation of verses 1–2. Attempts to see metrical form in them have not been convincing, and they must be regarded as prose. Although they contain a number of phrases reminiscent of Deutero-Isaiah, there is no clear train of thought, and they are probably best seen as a series of later additions inspired by reflection on his words.

3. The meaning of this verse is similar to that of 50 : 1, which may have been its inspiration. Yahweh's handing over of his people to the Babylonians was not really a sale (see on 50 : 1), since Yahweh gained nothing from it. There is therefore nothing to hinder him from 'redeeming' them: the verb *gā'al* here retains something of its original meaning: see on 43 : 1.

4. The repetition of **For thus says the LORD** suggests a new beginning. The verse makes brief references to Israel's earlier 'exiles', the sojourn of the patriarchs in Egypt and the deportation of the northern Israelites to Assyria in the eighth century. Presumably these were believed by the author to be relevant to what he had to say about the present Exile in verse 5; but the connexion is not obvious. Probably what he intended to convey in this verse was that the former oppressions were undeserved: the verb *gûr*, **sojourn**, may imply that the Israelites in Egypt were there as guests; and the phrase *be'ep̱es*, **for nothing**, should probably be translated 'without any reason'. The view that Israel did not deserve its fate at the hands of Assyria is in direct contradiction to that of the prophet Isaiah.

5. says the LORD (twice) again suggests a lack of literary unity. **what have I here:** the meaningless 'whom have I here?' of Kethib is corrected by Qere. The phrase is probably intended to make a connexion with the previous verse. **here** means 'here in Babylonia': Yahweh is represented as saying 'What do I find here?'. **for nothing:** it is difficult to reconcile this with the constantly reiterated statements of Deutero-Isaiah that the Exile was deserved. **Their rulers wail:** no satisfactory interpretation of this phrase has yet been found. The Jews at this time had no **rulers** except the Babylonians, and these would more naturally be referred to by some other term such as 'conquerors' or 'oppressors'. Some commentators nevertheless interpret the phrase in this sense, and emend *yᵉhêlîlû*, 'wail', to *yᵉhallēlû*, 'boast'. Others emend to *yᵉḥullēlû*, 'are profaned', giving the verb a past sense and taking **rulers** to mean the political and religious leaders of Judah at the time of the destruction of Jerusalem (cf. 43 : 28). **is despised:** the form *minnōʾāṣ* is anomalous. It may be a combination of two distinct readings, *mᵉnōʾāṣ* (Pual participle) and *miṯnōʾāṣ* (Hithpoel participle).

6. Therefore: on its second occurrence this word is probably to be omitted. It is lacking in 1QIsᵃ and several Versions. This verse seems to have no connexion with what precedes. **in that day:** this phrase, which occurs frequently in post-exilic prophecy, is not used elsewhere by Deutero-Isaiah, whose prophecies always concern the immediate rather than the distant future. It is a further indication of later authorship.

THE MESSAGE OF REDEMPTION

52 : 7–10

This passage is adapted from the hymn of praise, whose structure is clearly seen in verses 9–10: a summons to rejoice, followed by a joyful proclamation, introduced by *kî*, **for**, of God's act of redemption which provides the grounds for praise. This is another example of what Westermann calls the 'eschatological song of praise', in that the verbs describing God's action, though in the perfect tense—**has comforted**, **has redeemed**, **has bared**—

refer to the future. The prophet speaks of it with absolute certainty, as if it had already taken place. The grounds for this certainty are apparent from verses 7–8: he has seen in a prophetic vision the arrival in Jerusalem of the messenger who comes to announce Yahweh's victory.

7–8. The imagery is similar to that of 40 : 9–11. The word rendered (**him**) **who brings good tidings** (*m^e^ḇaśśēr*) is that rendered 'herald of good tidings' in 40 : 9, where it is fem. because it refers to Zion. The present scene is slightly different: Jerusalem —here primarily the city—is portrayed as the recipient of the message. In 40 : 9, she is told to proclaim it to the other cities of Judah. But the message itself is essentially the same.

7. How beautiful: better, 'How welcome!' The one **who brings good tidings** is a military runner, on whose function see on 40 : 9. He is an anonymous figure, whose significance lies in his function rather than in his identity. **feet:** this concentration on the significant part of the body rather than on the person is characteristic of Hebrew thought. **peace** (*šālôm*)**:** the meaning of this word here is best illustrated from 2 Sam. 18 : 28, where *RSV* renders it, "All is well!". **salvation:** better, 'victory'. **Your God reigns:** this phrase is adapted from 'The LORD reigns' of the so-called 'enthronement psalms', e.g. Ps. 97 : 1. The acclamation of Yahweh's appearance or theophany in the cult as supreme King is here boldly transferred by Deutero-Isaiah into a concrete, historical event: he is assuring the exiles that what they have previously acknowledged in faith is now about to be enacted before their eyes in a victory over Babylon which will set God's people free and restore Jerusalem to its former glory.

8. The vision is followed by the sound of voices. The **watchmen** on the walls of the city (see on 40 : 9) are the first to see the approach of the runner, or to hear his message, and they burst into a shout of joy. **eye to eye:** better, 'at close quarters' (cf. Num. 14 : 14; Jer. 32 : 4). At the end of the verse 1QIs^a adds 'in love'—a gloss, but one which gives a correct interpretation.

9. Break forth . . . into singing: this is the language of the cultic hymn of praise. **you waste places:** Jerusalem was in ruins; it had at this time no city walls on which watchmen could take their stand, as is implied by verse 8. This is poetic licence, or even deliberate paradox.

10. has bared his holy arm: in other words, he has thrown back the encumbering folds of his garment in order to be able to use his sword. Cf. Ps. 74 : 11. The defeat of Babylon, and the return home of the exiles which is implied in this passage, will amaze the nations of the world. **salvation:** better, 'victory'.

THE COMMAND TO DEPART

52 : 11–12

Here again the prophet speaks as a visionary. He sees Babylon as already falling: the order is given to the exiles to leave the stricken city. The new Exodus is about to begin, and it will be more glorious than the old.

11. The argument of some commentators that the phrase **go out thence** shows that the prophet is situated, whether in reality or in imagination, not in Babylonia but in Palestine, is hyper-critical. The choice of 'thence' rather than 'hence' may be due to any one of a number of circumstances of which we are ignorant. The exiles are to take with them on their journey the sacred temple **vessels** removed by Nebuchadnezzar (2 Kg. 25 : 14–15) which had, it seems, been carefully preserved in Babylon (Ezr. 1 : 7–11; 5 : 14–15). The journey thus has the character of a solemn religious procession, necessitating ceremonial purity, especially on the part of the priests, whose function it was to carry these vessels.

12. Both the similarities and the differences between the old and the new Exodus are emphasized in this verse. The promise that Yahweh will both **go before** his people and also be their **rear guard** is a clear reference to the pillar of cloud and of fire which had both guided and protected the Israelites in their flight from Egypt (Exod. 13 : 21–22; 14 : 19–20). But whereas the departure from Egypt had had to be carried out **in haste** and **in flight** (Exod. 12 : 11; Dt. 16 : 3), the new Exodus is to be an orderly march, since the power of Babylon will no longer exist. The extent of Deutero-Isaiah's familiarity with the traditions of the Exodus in a form similar to that preserved in the Pentateuch is shown not only by the reference to the pillar of cloud, but also by the use of the word *ḥippāzôn*, **haste**, which elsewhere occurs only in the two verses already referred to (Exod. 12 : 11; Dt. 16 : 3) and thus has the character of a technical term.

FROM HUMILIATION TO HONOUR

52 : 13–15

The great majority of commentators support the view that these verses are part of a larger whole, the fourth 'Servant Song', 52 : 13–53 : 12. But the minority view, held by Coppens, Snaith, and Orlinsky among others, that 52 : 13–15 constitute a separate piece, has much to commend it. Chapter 53 by itself, though not without its own problems, makes good sense as a song of thanksgiving for the deliverance of God's servant, Deutero-Isaiah, from mortal danger (see below). But 52 : 13–15 are an oracle spoken by Yahweh which can hardly be regarded as a 'preface' to this. The **many nations** and **kings** of verse 15 suggest that the Servant here is not the prophet, but Israel. The fact that the phrase **my servant** is applied to the person referred to in both cases (52 : 13; 53 : 11), the similarity of the description of the servant's exalted status in those verses, and the close similarity between the thoughts expressed in 52 : 15*b* and 53 : 1*a* are sufficient to account for the editorial juxtaposition of the two passages. 52: 13–15, then, is a short promise of salvation assuring the exiles of a reversal of their fortunes and a new pre-eminence in the world which will astonish the other nations.

13. shall prosper (*yaśkîl*)**:** the suggestion of Budde that this is a corruption of 'Israel' (*yiśrā'ēl*) is quite arbitrary. The most frequent meaning of this verb is 'understand, be wise or prudent'; but it can also have the sense of 'be successful': success was believed to be the normal outcome of the possession of wisdom. The two meanings may be combined here, but the context suggests that it is 'prosper, be successful' which predominates. **he shall be exalted:** there is a superfluity of synonyms here, and the metre is overloaded. This word is not represented in LXX, and may be a gloss, although the reasons advanced for its later insertion are not very convincing.

14–15. These verses have suffered some textual dislocation: the first line of verse 14 (**As many . . . at him**) is metrically too short, and the remainder of the passage can only be translated if the words included between dashes in *RSV* are treated as a parenthesis. These lines have much in common with 53 : 2–3, and Duhm's suggestion that they have been misplaced from the end of 53 : 2 has been widely adopted, and is probably correct.

14. As has been suggested above, the bulk of this verse (from **his appearance**) refers to the 'Servant' Deutero-Isaiah and is an insertion from ch. 53. The remaining line, **As many were astonished at him**, refers to the present wretched state of the exiles (cf. 42 : 22) and forms the first part of a contrast between present and future of which verse 15*a*, which originally followed directly upon it, forms the second. **were astonished:** better, 'were horrified'. In Israel and among her neighbours the shame of dishonour, whether individual or corporate, was deeply felt and added to the suffering which had been inflicted: cf. the book of Job and the lamentations generally, e.g. Lam. 2 : 15. **at him:** Heb. has 'at you'. *RSV* has adopted an emendation suggested by Syr. and Targ. But Heb. may be correct: such abrupt changes of person are not uncommon in Hebrew poetry.

so marred: the use of *kēn* (**so**) in this sense is very unusual, but just possible (cf. Jer. 14 : 10). The word translated **marred** (*mišḥaṯ*) is an otherwise unattested noun in the construct. The root shows that its meaning would be 'a disfigurement'. The construction is just possible, but the word should perhaps be repointed to give the Hophal participle *mošḥāṯ*. **beyond human semblance:** literally, 'from (being) a man'.

15. so here picks up **As** in verse 14. Unfortunately the meaning of the word translated **startle** (*yazzeh*) is uncertain. The traditional derivation from *nāzāh* (Hiphil), 'sprinkle', that is, 'purify', used in connexion with sacrificial and purificatory rites, although recently defended by E. J. Young (*Studies in Isaiah*, 1955, pp. 199–206) is rather forced. LXX has 'many nations shall be astonished at him'; and, since this fits the context well, various emendations yielding a similar sense have been proposed. The suggestion that *yazzeh* is derived from an otherwise unattested root cognate with Arabic *nazā* has also found many adherents: this might be made to yield either 'he will startle many nations' (*RSV*) or, by repointing the verb as Qal, 'many nations will leap to their feet (in respect)'. **kings shall shut their mouths:** also in token of respect. Cf. Job 29 : 8–9. The last two lines of the verse (**for that . . . understand**) express the suddenness of the transformation of the status of the exiled Israelites, which catches the world unprepared.

THE PROPHET'S SUFFERINGS AND RELEASE

53 : 1–12

The person referred to throughout this chapter is the same as the 'servant' of the three earlier 'Servant Songs', 42 : 1–4; 49 : 1–6; 50 : 4–9—that is, the prophet Deutero-Isaiah himself. Except in verses 11*b*–12*a*, on which see below, Yahweh is referred to also in the third person. The speakers, who refer to themselves throughout as 'we', are a group of the prophet's fellow-exiles, possibly an intimate group of his disciples, though they speak for the whole exilic community.

It is held by most commentators that the passage refers to the Servant as one who has been put to death by his enemies, but who will, astonishingly, be restored to life by Yahweh, who accepts his suffering and death as vicariously atoning for the sins of others. This view might be tenable if the Servant were an allegorical figure representing the nation of Israel, though it would then ascribe to Deutero-Isaiah a view of the mission of Israel to the world which would be quite unparalleled. But it has already been argued (see on 42 : 1–4; 49 : 1–6) that the Servant in this group of passages cannot be Israel. If on the other hand this passage is interpreted as referring to a historical individual whose death is regarded as bringing atonement for the sins of others, the difficulties are even greater. The concept of an innocent person's suffering the death penalty so that the guilty might go free would not only be an unheard of and inexplicable innovation, but would also be contrary to the principles of justice constantly reiterated in the *OT*. Further, who is it that goes free? The speakers can hardly be representatives of the heathen nations; and if they are Israelites, they have *not* escaped punishment for their sins, but have on the contrary, as Deutero-Isaiah frequently states elsewhere, paid in full. A further difficulty concerns the supposed resurrection of the Servant. As a metaphor of the restoration of Israel after exile this might be conceivable (cf. Ezek. 37 : 1–14), but with reference to an individual it is totally foreign to the Judaism of the sixth century BC. All these difficulties are removed, however, when it is realized that the supposed references to the Servant's vicarious suffering and death and resurrection are illusory, due partly to a misunderstanding of the language of a particular kind of religious poetry and partly to the determination of Christian interpreters to find here a prefiguration of the suffering, death and resurrection of Christ. See especially H. M. Orlinsky in *Studies on the Second Part of the Book of Isaiah* (*VT* Suppl. 14), 1967; G. R. Driver, *In Memoriam Paul Kahle* (*BZAW* 103), 1968, pp. 90–105.

The basic form of the chapter is that of the thanksgiving of the individual for deliverance from trouble, with the unusual feature that it is not the former sufferer himself but his friends who give thanks. This feature is not, however, entirely unique: according to Ps. 22 : 22–25 (MT 23–26); 35 : 27 it is the function of the 'great congregation' to offer such praise, and Ps. 107 is in fact such an act of thanksgiving for the rescue of others from trouble, though expressed in general terms, while in Ps. 118 there is a dialogue of praise in which both the former sufferer and the congregation participate. In Isa. 53 the allusiveness of the language does not permit us to say precisely what was the occasion of this giving of thanks, but it may be surmised that it was the release of Deutero-Isaiah from a Babylonian prison, where he had been subjected to the suffering of which the third 'Servant Song' (50 : 4–9) also speaks. The reason for his release is not known; but it would appear that his friends took it as a miracle and as a sign that the tide of their own sufferings had turned, and that the deliverance of the exiles which he had constantly promised was about to begin. This, together with his exalted role as the bearer of Yahweh's word, would account for the exalted language in which they speak of him.

1. As in Ps. 34, where an individual expresses his thanks for his own deliverance from affliction, and Ps. 107, where as here it is others who speak, the speakers throughout this chapter do not address Yahweh directly, but simply narrate the sequence of events which has led to the happy conclusion, referring both to Yahweh and the sufferer in the third person. This is therefore not a prayer, but an act of confident faith in Yahweh based on the knowledge of what he has done. Since this is something totally unexpected, they begin with a rhetorical question which stresses their intense and joyful astonishment. **Who has believed:** probably better, 'Whoever would have believed?' (cf. Ps. 118 : 23). **what we have heard:** that is, 'what we have *just* heard'. This may refer to the news of Deutero-Isaiah's release; the setting is probably an act of worship at which the prophet has just told the tale of his miraculous deliverance. We may compare the reception of the news of Peter's release from prison in Acts 12 : 12–17. The deliverance is seen as the manifestation of the **arm of the LORD** (cf. 52 : 10; Ps. 98 : 1) to, or **upon** (*'al*) the prophet.

2–9. These verses correspond to the narrative section in the individual thanksgiving, in which the speaker describes his lamentable state before Yahweh rescued him, using the language of the individual lamentations. Much of the language used here is similar to that of those two types of psalm.

2–3. In these verses we encounter for the first time one of the main difficulties in the interpretation of the chapter: that of determining which phrases are to be understood literally and which as poetical hyperbole in the manner of the individual lamentation. These two verses should be interpreted in relation to the expression of astonishment in verse 1. They are concerned to make the point that the speakers—or those on whose behalf they speak—had formerly failed to recognize any special qualities in the prophet, and consequently had not been moved by his acute distress.

2. The similes of the **young plant** and the **root** growing **out of dry ground** are examples of a symbolism commonplace in the ancient Near East, including Israel: just as the man who has the divine blessing and consequently prospers is compared to well-watered vegetation, so the man from whom the divine blessing has been withheld is like a parched plant destined to wither and die (cf. Ps. 1; Jer. 17 : 5–8). There is no justification for the contention of H. S. Nyberg (*Smärtornas Man*, 1942) and I. Engnell, ('The "Ebed-Yahweh Songs" ', *BJRL* 31, 1948, pp. 54–93) that the language used here and elsewhere in the Servant Songs is derived from the pagan fertility-mythology concerning Tammuz. **he grew up:** this is not a reference to the Servant's early life. **grew up** is simply a metaphor taken from plant life. The emphasis is on the apparently blighted career of the Servant. **before him** (*l^epānâw*): the obvious meaning of this phrase is 'in Yahweh's presence'; but some commentators have emended it to *l^epānênû*, 'before us', on the grounds that **before him** would imply that Yahweh was seen to give the Servant his special protection, which is the contrary of what the speakers intend to say. But this emendation, which has no support from the MSS or Versions, is unnecessary. **before him** simply means that Yahweh was aware of the Servant's misfortunes, yet appeared to do nothing to remedy them. The earlier contention of G. R. Driver that *l^epānâw* should be translated 'straight up' has now (*In Memoriam Paul Kahle*, pp. 92, 103) been withdrawn by its author.

In the second half of the verse (**he had no form . . . desire him**) the speakers refer to their own former reaction to the person of the prophet. They do not state that his appearance was repulsive, but only that he lacked any impressive appearance (*tō'ar, mar'eh:* not **form** and **beauty**) or majestic manner (*hāḏār*: hardly **comeliness**) which might have commanded their attention or attracted their devotion. **that we should look at him:** in MT this word is taken with the words which follow; but the sense is greatly improved by the punctuation given in *RSV*. On the lines, **his appearance . . . sons of man** in 52 : 14, which probably originally stood here, see above on 52 : 14–15.

3. This description of the Servant's rejection by his fellows, suffering, and ostracism is clearly dependent both in thought and vocabulary on similar descriptions in the individual lamentations and thanksgivings: cf. Pss. 22; 38; 69. **rejected by men** (*ḥ^aḏal 'îšîm*)**:** some scholars maintain that 'shunning the company of men' is a preferable translation. **sorrows**; **grief:** rather, 'pain(s)', 'sickness': the results of his ill treatment. **acquainted with** (*y^eḏûa'*)**:** this use of the passive participle Qal raises difficulties if the verb is *yāḏa'* = 'know'. 1QIs^a, supported by the Versions, has the act. part. *yôḏēa'*, 'knowing'. But MT may be retained if the theory of D. W. Thomas is accepted that there is another *yāḏa'* in biblical Hebrew, cognate with Arabic *wadu'a*, which would here yield the meaning 'humbled by'. **and as one from whom men hide their faces** (*ûk^emastēr pānîm mimmennû*)**:** literally, 'and like a hiding of face from him' (or, 'from us'). This is hardly acceptable Hebrew. Skinner compares it with Job 17 : 6, 'I am a spitting in the face'; but even so *mimmennû* remains a difficulty. *mastēr* may be a defective spelling of the Hiphil participle *mastîr*, which, in addition to its usual meaning 'one who hides', might perhaps have the sense of 'one who causes (others) to hide': the Servant would then be 'like one who causes (others) to hide (their) faces from him'. Alternatively, J. Heller (*Communio Viatorum* 1 (1958), pp. 263–6) has suggested that *k^e* may have the sense of 'as if', and that Targ. and Aquila are right in taking Yahweh to be the (unexpressed) subject: 'And as if (Yahweh) were hiding his face from him': cf. Ps. 22 : 24 (MT 25). **he was despised** (*nibzeh*)**:** here we should perhaps read *nibzēhû* or *nibzēhū*, 'we despised him': cf. 1QIsᵃ and Syr.

4–6. The speakers now go further and recognize that the prophet's suffering was an integral part of a ministry which brought Yahweh's healing word to them. The distinctiveness of this ministry of suffering is brought out in a series of clauses which make a sharp contrast between **he** and **we.**

4. Surely (*'āḵēn*)**:** or perhaps, better, 'Yet'. **griefs; sorrows:** see on verse 3. The speakers now recognize that the prophet's suffering, though more intense than theirs, was fundamentally due to the same cause. They speak of his identification with them in their suffering: there is nothing to suggest that he suffered in their place. They—that is, the whole exilic community in whose name they make their confession—had previously thought of him quite differently, dismissing him simply as a person who had undergone unusually intense misfortune, with the implication (though **smitten by God** perhaps means no more than 'terribly smitten') that he had brought divine punishment on himself through his own wickedness—possibly as a false prophet. See further on **he bore the sin of many** in verse 12.

5. for our transgressions; for our iniquities: these phrases are usually interpreted as implying vicarious suffering: the people sinned, but the Servant was punished. But this is made improbable by the choice of the word translated **for.** If the author had intended to imply such a transference of guilt, he would almost certainly have used the particle *bᵉ*, which denotes an exchange. The fact that he chose instead the particle *min* indicates that he regarded the Servant's ill treatment as the *result* of the people's sin but not as a *substitute* for the punishment which they had deserved. If there had been no sin, and consequently no exile, the prophet's dangerous vocation would not have been necessary. He suffered with his fellow-exiles, but his prophetic calling exposed him to additional and peculiar danger, whose cause was ultimately derived from Israel's sin. We may compare the experiences of Jeremiah and Ezekiel, who also suffered from a similar cause.

In the second half of the verse the speakers assert that the prophet's suffering has not been in vain. In saying that they have been **made . . . whole** and **healed**, they are summarizing

Deutero-Isaiah's own essential message, that Yahweh has forgiven them and is on the point of rescuing and restoring them. They affirm their faith in this message, and recognize that without his readiness to suffer in the course of his prophetic duty, the prophetic word, which was the means used by Yahweh to achieve his purpose (55 : 11), would not have been pronounced.

6. All we like sheep: the use of the word **All** indicates that the speakers identify themselves with the whole community. The simile of the straying **sheep** is found frequently in the *OT*. **laid on him** has overtones lacking in the Heb. *hipgîaʿ bô*, which probably simply means 'caused him to suffer', while the following word (*ʿāwōn*) would be better translated by 'punishment' here. The point is that the whole people had deserved to suffer, but only he had borne the full measure of suffering. See on **he bore the sin of many** in verse 12.

7–9. The speakers now emphasize that the prophet, though innocent, accepted his misfortunes uncomplainingly. This may well be a historical fact; but the occurrence of this theme in Ps. 38 : 13–14 (MT 14–15) suggests that it may also have belonged to the stock of themes available to authors of individual psalms of lamentation or thanksgiving.

7. He was oppressed: the word (*niggaś*) denotes physical brutality. **and he was afflicted:** probably better, 'although (or, 'but') he made no resistance'. In the similes of the **lamb . . . led to the slaughter** and the **sheep . . . before its shearers** the point of comparison is the silence of the victim. The fact that only one of the similes speaks of **slaughter** shows, if proof were needed, that there is no implication here that the Servant was put to death. Jeremiah, in referring to plots against his life which had failed, says of himself, 'But I was a gentle lamb led to the slaughter' (Jer. 11 : 19). **so he opened not his mouth:** commentators are divided on the question whether the phrase was deliberately repeated by the author for poetical effect or whether the duplication is a copyist's error.

8. By oppression and judgment he was taken away: every word in this phrase is of uncertain meaning. In view of the context it is probably best to give to *ʿōṣer* (*RSV* **oppression**) a specific meaning such as 'arrest' or 'imprisonment'; the verb *ʿāṣar* is used in both these senses. Since one of the meanings of *mišpāṭ* (*RSV* **judgment**) is 'trial', the most probable meaning of the phrase is 'after arrest and trial he was led away'. There is no reason to suppose that this verb (*lukkāḥ*) means 'died' or 'was executed'. The passive Qal of *lākaḥ* is never used of death in the ordinary sense, although it is used once of God's mysterious removal of Elijah, who was 'snatched away' into heaven (2 Kg. 2 : 10). Deutero-Isaiah uses it elsewhere (52 : 5) of the taking of the Jewish people into exile, and here it probably has a similar meaning: the prophet was taken away to prison.

as for his generation (*weʾeṭ-dôrô*): the particle *ʾēṭ* normally designates the object of a verb. But 'who considered his generation?' makes little sense. We should probably accept the suggestion of G. R. Driver (first made in *JTS* 36 (1935), p. 403) that *dôr* here corresponds to Accadian *dûru* and Arabic *dauru(n)* and means 'fate' or 'plight'. We may then translate 'but who gave a thought to his plight?' The following word *kî* (*RSV* **that**) should then be translated 'for'. **cut off out of the land of the living:** interpreted literally, this phrase almost certainly means that the Servant died. But a literal translation is not mandatory. In the psalms of lamentation and thanksgiving reference is frequently made to severe suffering in terms of death; and in Lam. 3 : 54 the worshipper says of himself: 'I have been cut off' (*nigzārtî*; *RSV* 'I am lost'). So here the speakers are concerned to emphasize the Servant's nearness to death: he was 'as good as dead' (see also on verse 9). **stricken:** Heb. has 'a blow to them' (*negaʿ lāmô*), which makes no sense. We should probably read something like *yenuggaʿ* / *nuggaʿ lammāweṭ*, a reading suggested by LXX. A literal rendering of this would be 'he was smitten to death'; but 'death' here may be used simply as a superlative: 'he was grievously smitten'. See D. W. Thomas, *VT* 3 (1953), pp. 219–22; *Ephemerides Theologicae Lovanienses* 44 (1968), p. 84. **for the transgression of my people** (*mippešaʿ ʿammî*): see the note on **for our transgressions**; **for our iniquities** on verse 5 above. **my people** (*ʿammî*): 1QIsᵃ has 'his people' (*ʿammô*). Possibly the suffix **-î** (**my**) was intended to be the first letter of the next word, which, as has been suggested, may have been *yenuggaʿ* (imperf.). If so the phrase would read, 'for the people's transgression he was grievously smitten'.

9. they made: the sing. verb *yittēn* here has an impersonal sense. 1QIsᵃ has the plur. A better translation would be 'they assigned'. The Servant was regarded as being 'as good as dead'; and as a convicted criminal he was to be buried among the criminals. This, for a Jew, would have been a terrible fate. But in fact it is not stated that he died. One of the features of the descriptions of past suffering in the psalms of lamentation is that the worshipper's enemies had gleefully supposed him to be at the point of death. Compare also the line 'My grave was waiting, and my funerary paraphernalia ready' from the Babylonian *Poem of the Righteous Sufferer* (W. G. Lambert, *Babylonian Wisdom Literature*, 1960, p. 46). **and with a rich man** (*ʿāšîr*)**:** that the burial places of rich men and criminals should have been identical is highly improbable, and makes the lines meaningless. Of the emendations which have been proposed, *ʿōśê raʿ*, 'doers of evil' and *śeʿîrîm*, 'demons', are the most plausible, but the text may be correct: it has been suggested that *ʿāšîr* here is unconnected with *ʿāšîr* meaning 'rich', but related to an Arabic word meaning 'refuse, rabble'. **in his death:** MT has the meaningless *bemōṯâw*, 'in his deaths'. Most modern scholars, following W. F. Albright (*VT* Suppl. 4 (1957), pp. 242–58) now accept an ancient emendation to *bāmāṯô*, 'his burial mound', a reading which perhaps gains some support from 1QIsᵃ. The line would then mean 'and his burial mound among the dregs of society'.

10–12. The main concern of the speakers in these verses is to express their joy and thanks that Yahweh has delivered his Servant from danger of death to enjoy a long and prosperous life, and to reiterate their newly found appreciation of his prophetic ministry. Unfortunately, however, the text of verses 10–11 is seriously corrupt and its meaning in some places not clear in spite of many attempts to restore it.

10. The first half of this verse (to **sin**) is particularly obscure. As translated in *RSV* it appears to continue the account of the Servant's sufferings and to assert that these were part of the divine plan. But this translation glosses over a number of difficulties. **he has put him to grief** (*heḥelî*)**:** it might just be possible to render this word by 'he made (him) sick'; but the irregularity of the form and the absence of the pronominal object make this unlikely. LXX may have understood it as an adverbial phrase, 'with sickness' (perhaps *heḥolî*). But the introduction of a reference to sickness is strange at this point. It would seem that we have here the first of a group of words (up to **offering for sin**) whose letters have been accidentally jumbled at a very early stage (before the LXX translation was made). **when he makes him-**

self an offering for sin: the Heb. has 'if' (*'im*), not **when**; but this conditional clause is difficult to reconcile with earlier statements that the Servant's suffering is past. J. Begrich (*Studien zu Deuterojesaja*, 1938, p. 58; reprinted in *Theologische Bücherei* 20, 1963, p. 64) regarded the words *heḥ^e^lî 'im-tāśîm 'āšām napšô* as a corruption of *heḥ^e^lîm 'eṯ-śām 'āšām napšô*, 'he healed him who made his life a guilt-offering'. If this is correct, the thought of Yahweh's desire that the Servant should suffer disappears from this line; and it may be that this is true of the previous line also: here Begrich proposed the reading *dakkā'ô*, 'his crushed one', for *dakk^e^'ô*, 'to crush him', so 'But Yahweh was pleased with his crushed one'; while G. R. Driver, who earlier accepted Begrich's emendation, now suggests that the Piel of *dāḵā'* here may mean 'declare innocent' (a late spelling of *zāḵāh*) rather than 'crush' or 'bruise'.

The above emendations remain conjectural; others are even more radical. In view of the great uncertainty about the text, it is unwise to press the significance of the reference to the Servant's having been made **an offering for sin** (*'āšām*). Although the majority of commentators retain this statement in some form some scholars (e.g. Marti; H.-P. Müller, *ZAW* 81 (1969) pp. 377–80) regard it as a later interpolation, while others (e.g. Duhm; I. Sonne, *JBL* 78, 1959, pp. 335–42) have eliminated the word *'āšām* altogether in their textual reconstructions. Nowhere else in the *OT* is it stated that a man's life can be a guilt-offering, whether in a literal or a metaphorical sense, and the idea would appear to be entirely foreign to *OT* thought. If the author had intended to introduce such a novel and astonishing idea, we should expect him to have stated it more clearly. (It should also be noted that even if the verse *did* speak of the Servant as having in fact made himself an offering for sin this would not necessarily imply more than that he was *ready* to die: for example, both Begrich and Driver hold that the poem does not speak of his death, and that he was still alive when it was written. See on 'he poured out his soul to death' in verse 12.

his offspring: Heb. has simply *zera'*, 'seed', without the pronominal suffix **his**. **he shall prolong his days** is a relative clause: the whole line might be paraphrased 'he will live to see his own descendants living to a great age'. This implies an exceptionally long life for the Servant himself. A long and happy life was the greatest blessing imaginable to the Jew of this period. **the will of the LORD** (second occurrence): perhaps better, 'Yahweh's cause'. **in his hand** (*b^{e}yāḏô*): that is, through his agency as a prophet. The phrase *b^{e}yaḏ*, 'by the hand of', is frequently used of the prophetic function of the communication of Yahweh's word to the people.

11. he shall see: both 1QIs^a and LXX add the word 'light' (Heb. *'ôr*), and this is certainly correct. The word was probably omitted by a copyist who was confused by the similarity of the consonants *'wr* with those of the previous word, *yr'h* (**see**). **the fruit of the travail of his soul** (*mē'^{a}mal napšô*): better, 'after his terrible suffering'. *napšô* (*RSV* **his soul**) simply indicates the intensity of the suffering. So the whole phrase may be translated, 'after his terrible suffering he will see light': that is, he will resume his normal happy life. It has been suggested on the other hand that *yir'eh* here does not mean 'see', but is an alternative spelling of *yirweh*, from *rāwāh* meaning 'be filled, saturated': so *NEB*, following Driver, renders the phrase by 'he shall be bathed in light'.

and be satisfied . . . accounted righteous: these lines are exceptionally difficult, and no attempt to elucidate them can be regarded as more than tentative. It is difficult to understand how the Servant's **knowledge** should **make many to be accounted righteous**; and the proposal to take **by his knowledge** with the preceding phrases ('he shall be satisfied through his knowledge') is hardly an improvement. A further difficulty is the position of *ṣaddîḳ*, **the righteous one**, which, as an adjective, ought to follow rather than precede the noun **my servant**. The proposal of D. W. Thomas that the word *da'aṯ* here does not mean 'knowledge' but 'humiliation', being derived from a verb *yāḏa'* cognate with Arab. *wadu'a* rather than from the more familiar *yāḏa'* (cognate with Accadian *idû*), 'to know' (see on **acquainted with** in verse 3) would greatly alleviate the first of these problems. The second problem might be solved by the omission of *ṣaddîḳ* as an accidental repetition of the last five consonants of the previous word *yaṣdîḳ*; but it may simply have been misplaced. If it preceded *yaṣdîḳ* instead of following it it would be possible to take it with the previous phrase: literally, 'after his humiliation he shall receive satisfaction as a righteous (i.e. innocent) person'. This would also improve the metre and, in addition, produce a parallel couplet:

after his terrible suffering he will see light;
after his humiliation he will be vindicated
(declared to be entirely innocent).

my servant: it would seem that Yahweh begins to speak at this point a divine oracle which continues, probably, until **strong** in verse 12, reasserting the prophet's status and making a formal declaration of his innocence. Such a divine oracle, confirming the confident faith of the worshippers, is rare but not entirely unknown in the psalms: cf. Ps. 46: 10 (MT 11). **make many to be accounted righteous** (*yaṣdîḳ . . . lārabbîm*): elsewhere the Hiphil of this verb means either 'acquit' or 'render justice to'. But here, since the **many** are presumably the Jewish exiles who are guilty and being justly punished for their sins, it can hardly have either of these meanings. To 'acquit the wicked' (*hiṣdîḳ rāšā'*) was not a virtuous action but a heinous crime, comparable with condemning the righteous. *God* might *forgive* the wicked, but *man* must not *acquit* him. The best answer to this problem is probably that of Mowinckel, who regards *yaṣdîḳ* as a so-called 'internal Hiphil'. The meaning would then be 'he showed himself to be righteous with regard to the many' (the imperf. being rendered as a past tense). The oracle of Yahweh picks up the word *ṣaddîḳ*, 'righteous, innocent', from the words of the previous speakers and gives their statement the weight of divine authority. **and he shall bear their iniquities:** this verb (an imperf.) should also be rendered as a past tense. This statement, like **he bore the sin of many** in verse 12 (see below), is usually interpreted as a statement that the Servant's suffering was vicarious and atoning. But there is no evidence for this. The phrase 'bear iniquities' (*sāḇal 'ᵃwōnôt*) occurs in only one other passage in the *OT*: 'Our fathers sinned, and are no more; and we bear their iniquities' (Lam. 5 : 7). Here it is clear that although the speakers complain that their punishment is the *consequence* of their dead ancestors' sins, they can hardly claim to be vicariously atoning for them. So also here the Servant, though innocent, has suffered punishment which is the consequence of the sins of others, and which should rightly have fallen only on his guilty compatriots (compare verses 2–6); but he has not suffered in their stead. The meaning of the phrase is 'yet *he* suffered punishment which only *they* deserved'.

12. Therefore (*lāḵēn*)**:** see on 51 : 21. Yahweh now announces the reward which the prophet is to have for his faithfulness. **I will divide him a portion** (*'ahallek-lô*)**:** the words **a portion** are lacking in the Hebrew. Either the object is to be understood without need for its specific mention, or **the spoil** functions as the object of both verbs. The phrase *ḥillēḵ šālāl*, 'divide the spoil', is primarily a military expression denoting the apportionment of captured booty among the members of a victorious army. But **spoil** (*šālāl*) can also have a general sense of 'profit, gain' (Prov. 31 : 11), and the phrase itself has a non-military sense in Prov. 16 : 19. Here **spoil** is to be taken in a metaphorical sense, simply as 'reward'. The nature of this reward has already been described in verses 10–11. **he shall divide the spoil:** the word **divide**, indicating the distribution of spoil, is on both occasions in the Piel. But in the second occurrence it is probable that the vowels of the Qal were intended: *yaḥalōḵ*, 'he will receive', rather than *yeḥallēḵ*, 'he will distribute'. (So Driver). **with the great; with the strong:** each of these two adjectives (*raḇ*, *'āṣûm*) can mean either 'many' or 'strong'. Here the latter meaning is intended: the triumph of the Servant and his new strength are contrasted with his former reputation as pitifully weak. The one who had appeared to be crushed beyond hope of recovery will now take his place among the **great** ones (*bārabbîm*) and with the **strong** ones (*'et-'aṣûmîm*) of the world. The choice of metaphor is probably an indication of the fact that the author saw in the triumph of the Servant an anticipation of the coming triumph of the Jewish exiles as a whole. (The fact that the word *rabbîm* later in this verse and also in verse 11 means not 'great' but 'many' does not constitute an objection to the above interpretation: double meanings of this kind are characteristic of Deutero-Isaiah himself, and it is not surprising to find the same trait in the work of one of his close associates.)

because: what follows may be a continuation of the divine oracle, but is more probably a final comment by the earlier speakers. **he poured out his soul to death:** better, 'he exposed his life to (danger of) death'; or perhaps, following D. W. Thomas' interpretation of *lammāweṯ* (see on **stricken** in verse 8), simply 'to the uttermost'. **was numbered:** perhaps better, 'allowed himself to be numbered' (Niphal tolerativum). **he bore the sin of many** (*ḥēṭ'-rabbîm nāśā'*)**:** see on **and he shall bear their iniquities**

in verse 11. Like other expressions in verses 4, 6, 11, this phrase has frequently been interpreted as referring to the Servant's suffering and/or death as vicariously borne for the sake of others. Yet the phrase 'bear sin' (*nāśā' ḥēṭ'*), which occurs almost exclusively in the laws of Exodus and Leviticus, always refers to a person's responsibility for his own sin, and is never used in connexion with atoning sacrifice. Here it means that the Servant shared with others a penalty which was appropriate for them but not for him.

It may be noted here that several phrases in this chapter—**he has borne our griefs and carried our sorrows** (verse 4); **and the LORD has laid on him the iniquity of us all** (verse 6); **and he shall bear their iniquities** (verse 11); **and he bore the sin of many** (verse 12)—have been discussed by some commentators as if they were identical in meaning with another phrase, *nāśā' 'āwôn*, 'bear guilt' or 'bear punishment', which does not occur in this chapter. But even if we can assume that the phrases are virtually interchangeable, *nāśā' 'āwôn* does not in fact refer to vicarious punishment or suffering. In the four passages from the laws (Exod. 28 : 38; Lev. 10 : 17; 16 : 22; Num. 18 : 1) which have been cited as proof of this meaning, the subject of the verb 'bear' is not involved in suffering at all. Rather these passages express a belief that certain ritual actions neutralize or take away a punishment which would otherwise fall on the people. They have nothing in common with the idea of one person's suffering instead of another. Further, in Ezek. 4 : 4–6, where the prophet Ezekiel 'bears the punishment' of the house of Israel, his suffering is in no sense a vicarious punishment: on the contrary, it is a sign of the punishment which the people are themselves called upon to bear. The roles of Deutero-Isaiah and Ezekiel are here similar in the sense that both share the suffering of the people rather than suffering in their stead.

and made intercession (*yapgîa'*) **for the transgressors:** in verse 6 this verb is used in the sense of 'cause to suffer'; but here it means 'plead for, intercede', as in Jer. 15 : 11. Both passages illustrate the prophetic role of intercession with God on behalf of the people.

FUTURE EXPANSION AND PROSPERITY

54 : 1–10

This passage resembles 49 : 14–23 in theme and also to some extent in form. Zion is addressed, though not specifically named; and the reassurances about her future prosperity which are made are Yahweh's answer to her specific lamentations, which underlie the whole passage, although they are not expressed directly. Zion has cast herself in the role of a barren woman and of a forsaken wife (verse 1); she laments that she has been humiliated and put to shame (verse 4); and that Yahweh has forsaken and forgotten her (verse 6; cf. 49 : 14). The reply to these complaints has basically the form of a promise of salvation, although other forms have also been used. The poem may originally have ended with verse 8: verses 9–10 introduce a slightly different theme, although one not entirely unconnected with what precedes.

1. The exhortation to **Sing** is characteristic of the hymn of praise (cf. 44 : 23; 49 : 13; 52 : 9). **into singing:** some commentators wish to omit this word (*rinnāh*) as superfluous to the metre. It is not strictly necessary to the sense. Yahweh's answer to Zion's complaint of barrenness takes the same form as in 49 : 19–23. The paradox of the last half of the verse may have been taken by Deutero-Isaiah from a stock of hymnic motifs: cf. 1 Sam. 2 : 5; Ps. 113 : 9.

2. As in 49 : 19–20 the promise is given that the returning exiles will be so numerous that there will hardly be room for them. This is first expressed in the form of a command to Zion, now pictured in the role of wife and mother in a family of tent-dwellers, to enlarge the family **tent**. New sections (**curtains**) must be added, and the ropes (**cords**) lengthened and the tent-pegs (**stakes**) strengthened to support the more ponderous structure. All this was women's work. The nomad's tent was a complex affair with many compartments. **let . . . be stretched out:** the Heb. has *yaṭṭû*, literally 'let them stretch out'. Possibly either the passive *yuṭṭû*, 'let . . . be stretched out' or the fem. imperative *haṭṭî*, 'stretch out', may have been the original reading.

3. The fem. forms show that Zion is still being addressed, but the promise is now put into plain language. **you will spread abroad:** the same verb is used in Gen. 28 : 14, where Yahweh promises the land of Canaan to Jacob. This promise was probably in Deutero-Isaiah's mind: the return from exile was to be the definitive fulfilment of Yahweh's promise of the land to the patriarchs. **to the right and to the left:** it is not certain whether this means 'to the north and to the south', or simply 'in all directions'. **will possess the nations:** better, 'will dispossess (drive out) the nations'. Some commentators hold that this is a promise of a future imperial rule by Israel of the nations beyond the borders of Palestine: a revival of the old Davidic empire; but this is improbable: the phrase 'dispossess the nations' (*yāraš (hag)gôyîm*), which occurs elsewhere only in Deuteronomy, always refers to the conquest of Canaan itself by Israel, in the course of which they will drive out the 'nations' or peoples formerly in possession of that land. It should also be noted that the phrase here is parallel with **people the desolate cities**, which certainly refers only to the cities of Palestine itself.

4. Yahweh now announces the end of Israel's humiliation, still under the figure of Zion as a woman who feels that her troubles are due to her abandonment by her husband. **Fear not:** see on 41 : 10. **the shame of your youth:** this probably refers not to Israel's bondage in Egypt in days gone by, but to more recent events such as Israel's oppression by Assyria during the period of the monarchy. **the reproach of your widowhood:** this clearly refers to the present, that is, to the Babylonian exile. The form *'almenûṭayiḵ* (**widowhood**) is slightly anomalous.

5. The reason is now given why Zion need no longer feel shame. **your Maker is your husband:** better, 'your husband is your Maker'. The point in both parts of the verse is that the husband whose absence Zion laments is not absent through any coercion which has been placed on him: he is **the Holy One of Israel** and **the God of the whole earth**. It therefore cannot be that he is *unable* to come and rescue his wife. (In verses 6–8 the further point is made that he is not only able, but also *willing* to do so.) **your Maker:** compare the similar statements in 43 : 1, 15. **your husband:** MT has *bō'alayiḵ*, 'he who marries you'. Possibly *be'ālayiḵ*, 'your husband', was intended ('plur. of excellence', G–K §124k). The following word (*'ōśayiḵ*) has what appears to be a plur. form also, but this is probably not so (G–K §93ss). In this and the following verse Yahweh refers to himself in the third person.

6. The precise nuances of this verse are elusive. Perhaps *ke* (**like**) should be regarded as the so-called *kaph veritatis* (G–K

§118x): 'called you who were truly a wife forsaken'. *kî* (**when**) should perhaps be given the sense of 'although': Yahweh regards Zion as if she were a fresh young bride (**wife of youth**), although in fact she had already been 'married' to him and subsequently separated from him. **has called you** would then be a promise (the 'prophetic perfect') that Yahweh would now recall Zion once more to himself.

7. Yahweh now replies to Zion's complaint that Yahweh has forsaken her. As in 50 : 1 he does not deny that the Exile constituted a separation from him, but he emphasizes that this separation was not only not permanent, but even insignificant in comparison with the immensity of the love with which he will take her back.

8. for a moment (*beše̢ṣep̱*): the word *šeṣep̱*, which was no doubt chosen for reasons of alliteration (*bešeṣep̱ ḳeṣep̱*), occurs only here in the *OT*, and its meaning is unknown. But this is no reason for omitting or emending it. North's suggestion that it may be related to the verb *šaṣap*, 'to cut, slash' in rabbinic Hebrew may be right: a meaning such as 'a fragment of time' would fit the context, and is perhaps supported by Aquila's 'in an atom of time'. The idea that God's wrath is only momentary is found in Ps. 30 : 5 (MT 30 : 6) in an individual thanksgiving, and may therefore have been part of the liturgical stock on which Deutero-Isaiah was able to draw.

9–10. In these verses Yahweh seeks to assure his people that his promises may be relied upon.

9. Yahweh reminds his listeners of the promise which he made to **Noah** (Gen. 8 : 21; 9 : 1) after the Flood, and now swears a similar oath (the second *nišbaʿtî* should be translated by 'I swear' rather than by **I have sworn**). The two situations were indeed analogous: fears of the repetition of a terrible disaster allayed by a divine promise. Deutero-Isaiah was evidently familiar with the patriarchal traditions, though not necessarily in exactly the form in which they now appear in Genesis (where nothing is said specifically about an oath), and used them in an extremely effective way: cf. his use of the Abraham traditions in 41 : 8; 51 : 2. **this** (*zōʾṯ*): that is, 'the present situation'. **like the days of Noah:** Heb. has 'For this is the waters of Noah (*kî-mê nōaḥ*)'. *RSV* follows a widely accepted emendation to *kîmê*, 'like the days'.

10. It may be the thought of the disappearance of the mountains beneath the waters of the Flood (Gen. 7 : 19–20) which inspired the prophet to make this second comparison: the story of Noah shows that God protects those who enjoy his favour even when the mountains, usually regarded in the *OT* as symbols of strength and permanence, disappear. But the thought itself is independent of the comparison with the Flood, and is found also in 51 : 6. Although the verse is not eschatological in the sense of envisaging a period of eternal blessing after the end of the world, it expresses a view of divine transcendence which goes beyond earlier *OT* theology. **For:** perhaps better, 'Although'. **my covenant of peace** (*b*e*rîṯ š*e*lômî*)**:** the story of Noah is still in the prophet's mind. In Genesis the earlier reference to Yahweh's promise to Noah after the Flood (Gen. 8 : 22, J) becomes in the later version (P) an 'everlasting covenant' (Gen. 9 : 8–17). Here Deutero-Isaiah is close to the Priestly writer, and uses his 'covenant theology' in his affirmation about the new era which is about to begin. Yet again God will make an eternal **covenant**, this time guaranteeing not merely the survival of mankind but his eternal favour towards his own people. The basis of the covenant is his **steadfast love** (*ḥeseḏ*) or faithfulness to his promises. Deutero-Isaiah's near-contemporary Ezekiel also prophesies a 'covenant of peace' (Ezek. 37 : 26); cf. also Jeremiah's 'new covenant' (Jer. 31 : 31). The word *šālôm* (**peace**) has a much more positive meaning in Hebrew than its counterpart in English, and signifies well-being of every kind.

THE NEW JERUSALEM

54 : 11–17

Some commentators have suggested that these verses comprise two originally independent pieces, but the lack of agreement about the extent of these shows that a division of this kind can hardly be made. The passage deals with two closely related themes: the glory of the new Jerusalem which is to be built, and its protection by Yahweh from all harm. The first line of verse 14 (**In righteousness you shall be established**) appears to mark the point of transition from the first theme to the second. Yahweh is the speaker throughout, and he addresses Zion as the devastated city which is to be built more glorious than before. At the same time the image of Zion as the forsaken wife who is to be restored to her former dignity and beauty underlies some of the language used. The passage has some of the characteristics of the promise of salvation, but, as Westermann has pointed out, the last part (verses 14–17) has the form of the divine blessing, a form which lays stress not merely on the imminent act of salvation itself but on the permanent quality of life which will be conferred on God's people by his constant protection.

11–12. This description of the dazzling beauty of the new Jerusalem may to some extent have been inspired by the idea that even the beauty and luxury of Nebuchadnezzar's Babylon, now doomed, would be outshone by that of the city which Yahweh would build for his people. It is also possible that the motif of precious stones may be connected with a Paradise myth like that preserved in Ezek. 28, especially verse 13. In some sense what is promised here is Paradise Regained. The theme of the New Jerusalem was taken up in later literature, especially Tob. 13: 16–18; Rev. 21: 19–21. It should be noted that Deutero-Isaiah here makes no mention of a rebuilt Temple: his thought is entirely concentrated on the renewed community itself.

11. O afflicted one: the same phrase is found in 51: 21, where it is preceded by 'Therefore hear this'. Some such introductory phrase may have originally stood here also. **not comforted:** once more the oracle of salvation takes up the exiles' own words of complaint: cf. Lam. 1: 16; 2: 13. **antimony:** in 2 Kg. 9: 30; Jer. 4: 30 this word (*pūḵ*) means a kind of powder used by women for darkening the appearance of their eyes, and it may have been chosen here to suggest, together with the mention of jewels in verse 12, the image of Zion as a splendidly groomed woman; but in 1 Chr. 29: 2 it seems to be a kind of mortar for setting stones in a mosaic pattern, and this is probably the primary meaning here. **sapphires:** probably the semi-precious *lapis lazuli*, as suggested by *RSV* mg.

12. agate; **carbuncles:** these two stones cannot be identified with certainty. Both words suggest a reddish or fiery colour.

13. taught: this probably refers to the skills required for the building of the city, which Yahweh will supply as needed, rather than to some deeper or more religious kind of knowledge. It has been suggested that the first line of verse 14 originally followed **the LORD**. This would provide a better parallelism in both verses. **your sons** (second occurrence): it is unusual for the same word (here *bānayik*) to occur in both parts of a parallel couplet. In 1QIs[a] the word has been corrected on its second occurrence to *bwnyky*, i.e. *bônayik*, 'your builders', and this is probably correct. Deutero-Isaiah is again playing on the sound of words: Zion's **sons** and her builders are in fact the same people.

14. In righteousness: Zion (Jerusalem) seems to have been traditionally known as the 'city of righteousness' (cf. 1 : 26). Elsewhere in Deutero-Isaiah this word (*ṣᵉdāḳāh*) is equated with salvation, and this meaning is certainly intended here, as it stands in parallelism with *šālôm* (**prosperity**) in verse 13. But a moral sense is probably also included. **you shall be established** (*tikkônānî*): on the form see G–K §54c. **you shall be far from:** in Heb. the word is imperative (*raḥᵃḳî*). The effect of this imperative is to emphasize the force of the divine promise (cf. G–K §110c), and no emendation is necessary. **for it shall not come near you:** cf. the similar divine promise in Ps. 91 : 9–16 (MT 10–17).

15. The Heb. of this verse is difficult, but the wholesale emendation proposed by *BHS* is hardly justified. **stirs up strife:** the verb in both occurrences is *gûr*, which is not otherwise attested in this sense. It may be an alternative form of *gārāh*, which can have this sense in the Piel. **not:** one of the functions of *'epes* is to indicate a negative: cf. Isa. 5 : 8, *'ad 'epes māḳôm*, 'until there is no place'. **from me:** *mē'ôṯî* is found elsewhere as a variant of *mē'ittî*, and no emendation is necessary. **because of you** (*'ālayik*): this is probably a better translation than 'upon you'. Attacks on Zion will fail because she is what she is, a city under God's protection. The meaning of the verse is therefore that Yahweh promises that he will never again incite enemies to pick a quarrel with Jerusalem; and consequently any attempts to do so are bound to fail.

16–17a. These verses explain the reason why no attack on Zion can succeed. Both the smiths who forge weapons of war and the warriors who use them are Yahweh's creatures and therefore under his control. Since he will never permit them to attack his people, Jerusalem will always remain secure.

16. Behold: Kethib has *hēn*; Qere and 1QIs[a] *hinnēh*. The meaning is the same. **for its purpose:** this is a better translation of *lᵉma'ᵃśēhû* than 'for his (the smith's) purpose'. Each type of weapon has its own purpose. **the ravager** (*mašḥîṯ*): the word is simply descriptive of the function of the warrior, and does not necessarily refer specifically to the Babylonians or to any other of Israel's former enemies.

17. and you shall confute . . . judgment: the power of the **tongue**, here used in making false accusations, was considered to be as great as that of the sword, and Yahweh also promises protection against this. **in judgment:** better, 'in court' (to be taken metaphorically). The last part of the verse (from **This is the heritage . . .**) rounds off the whole poem. **heritage** (*naḥ^a^lāh*), originally the land given by Yahweh to his people, probably means no more here than 'free gift' (cf. Ps. 127 : 3), though the idea that Yahweh is now about to repeat his gift of the land of Palestine to the returning exiles may lie in the background. **the servants of the LORD:** the use of this word in the plur. to designate Israel is characteristic of Isa. 56–66, and may perhaps indicate that the author here is not Deutero-Isaiah. **vindication** (*ṣ^e^ḏāḳāh*)**:** or, 'deliverance, salvation'.

THE EVERLASTING COVENANT

55 : 1–5

Here Yahweh addresses his people, urging them to detach themselves from their involvement with the daily life of Babylon and to accept the promise which he gives them of true satisfaction in their own land, when they will once more take their place, under his protection, as a prosperous and imperial nation, as in the days of David.

1. The form of the address is unique in Deutero-Isaiah. It has been compared on the one hand with the invitation made by Wisdom to passers-by to enter her house and partake of the 'banquet of life' (Prov. 9 : 1–6) (Begrich) and on the other with the cry of the water-seller, familiar in the Near East (Volz). The phraseology suggests that the prophet may have had both these models in mind. In any case the point of the metaphor lies in the paradoxical theme expressed in the words **buy** and **without money**. Volz suggested the possibility that the prophet may have been thinking of the action of a rich man who, in time of famine, buys up all the food available and then generously offers it to the people free. The lesson is that Yahweh requires no payment for the grace which he offers.

There is some repetition here. **come** (literally, 'go': *l^{e}k̲û*) occurs three times; **buy** twice; **no** (**without**) **money** twice. It has been argued that such repetitions are natural in the speech of a street vendor (Westermann); but the metre is overloaded, and it is perhaps best to accept the reading of 1QIs^{a}, which is partly supported by some of the Versions, and omit **and eat! Come, buy**.

2. Here the metaphor is continued, and some hint is now given of the nature of what Yahweh has to offer. The **what is good** and the **fatness** (i.e. rich food) are not entirely metaphorical: Yahweh's promise to Israel includes material gifts; but the verses which follow make it clear that these are symbolic of further gifts. A more difficult problem is the meaning of **that which is not bread** and **that which does not satisfy**. It can hardly mean material things as opposed to spiritual ones, since this modern contrast would have no meaning for the ancient Israelite. The 'good life' included both, and Yahweh is in fact offering both. It is more probable that the reference is to the exiles' preoccupation with the everyday concerns of life in Babylon, to which they have become accustomed. Such a life, lived away from the holy city and among unclean people (52 : 1) can never offer true satisfaction.

3. The metaphor is now dropped, and Yahweh explains what he is offering in plain language. **that your soul may live:** the Christian concept of the **soul** was unknown to the ancient Israelites. The word so translated here (*nep̄eš*) means either a living being, life, or the 'self'. But it is frequently used, as here, in place of the personal pronoun to add a note of emotion or of intensity to the verb. Thus Deutero-Isaiah could have said 'that *you* may live'; but the addition of *nap̄š^{e}k̲em* intensifies the thought: 'that you may have the very fullness of life'. The quality of this life is then expressed in terms of **an everlasting covenant** (*b^{e}rît̲ ʿôlām*; cf. 54 : 10), and further defined by God as **my steadfast, sure love for David** (*ḥas^{e}d̲ē dāwîd̲ hanne'^{e}mānîm*). **steadfast . . . love** (*ḥesed̲*) is faithfulness to a covenant (see again 54 : 10); but here it is in the plur., referring to the many acts of faithfulness which God performed for David in protecting him and giving him victory and success. The phrases **everlasting covenant** and **my steadfast, sure love for David** both recall God's promises to David and his line in 2 Sam. 7 : 8–16; 23 : 5;

1 Kg. 8 : 23–26; Ps. 89 : 27–37 (MT 28–38). But these verses contain no promise of the restoration of the Davidic monarchy in the person of one of David's descendants; rather what is stated here is that the covenant promises, originally made to David as the leader of the nation, are now to be transferred directly to the whole people. Deutero-Isaiah thus differs from that other line of exilic and post-exilic prophecy which looked forward to a 'new David'.

4–5. Behold . . . Behold (*hēn . . . hēn*)**:** the repetition of this word serves to draw attention to the similarities, and also to the differences, between the past glories of the time of David and the age which is about to dawn. What was once given to the individual David will now be given to the people as a whole.

4. In speaking of David as **a leader** (*nāgîḏ*) **and commander for the peoples**, Deutero-Isaiah is simply drawing upon the historical tradition of David's imperial power. But nowhere else in the *OT* is he spoken of as **a witness to the peoples** (*'ēḏ le'ûmmîm*). However, the idea that his conquest of other nations constituted a witness to them of the power of Yahweh is found in Ps. 18 : 43–50 (MT 44–51), and also, with regard to other periods in Israel's history, elsewhere in the *OT* (e.g. Exod. 15 : 14–16; Jos. 2 : 9–11). Deutero-Isaiah uses the word **witness** (*'ēḏ*) of Israel in 43 : 10, 12; 44 : 8. In the phrase **witness to the peoples** some commentators have proposed the emendation of *le'ûmmîm*, **the peoples**, to *le'ammîm*, on the grounds that the repetition of the same word is improbable in parallel couplets.

5. you shall call: although the verb is in the sing., it is Israel which is addressed. As in the days of David, other **nations** (*gôy*, sing., stands for plur.) will be Israel's servants, and will **run** to him when he summons them. There is no reason to suppose that this domination is purely spiritual: as elsewhere, Deutero-Isaiah envisages political domination by Israel. **because . . . glorified you:** this line is very similar to 49 : 7*b*.

YAHWEH'S IRRESISTIBLE WORD

55 : 6–13

This passage stands here as an epilogue to the book of Deutero-Isaiah. Like the prologue (40 : 1–8) it has the effect of summarizing his message, so that the rest of the book is enclosed between passages which set the tone for the whole. It is not entirely clear whether this was originally a single poem, or whether verses 12–13 are to be distinguished from what precedes. But in its present form the passage possesses a logical structure. In anticipation of the imminent appearance of Yahweh to save his people, the prophet urgently calls upon them to prepare themselves by repentance (verses 6–7). Then, in order to persuade the doubters, he supports his assertion of imminent salvation by means of two arguments: those who object that they see no signs of a reversal of Israel's fortunes are reminded that God 'moves in a mysterious way, his wonders to perform' (verses 8–9); and those who doubt God's power or the credentials of his prophet are silenced by a solemn divine assurance that it is his Word to which they are listening, and that nothing can prevent its effective operation (verses 10–11). Finally the promise of salvation is set out in specific terms (verses 12–13). An oracle of Yahweh (verses 8–11) has been enclosed within the prophet's own words of assurance to his people.

6. Seek the LORD: in pre-exilic times this was a technical expression for the sacrificial worship of Yahweh or his consultation through an oracle; but already in Amos it had acquired a more spiritual or moral sense (Am. 5 : 4, 6; cf. Am. 5 : 14). In the literature of the exilic period it is made clear that Yahweh can be sought, and is to be found, through prayer by those Israelites who seek to do his will, and that, when appealed to in this way, he will restore their fortunes (Dt. 4 : 29; Jer. 29 : 12–14). What Deutero-Isaiah is saying here is that the appropriate moment has arrived (cf. 49 : 8): now is the time when **he may be found**, when **he is near:** he is about to manifest his redemptive power to those who genuinely seek him.

7. Some commentators (e.g. Duhm, Westermann) regard this verse as an interpolation by a pious reader, on the grounds that it seems to set conditions for the operation of God's grace. But it is rather to be seen as a call to the exiles to prepare themselves through personal repentance for the awesome approach of the holy God. See especially on this verse and on the whole passage H.-G. Troadec, 'La parole vivante et efficace', *Bible et Vie Chrétienne* 11 (1955), pp. 57–67.

8–9. The point of the contrast between the **thoughts** and **ways** of God and of his human servants is that the inability of the latter to imagine, from their knowledge of earthly events and circumstances, that divine salvation is at hand is entirely irrelevant to the truth of the divine message. The events of history are set in motion by Yahweh, whose **thoughts** (better, 'intentions, purposes') and modes of operation are entirely concealed from human observation. Apparent lack of external evidence is therefore no reason to doubt the truth of the prophetic message.

9. For as the heavens are higher: MT has the perfect tense and nothing corresponding to **as** (*kî-gāḇ*ᵉ*hû*). We should probably accept the reading presupposed by LXX (*kig*ᵉ*ḇōah*), or possibly that of 1QIsᵃ (*k*ᵉ*gōḇah*, 'according to the height of . . .').

10–11. The reliability of the prophetic **word** is further demonstrated by a comparison with another of God's gifts, of the **rain** and **snow**. Neither the idea of the fertilizing activity of the rain as sent by God, nor that of his sending his creative word on the earth (cf. Gen. 1) was new; but it was the achievement of Deutero-Isaiah to link the two and so to make the most profound statement about God's word to be found in the *OT* (cf. also 40 : 8). What God has spoken cannot fail to achieve its purpose.

10. but water the earth: probably better, 'without watering the earth'. Similarly in verse 11 it seems to be implied that Yahweh's **word** *does* return to him, but it does not return *empty*: that is, it achieves its purpose first, and then returns to him who has spoken it. So also in Job 36 : 26–29 it would seem that the rain returns to heaven. This idea seems to have been dimly perceived by the ancient Israelites, even though the mechanism of evaporation was probably unknown to them.

11. goes forth (*yēṣē'*)**:** some commentators prefer to point this word as the perfect *yāṣā'*, 'has gone forth'.

12–13. The prophecy ends as it begins (40 : 3–5) with a promise of the return of the exiles to their own land.

12. That nature rejoices at the presence of Yahweh is part of the tradition preserved in the Psalms (e.g. Ps. 96 : 12–13; 98 : 8). See on 44 : 23. Nature is now to join in rejoicing at the triumphant revelation of Yahweh's glory (cf. 40 : 5) as he leads his people home.

13. In this final verse, with which we may compare 41 : 19, the theme of nature's rejoicing is carried still further. Here we have a transformation of nature which reverses the curse upon nature pronounced in Gen. 3 : 18: Israel's return home will be

'Paradise Regained'. **cypress** and **myrtle** are among the trees listed in 41 : 19. The precise identity of the **thorn** (*naʿaṣûṣ*, which occurs elsewhere only in Isa. 7 : 19) and the **brier** (*sirpaḏ*, which occurs only here) is uncertain, though the context gives a general indication of their nature. In the final lines the promise is backed by a further assurance: the miraculous fertility of the desert region through which the exiles are to travel will not be a merely temporary phenomenon: the region will be preserved in that state for ever as a kind of 'national park', as a reminder (**memorial:** *šēm*, literally, 'name'; **everlasting sign:** *'ôṯ ʿôlām*) not only to Israel but also to Yahweh himself, of the promise which he has made. The idea is similar to that of the establishment of the rainbow in Gen. 9: 8–17 (P), where some of the same terminology is used: there **sign** (*'ôṯ*) and 'everlasting covenant' (*berîṯ ʿôlām*, verse 16), correspond to Deutero-Isaiah's *'ôṯ ʿôlām*, and the phrase **shall not be cut off** (*lō' yikkārēṯ*), which in Deutero-Isaiah refers to the permanence of the sign, is used in Gen. 9 : 11 of the recipients of the promise. The prophecy ends on a note of firm confidence which epitomizes Deutero-Isaiah's whole message.

CHAPTERS 56–66

THE TRUE PEOPLE OF GOD

56 : 1–8

The tone of this passage is strikingly different from that of chapters 40–55. Nowhere in those chapters do we find attention given to particular problems arising within the Jewish community as we do here. Moreover the character of these problems—questions concerning the admissibility of certain classes of person into the religious community—presupposes a different historical situation. Groups of exiles have now returned to Palestine, and regular worship has been re-instituted. The Temple has been rebuilt, or at least its rebuilding is projected. The date of the passage therefore, at least in its present form, can hardly be much earlier than 520 BC.

Other considerations make it clear that this is not the work of Deutero-Isaiah. In fact, its uneven literary character suggests that it was not composed by a single hand but has undergone expansion, perhaps more than once. (See especially D. Michel, 'Zur Eigenart Tritojesajas', *Theologia Viatorum* 10 (1966), pp. 220–225.) This view is confirmed rather than weakened by the fact that genuine oracles of Deutero-Isaiah are twice quoted, or at least clearly alluded to (verse 1*b*; cf. 46 : 13, and verse 5*b*; cf. 55 : 13). As will be shown below, these words of Deutero-Isaiah are here used in quite a new sense. Such re-interpretation of the message of Deutero-Isaiah is characteristic of chapters 56–66. It has even been suggested (by Michel) that the author(s) of these chapters already regarded the oracles of Deutero-Isaiah as a 'canonical' sacred text which must be re-interpreted to fit a new situation.

1. Thus says the LORD: the messenger-formula, repeated in verse 4, suggests that the whole passage is a divine oracle. Yet this is clearly not so: there is a constant oscillation between the first and third persons in reference to Yahweh. In this verse re-interpretation of Deutero-Isaiah is evident. The second half (from **for soon**) is virtually a quotation from Deutero-Isaiah (cf. especially 46 : 13). But his characteristic word *ṣᵉḏāḳāh*, **deliverance**, occurs also in the first half, where it has a quite different meaning: **righteousness**. By punning on the ethical and soteriological senses of the word the author has contrived to imply that **salvation**

is to be achieved through the perfecting of human behaviour within the Jewish community. The Deutero-Isaianic note of expectancy of an imminent divine act of deliverance has been lost. **Keep justice** (*šimᵉrû mišpāṭ*); **do righteousness** (*ʿᵃśû ṣᵉḏāḵāh*): the phraseology perhaps suggests that the author is thinking of obedience to a codified Law.

2. This verse sets out the meaning of the admonition in verse 1*a* in specific terms. **this** and **it** have both a backward and a forward reference. **Blessed** (*'ašᵉrê*): this formulaic beginning perhaps indicates a second hand, expanding the preceding oracle. *'ašᵉrê* is not, as some writers have asserted, a word primarily associated with the wisdom literature. **who keeps the sabbath:** the author regards this as epitomizing righteousness. Although the observance of the sabbath was an ancient custom in Israel, it was only from the time of the Exile that it acquired this cardinal importance as a distinguishing mark of the Jew (Ezek. 20 : 12, 20; 22 : 8, 26). It is, however, never mentioned in the oracles of Deutero-Isaiah. That one can speak of **profaning it** shows that it had now come to be regarded as belonging to the category of the 'holy', with which men tampered at their peril. **doing any evil:** the strange pairing of such a general reference to moral conduct with sabbath-keeping is a further indication of the crucial importance of the latter.

3–7. Here the prophet gives a divinely dictated decision or *tōrāh* on the admissibility of certain classes of person to full status within the religious community. The *tōrāh* provides a clarification of the meaning of **the man** and **the son of man** in verse 2, and may have been added subsequently. The attitude adopted is liberal and clearly intended as a riposte to those whose who adopted a rigorist view.

3. Here words of comfort are addressed to two classes of person. **the foreigner who has joined himself to the LORD** (reading the participle *nilweh* for MT *nilwāh*) is the individual convert to Judaism known in later times as the proselyte. Deutero-Isaiah had envisaged and approved such a phenomenon (44 : 5); but now, probably in the early years after the Return, this newly acquired status is being threatened by Jewish rigorists (cf. Ezr. 4 : 1–3). This situation should not be confused with the later rigorism of Ezra and Nehemiah, which was directed against the association of Jews with unconverted pagans (so Volz). For a position between the two extremes see Dt. 23 : 3–8. The position of the Jewish **eunuch**—probably the man who had accepted this condition on entering Babylonian or Persian official employment such as that of Nehemiah or Daniel—was somewhat different. Dt. 23 : 1 specifically excludes such persons from admission into the religious assembly; but that does not appear to be the issue here. What the eunuch complains of is that his lack of posterity puts him at a disadvantage in that his name will die with him (cf. verse 5). In a time when a belief in personal resurrection or immortality was not yet part of the Jewish faith great importance was attached to the continuance of the family name through pious descendants, and the lack of it was regarded as a kind of personal extinction tantamount to exclusion from divine blessing.

4–5. The case of the eunuch is taken first. The three conditions of his full acceptance by God really amount to two: both **choose the things that please me** and **hold fast my covenant** probably refer to the keeping of God's laws prescribed in the Mosaic covenant. In verse 5 **my house** and **my walls** refer to the Temple buildings. The **monument** (*yāḏ*) and the **name** are to be interpreted literally. The phrase is a hendiadys: 'a memorial stele', such as was set up by the childless Absalom (2 Sam. 18 : 18). The decision that eunuchs were to be permitted to erect such monuments in the Temple or its precincts (for such a custom see Y. Yadin, *Hazor* (Schweich Lectures, 1970), 1972, pp. 71–4) would ensure the continued memory of their names even **better than sons and daughters. them:** this reading of 1QIs[a] is preferable to MT's 'him'. **an everlasting name . . . cut off:** probably a reminiscence of 55 : 13*b*.

6–7. These verses pick up verse 3*a* and assure the proselytes that any attempt to exclude them from full religious status with native-born Jews is contrary to the will of God. The same pattern is followed as in the case of the eunuchs: first the conditions and then the promise.

6. Since the proselytes, unlike the eunuchs, are converts, the conditions of their acceptance are laid down more comprehensively. The qualification of circumcision seems to be taken for granted or to be included in the phrase **who join themselves to the LORD**. The next three phrases are apparently of a general character indicating a total readiness to put oneself at the disposal of Yahweh.

7. Here it is emphatically stated that the status of proselytes is to be exactly the same as that of native-born Jews, including the right to present acceptable **sacrifices** to Yahweh at the Temple. **I will bring:** this phrase perhaps suggests that the prophet is thinking mainly of proselytes living outside Palestine who make pilgrimages to the Temple. **in my house of prayer** (*b^{e}ḇêṯ t^{e}p̄illāṯî*)**; a house of prayer for all peoples:** the thought of the Temple as a place where God answered prayer is expressed most fully by the Deuteronomic Historian in Solomon's prayer at the dedication of the first Temple (1 Kg. 8 : 27–53), and there also it is stated that God will hear the prayer of 'a foreigner, who is not of thy people Israel, who comes from a far country for thy name's sake' (verses 41–43). This is the sense in which **all peoples** is to be interpreted here. **will be accepted:** these words are not directly represented in MT. Torrey's suggestion that *ya'^{a}lû,* literally '(they) shall go up', which occurs in a similar phrase in 60 : 7, has fallen out is now supported by 1QIs^{a}.

8. This verse, though not inappropriate as a summing up of the preceding passage, may have originally been a separate oracle. It is not clear whether it is a promise that the numbers of the Palestine community will be increased by further Jewish arrivals (cf. the post-exilic Isa. 11 : 12), or whether it refers to non-Jewish converts.

UNWORTHY LEADERS AND IDOLATERS

56 : 9–57 : 13

There is no agreement among the commentators about either the literary unity or the date(s) of this section. The harshness of its tone throughout and its similarity to pre-exilic prophecy has suggested to some that it is pre-exilic, and this view has been defended recently by Westermann, who regards it as 'a short, self-contained collection of prophetic oracles of doom dating from the pre-exilic era' which a post-exilic editor found applicable to his own times. Such a view requires more positive evidence to support it than its advocates have produced. There is nothing here which compels a pre-exilic date: the sins condemned are not exclusively characteristic of any one period, and there is no proof that such unrelieved prophecies of disaster cannot have been pronounced after the Exile.

Two distinct groups of people are the object of the prophet's attack, the leaders of the community (56 : 10–12) and idolaters (57 : 3–13*a*). The short, almost certainly corrupt passage (57 : 1–2) which separates the two denunciations is not closely linked to either. The message itself contains nothing which either suggests or precludes unity of authorship. Since Fohrer's view that the whole forms a 'prophetic liturgy' suffers from the difficulty that the form and function of such a composition have never been defined, nor indeed its existence proved, it may perhaps best be regarded as either two or three independent compositions.

9–12. This is a prophetic oracle condemning a group of men referred to as **watchmen** (verse 10; glossed in verse 11 as **shepherds**). Elsewhere in the *OT* the word 'watchman' (*ṣōp̱eh*) when used metaphorically and in a specific sense always designates prophets (Jer. 6 : 17; Ezek. 3 : 17; 33 : 2–7) as set over the people to warn them of God's imminent wrath; however, such a function might be attributed to other religious leaders such as priests, or even to political leaders. We cannot therefore say more than that this is a condemnation of leaders of the community. They are accused of incompetence, laziness, greed, self-indulgence, and complacency. Similar accusations occur elsewhere in post-exilic literature: Malachi (*passim*); Nehemiah (5: 7–12, 15–16).

9. The announcement of divine punishment precedes the description of the offence. Because of the failure of the watchmen to do their duty it is to fall on the whole community. The speaker —perhaps Yahweh himself—grimly calls upon the **beasts of the field** and of **the forest** to devour the unprotected population. The metaphor and language strongly resemble Jer. 12 : 9*b*, although Duhm is hardly justified in calling the verse a 'slavish imitation' of that passage. The **beasts** are probably a generalized symbol of the divine anger and have no more specific reference.

10. His watchmen: this is the reading of Qere, and it is supported by 1QIs[a]. But **His** has no antecedent. The suggestion that the original text may have had '*my* watchmen', with Yahweh as the speaker, may be correct. **they are . . . without knowledge:** literally, 'they do not know'. The phrase (*lō' yāḏᵉʿû*) occurs twice more in the oracle (**they never have . . .**; **have no . . .**, verse 11), but on both occasions followed by a further word. It has been suggested that here also we should read 'have no understanding', following LXX (but see also on verse 11). **dogs:** the word suggests both that the **watchmen** are contemptible and that they are incompetent: they are 'watchdogs' who are both **blind** and unable to **bark**. **dreaming:** this word (*hōzîm*) occurs only here. Cheyne suggested that it is a pun on *ḥōzîm*, 'seers'.

11. The shepherds also have no understanding: literally, 'and those are (the) shepherds; they cannot understand'. The first half of the line reads like a gloss identifying **watchmen** or **dogs** with **shepherds** (*rō'îm*), a word regularly used in the sense of 'rulers'. If this is so, the second half is metrically redundant. It is possibly the misplaced original of the line **they are . . . without knowledge** in verse 10. **one and all:** some commentators propose the deletion or emendation of this word (*miḳḳāṣēhû*); but it makes perfectly good sense.

12. The prophet here quotes or adapts a senseless drinking-song. **let us get wine:** the Heb. has 'let *me* get wine'. The verse is missing from LXX, but there is no reason to doubt that it is original. The culminating sin of these men is their complacency.

57 : 1–2. It is impossible to make sense of these verses as they stand. Only verse 1*a* (to **understands**) is free of difficulties. The statement, repeated in parallelism, that the **righteous man** (*haṣṣaddîk*) and the **devout men** (*'an*ᵉ*šê-ḥese*ḏ) disappear with no one to mourn their fate, may be a commonplace of the lamentation of the pious man (cf. Ps. 12 : 1 (MT 12 : 2); Mic. 7 : 2) added at the end of 56 : 9–12 as a general comment on the situation described, though it is just possible that it is the original conclusion of that oracle. It has been asserted that these are technical expressions denoting a particular religious party rather than general terms expressing fidelity to God's moral requirements; but this is by no means certain.

The remainder of these verses (**For the righteous man . . . their uprightness**) appears to be both unconnected with what precedes and also lacking in inner unity. One of the difficulties is grammatical: **they rest in their beds** refers to a number of persons, while the remainder refers only to one (Heb. has the singular 'who walks in his uprightness' in the last line of verse 2). There are also ambiguities: in verse 1 **For** (*kî*) could also be translated by 'that'; **from calamity** might equally be rendered by 'because of evil'. It is generally agreed, however, that in verse 2 **peace** and **beds** refer to death. The word **peace** would seem to imply that the final state of the righteous man (whether here or hereafter) will be pleasant. However these phrases are interpreted they hardly seem to form a logical continuation of verse 1*a*. It may be best, with Odeberg, to regard everything from **For** in verse 1 as 'a series of glosses'.

3–13. This passage has every appearance of being a single composition. Yahweh summons the idolaters to appear before him for judgment. The forms of heathen worship described here correspond in general to the Canaanite practices condemned by pre-exilic prophets, but this is no reason to suppose that the oracle is itself pre-exilic: we may suppose that those who remained in Palestine during the Babylonian exile continued in their own ways, and that their post-exilic descendants still continued to do so for some time after the first return of the Jewish exiles in 538 BC. It has therefore been argued that this is a condemnation of these people by the orthodox Jews, who had purified their religious beliefs in exile. Certainly the idolaters are contrasted with those who are faithful to Yahweh (verse 13*b*); but we cannot be certain that the religious differences were drawn so sharply between the immigrants and the native inhabitants in the early years after the return from exile. This is not a dispute about different understandings of Yahweh's requirements like 56 : 1–8, but an attack on heathenism, or rather on syncretism: these people evidently claim to worship Yahweh as well as other gods; otherwise there would be no point in the prophet's attack.

3–4. The idolaters are summoned and rebuked in general terms.

3. draw near hither: the summons is reminiscent of the trial speeches in Deutero-Isaiah. **sons of; offspring of:** the meaning is not that they are held responsible for their parentage. The phrases are not to be taken literally, but are used to indicate the characteristics of these people themselves: cf. 1 : 4, 'offspring of evildoers'. **sons of the sorceress:** the accusation of sorcery or magic is to be taken literally: cf. Isa. 2 : 6; Mic. 5 : 12 (MT 5 : 11); Jer. 27 : 9. **the adulterer:** this word is masc. in the Heb., and it is unnecessary to emend it to fem.: according to the metaphor, their father was an **adulterer** and their mother a **harlot** (cf. Ezek. 16 : 45). Adultery and harlotry stand for the worship of Canaanite or other deities with sexual overtones, as in the pre-exilic prophets. **the harlot:** reading *wᵉzōnāh* for MT's *wattizneh*, following a number of Versions.

4. The purpose of these questions may be compared with that of similar questions in 37: 23. As Sennacherib's mockery of his victims is there castigated as amounting to mockery of Yahweh, the Lord of history, so also here: the idolaters have mocked and made rude gestures of contempt to the faithful followers of Yahweh; but in doing so they have committed blasphemy against Yahweh himself. **deceit:** this word (*šeḳer*), often translated 'lie', is the opposite of *'emet*, 'truth'. It is a favourite word of Jeremiah, who also uses it in some passages with reference to idolatry. See T. W. Overholt, *The Threat of Falsehood*, 1970.

5–10. The idolatrous practices are now described in detail.

5. This verse is probably not the continuation of the second question in verse 4 but the beginning of a new sentence addressed to the idolaters. Two distinct practices are referred to: sexual fertility-rites and child sacrifice. Both are condemned by the pre-exilic prophets, especially Jeremiah and Ezekiel. **oaks** (*'ēlîm*): this is an unusual spelling. It is possible that the word means 'the Els', i.e. the Canaanite gods. **under every green tree:** this is a stereotyped expression used in connexion with these rites, especially by Jeremiah. **who slay your children in the valleys:** child sacrifice is known to have been practised by the Canaanites. In pre-exilic Israel it does not appear before the time of Ahab, and was resorted to only rarely, in times of crisis; but under Ahaz and Manasseh it may have been widely practised, particularly in the valley of Hinnom (e.g. Jer. 7: 31). It was suppressed by Josiah (2 Kg. 23: 10). Its revival thereafter may have been due to the crisis of faith caused by the terrible sufferings of the Jewish population which remained in Palestine during the Exile. It was offered to Baal and to Molech (see on verse 9). **under the clefts of the rocks:** nothing is known about the reason for the choice of such places for sacrifices. It is unnecessary to emend **under** (*taḥaṯ*) to 'among' (*beṯōḵ*). The meaning is perfectly clear.

6. The idolaters are told that their apostasy is unforgivable. **smooth stones:** the Heb. word simply means 'smooth (ones)'. That these were stones is a conjecture based on the fact that large smooth boulders are a characteristic feature of this kind of valley (*naḥal*)—the torrent-valley or *wadi*. But although worship might be offered in connexion with tall standing stones (e.g. Gen. 28: 18), there is no evidence that such smooth stones were ever used in this connexion. A variety of other interpretations has been offered (e.g. serpents, 'slippery' or deceitful gods, stone images) but the reference remains obscure, though some kind of pagan rite is clearly intended. However, the prophet certainly chose the word (*ḥalleḳê*) because of its close resemblance to the word translated by **your portion** (*ḥelḳēḵ*). The jingle emphasizes the fatefulness of the choice made by the idolaters. Both **portion** (*ḥēleḳ*) and **lot** (*gôrāl*) combine the ideas of choice and its consequences: as these men have chosen, so will be their fate. It should be noted that from this point onwards the idolaters are addressed in the fem. sing. Since idolatry is spoken of under the figure of sexual licence, the idolatrous community is addressed collectively under the figure of a woman, as in other similar prophetic oracles. **to them:** M. Weise (*ZAW* 72 (1960), pp. 25–32) has plausibly argued that this refers not to the 'smooth (stones)' but to the false gods of verse 5*a*. **drink offering** (*neseḵ*); **cereal offering** (*minḥāh*)**:** these were not in themselves forbidden: they were used in the legitimate cult of Yahweh. The sin lies in their being offered to false gods. **Shall I be appeased for these things?:** there is nothing inappropriate in this interjection, as some commentators have supposed; nor is anything to be gained by transferring this line to a position after verse 7 (*BHS*).

7. The prophet now turns to idolatrous cults practised on mountains, which were regarded as particularly propitious locations for offering sacrifice, whether legitimate or illegitimate (cf. Jerusalem and other well-known Israelite sanctuaries). The use of the word **bed** indicates that it is once again cults with sexual aspects that he has in mind: cf. the very similar use of the word in Ezek. 23 : 17, in a passage which is reminiscent of this passage also in other ways.

8. The reference to **door** and **doorpost** has led most commentators to see this verse as referring to yet another form of idolatrous worship practised privately at home. **your symbol:** the word (*zikkārôn*) normally means 'memorial', 'reminder', and can be applied, as in Jos. 4 : 7, to objects which remind the believing Israelites of Yahweh's actions on their behalf. Here therefore it may refer to a pagan cult-symbol displayed in the house of the worshipper. An alternative explanation of *zikkārôn* here is that it may be connected with the word *zāḵār*, 'male', and refer to an image of the male sexual organ. Such objects were not unknown in the ancient Near East, and there may be a reference to them in

Ezek. 16 : 17 in the phrase *ṣalᵉmê zāḵār*. **you have uncovered** (*gillîṯ*)**:** in MT this is the first of three verbs whose object is **your bed**. However, this leaves unexplained the word which *RSV* translates by **deserting me** (*mē'ittî*, literally 'from me'). It has therefore been suggested, on the basis of one MS and some of the Versions, that *gillîṯ* should be pointed as *gālîṯ*. The phrase *gālîṯ mē'ittî* could then be rendered as 'you have departed from me'. Duhm, on the other hand, suggests the emendation of *mē'ittî* to *mē'ittô*, 'in consequence of it', i.e. of the above-mentioned **symbol**. **and you have made a bargain:** Heb. *wattiḵroṯ*, literally 'and you have cut', though the masc. form is surprising: we should expect the fem. *RSV* takes the word as the equivalent of *wattiḵroṯ bᵉrîṯ*, 'and you made a covenant', with the omission of *bᵉrîṯ*, an abbreviated form attested elsewhere. But this translation is rendered doubtful by *mēhem*, for which *RSV*'s **with them** is hardly a possible translation. For this reason Duhm, followed by a number of commentators, suggests emendation to *wattiḵrî*, 'and you bought', i.e. 'and you bribed', from *kārāh*. *mēhem* would then mean 'some of them'. The idea that Israel, in distinction from other harlots, gave gifts to her (male) lovers (i.e. made gifts to pagan deities) rather than receiving gifts from them is also found in Ezek. 16 : 30–34. But the emendation is no more than a guess. **nakedness:** the Heb. has *yāḏ*, which normally means 'hand'. But there is reason to suppose that here the word is a euphemism for the male sexual organ (M. Delcor, *JSS* 12 (1967), pp. 230–40). (Cf. on **symbol** above.) **you have looked on** (*ḥāzîṯ*)**:** the word can also mean 'look on with satisfaction' or 'experience'.

9. This verse appears to describe the attempts of the 'harlot' to attract lovers to herself. But the meaning of the first line is very uncertain. **You journeyed to Molech with oil:** MT has *lammeleḵ*, 'to the king'. The older view that this refers to an actual embassy to a foreign king is very unlikely, and *RSV* follows a number of commentators in repointing the word as *mōleḵ*, or in regarding *meleḵ* as an alternative (and probably more original) form of the name of this god. Duhm suggested that the god in question was the Ammonite god Milcom, but there was a Canaanite god *mlk* who is perhaps more likely to be referred to here. However, the *RSV* translation is not very satisfactory: *baššemen* can hardly mean **with oil** in this sense of 'with'. It has been suggested by P. Wernberg-Møller (*VT* 8 (1958), pp. 307f.;

see also G. R. Driver, in *Studies in Old Testament Prophecy*, 1950, pp. 58f.) that **You journeyed** (*wattāšūrî*) should be repointed as a form of a verb cognate with Arab. *ṯarra*, giving 'You lavished oil on Melek'. LXX and the spelling of 1QIs[a] give some colour to this proposal. *BHS* goes further and repoints *lammelek̠* as *l*[e]*mallēk̠* or *l*[e]*millēk̠* with the meaning 'to your hair', rendering the whole phrase by 'you drenched your hair with oil'. This provides a parallel for the following line, though both these interpretations are based on speculative additions to the vocabulary of biblical Hebrew. **perfumes:** perhaps better, 'ointments'. **you sent your envoys:** similarly in Ezek. 23 : 16, 40, the woman Oholibah, a figure standing for pre-exilic Judah, is represented as sending messengers to the Babylonians for the same purpose of obtaining 'lovers'. **even to Sheol:** that is, to the god of the underworld: here necromancy is suggested (cf. 1 Sam. 28 : 11–14).

10. This verse describes the pertinacity with which the idolaters continued to practise their rites in spite of their inefficacity. It perhaps reflects the disappointments of the early post-exilic years. **your way:** this probably refers to the entire conduct of the idolaters described in verses 5–9. **you found new life for your strength:** this is a difficult phrase. Heb. has 'you found life for your hand'. This has generally been interpreted in the manner of *RSV*; but some commentators have been unable to accept this as a possible translation, and have emended *ḥayyaṯ yāḏēk̠* to *dê ḥayyāṯēk̠*, rendering the phrase by 'you found a sufficient livelihood for yourself'.

11–13. The note of divine judgment already adumbrated in the last line of verse 6 is now sounded clearly, although it is somewhat more muted than in the pre-exilic prophets.

11. This verse is transitional in function: Yahweh, who has been thrust into the background by the idolaters and regarded by them as irrelevant because he has not made any protest against their behaviour, now breaks his silence and prepares to pronounce their fate. **Whom did you dread and fear . . .?** may mean either that they have exhibited a senseless and dangerous bravado or that they feared their false gods instead of the true God. The use of the word **dread** (*dā'ag:* 'be anxious, concerned') suggests that the former is the correct interpretation. **you lied:** that is, 'you were unfaithful (to me)'. The word is used somewhat similarly in 58 : 11 of a spring of water which 'fails' those who rely on it.

remember me: the word **me** is emphatic. **did not give me a thought: me** is not expressed in the Heb. of MT. 1QIs[a] has 'you did not give a thought to these things' (adding *'ēlleh*). The arguments in favour of the two readings are very evenly balanced. **Have I not . . .?:** the meaning is 'Is it not because . . .?'. The precise interpretation of Yahweh's silence depends on the date of the oracle. But it is clear that the Jerusalem community must have been passing through a period when no prophetic voice had been raised against contemporary idolatrous practices. **even for a long time:** Heb. has 'and for a long time' (*ūmēʿōlām*). LXX and other Versions may have read this word as *maʿlīm*, which means something like 'hiding myself'; but this departure from MT, though accepted by many commentators, does not seem to be really necessary. This is probably a conscious adaptation of part of 42 : 14.

12. I will tell of your righteousness: the intention is clearly ironical. We must presume that the idolaters combined their idolatrous practices with assiduous performance of the outward forms of the worship of Yahweh (on **righteousness** see on 56 : 1), and so claimed to possess righteousness, and consequently the right to call on him for help. Such syncretism was, however, a 'lie', and tantamount to total abandonment of Yahweh (verse 5). Yahweh warns them that it will not help them when the crisis comes.

13. Equally useless will be their attempts to **cry out** in an appeal to their idols, who are unable to help them. The thought of the helplessness of idols may have been taken from Deutero-Isaiah, who uses it in the context of the polemic against the Babylonian gods. Here it has been put to a different use. **your collection of idols** (*ḳibbûṣayiḵ*): the word *ḳibbûs* (from the root *ḳbṣ*, 'gather') occurs only here. The words **of idols** do not occur in the Heb. Torrey's suggestion that the word was originally *mᵉḳabbᵉṣayiḵ*, 'those who gather you (in their arms)', with a reference to such passages of Deutero-Isaiah as 46 : 3–7, and that this was deliberately changed to *ḳibbûṣayiḵ* on the analogy of *šiḳḳûṣ*, 'abomination', by the Massoretic editors has some plausibility. In any case the word is intended to express contempt. In the last two lines (**But he who takes refuge in me . . . my holy mountain**) the prophet suddenly takes leave of the idolaters and refers, in the third person, to the blessing which is reserved for those who trust

Yahweh. The idea of taking refuge (*ḥāsāh*) in Yahweh is found predominantly in the cultic tradition of the Psalms. Although the style of these lines is different from what precedes, and they may indeed be a quotation perhaps taken from a psalm (Westermann) or perhaps adapted from a wisdom saying (cf. Prov. 2 : 21; 30 : 5), there is no sufficient reason for regarding them as a later interpolation. Their presence here shows that there is an element of appeal in the denunciation: there is still time for the idolaters to abandon their idolatry and join the ranks of Yahweh's true worshippers. **shall possess the land:** Yahweh, always seen in the *OT* as the giver of the land of Israel to his people, makes this promise to those who trust him. As applied to individuals this promise became in post-exilic Judaism something of a fixed formula of promise meaning little more than 'live to enjoy fully the good land' (e.g. Ps. 37 : 9); but here it may refer to the future of the nation: the time will come when the righteous Jews will once again enjoy full possession of the land as an independent people: cf. 60 : 21; 65 : 9. **my holy mountain:** although this phrase meant primarily the mountain of Zion where the Temple stood (as it does in 56 : 7), its meaning later became extended to the whole of Palestine, or even to the whole earth (cf. Isa. 11 : 9). Here the context suggests that it may mean the land of Palestine, although this is not certain.

COMFORT FOR THE HUMBLE

57 : 14–21

This passage is basically a promise of salvation similar to those of Deutero-Isaiah (see on 41 : 17–20) and, like them, it clearly refers to the words of a corporate lamentation to which it is a reply (cf. verses 16*a*, 17*a* with, e.g., Ps. 44 : 23–24 (MT 24–25); 74 : 1; 79 : 5; Lam. 5 : 20, 22). But it is equally clear that it is not the work of Deutero-Isaiah but rather of one who consciously stands in his tradition while facing an entirely different situation. It begins with a command to **build up . . . the way** which is a conscious adaptation of 40 : 3, and the remainder of the oracle is an interpretation of that 'text'. The passage provides no clear indication of date. It is apparently addressed to the whole community in Palestine after the Return. The mention of **the wicked** in verses 20–21, which is characteristic of post-exilic prophecy, shows that, as in the previous passage, apostasy within the community was prevalent. The main problem, however, was God's apparent failure even now to forgive his people for their past sins and to restore his favour to them. The point of the oracle is that the time for this has now come; and the earlier words of Deutero-Isaiah are cited as prophecy which is now, belatedly, to be fulfilled.

14. And it shall be said (*wᵉʾāmar*): literally, 'and someone will say'. The consonants could equally well be read as 'and I shall say' (so Vulg.) or as 'and I said'. Most commentators dismiss the word as a connecting link added when the oracles were arranged in their present order. 1QIsᵃ has 'and he (or, "someone") said'. If it was intended to represent a third person verb, the word may have been an introductory formula introducing the 'text' (although it is not an exact quotation) from Deutero-Isaiah. The **way** which is to be prepared is no longer, as in Deutero-Isaiah, to be understood as a road built to convey the returning exiles from Babylon to Palestine, nor is the prophet thinking of the gathering of the Jews from Dispersion: there is no reference in the passage to a physical journey. The key to the verse is given by the word **obstruction** (*miḵšôl*), elsewhere translated in *RSV* by 'stumbling block'. This word is most frequently used in the *OT* not in a literal sense but, especially in Ezekiel, of sin (especially idolatry) or guilt leading to divine punishment. The command to **remove every obstruction** expresses God's insistence that the sinful elements in the community must be purged, since he is determined not to delay any more in bringing relief to those who are faithful to him. Unfortunately no indication is given of the identity of those addressed.

15. The interpretation of the former oracle of Deutero-Isaiah is presented as a new oracle. The style of this, too, is reminiscent of the style of Deutero-Isaiah: the messenger-formula is expanded with epithets which already foreshadow the message which is to follow. The purpose of the oracle is to overcome the despondency of those who, though still hoping that God would intervene on their behalf, tended to attribute his failure to do so to his awe-inspiring transcendence which set him apart from such insignificant creatures as themselves. The point made here is of considerable theological importance. **the high and lofty One** (*rām wᵉniśśāʾ*: this phrase, taken from Isa. 6 : 1, already reminds those familiar with it in its original context of God's readiness to help his servants. **who inhabits eternity** (*šōḵēn ʿaḏ*): better, 'who abides for ever'. **the high and holy place** (*mārôm wᵉḳāḏôš*): we should perhaps read *mārôm wᵉḳōḏeš*. The meaning is unaffected. *mārôm* (literally, 'on high'), does not refer to any particular place but expresses Yahweh's transcendence. **him who is of a contrite and humble spirit** (*dakkāʾ ûšᵉp̄al-rûaḥ*): *RSV* suggests the idea of repentance; but two other passages where these or similar phrases occur (Ps. 34 : 18 (MT 19); Prov. 29 : 23) make it probable that what is meant is rather the humble attitude towards God which comes from acceptance of adversity. The same is true of **the contrite** (*niḏkāʾîm*). God offers new hope to such persons.

16. contend: i.e. 'punish'. **for from me . . . breath of life:** the meaning of these lines is far from clear. The main problem is the meaning of *yaʿᵃṭôp̄* (*RSV* **proceeds**). The usual meaning of *ʿāṭap̄* is 'to be weak': hence the older EVV have 'for the spirit should fail before me, and the souls (Heb. has the plur. *nᵉšāmôṯ*) which I have made' or the like, suggesting what would be the consequence if God did not withdraw his anger. The rendering of *RSV* is based on LXX, Vulg., Syr., together with a somewhat dubious analogy from the use of the root in Syriac.

17–18. God now justifies his past anger and promises that he will turn and bless his people even though its sin remains unrepented. This is the 'obstruction' of verse 14. The sin of one group within the community has hitherto tainted the whole, so that it can be referred to in verse 17 as a single guilty person (**he**) deserving of wrath. In this re-interpretation of verse 14 the task of 'removing every obstruction' will now be performed by Yahweh himself out of his love: he will save *despite* the continued existence of the sin. The thought is similar to that of Deutero-Isaiah in 54 : 7–8, which may have been in the prophet's mind.

17. Because of the iniquity of his covetousness (*baʿᵃwōn biṣʿô*): since the mention of **covetousness** (also found, however, in 56 : 11) has seemed inappropriate to such a general reference to Israel's sin, some commentators have proposed to transfer **his** from the second to the first word (giving *baʿᵃwōnô ḇeṣaʿ*) and to translate *beṣaʿ* by 'for a little while': 'For a little while I was angry'. This would also increase the similarity to 54 : 7–8. But it is doubtful whether *beṣaʿ* can have this meaning, and the supposed support of the LXX here is dubious. In fact *beṣaʿ*, which is frequently associated with violence and even with murder (Jer. 22 : 17), and in Ps. 119 : 36 appears to denote the opposite of obedience to God, is not as inappropriate as has been thought. **I smote him:** *RSV*'s repointing of this verb as a past tense is required by the sense. **and was angry:** here the infinitive absolute *ḳāṣôp̄* is probably to be preferred to MT's *we'eḳṣōp̄*.

18. I will lead him (*we'anḥēhû*): LXX and Targ. suggest the reading *wa'anīḥēhû*, 'I will give him rest', which may be correct. **creating for his mourners the fruit of the lips:** in Heb. the whole of this phrase except for **his mourners** belongs to verse 19; but the whole phrase clearly belongs together. It is a difficult phrase, and is lacking in LXX. If original it is probably an oblique way of saying that those who now mourn will from henceforth have songs of praise on their lips.

19. Peace (*šālôm*): for the meaning see on 54 : 10. The word is repeated for emphasis. **to the far and to the near:** not in the spiritual sense of Eph. 2 : 13, but in a physical sense: the Jews in Jerusalem and the Jews scattered throughout the world. **and I will heal him:** this may be an intrusion from verse 18, where the same word occurs in a slightly different form. It may have originally been a variant reading which has strayed from its original position.

20. Some commentators regard this verse as a later comment. But the passage would hardly be complete without it. It is **the wicked** who are the 'obstruction' of verse 14. Yahweh's love for his people has overcome this, but clearly this does not mean that the sinful element itself is to share in his blessing. Indeed, the verse suggests that they cannot do so by their own nature.

21. See on 48 : 22, which is almost identical with this verse. Although it fits the context here better than in 48 : 22, its repetitiveness and the rather incongruous **my God** suggest that it is a gloss added by a reader, which was then slightly adapted and inserted into 48 : 22.

GOD'S TRUE SERVICE

58 : 1–14

It has long been recognized that in spite of its apparent unity of thought this passage shows clear signs of composite authorship. The most thorough investigation of it is that of D. Michel, who sees verses 1–3*a*, 5–9*a* as the original kernel of the passage. This is a prophetic reply to a lamentation on the part of Jews who are disappointed that their pious observance of the customary fast-days seems to have gone unheeded by God, who still withholds his blessing from them. The prophet replies that God does not desire such fasts, and gives a new definition of the word 'fast', in which he specifies conduct acceptable to God which alone will move him to answer their cry. Within this section verses 3*b*–4 are an interpolation which entirely misses the original point. Verses 9*b*–12, which repeat the contents of verses 6–9*a* in different words, seem to be a further addition whose purpose is somewhat different. Finally verses 13–14, in a somewhat different mood and concerned with the sabbath rather than with fasting, are a further expansion. It is difficult to assign a date to any part of this chapter. The conditional promise in verse 12 that **ancient ruins** will be **rebuilt** and ancient **foundations** raised up does, however, suggest a time fairly soon after the Return in 538 BC, and this is perhaps confirmed by the mood reflected in verse 3*a*.

1. The oracle begins with a call from God to a prophet to denounce the people for **their sins** in the manner of pre-exilic prophecy. **like a trumpet** recalls Hos. 8 : 1, and the second half of the verse (from **declare to my people**) is almost identical with Mic. 3 : 8*b*. But the verses which follow are far milder in tone than the denunciations of a Hosea or a Micah, so much so that some interpreters (e.g. Volz, Morgenstern) have thought of the passage as a sermon or instruction to a pious synagogue congregation. This abrupt change of tone, which leaves the command of verse 1 unfulfilled, is probably to be explained by regarding the verse as a quotation or 'text' from earlier prophecy designed to shock the hearers out of their complacency. The situation appears to be quite different from the denunciations found in such passages as 57 : 1–13.

2. There is no reason to take this verse as ironical in intention. The derogatory **as if they were** of *RSV* is simply 'like' in Heb. The picture is that of a people which sincerely seeks to know and to do God's will. They are entirely unaware that their conduct is displeasing to God. **seek me daily**; **know my ways:** they are scrupulous in their efforts to learn God's will through the oracles of priests and prophets. There is nothing to indicate that they limit their concerns to matters of outward ceremonial. **righteous-**

ness (*ṣᵉḏāḳāh*); **ordinance** (*mišpāṭ*): probably in the same sense as in 56 : 1. **righteous judgments** (*mišpᵉṭê-ṣeḏeḳ*): that is, decisions on matters connected with their communal or personal life. **draw near to God:** that is, for worship; whether sacrificial or not is not stated.

3a. The main subject of the oracle, fasting, is now introduced in the form of a quotation from a lamentation which was probably made on one of the regular fast-days observed by the Jews since the destruction of Jerusalem in 587 BC. The practice of public fasting, formerly reserved for times of national calamity (e.g. Jer. 36 : 9; Jl 1 : 14; 2 : 12, 15) became at that time a regular item in the liturgical calendar (Zech. 7 : 1ff.; 8 : 19), an occasion when the whole community besought God for the restoration of his blessing. The people's lamentation here reflects their disappointment with the incompleteness of their restoration: they are living once more in their own land, but the fullness of the expected blessing has not been realized, and they demand to know why God has not accepted their fasting and prayer. It was the function of the prophet to answer them. **humbled ourselves:** this phrase is used frequently in the laws of Leviticus and Numbers as a synonym for fasting.

3b–4. Here, beginning with **Behold** in verse 3, we have what at first appears to be the prophetic reply to the questions of verse 3*a*. But as we read on it becomes clear that another, quite different reply is given in verses 5–7, and that it is the latter which gives the better sense. Verses 3*b*–4 implicitly make an accusation of gross insincerity and hypocrisy against those who observe the fast which is not in any way suggested either by the preceding or by the subsequent verses. It is clear that the original oracle has been expanded to make it fit a quite different and much more serious situation—another example of the use of the words and authority of earlier prophecy as a basis for the proclamation of a new message. **Behold** (twice): better, 'if' or 'when'. The last two lines of verse 4 (from **Fasting like yours**) then form the main clause of a conditional sentence.

3b. you seek your own pleasure: Heb. has 'find', not **seek. pleasure:** it is not certain whether this word (*ḥēp̱eṣ*) means 'pleasure' or 'business': that is, whether the phrase means 'you do what you like' or 'you pursue your own affairs'. The cessation of all normal pursuits was not the primary characteristic of the observance of fasts as in the case of the sabbath; but a fast-day was intended to be spent in gatherings for prayer and worship which ought not to have left time for thinking about or practising either business or pleasure. Utter devotion to God was its keynote (cf. Jl 2 : 15–16). **all your workers** (*ʿaṣṣeḇêḵem*)**:** the word *ʿāṣēḇ* or *ʿaṣṣāḇ*, 'toiler', from the same root as *ʿeṣeḇ*, 'pain, toil', occurs only here (on the form see G–K §20h), but it is unnecessary to emend it in imitation of some of the Versions to *ʿōḇeṭêhem*, 'debtors' and to translate *tingōśû* (**oppress**) as 'press' or 'demand repayment from' on the dubious analogy of Dt. 15 : 2–3.

4. Behold, you fast only to quarrel and to fight and to hit: better, 'If your fasting leads to quarrelling' etc. The meaning can hardly be that quarrelling is actually these people's aim when they fast, or even that it is its direct result. The meaning is rather that they have ignored the true intention of the fast-day and have pursued their own secular activities, not even refraining from wicked behaviour which would be wrong at any time. **Fasting like yours:** better, 'then your fasting . . .'

5–7. These verses are the continuation of the oracle broken off at verse 3*a*. **humble himself** picks up the similar phrase in that verse. Here there is no accusation of insincerity or hypocrisy, but rather a radical questioning of the practice of fasting as a way of pleasing God which is reminiscent of some of the words of pre-exilic prophets about sacrifice (e.g. Isa. 1 : 12–17; Am. 5 : 21–25; Mic. 6 : 6–8), although the tone is much less harsh. The passage is somewhat similar to Zech. 7 : 1–14, which may be an indication of a relatively early post-exilic date. The prophet, speaking in Yahweh's name, seeks to answer the people's questions (expressed in verse 3*a*) by asserting that they have misunderstood what is and what is not **acceptable to the LORD** (verse 5). The old concept of fasting as a way of drawing God's attention to one's plight is inadequate because it is negative and selfish, concentrating on self rather than on others. We are probably to see verse 6 not as a condemnation of the traditional practices in themselves, but as a warning against the danger of regarding them as a substitute for compassion and kindness towards the poor and unfortunate, which are much closer to Yahweh's heart.

5. choose: better, 'require' or 'prefer'. The phrases which follow refer to mourning ceremonies which traditionally accompanied fasting: cf., e.g., 2 Sam. 12 : 16; Jl 1 : 13; Jer. 6 : 26.

spread . . . under him (*yaṣṣîaʿ*): the verb signifies the making of a bed or couch.

6. To use the word **fast** in the sense in which it is used in this and the following verse is of course to use it in a sense unrelated to its normal meaning, and amounts to saying that God does not primarily want fasting but something else altogether; though there may be some connexion between the two concepts of his requirements in that the positive acts listed here doubtless also involve some kind of self-sacrifice. It is better to choose a form of self-sacrifice which benefits others than one which has no relevance to society. After **Is not this the fast that I choose?** LXX has 'says the LORD', perhaps rightly. The four actions required by Yahweh are basically one: the rescue of the **oppressed** members of the community from harsh treatment by the powerful and unscrupulous. The expressions are metaphorical and the references general, but the action required positive and particular. The requirement to protect the helpless was not new but was already a feature of Israel's most ancient laws. But social injustice was always present; and here the prophet once again urges the community to get its priorities right. **bonds of wickedness:** better, 'fetters of injustice' (*NEB*).

7. The rescue of the oppressed is to be followed by positive actions: the provision of food, shelter and clothing to those in need of them. Obligations such as these were widely recognized among other peoples of the ancient Near East as well as Israel. In the *OT*, cf. especially Ezek. 18 : 7–8; Job 31 : 13–23. **the homeless poor:** the word translated by **homeless** (*meʳrûḏîm*) appears to be derived from the root *rwd*, denoting wandering or restlessness; but elsewhere (Lam. 1 : 7; 3 : 19) it appears to be an abstract noun rather than an adjective. Here it probably means 'homelessness', but the abstract is used in place of the concrete, so we may translate 'the homeless ones'. The word **poor** (*ʿaniyyîm*) may be a gloss added to explain the meaning of an unusual word. The reference is to persons whose lands and houses have been expropriated in payment of debts, a common occurrence not confined to any one period. **when you see . . . and not to hide yourself:** similar expressions are used in Dt. 22: 1, 3, 4, where deeds of kindness are given the force of law. **your own flesh:** that is, from your own kinsfolk.

8–9a. The promise of blessing to be conferred by God when all these conditions are fulfilled (**Then**) is expressed in somewhat stereotyped terms, some of which are borrowed and adapted from Deutero-Isaiah. It is characteristic of this re-interpretation that the divine promise which in the earlier prophet spoke of specific miraculous events in the near future has here lost its precise contours and has become a rather general promise of well-being.

8. light, parallel with **healing**, has here as elsewhere in Trito-Isaiah (58 : 10; 59 : 9; 60 : 1, 3) the meaning of 'prosperity' or 'state of blessedness'; for its different meaning in Deutero-Isaiah see 49 : 6; 51 : 4. See also on 60 : 1. **healing** (*'arūḵāh*): the literal meaning seems to be the growth of healthy tissue over a healing wound: cf. Jer. 8 : 22. The use of the verb *ṣāmaḥ* (**spring up**) instead of the usual 'grow' (*'ālāh*) is perhaps a reminiscence of 42 : 9; 43 : 19. **your righteousness . . . rear guard:** this is clearly adapted from 52 : 12*b*; but since no journey is involved here the phrases lose their original force. Moreover, the substitution of **your righteousness** (*ṣiḏḳeḵā*) for 'Yahweh' as the subject of the first verb changes the meaning even more: the people's righteous behaviour (specified in verses 6–7) will go to meet Yahweh as a kind of ambassador to plead their cause. He will then protect them with his **glory**.

9a. The original oracle ends with an assurance that from henceforth the people's prayers will no longer go unanswered (cf. verses 2, 3*a*).

9b–12. In spite of the somewhat similar structure there are substantial differences between these verses and verses 5–9*a*. There are no more references to fasting; the proportions of the component parts are quite different; and in verse 12 a specific promise is introduced which has no parallel in the previous section. At the same time, there are substantial parallels in phraseology. These facts suggest that these verses are an addition to the original oracle but modelled upon it.

9b. The tone is harsher than in verses 5–9*a* and not unlike that of verses 3*b*–4. The nature of the sins specified here as hindering the coming of God's blessing is not entirely clear, but the view that they are all examples of malicious behaviour is plausible. **yoke** (*môṭāh*), if correct, is a metaphor for social oppression as in verse 6; but the line is then somewhat unsatisfactory; and the original reading was perhaps *muṭṭeh*, a rare word which may denote some kind of dishonest practice. **the pointing of the finger** (cf. a similar expression in Prov. 6 : 13) has been interpreted as a maleficent gesture intended to bring misfortune on others by magical means; but more probably it signifies the making of a legal accusation. See C. Hauret, *Revue de Science Religieuse* 35 (1961), pp. 369–77. **wickedness** (*'āwen*) may also have the more specific sense of malicious speech.

10. The first half of this verse corresponds to verse 7 and the second to verse 8*a*. **pour yourself out:** a rather dubious translation. It is probably best to read *laḥmeḵā*, 'your bread' for *napšeḵā*, with some MSS, and to translate 'bestow your food upon the hungry'. **desire:** better, 'appetite'. **then shall your light rise in the darkness:** see on verse 8 above and on 60 : 1.

11. good things: the derivation and meaning of this word (*ṣaḥṣāḥôṯ*) are obscure, and the commentaries and translations are divided. Some, deriving it from the root *ṣḥḥ*, take it as denoting the circumstances in which the blessing will be given: e.g. *NEB*, 'in the shimmering heat'. Others, including *RSV*, explain it by an Arabic root *ṣaḥ*, 'good, healthful'. **and make your bones strong:** emendation is unnecessary here. Although this is the only occurrence of the Hiphil of *ḥlṣ*, the idea of strength seems to be included within the range of meanings of this verb. The similes of the **watered garden** and the perennial **spring** standing for prosperity are a commonplace of Semitic poetical speech.

12. This verse presupposes a situation in which the people returned from exile have not yet found time, energy or resources to rebuild their towns. To interpret the phrases **ancient ruins** and **foundations of many generations** as necessarily or exclusively referring to the walls of Jerusalem or to the Temple is to go beyond the evidence. A general rebuilding activity, repairing the ravages caused many years ago by Nebuchadnezzar's troops and by subsequent neglect would be both a vital part of a renewed prosperity and also a heartening outward symbol of it. **ancient** (*'ôlām*); **of many generations** (*dôr wāḏôr*)**:** these phrases refer to the length of time since the buildings were destroyed; but they are not to be taken as indicating a date of authorship long after the return from exile. This is the exaggerated, or vague, language of poetry. **shall be rebuilt:** MT has 'and they shall build'. But this leaves the following word *mimmeḵā*, 'of thee', untranslatable. *RSV* follows some of the Versions which suggest a passive verb

(Pual or Niphal) as the original reading. **streets to dwell in:** it is probably unnecessary to emend **streets** (*n*e*ṯîḇôṯ*) to *n*e*ṯîṣôṯ*, 'ruins' or to understand it as meaning 'what has been torn down' on the analogy of an Accadian word. Although strictly speaking one does not **dwell** in **streets**, streets and roads are essential for the life of a prosperous community. *lāšāḇeṯ* (**to dwell in**) may have a wider reference: 'so that (you) may dwell (in the land)'. On the whole verse see on 61 : 4.

13–14. Although the structure of these verses (**If . . . if . . . then**) is the same as that of verses 9*b*–12 the mood is quite different. It is also difficult to see them as a continuation of verses 1–3*a* + 5–9*a* or of 3*b*–4. The subject is the observance not of fast-days but of the sabbath. It is not suggested as in verses 5–7, 9*b*–10 that the observance of such special days was not in itself pleasing to God, and there is no re-interpretation of their meaning in terms of compassion for the unfortunate; nor on the other hand is there any condemnation of sin as in verses 3*b*–4, 9*b*. The mood, which resembles that of 56 : 2, is rather that of a sabbath sermon than of a prophetical oracle. But the verses are clearly modelled on the previous oracle. It may be significant that in the consonantal Heb. text the final word of verse 12, *lāšāḇeṯ*, to dwell in, could also be read as *laššabbāṯ*, 'on (or "for") the sabbath'.

13. On the importance of the **sabbath** in post-exilic times see on 56 : 2. Here as in Ezekiel (20 : 12, 20), where it is a 'sign' of the covenant between Yahweh and Israel, the sabbath is seen purely as Yahweh's **holy day** which, because he has ordained it, is to be observed as **a delight**, rather than (as in Dt. 5 : 14–15) a day set aside to allow men and animals to rest from their work. This change seems to have taken place during the Exile. **turn back your foot from:** that is, be careful not to trespass on the holiness of the sabbath. **from doing your pleasure:** here *ḥēp̄eṣ*, which also occurs in verse 3*b*, probably means 'business'. Probably read the sing. with 1QIs[b] and some Versions. **and the holy day of the LORD:** Heb. has 'the holy *one* of Yahweh'. This is probably corrupt. Vulg. has 'the holy thing of the Lord'. LXX has a substantially different text from here to the end of the verse.

14. The promise is expressed in a series of conventional or traditional phrases. **then you shall take delight in the LORD:** the verb (*tiṯʿannag*) refers back to the noun **delight** (*ʿōneg*) in verse 13; but the phrase itself occurs in an almost identical form in Job 22 : 26, and in a similar context. A better translation would be: 'then you shall find Yahweh a delight'. **I will make you ride upon the heights of the earth:** this is a quotation, slightly adapted, from Dt. 32 : 13 (the Song of Moses), and the next line, **I will feed you with the heritage of Jacob your father**, is inspired by the second half of that verse ('and he ate the produce of the field') together with verse 9 of the same Song ('Jacob (is) his allotted heritage'). The author is drawing upon well-known phrases and traditions which express divine promises of well-being. As elsewhere in Trito-Isaiah and in contrast with Deutero-Isaiah the expectation of a specific future event appears to be lacking. **I will make; I will feed:** 1QIs^a and some Versions have the third person. In view of the oscillation between first and third person in verse 13 it is impossible to determine which was the original reading. 1QIs^b even has 'I will make . . . he will feed'. **for the mouth of the LORD has spoken:** perhaps a quotation from 40 : 5, although the phrase occurs elsewhere. This concluding phrase gives these verses the appearance, if not the reality, of a prophetic oracle.

ALIENATION FROM GOD

59 : 1–8

Chapter 59 comprises several distinct units. In verses 1–8 a prophet or other spiritual leader addresses the community, defending God against the charge that he is incapable of delivering them from their wretched situation and asserting that the real reason for his failure to come to their help is that they are sunk in sin. In verses 9–15*a* a group of persons make a confession in which they admit that it is their sins which are the cause of their misery. In verses 15*b*–20 once again a prophet or leader speaks, this time giving an assurance to his audience that God has taken pity on his people and is already preparing to intervene on their behalf to destroy their enemies and to redeem those who are faithful to him. In this section there is no reference to the people's sins except for their characterization in verse 20 as **those . . . who turn from transgression**. Otherwise it is implied that they have not deserved their present state of wretchedness. Finally, verse 21, which is in prose, is, as is generally agreed by the commentators, unrelated to the previous verses.

There is in verses 1–20 at first glance a logical progression of ideas: the sinful people are reprimanded, repent, and are restored to God's blessing. Consequently some commentators hold that these verses form a single unit, though they differ with regard to its character: some regard it as a 'prophetical liturgy', others as a sermon. But the differences between the situations presupposed by the three sections, and especially between the first two and the last, are too great to allow such an interpretation. Even if, as may well be the case, verses 5–8 are an interpolation, it is difficult to conceive of a liturgy in which the simple confession of sin in verses 12–13 would be regarded as sufficient to cancel the effect of the extremely grave sins condemned in verses 1–4 and so to open the way for the joyous promise of verses 15*b*–20. Equally great difficulties attend the theory of a sermon incorporating a long quotation from a liturgical prayer. It must be concluded that the chapter does not form a single unit, although an original connexion between the first two parts is possible.

It is probable that some expansion has taken place in verses 1–8. The indictment of the people's sins here changes after verse 3 from an address in the second person to a description in the third person, and there is a further stylistic change at the beginning of verse 5. The verses as they stand now are a hotchpotch of the general and the particular, of the literal and the metaphorical, and there are repetitions. The whole of verses 5–8 (4–8 according to Volz) is probably a rhetorical 'embellishment' added subsequently to a piece which was originally not primarily a condemnation, whether prophetic or sermonic, but a disputation in which the speaker gave reasons for God's apparent inactivity.

1–2. The speaker's intention is clearly to give a reply to complaints about God's inactivity; but it is equally clear that he does so with a passage from Deutero-Isaiah in mind: 50 : 1–3. In verse 1 **the LORD's hand is not shortened, that it cannot save** is a citation from 50 : 2*b*, and in verse 2 the emphasis on **your iniquities** and **your sins** is a reminiscence of 50 : 1*b*. But the way in which the two thoughts are combined is new: another reinterpretation to fit a new situation.

2. his face: Heb. has *pānîm*, '(the) face'. It is unlikely that this is an example of the absolute use of the word as a substitute for a more direct reference to God or of the personification of one of his attributes, as 'Word' and 'Glory', etc. were used in later times.

It is more probable that this is a corruption of *pānāw*, 'his face'.

3. The accusations which begin here and continue to the end of verse 8 are addressed not to a group within the community, as in chapter 57, but to the whole people. However, not all of them are to be taken literally: we have here something of the sermonic style which gathers up all kinds of traditional phrases and themes from the earlier prophets and elsewhere and piles one upon another. **your hands are defiled with blood** is taken almost word for word from 1 : 15, where already it is unlikely that it is to be taken literally as an indictment of murder. Here it is probably used in a very loose sense (so Westermann).

4. This verse also consists mainly of generalities, although the accusations of dishonesty in the lawcourts—a commonplace of the pre-exilic prophets—are perhaps intended literally. Such accusations would find their mark in almost any period. **enters suit justly:** for this use of *ḳārā'*, literally 'call', see Job 5 : 1; 9 : 16; 13 : 22. **empty pleas; lies** (*tōhû; šāw'*)**:** both words signify what is empty or unreal, hence also what is false. **they conceive . . . iniquity:** the phrase is almost identical with Job 15 : 35*a*, and was probably a traditional expression signifying deliberate, planned wickedness. The last four verbs in the verse are infinitive absolute, probably implying that these actions were frequent or habitual.

5–8. These verses deal entirely in generalities at least partly derived from traditional sources. Much of what is said here is elsewhere attributed to the party of the 'ungodly' who are the enemies of the 'righteous'. It is difficult to believe that the whole Jewish community in Palestine was guilty of such great wickedness as is described here. On the other hand such denunciations may well have figured in the kind of rhetorical preaching known in modern times as the 'hell-fire sermon'.

5. The two metaphors of **adders' eggs** and **spider's web** are presumably both intended to illustrate the deliberate, planned wickedness mentioned in verse 4, though only the first is in fact developed along those lines. **adders' eggs:** the common adder or viper found in Europe is viviparous. Since the exact meaning of the Heb. *ṣip̱'ōnî* is unknown, it would be better to translate it by 'serpent'. **he who eats . . . is hatched:** if the *RSV* translation is right the point is that the plots of the wicked catch both the unwary who do not perceive the danger and also those who attempt to crush it. But **one which is crushed** (*hazzûreh*) is doubtful both in meaning and in grammar (masc. where a fem. would be expected), and should perhaps be translated by 'stinking', giving 'the stinking (egg) hatches out (as) a serpent' (P. Wernberg-Møller, *VT* 4 (1954), pp. 322–5). *NEB* (following G. R. Driver) goes further and translates *'ep̱ʿeh* (**viper**) as 'rottenness': 'for rotten eggs hatch only rottenness'.

6. Their webs will not serve as clothing: the point seems to be the futility of the plots of the wicked. But the spider's web is not intended to be used for this purpose. This verse entirely fails to develop the reference to the spider in verse 5, whose web is intended to ensnare the righteous. The remainder of the passage (from **Their works** to the end of verse 8) employs the characteristic terminology of the general descriptions of the wicked to be found in Proverbs, the 'wisdom psalms', and the book of Job.

7. The first half of this verse (to **blood**) is almost identical with Prov. 1 : 16 which is, however, lacking in LXX. The second half may be compared with Prov. 16 : 17.

8. In this verse and verse 7 there are four nouns meaning 'road, path', all of which are used in Proverbs metaphorically, as here, of human conduct. Cf. also Ps. 14, which throughout expresses sentiments similar to those of the present passage. **they have made their roads crooked:** the same verb (*ʿḳš*) is used in Prov. 2 : 15; 10 : 9; 28 : 18 in connexion with the 'road' of the wicked and in contrast to the behaviour of the righteous. **in them:** Heb. has 'in it'. **no one . . . peace:** the virtual repetition of the first line of the verse in the last is not without meaning: those who deny **peace** (*šālôm*, 'happiness, well-being') to others will find that they are themselves deprived of it. Cf. 57 : 21 = 48 : 22.

A CONFESSION OF SIN

59 : 9–15a

This passage, which has been editorially joined to the preceding section by the initial word **Therefore** (*ʿal-kēn*), is basically a corporate confession of sin (verses 12–15*a*) preceded by a description of the present lamentable situation which is the result of this state of sin (verses 9–11). The central point is the general confession (verse 12) which is then elaborated in the verses which follow. It thus contains two characteristic elements of the corporate lamentation found in the Psalms and the book of Lamentations—or at least, of those few corporate lamentations which admit guilt rather than maintaining innocence. But other characteristic elements are lacking: the cry for help, the appeal to God on the basis of the covenant or of his past acts of salvation, the expression of confidence, etc. It appears to be taken for granted that God is able to help and that he refrains from doing so only on account of the people's refusal, up to the present moment, to repent. In this respect the passage adopts the same point of view as verses 1–2, and it is possible that it may have been the people's response to the first section of the chapter in its original, shorter form. There can be little doubt that it is a liturgical piece, perhaps part of a longer liturgical prayer. It might have been used in a variety of historical situations, but the period shortly after the return from exile provides a very appropriate background.

9–11. The lamentation is expressed in general terms and in traditional phraseology much of which has parallels elsewhere. It is a well-rounded composition consisting of a series of metaphors and similes in which the speakers describe their present misery preceded and followed by statements about the lack of divine vindication expressed in similar but not identical terms (verses 9*a*, 11*b*). Taken by themselves these complaints are extremely similar to those made by the Babylonian exiles of a previous generation, to which Deutero-Isaiah had replied with arguments and divine assurances.

9. justice (*mišpāṭ*); **righteousness** (*ṣᵉḏāḳāh*): primarily these two words, together with **salvation** (*yᵉšûʿāh*) in verse 11, denote the divine saving activity, although there may be a double meaning here as in 56 : 1. (See also on verse 14 below.) There is almost certainly an allusion to 46 : 13: the salvation said by Deutero-Isaiah to be about to arrive has still not come. **overtake:** see on 51 : 11. **we look for light . . . gloom:** a traditional way of expressing disappointment: cf. Jer. 14 : 19 *b*; Lam. 4 : 17. **light** and **darkness** were also traditional expressions for happiness and misery respectively.

10. We grope . . . like the blind: the same expression, combined with **at noon** (*baṣṣohᵒrayim*) is found in Dt. 28 : 29 except that there the verb is *mšš*, here *gšš*. The latter verb occurs only here in the *OT*, but is found more frequently both in Hebrew and Aramaic in the rabbinic literature. **among those in full vigour** (*bā'ašmannîm*: the meaning of this word is obscure. It has been taken as an elative form derived from *šmn* 'be fat'; but even if this is so the meaning of the line still remains unclear. Probably the text is corrupt. Proposed emendations of this word or of both this and the following word have produced, among others, the following translations: 'in darkness'; 'groping, reeling'; 'we sit astonished'; 'in the underworld'. There is little to choose between them.

11. we moan and moan like doves: a traditional image of great distress found both elsewhere in the *OT* (Isa. 38: 14; Ezek. 7: 16; Nah. 2: 7) and in Babylonian lamentations. **growl like bears:** this image, probably also traditional, does not occur in any other extant text. **we look . . . far from us:** see on verse 9 above.

12. In this verse, which is a formal confession of sin, the liturgical note is very clear. The expressions used are extremely similar to the wording of Ps. 51: 3 (MT 51: 5), which is an individual lamentation, and Ps. 90: 8, which has the form of a corporate lamentation. A direct literary relationship is, however, improbable: this is simply the language of the cult. **testify against us:** this vivid personification of sins is found also in Jer. 14: 7. **with us:** that is, within our knowledge. **with** is used in this sense also in Job 12: 3; 14: 5.

13–15a. The sins confessed in verse 12 are now described more precisely. Although the passage is stylistically somewhat uneven Volz' opinion that it is a subsequent addition taken from a list of sins drawn up for use in the synagogue is hardly justified.

13. The first three verbs refer to apostasy: not idolatry, but indifference to or contempt for God. **transgressing** (*pāšōa'*) means 'rebellion'; **denying** (*kaḥēš*) 'disavowal' of God. In the second half of the verse the sins mentioned are sins against society. **speaking oppression** is a strange phrase, and **oppression** (*'ōšeḳ*) may be a mistake for *'iḳḳēš*, 'that which is crooked' (the corresponding verb occurs in verse 8). **revolt** (*sārāh*) here refers, as in Dt. 19: 16, where *RSV* translates it by 'wrongdoing', to abandonment of honest behaviour rather than to rebellion against God. **conceiving and uttering:** the pointing of the verbs *hōrô* and *hōgô* is puzzling, and various explanations have been offered of what the Massoretes intended. They should probably be pointed as Qal inf. abs.: *hārô wᵉhāgô*. But 1QIsᵃ omits *hārô*, which may be an addition arising from dittography.

14. Here it is clear that **Justice** (*mišpāṭ*) and **righteousness** (*ṣᵉdāḳāh*) refer to ethical conduct (see on verse 9 above). Together with **truth** and **uprightness** they are personified as righteous men pushed aside and knocked down by those who are intent on wickedness in the city.

15a (up to **a prey**): the connexion of these lines with verse 14 is not entirely smooth, but the difficulty is hardly enough to justify their rejection as a later addition. **makes himself a prey:** the word in Heb. is *mištôlēl*, the Hithpoel participle of *šālal*, 'plunder', and might mean 'is treated as spoil'. But the word is regarded as doubtful by some commentators, and the abrupt introduction of a concrete human figure after a series of personifications of abstractions has also been judged improbable (Duhm). If the text is corrupt, it may be significant that LXX, which differs from Heb. in other respects also, may have read *haśśeḵel*, 'understanding', in place of *mištôlēl*, and the line might then be translated 'and understanding has departed because of evil'. But this is very uncertain.

GOD REDEEMS HIS LOYAL SERVANTS

59 : 15b–21

This section (from **The LORD**) begins abruptly with a description in the perfect tense of an intervention by God to help his people (verses 15*b*–17). This is followed by a promise (imperfect tenses with future meaning) that he will defeat his enemies, inspiring terror and awe among the nations, and redeem those of his people who are loyal to him (verses 18–20). The way in which a number of separate traditional themes have been combined creates the impression of patchwork, and this raises the question whether this was originally a single composition; however there is a certain consistency in the situation presupposed which contrasts sharply with the earlier part of the chapter. Whereas both in verses 1–8 and 9–15*a* the community is regarded, both in condemnation and in its own confession, as a single unit, whose present state of misery is due entirely to its own shortcomings, here we have an intervention of Yahweh to redeem a loyal, or at least repentant (verse 20) group of people from their—and consequently his—enemies who are evidently the cause of their distress. Whether these enemies are external or, as is much more probable, a group of wicked and unrepentant Jews within the community itself, the situation is quite different from that of the preceding verses; and simply to regard this passage as the answer to the confession of verses 9–15*a* and so as part of a larger liturgical whole (so e.g. Jones, Muilenburg, Westermann) is to ignore this fact. This passage is clearly in intention a promise of salvation, but not the one which verses 9–15*a* would have led us to expect.

15b–16. The abrupt announcement, expressed in verbs in the perfect tense, of Yahweh's intervention to save his people immediately following a corporate lamentation has been compared with Jl. 2 : 18. There is certainly a superficial similarity between the two passages; but to deduce from this that this transition is to be explained in terms of a liturgical sequence is not justifiable since there is no consensus of opinion regarding the structure and function of the book of Joel beyond the universal recognition that it contains much liturgical material. More to the point is the similarity to Isa. 63 : 5. Here the points of comparison, especially of vocabulary and syntax, are so numerous that a direct literary connexion between the two passages is beyond doubt. 63 : 5, where it is Yahweh himself who is the speaker, is entirely at home in its context; moreover the traditional picture of Yahweh as warrior, appropriate when the enemies in question are foreign peoples, as they are in 63 : 1–6, is strange and hardly appropriate in a context of internal struggles within the Jewish community. The author has probably borrowed these verses and adapted them somewhat clumsily to a quite different situation in order to form, together with his expansion of the theme in verse 17, a 'text' on which to hang his message of encouragement (verses 18–20): as in the past Yahweh saved his people from their foreign enemies, so now he will intervene to save his loyal servants from a new kind of danger. The situation may be the same as that of chapters 57–58.

15b. and it displeased him: the sequence of thought is entirely satisfactory, and emendation is unnecessary. **justice:** probably *mišpāṭ* is used here in a quite general sense of a properly ordered community life.

16. no man: that is, no leader willing and able to put things right, such as was Nehemiah at a later time. **no one to intervene**

(*'ên mapgîaʿ*): the thought is well expressed in a similar passage in Ezek. 22:30. **his righteousness** (*ṣiḏᵉḳāṯô*): possibly 'his righteous purpose'; more probably 'his salvation' or 'his victory', as in 46:13; 51:6, 8. The expression is somewhat strange and the text has been questioned; but the proposal to substitute *'ammāṯô*, 'his forearm' (A. Rubinstein, *JSS* 8 (1963), pp. 52–4) is based on arguments too speculative to be convincing.

17. Yahweh is frequently represented as a warrior in the *OT*, though generally against foreign enemies. In Deutero-Isaiah the theme appears in 42:13; 49:24–25; 52:10. The figurative language used here is characteristic of Hebrew poetry, but the images themselves have no parallels except in later biblical literature: Wis. 5:17; Eph. 6:14–17. **for clothing:** this word (*tilbōšeṯ*) is unrepresented in the major Versions and is probably to be deleted as an example of dittography.

18. According to their deeds . . . enemies: it is recognized by most commentators that there is corruption here. LXX has a shorter text. In *RSV* **according to** and **so** represent the late and rare word *kᵉʿal*, which occurs twice. It is not certain that *RSV*'s rendering **According to . . . so** is a possible translation. Moreover, **their** is not represented in the Heb. It is possible that the second *kᵉʿal* is a corruption of a noun; but *BHS*' opinion that this was *gᵉmûl* is not really supported by Targ., as the note suggests, since Targ.'s reading differs from the Heb. in other ways. Volz suggested that the first words of the line are a proverbial saying written in the margin of a MS and later incorporated into the text. It has also been suggested that the final words **requital to his enemies** are an interpolation from 66:6, where the identical words occur. They are missing from LXX here. The problems are so numerous that some commentators have abandoned the attempt to reconstruct the original text. The final words of the verse (**to the coastlands he will render requital**) are also lacking in LXX and are rightly rejected by most commentators as an interpretative gloss interpreting **adversaries** as foreign enemies of the Jews. It is only here that this identification is made. The genuineness of these words is also doubtful on other grounds: this is the third time that *gᵉmûl* occurs in this verse, and the second occurrence of *yᵉšallēm*.

19. The first half of the verse (to **the sun**) refers to the nations of the world: not, however, as enemies, but as seeing God's action described in verse 18 and so being constrained to acknowledge this manifestation of his power—an idea frequently found in Deutero-Isaiah. **fear:** many commentators, following a large number of MSS, prefer to read 'see' (*yirᵉʾû* for *yîrᵉʾû*), in view of the similarity of the thought of 66 : 18, where the phrase **see my glory** occurs. A similar proposal is made with regard to Ps. 102 : 15 (MT 16). Otherwise, however, the phrase 'to see Yahweh's name' does not occur; and 'fear Yahweh's name', which makes perfectly good sense, is a more natural expression. The second half of the verse (from **for he will come**), comparing Yahweh's imminent coming to save his people with natural forces, uses the motifs of the theophany. **like a rushing stream** (*kannāhār ṣār*)**:** the pointing of *kannāhār* (with the article) shows that the Massoretes understood *ṣār* (which has no article) as meaning 'adversary', and the whole phrase as 'an adversary will come like a river'. But this interpretation is most unlikely, and *kannāhār* should be repointed as *kᵉnāhār*. The meaning of *ṣār* (**rushing**) is not entirely certain. *RSV* takes it as the participle of *ṣārar*, 'to be confined': the river is pent up between its banks and so has additional force.

20. LXX here has a different text: 'And the deliverer shall come for Zion's sake, and shall turn away ungodliness from Jacob'. Paul in Rom. 11 : 26 agrees with LXX with the exception that he has 'from Zion'. But there is no reason to doubt the correctness of MT. **those . . . who turn from transgression:** *šāḇê pešaʿ* (literally, 'repenters of sin') is a unique phrase, but not impossible since *šûḇ*, 'turn away', can have the absolute meaning 'repent' without an accompanying *min-*, 'from'. **says the LORD:** probably a later addition.

21. It is generally agreed that this verse, which is in prose, was originally unconnected with the preceding passage. It may be a fragment of a larger composition: Westermann believes that it originally belonged to 66 : 20–24. Its present position may be due to the 'catchword' *rûaḥ*, which appears in verse 19 in the sense of 'wind' and here in the sense of 'spirit', both in association with Yahweh. The first phrase (**And as for me, this is my covenant**) is in the style of the Priestly document in the Pentateuch (cf. especially Gen. 9 : 8; 17 : 4) and reaffirms God's covenant with Israel as P understood that term; but the remainder of the verse is equally reminiscent of the Deuteronomic mode of thought (cf. Dt. 30 : 14; Jos. 1 : 8). The close association of Yahweh's **spirit** and his **words** suggests a date considerably later than that of the remainder of the chapter. The gift of the **spirit** has been compared with the prophetic claim to possession of the spirit in 61 : 1, and the phrase **my words which I have put in your mouth** with 50 : 4; 51 : 16, which would suggest that the verse is addressed to an individual prophet or spiritual leader (so Klostermann, Volz); but the two phrases taken together point rather to its being a promise of the gift of prophecy to all God's people such as is found in Jl. 2 : 28–29, with perhaps the additional idea of the Spirit as guiding the people of God which we find in 63 : 14. **with them:** MT has *'ōṯām*, 'them'; but *RSV* correctly emends to *'ittām*. **them**; **you:** this change from third to second person is not unusual in prophecy and is not necessarily an indication of composite authorship.

ZION GLORIFIED

60 : 1–22

Chapters 60–62, which Westermann regards as the kernel around which the remainder of the book of Trito-Isaiah took shape, have much in common, and most commentators regard them as the work of a single author, though this cannot be regarded as certain. They contain no word of condemnation, but are entirely devoted to promises of a wonderful future for Jerusalem which derive their main inspiration from Deutero-Isaiah. However, they are addressed not to a body of exiles far from their land but to Jews who have returned to Palestine but have subsequently awaited in vain the fulfilment of Deutero-Isaiah's other prophecies. The city is still in ruins; and the people, far from prosperous, regard themselves as still forsaken by God. In addition to a variety of themes from Deutero-Isaiah there are numerous allusions to other earlier traditions and sources, including perhaps quotations from prophecies not elsewhere preserved, used as texts to be reinterpreted to form a picture of a marvellously glorified Jerusalem (on this see D. Michel). The words of Deutero-Isaiah are detached from their original contexts and have lost the sharp outlines of a concrete expectation. What is depicted is a future *state* of Jerusalem rather than a concrete *act* of salvation.

The allusions to the contemporary state of affairs suggest that these chapters were composed not many years after the return of the first exiles from Babylon. The rather imprecise allusions to the rebuilding or adornment of the Temple and to the offering of sacrifice fail to make it clear whether the Temple is still to be rebuilt, is being rebuilt, or has already been rebuilt; similarities to Haggai and Zech. 1–8 suggest a date not far from that event.

In spite of their close mutual affinities these chapters do not give the impression of being a single literary composition; nor have attempts to reconstruct such an original unity by rearranging their component parts been convincing. Chapter 60 in its present form seems to be a self-contained unit: 61 : 1 marks the beginning of a new section. However, the lack of a clear structure and the occurrence from time to time of pronouncements by Yahweh suggest that chapter 60 itself is the product of a process of gradual development in which reinterpretation and development of earlier prophecy played a part.

1–3. These introductory verses present the themes to be developed in the form of an address to Zion, that is, the city of Jerusalem (cf. verse 14), personified (as in Deutero-Isaiah) as a woman.

1. Arise (*ḳûmî*)**:** this recalls similar addresses to Zion in the fem. imperative in Deutero-Isaiah (51 : 17; 52 : 1). In spite of the return from exile Zion still lies prostrate and must pick herself up to hear the news of her restoration to prosperity. **your light** and **has risen** are used together in 58 : 10, where the rising of the sun is a metaphor of the dawning of a new age of prosperity; but here the metaphor is given a further significance through its combination with **the glory of the LORD**, a theophany theme and a reminiscence of Isa. 40 : 5, where Yahweh's glory is to be revealed. The image is characteristically detached from its original precise context. **has risen:** the reference is future; the perfect tense expresses the certainty of the promise. **shine:** the image of Zion as not only the recipient of God's light but as herself shining with the reflected light of Yahweh's glory is an original contribution by this author.

2. The theme of God's giving light to his own people while the heathen world remains in **darkness** is derived from the Exodus traditions (Exod. 10 : 23). The metaphor of light shining on those who were formerly in **darkness** already occurs in Isa. 9 : 2 (MT 9 : 1). It has been suggested that this theme of light in connexion with Jerusalem points to the Feast of Tabernacles or New Year's Day as the original setting for the chapter; however, there is no direct evidence of such ceremonies involving the use of lights in this period, although such was the case in later times. **darkness:** in Heb. this word has the article (*haḥōšeḵ*); but the article is almost certainly an addition due to dittography.

3. The theme of **light** is now combined with another: that of the coming of the **nations** (and their **kings**) to Jerusalem, a theme which occurs already in Isa. 2 : 2–4 (Mic. 4 : 1–4) and may be even older. But the author is thinking primarily of themes and passages from Deutero-Isaiah: 40 : 5, where 'all flesh' shall see Yahweh's glory; the giving of 'a light to the nations' (42 : 6; 49 : 6); and the prophecies that 'kings will see and arise' (49 : 7) and will come to Zion as slaves (49 : 23). Whereas in Isa. 2 : 2–3 the nations will come to learn Yahweh's ways, here they come to bring tribute to Zion and to serve her, as is made clear by verses 4–14. If the idea of a *pilgrimage* of the nations to worship Yahweh was in the author's mind at all, it was not his primary thought. Not universalism, but the glorification of Zion is his main theme.

4–9. The thought of the coming of the nations to Zion is now developed further: they will come to bring Zion's children home to her and also to bring tribute to increase her wealth and for the adornment of the Temple and for its sacrifices. It is difficult to understand why some commentators insist on spiritualizing these promises. The author is saying that the promises of world dominion which go back ultimately to the time of David, but which had much more recently been confidently reiterated by Deutero-Isaiah, remained valid and would soon be amply fulfilled. The note of nationalism—albeit of 'religious nationalism'—is unmistakable.

4. The first half of this verse (**Lift up . . . come to you**) is an exact quotation of 49 : 18*a*, and in the second half **shall come from far** is taken from 49 : 12, while **and your daughters shall be carried in the arms** is a reminiscence of part of 49 : 22. The subject of **gather together** and **come to you** is the **nations** and **kings** of verse 3, who appear in the same role in 49 : 22–23. In their original context these phrases refer to the repopulation of 'bereaved', that is, uninhabited, Jerusalem who is pictured as watching with amazement the arrival of her 'children', the exiles and other dispersed Israelites. Here Zion is the community of Jews already returned from exile and living in and around Jerusalem, and the promise is of the completion of this return: the restoration of all the people of God to their land. Only then, it is implied, will the promised wealth and power be restored to them. This is a notable shift of emphasis. **shall come:** the proposal to repoint this verb (*yāḇō'û*) as the Hiphil *yāḇî'û*, 'they shall bring', is unnecessary, and improbable in view of 49 : 12. **shall be carried:** literally, 'shall be held firm' (by a nurse). This meaning of the Niphal of *'mn* is unique, but plausible, and neither emendation nor derivation from a different and hypothetical root (as proposed by *BHS*) seems necessary or probable. On the unusual form see G–K §51m. **in the arms:** literally, 'on the side'. The reference is to a mode of carrying children familiar in the Near East.

5. The first half of the verse describes Zion's strong emotions at being reunited with her children. **you shall see:** many MSS read 'you shall fear' (*tîrᵉ'î* for *tirᵉ'î*); but MT is certainly right. **and be radiant:** this verb, which occurs only here and in Ps. 34 : 5 (MT 34 : 6), is an original touch, in keeping with **shine** in verse 1. **rejoice:** literally, 'be enlarged'. With the second half of the verse (from **because**) begins a description of the arrival of the wealth of the nations by land and sea. There is a very similar promise in Hag. 2 : 7. **the abundance of the sea:** that is, goods brought by sea, referring to the maritime traffic of coastal cities such as Tyre and the other Phoenician cities. **abundance:** the word *hāmôn*, usually 'tumult, confusion', seems to have acquired this sense of 'abundance, wealth' in the post-exilic period. This is probably one of the earliest examples of this development. **shall come:** the verb is plur. but the subject singular. We should probably either follow 1QIs[b], which reads the singular, or repoint as Hiphil, 'they shall bring (the wealth . . .)' (*yaḇî'û* for *yāḇō'û*).

6. This and the succeeding verses refer to transport by land. **shall cover you:** that is, Jerusalem and the surrounding district will swarm with caravans of camels converging on the city. **Midian:** the Midianites, whose traditional home was in the north Arabian desert east of the Gulf of Aqabah, were especially known as caravan leaders and traders (cf. Gen. 37 : 28, 36). **Ephah** is mentioned as a 'son of Midian' in Gen. 25 : 4. **all those from Sheba shall come:** literally, 'all of them shall come from

Sheba'. It is not clear whether it is meant that the wealth of Sheba will be carried by Midianite camels, or whether the Sabaeans themselves will bring their tribute to Jerusalem. The Sabaeans of Sheba in south Arabia, whose queen's visit to Solomon is recorded in 1 Kg. 10 : 1–13, were in later times known as suppliers of gold, frankincense, and spices. The theme of tribute brought from Sheba is found also in Ps. 72 : 10. **and shall proclaim the praise of the LORD:** if this line is original it sets the tone for the whole passage. But from the points of view of both sense and poetical parallelism it stands out in isolation; and since the verse as a whole is metrically overloaded it may well be a later addition (so Skinner; cf. also Volz).

7. In addition to the camel caravans, the **flocks of Kedar** and **Nebaioth** in north Arabia will be driven to Jerusalem to serve as sacrificial victims in the Temple. **shall minister to you:** the same word occurs again in verse 10. But there is no overwhelming case for its omission or emendation here. The image of the animals 'serving' Zion by becoming sacrificial victims is not beyond the normal range of poetical imagination. **they shall come up with acceptance on my altar:** that is, Yahweh will accept them as offerings. Here the reading of 1QIs^{b} (*wyʿlw lrṣwn ʿl mzbḥy*) is preferable to that of MT. **and I will glorify my glorious house:** whether this refers to the rebuilding of the Temple or to the adornment of the rebuilt Temple cannot be determined. It should be noted that Yahweh himself is speaking here.

8. The speaker, whether Yahweh or the author, now turns once more to the maritime scene and pictures ships sailing along the Mediterranean coast towards Palestine, their sails giving the appearance of a fast-moving **cloud** or of **doves** returning to their dovecotes (**windows**).

9. For the coastlands shall wait for me (*kî-lî 'iyyîm yeḳawwû*)**:** the present text is a reminiscence of 51 : 5 (cf. also 42 : 4). But this is almost certainly the result of subsequent alteration during the transmission of the text. The thought is somewhat out of place here, and there is a strong case for emending *'iyyîm* to *ṣiyyîm*, 'ships', and repointing *yeḳawwû* as *yiḳḳāwû*, which may then be translated 'will be assembled': 'for me (the) ships will be assembled'. This still leaves Yahweh as the speaker, though he is referred to in the third person later in the verse. An alternative emendation is *kelê 'iyyîm yiḳḳāwû*, 'the ships (literally, 'the vessels') of the coastlands will be assembled'. **the ships of Tarshish:** that is, large ocean-going ships (as in 1 Kg. 10 : 22 and elsewhere), named after **Tarshish** (Tartessus), a Phoenician colony probably in southern Spain. **first:** that is, leading the way. **for the name . . . glorified you:** this is an exact quotation from 55 : 5*b* except that **for the name of** (*lešēm*) has been substituted for 'because of' (*lema'an*). The phrase 'the name of Yahweh' does not occur in Deutero-Isaiah. **name** here probably has the sense of 'renown'. Zimmerli remarks that these lines are less integrally related to their context here than in 55 : 5, and sees in this an example of the beginning of a process in which the language of earlier prophecy came to be used as a kind of conventional, pious language.

10–11. It is now further promised that **Foreigners** and **their kings** will be obliged to serve as workmen to rebuild the **walls** of Jerusalem under Israel's direction. This goes beyond the expectation of Deutero-Isaiah (49 : 17), although as a reversal of the roles of Israel and the nations it is entirely in agreement with the promises of 45 : 14; 49 : 22–23.

10. The second half of this verse (from **for in my wrath**) expresses very much the same thought as 54 : 7 and emphasizes the reversal of roles: the walls which were destroyed by foreigners will now be rebuilt by them.

11. The statement that the **gates** of the city will remain **open continually** follows on from the promise that the walls will be rebuilt. Two thoughts appear to have been combined here: the fact that Jerusalem will not need to close its gates even at night is an indication of its complete security from the possibility of hostile attack (cf. 54 : 14–17); at the same time the great influx of tribute-bearing visitors will actually necessitate the leaving of the gates open permanently. **shall be open:** MT has *pittᵉḥû*, 'they shall open'. Either the subject is impersonal or the word should be pointed as passive: *puttᵉḥû*. **wealth:** another possible translation of *ḥayil* is 'multitude'. **led in procession:** this is hardly a possible translation of *nᵉhûḡîm*. The verb *nāhaḡ* means 'drive' (of flocks) or simply 'lead'. If the text is correct it must mean, as the Versions understood it, that the peoples will bring their own kings to Jerusalem as captives. This hardly makes sense, and the proposal to emend to an active participle, *nôhᵉḡîm*, yielding the translation 'with their kings leading them', may be right.

12. This verse is in prose and is almost certainly a gloss as most commentators agree, although it is not as far removed from verses 10–11 in tone as many have held. The thought is not, as has frequently been asserted, the same as that of Zech. 14: 16–19 where punishment is decreed for the nations which refuse to go to Jerusalem to worship Yahweh. Here the reference is not to the worship of Yahweh but to the service of Israel. **those nations:** Heb. has simply 'the nations'. A word seems to be missing from the text.

13. The author now turns from the city to the Temple within it, expanding the reference to it in verse 7. The foreign nations will come bringing timber for its construction or adornment. He refers first to the cedars of Lebanon under the name **The glory of Lebanon**, which he has borrowed from 35: 2 and, as Torrey remarks, 'slightly misunderstood'. He was then, it would seem, unable to resist adding a quotation from 41: 19 which mentions three other kinds of tree but in an entirely different sense: there they are living trees made to flourish in the desert, here simply timber. **the place of my feet:** almost the same expression occurs in Ezek. 43: 7; it is also to be noted that Ezekiel frequently uses the word **sanctuary** (*miḳdāš*), which never occurs in Deutero-Isaiah. Traditionally it was the Ark which was identified with or closely associated with Yahweh's footstool (Ps. 132: 7; cf. 1 Chr. 28: 2). The Ark had perished in the destruction of 587 BC; but now (so also in Ezek. 43: 7) it is the Temple which is his footstool, Yahweh himself dwelling in heaven. For a different view see 66: 1.

14. In this and the following two verses the author clearly had 49: 23 in mind, though most commentators here accept the reading of LXX, which lacks **all** and **shall bow down at your feet**, making (those) **who despised you** a second subject of the verb **shall come bending low**. Zimmerli regards the piling up of epithets at the end of the verse and at the end of verse 16 as an indication of merely pious, conventional language in contrast with the outwardly similar but deeply significant epithets used by Deutero-Isaiah.

15. A general statement about the transformation of Jerusalem from wretchedness to splendour. **forsaken and hated:** the idea of Jerusalem as abandoned by Yahweh, ultimately derived from the community's lamentations, is here taken up in the figure of the abandoned wife, which was the form in which it was expressed by Deutero-Isaiah (49 : 21; 50 : 1; 54 : 6), and the author almost certainly had these passages in mind. The fem. participle *ʿazûḇāh*, **forsaken**, also occurs in 54 : 6 with reference to Zion. **hated** (*śenû'āh*), which does not in fact occur in Deutero-Isaiah, is a technical term for a wife repudiated by her husband. **with no one passing through:** the situation is now expressed in concrete terms. In the years since the destruction of the city Jerusalem has been 'off the map'. **I will make you majestic for ever:** characteristically the author uses the Deutero-Isaianic idea in a more imprecise way than his source: a future God-given *state* is promised rather than a precise act of salvation.

16. This verse is clearly modelled on 49 : 23, but the second half is expanded with phrases from 49 : 26*b*. The phrase 'and their queens your nursing mothers' (49 : 23) has, however, been entirely reinterpreted. Whereas Deutero-Isaiah uses the metaphor simply to indicate that the foreign nations will be slaves to Zion's 'children', the present author appears to be using it to express the idea that Zion will drain the foreign nations of their wealth. In so doing he commits the absurdity of saying **you shall suck the breast of kings** (there is no justification for emending **kings** to 'queens'!). **breast** (*šōḏ*)**:** usually *šaḏ*. This spelling is found only here and in 66 : 11.

17. It is not stated for what purpose the **gold**, **silver**, and **iron** are to be used. If it is for the reconstruction of the city this is poetical hyperbole: no city could be built entirely of metal. But precious metals (of which, at that time, **iron** was one) symbolized spiritual as well as material worth, as many references to them in the *OT* show. On the material level there is perhaps an allusion to the golden age of Solomon (1 Kg. 10 : 21, 27), and possibly also to 1 Kg. 14 : 26, 27, which relates how king Rehoboam, threatened by Shishak king of Egypt, was obliged to replace his golden shields with shields of an inferior metal. Now the situation in Jerusalem is to be reversed. This verse and verse 18 reflect the present wretched state of the Jewish community and its aspirations, which have up to now been thwarted. So in the second half of the verse the present foreign rule is to be replaced by **peace** and **righteousness**, personified qualities which symbolize the character of the state of perfection of the coming new age. **overseers:** the word *nōḡēś* signifies an oppressive rule, but this is an intentional paradox: a tyrant whose name was **righteousness** would be no tyrant at all.

18. The thought of the first half of this verse (to **borders**) is reminiscent of passages in Deutero-Isaiah such as 54 : 15–17. **you shall call your walls . . . Praise:** there is no suggestion here, as some commentators have argued, that the city will need no **walls** because Yahweh himself will protect it (as in Zech. 2 : 4–5 (MT 2 : 8–9)). The giving of a name to indicate or confer a certain character was not confined to human beings, as we see from the names Jachin and Boaz given to pillars in 1 Kg. 7 : 21 and (in a symbolic action) the naming of the sticks in Zech. 11 : 7. Jerusalem is given a variety of names in prophetical passages (Isa. 1 : 26; 62 : 12; Jer. 3 : 17; Zech. 8 : 3). Here the naming of the **walls** and **gates** of Jerusalem is a case of *pars pro toto*: the whole city, enclosed within its walls and gates, will be an embodiment of prosperity (*yᵉšûʿāh*, *RSV* **Salvation**; for this meaning cf. Job 30 : 15) and renown (*tᵉhillāh*; *RSV* **Praise**).

19–20. The theme of these verses, that in the age to come there will be no need of the **sun** and **moon** because Yahweh himself **will be your everlasting light**, is found in Zech. 14 : 7 and frequently in the apocalypses from the second century BC onwards. As Westermann has pointed out, the verses are an intrusion in a chapter which does not otherwise, once allowances have been made for poetic hyperbole, go beyond the possibilities of ordinary human existence. They also interrupt the theme of the future security and prosperity of Jerusalem, which is resumed in verse 21. It has been argued that they are in keeping with the theme of **light** in verses 1–3; but they are rather an interpretation of those verses in prosaic terms which show a misunderstanding of their poetic imagery. They should therefore be regarded as a later addition showing an apocalyptic tendency.

19. by night: this word is lacking in MT. *RSV* has added it, rightly following 1QIsᵃ, LXX, and other Versions. It should probably stand in the Heb. text before *lōʾ* (**nor**).

20. The first part of this verse (to **everlasting light**) is apparently an attempt to make clear the meaning of verse 19*a*, but it fails to do so. It is still not clear whether **sun** and **moon** will be abolished, or whether they will remain in the sky though no longer needed. The second part (from **and your days**) is a general promise unrelated to what precedes. The obscurity of the thought is due to inferior composition. The whole verse may be a further addition to verse 19.

21. Continuing the thought of verse 18, the author now turns from the future condition of the city itself to the state of its inhabitants. There has been much discussion of the meaning of **righteous** (*ṣaddîḳîm*) here. The only other occurrence of the word in Trito-Isaiah is in 57 : 1, where it seems to mean something like 'pious, devout'. The view of Volz, Muilenburg, and Fohrer that here it has the meaning of 'participating in salvation' can hardly be sustained in view of its usage elsewhere in the *OT*. It probably has the same meaning here as in 57 : 1, but the emphasis is on **all**: in contrast with the present situation (perhaps that described in chs. 57 and 59), the citizens of Jerusalem will be united in the sincere service of Yahweh. **they shall possess the land for ever:** the promise of the renewed gift of the land, which in Deutero-Isaiah (49 : 8; 54 : 3) means that the exiles in Babylon will be restored to the possession of their distant homeland, here has a quite different meaning: it is addressed to a people which has already returned home, only to find that whether because of the smallness of their numbers, or of the continuing foreign domination, or of other peoples who have settled there, or of internal dissensions, they do not really **possess the land. the shoot of my planting, the work of my hands** (*nēṣer maṭṭāʿay maʿaśēh yāḏay*): there is textual corruption here. All the ancient Heb. authorities have variant readings: Kethib has '*his* planting'; Qere (quoted above) 'my plantings'; 1QIsᵃ adds *yhwh* (Yahweh) after *mṭʿw*; 1QIsᵇ has *mṭʿyw* but omits *nṣr*. Both 1QIsᵃ and 1QIsᵇ have '*his* hands'. In view of the frequent confusion of *waw* and *yodh*, *RSV* may be right in conjecturing that the original had **my planting** (*maṭṭāʿî*) and **my hands** (*yāḏay*). For an entirely different interpretation see C. Brayley, *Biblica* 41 (1960), pp. 275–286. The idea of Yahweh as planting his people, which occurs also in 61 : 3, was a traditional one: see e.g. Isa. 5 : 1–7.

22. For the theme of the blessing of a greatly increased population, which derives ultimately from the promises to the Patriarchs, see 49 : 8, 19–21; 54 : 1–3. Such an increase in numbers would be necessary if the Jewish community were to **possess the land** (verse 21) in the full sense of that phrase. **I am the LORD:** as in Deutero-Isaiah, Yahweh uses this formula to seal his promises. The phrase both reminds the audience of Yahweh's power to help them and also, by virtue of its covenant associations, gives them an assurance of his readiness to do so. **in its time I will hasten it:** since the phrase **in its time** (*b^eʿittô*) means 'at the proper time' or 'when the time is ripe' there is a logical contradiction here: **I will hasten it** is an assurance that there will be no delay. Probably the intention is to urge patience upon the hearers while assuring them that they will not have to wait long. This modified expectancy strikes a different note from the urgency of Deutero-Isaiah. **it** comprises everything which has been promised in the foregoing chapter.

PROPHETIC CALL AND MESSAGE

61 : 1–11

The contents of this chapter are more varied than those of chapter 60. In verses 1–3 a prophet speaks of his divine call and mission, which is to bring God's word of healing and liberation to the disconsolate community. A more detailed interpretation of this word follows in verses 4–7. Then comes in verse 8 a word of Yahweh promising to the people a restoration of their rights, and the implications of this are expounded in verse 9. Two more elements complete the chapter: an individual thanksgiving in verse 10, and a final assurance that Yahweh will indeed keep his word in verse 11. It is probable that the chapter is neither a single, unified composition nor simply a collection of entirely disparate elements. The general similarity of themes and vocabulary together with an unusual degree of dependence on Deutero-Isaiah suggest that it has undergone a process of gradual development within the same prophetic circle as that which produced chapter 60.

1–3. There are close similarities between these verses and the Servant Songs of Deutero-Isaiah: so close that many of the older commentators held that this is a 'Song' belonging to the same group and the work of the same author. The speaker claims, like the Servant, to have received Yahweh's Spirit (cf. 42 : 1) in order to bring a message of hope to his people, and to restore their fortunes (cf. 49 : 6). Those who regard the second Servant Song as extending beyond 49 : 6 will also note two further similarities: **the year of the LORD's favour, and the day of vengeance of our God** (verse 2) corresponds to the 'time of favour' and the 'day of salvation' of 49 : 8, and the proclaiming of **liberty to the captives, and the opening of the prison** (verse 1) corresponds to 49 : 9*a*. On the other hand there are important differences. There is no mention in 61 : 1–3 of the Gentiles (though there is in the later verses of the chapter); more important, such characteristics of the Servant as his quietness, humility, sense of failure and suffering are entirely lacking. On the other side, the remarkable claim of the author in 61 : 1 that **the LORD has anointed me** finds no echo in the Servant Songs.

That these verses, like the rest of the chapter, are closely dependent on Deutero-Isaiah even apart from the Servant Songs there is equally no doubt. But in the case of verses 1–3 this dependence raises a curious problem. However dependent he may be on his predecessor, and however much he may use the thoughts and language of that predecessor in describing his own experiences and convictions about himself, there can be no doubt that the speaker's experiences and convictions are genuine and personal. What he says about himself he clearly sincerely believes. He must then be regarded as in some sense a prophet. Yet in spite of his high claims to have received the Spirit of Yahweh and to have been anointed and sent by him, his conception of his function is more restricted than that of earlier prophets, and perhaps characteristic of his age: he is an interpreter of an old message rather than an intermediary who transmits to the people a new message which he has received directly from God. His dependence on his predecessor shows that he regarded himself as one commissioned to assure the people that the earlier promises of prophets such as Deutero-Isaiah were still valid and would indeed be fulfilled (see especially Zimmerli).

1. It is interesting to note that in applying themes and phrases from the Servant Songs to himself this prophet shows that he understood the figure of the Servant to be Deutero-Isaiah himself. (According to Lk. 4 : 17–21 Jesus took this as a prophecy concerning himself). On the prophetic claim to possess the **Spirit of the Lord** see on 42 : 1. **has anointed me:** this is obviously to be taken metaphorically, like 'his anointed' in 45 : 1. The only persons to be actually anointed in Israel were kings and high priests (before and after the Exile respectively). Exceptionally Elijah was commanded to anoint Elisha to the prophetic office (1 Kg. 19 : 16); but there is no mention in the narrative which follows (1 Kg. 19 : 19–21) of his having done so, and it is possible that even at that time the word was already used figuratively of an appointing or commissioning by God to important functions: cf. **he has sent me** in the next line. The word **because** also suggests a close association between this 'anointing' and the gift of the Spirit (cf. 1 Sam. 16 : 13).

to bring good tidings (*l^eḇaśśēr*): for the original meaning of this verb, which (with its participial form meaning 'herald') occurs in three passages in Deutero-Isaiah, see on 40 : 9. With regard to one of those passages (41 : 27) it has been suggested that it may refer, as here, to the prophetic office. **the afflicted** (*'anāwîm*): this word, which may also be rendered 'humble' or (as in Lk. 4 : 18) 'poor' is, like **brokenhearted** (*nišbᵉrê-lēḇ*) used in the Psalms to denote those who in spite of their present distress confidently and steadfastly await the arrival of God's help. Like similar expressions in 57 : 15, both refer to the Jewish community in Palestine as it continues to hope for the fulfilment of the prophecies of Deutero-Isaiah and other exilic prophets. **he has sent me:** the metre suggests that this word is to be taken with what precedes. **the captives** (*šᵉḇûyīm*); **those who are bound** (*'ᵃsûrîm*): some commentators take these words literally as referring to the same situation as 58 : 6; but the context suggests that they are metaphors referring generally to the state of frustration in which the community finds itself. *'ᵃsûrîm* occurs in 49 : 9, where it refers to the Exile. The author is thus once more giving a new interpretation to traditional language. **to bind up:** that is, to bandage: a curious metaphor. **to proclaim liberty** (*likrā' dᵉrôr*): the word *dᵉrôr* is used in the *OT* exclusively—although sometimes in a metaphorical sense—in connexion with the 'year of release' (or, 'jubilee'), whose regulations are to be found in Lev. 25. This law prescribed, among other things, a general emancipation from slavery every fiftieth year. *ḳārā' dᵉrôr*, 'to proclaim a release', appears to have been the technical term for its official inauguration (Jer. 34 : 8, 15, 17). In the passage under discussion the prophet uses it metaphorically of the coming 'liberation' of the community from its frustrations. It has been surmised by some commentators that the choice of metaphor points to an actual jubilee as the occasion when the prophet spoke these words. **the opening of the prison:** in the Heb. (*pᵉḳaḥ-ḳôaḥ*) there is no reference to a prison. This is probably a single word *pᵉḳaḥḳôaḥ*, meaning 'opening' (cf. 1QIsᵃ). If the text of the remainder of the phrase is correct this probably means 'release', though some commentators, pointing out that the verb *pāḳaḥ* is used almost exclusively of the opening of the eyes, follow LXX (and Lk. 4 : 18) and emend *'ᵃsûrîm* (**those who are bound**) to *sanwērîm* or *'iwᵉrîm*, 'blind': 'opening of eyes to the blind'.

2. to proclaim the year of the LORD's favour: the metaphor of the year of release is now further developed: it is a time when Yahweh especially shows his **favour** (*rāṣôn*) to those in distress. **the day of vengeance** (*yôm nāḳām*): probably a traditional phrase (cf. Prov. 6:34; Isa. 34:8; 63:4). In the *OT* God is frequently said to take vengeance either against sinful Israel or against Israel's enemies. In the latter case **vengeance** is naturally seen as synonymous with salvation for Israel, and here and in 35:4 the thought of the enemies seems to have faded altogether, leaving only the positive thought of Israel's salvation. There is certainly no suggestion here of enemies who will suffer for their crimes against Israel—a contrast to the use of the word in Deutero-Isaiah (47 : 3) and in 63 : 4. The use of the verb **comfort** (*niḥam*), a keyword in Deutero-Isaiah, also shows a change of emphasis; and this is also true of **day**: the fact that **day** is here parallel with **year** shows that no single specific action is indicated (cf. a similar usage in Isa. 34 : 8). As elsewhere in these chapters the author is describing the future *state* of Zion.

3. to grant to those who mourn in Zion: this line is mainly a variant of the final line in verse 2. The acount of the prophet's commission then continues with a series of three images of joy to come which will replace the present dejection of the people. **garland** (*pᵉ'ēr*): better, 'head-dress'. To remove the head-dress was a sign of **mourning** (Ezek. 24 : 17, 23). Later in this chapter (verse 10) the head-dress is mentioned as part of the festive attire of the bridegroom. There is also a play on words here: a head-dress (*pᵉ'ēr*) will take the place of *'ēper*, **ashes**, which were traditionally sprinkled on the head as a sign of mourning. **oil of gladness:** anointing with oil (to be distinguished from the formal ceremony of appointment to an office) was a feature of festive occasions and appears to have been one of the attentions which a host lavished on his guests (Ps. 23 : 5). The phrase occurs again in Ps. 45 : 7 (MT 45 : 8). **praise:** better, 'splendour' or 'renown': cf. the use of the word in 60 : 18. **faint** (*kēhāh*): that is, discouraged; cf. the use of this word in 42 : 3 (*RSV* 'dimly burning'). **oaks of**

righteousness (*'êlê haṣṣeḏeḵ*): perhaps better, 'fine oaks'. **the planting of the LORD:** see on 60 : 21.

4. The close verbal similarity of this verse to 58 : 12 suggests a possible common source in some kind of traditional phraseology, perhaps in public lamentations of the period. The theme already appears in Deutero-Isaiah (49 : 8); cf. also 60 : 10. On the meaning of **ancient** and **of many generations** see on 58 : 12. **They shall build up . . .:** the subject is probably impersonal, less probably the Jewish community referred to in the previous verses. In either case there is no contradiction with 60 : 10, where it is the foreigners who are to undertake the actual manual labour. This does not mean that it is not the Jews who are the 'builders' in a more fundamental sense.

5. The change from third to second person is no rare phenomenon in prophecy, and neither this nor a supposed change of tone towards the foreigners justifies the view of Volz and others that this verse and verse 6 are an interpolation. The verse states that even the traditional tasks of the Jewish farmer are in future to be performed by foreign labour.

6. The promise that the Jews are to become **the priests of the LORD** is to be taken metaphorically. The priesthood here is seen primarily as a privileged status. In Israel the priests, who did not farm for themselves, were entitled by law to receive their livelihood from the laity. Now the Jews will all belong to a privileged class and the foreign nations will supply them abundantly with their needs. In return, it may be supposed, the Jews will condescend to perform on behalf of the foreign nations the role of intercessors and mediators. But this aspect of the matter is not emphasized, and it would be wrong to conclude that anything like a 'mission to the Gentiles' is here envisaged. **you shall glory** (*tiṯyammārû*): if this word is related to the differently spelled *yiṯ'ammᵉrû* of Ps. 94 : 4 the translation of *RSV* may be accepted. Other commentators prefer to derive it from a supposed root *ymr* = *mwr* ('receive in exchange') or to emend it, for example to *tiṯmārāyû* ('become fat') or *tiṯmayyārû* (cognate with Arab. *māra*—'be provisioned'.

7. Instead . . . lot: these lines, which are lacking in LXX, are quite unintelligible in the Heb. It would seem that **a double portion** (*mišneh*) which occurs again later in the verse is an intrusion. Two further emendations (*bōšeṯ*, 'shame', for *bošṯᵉḵem*,

your shame and *rinnāh*, 'rejoicing', for *yārōnnū*, 'they shall rejoice') would yield the translation 'Instead of shame and humiliation, rejoicing shall be their lot'. Though this must remain uncertain, there is much to be said for Volz' suggestion that this sentence has been misplaced from after **a faint spirit** in verse 3, where it would take its place together with the other phrases contrasting the present situation with the future and containing the word **instead. therefore in your land . . .:** *RSV*'s emendation of second person forms to third person in order to achieve consistency is unnecessarily pedantic. **a double portion:** a double allotment of land. The exact meaning is not clear. Perhaps it means that the Jews will receive full control both over their own land and also over that of the other nations. A connexion with 40 : 2 is improbable (see the commentary *ad loc.*). A great increase of population is implied, but the thought is different from that of 54 : 3.

8. Yahweh now speaks. In its present context, which may not be original, this oracle purports to give the reason why all these favours are to be conferred on his people: he is not willing to permit the continuation of a situation in which they are deprived of **justice** and are suffering **robbery and wrong**, that is, the denial to them by their foreign rulers of independence and self-respect. The word-pair *mišpāṭ/peʿullāh* (**justice/recompense**) has been taken over from 49 : 4, where the Servant expresses his confidence in Yahweh's help, and applied to the community. **wrong:** MT has *ʿôlāh*, which normally means 'sacrifice', but this makes no sense. Almost all commentators agree in pointing the word as *ʿawlāh* together with LXX and other Versions and a few MSS, though Delitzsch suggested that the pointing may be correct: this is an alternative spelling of *ʿawlāh*; cf. Job 5 : 16; Ps. 58 : 2 (MT 58 : 3); 64 : 6 (MT 64 : 7). The last line of the verse (from **and I will make**) is clearly dependent on 55 : 3 and is characteristic in its reinterpretation of Deutero-Isaiah: dissociated from its original context it seems almost like a stereotyped, conventional expression.

9. shall be known: that is, 'renowned'. The word is used in the same sense in Prov. 31 : 23. The second half of the verse (from **all who see them**) is perhaps a reminiscence of Gen. 12 : 2. Like Deutero-Isaiah (41 : 8; 51 : 2) the author has in mind the definitive fulfilment of the promises made to Abraham.

10. The form of this verse, in which an individual declares his intention to **rejoice in the LORD** and then states his reason in a series of clauses, introduced by **for** (*kî*), which recount God's gracious actions which he has performed on his behalf, is that of the individual psalm of thanksgiving: cf. especially Ps. 9 : 1–4 (MT 9 : 2–5); 30 : 1 (MT 30 : 2). Two questions arise here: the identity of the speaker and the relationship of this short psalm to the remainder of the chapter. In view of the similarity of the vocabulary to that of verse 3 (*pᵉʾēr*, 'head-dress', *RSV* **garland**, occurs in both verses; *śôś ʾāśîś*, **I will greatly rejoice**, is cognate with *śāśôn*, 'gladness', in verse 3; *yeʿāṭānî*, **he has covered me** (see below) is reminiscent of, if not cognate with, *maʿᵃṭeh*, 'mantle', in verse 3) it seems that the speaker is testifying that the action of God through the prophet announced in verse 3 has now been fulfilled in his own person: there appears to be a direct relationship between this verse and verse 3, if not between it and the immediately preceding verses. If this is so the balance of probability with regard to the identity of the speaker lies with the view that it is the community of 'those who mourn in Zion' which is here personified, an interpretation which is as old as the Targum. The metaphor of investiture as indicating a change of status or condition is commonly used in the *OT*: cf. 47 : 2; 52 : 1. The simile of the **bride** who **adorns herself with her jewels** is taken from 49 : 18, but in its new context the thought has lost its original precise sense. The thought of the verse as a whole is anticipatory, like Deutero-Isaiah's 'eschatological song of praise'. **he has covered me** (*yeʿāṭānî*)**:** the verb *yāʿaṭ* occurs only here. Unless it is a rare byform of *ʿāṭāh* it is probably a mistake for *yaʿᵃṭēnî* (Hiphil imperfect of *ʿāṭāh*) or possibly *ʿāṭānî* (Qal of *ʿāṭāh*), though in the latter case the use of the direct object would be unique. The meaning, literally 'wrap', is not in doubt. **decks himself:** the verb (*yeḵahēn*) means 'plays the priest', which makes no sense. It has been suggested that the original reading was either *yāḵîn* or *yeḵônēn*, either of which could mean 'fix on (his head)', so *RSV*. **righteousness** (*ṣeḏāḳāh*)**:** better, 'deliverance' as in 54 : 17.

11. In spite of the sudden change of imagery there is not, as some commentators have maintained, an impossible discontinuity between verse 10 and this verse, which is, however, probably not part of the psalm of thanksgiving. The speaker appears now to be once again the prophet, who concludes the composition with an assurance of the reliability of God's promises based on an argument similar to that of 55 : 10–11. As in 58 : 8 the choice of the word *hiṣmîaḥ*, 'cause to spring up', may have been dictated by Deutero-Isaiah's use of it in connection with the 'new things' prepared by Yahweh (42 : 9; 43 : 19), or by 45 : 8, where also Yahweh will cause *ṣᵉḏāḳāh* ('salvation'; *RSV* 'righteousness') to spring up. **before all the nations:** that is, the nations will be observers and witnesses of the salvation conferred upon God's people: cf. 52 : 10; 60 *passim*.

ZION REDEEMED

62 : 1–12

The alternation of oracles of Yahweh and prophetic comment characteristic of chapters 60 and 61 is also to be found in this chapter, suggesting a series of closely linked but not necessarily originally connected pieces on a common theme. Only in verse 8 is the presence of a divine oracle incontrovertible; but there is good reason to believe that the 'I' of verses 1*a* and 6*a* is also the divine 'I' (see below). Like the two previous chapters this chapter is wholly concerned with the restoration and glorification of Jerusalem (Zion), and the greater part of it is addressed to the city in the second person fem. Themes and language attach it closely to the two previous chapters. The dependence on Deutero-Isaiah is even more marked. The general historical situation appears to be the same.

1–5. Verse 1, in which God speaks in the first person, referring to Zion in the third, appears to be part of an oracle of salvation. Verses 2–5 are a prophetic comment on this which develops its theme by means of a variety of images but without adding anything fundamentally new. Here a prophet or other person is the speaker: he addresses Zion in the second person fem. and refers to Yahweh in the third person.

1. I will not keep silent (*lōʾ ʾeḥᵉšeh*)**:** the most frequent interpretation of the **I** here refers it to the prophet who states his determination to importune God until he intervenes to bring salvation to Zion. This interpretation is linked to a similar interpretation of verse 6. But the thought behind the verse is rather that of *God's* silence, that is, inactivity, which is the subject of the people's complaint in many Psalms including Ps. 28 : 1, and also in Isa. 64 : 12 (MT 64 : 11). It is in answer to this complaint that God promises—as also in 42 : 14; 57 : 11; 65 : 6—that he will now break his silence and intervene. (In all the passages cited above the same verb *ḥāšāh* is used, sometimes in the Qal and sometimes in the Hiphil.) **her vindication goes forth** (*yēṣē' . . . ṣiḏḵāh*): see on 58 : 8. **a burning torch:** it has been suggested by Volz that this is an allusion to ceremonies performed on the Feast of Tabernacles; but see on 60 : 2.

2. The nations . . . glory: the thought of these lines and of verse 1 is extremely close to that of 60 : 1–3. **your vindication** (*ṣiḏḵēḵ*): the repetition of *ṣeḏeḵ* from verse 1 confirms the view that verses 2–5 are to be seen as a deliberate expansion or exposition of verse 1. **a new name:** in the ancient Near East the giving of a new name to a person signified a radical change in his status or fortunes, and there are many examples of this in the *OT* both actual (e.g. the renaming of Jacob as Israel) and metaphorical (e.g. Isa. 60 : 14, 18, of Zion considered as a woman). The promise that Zion/Jerusalem herself will be so renamed is found a number of times (Isa. 1 : 26; Jer. 33 : 16; Ezek. 48 : 35), but on each occasion the **new name** itself is cited. This is also the case in verse 4 of this chapter. The repetition of the theme twice in this passage and the fact that only here in verse 2 is the name itself not cited has suggested to some commentators that these lines (**and you shall be called . . . will give**) are a later interpolation. This view, however, presupposes that the passage otherwise has a strict literary unity which it probably does not possess.

3. crown of beauty and **royal diadem** (better, 'turban') clearly indicate royal status. But the expressions are strange in two ways: Zion is not to *receive*, but to *be* a **crown**; and the crown is not worn upon the head but is **in the hand of the LORD**. With regard to the first point it may be that the city is to be regarded as a crown worn by Yahweh, its city walls having the appearance of a tiara. The phrase 'Borsippa is thy tiara', addressed to Bel (Marduk) in a Babylonian inscription, is frequently quoted in this connexion. The second point is more difficult to explain. It is possible that the idea of Yahweh as wearing a crown on his head like pagan deities was not acceptable to a Jew.

4–5. The restoration of Zion and her new status are now described in the familiar terminology of marriage.

4. Forsaken (*ʿᵃzûḇāh*) means 'abandoned (by your husband)' as in 60 : 15 and in 54 : 6, from which the metaphor was taken. **Desolate** (read *šōmēmāh* for *šᵉmāmāh*) is to be understood as meaning 'barren', as in 54 : 1. (**shall no more be termed** on its second occurrence is probably a later addition.) The new 'names' **My delight is in her** and **Married**, like the old names, are to be taken symbolically: none of them was ever actually used as a name of Jerusalem, although two of them, Azubah (**Forsaken**) and Hephzibah (**My delight is in her**) were actually in use as women's personal names (1 Kg. 22 : 42; 2 Kg. 21 : 1). The second half of the verse (from **for the LORD**) gives a rather pedestrian and unnecessary explanation of the change of names as symbolizing Yahweh's taking back of his estranged 'wife' (a theme derived from Deutero-Isaiah). **and your land shall be married:** this image, a variation on the theme of the city Jerusalem as Yahweh's spouse, has its origins in a Semitic concept of the procreator god who fertilizes the land. A similar phrase occurs in one of the Amarna Letters (fourteenth century BC).

5. For as . . . marries: read *kî-kiḇʿōl* for MT's *kî-yiḇʿal*, following 1QIsᵃ. **so shall your sons marry you:** this is an impossible thought, even as a metaphor. To repoint *bānāyiḵ*, **your sons**, as *bōnāyiḵ*, 'your builders' would be less offensive but still extremely odd. The most plausible solution is to emend to *bōnēḵ*, 'your Builder' (i.e. Yahweh). This involves the further change from a plur. to a sing. verb. Yahweh is called Jerusalem's Builder again in Ps. 147 : 2. The references here and in verse 4 to the ruined state of Jerusalem and of the surrounding land give no precise indication of date. One cannot speak of a full restoration before the time of Nehemiah.

6–7. The interpretation of this passage depends on the answers given to two problems concerning which there is no agreement among the commentators: the identity of the speaker(s) and that of the watchmen (and also of those **who put the LORD in remembrance**). There is the further problem of the **walls** of Jerusalem: whether they are to be taken as existing in reality or only in imagination. The most plausible interpretation of the passage is that of Michel, who regards the first part of verse 6 (to **silent**) as an oracle of Yahweh of which the remainder of the passage is a subsequent interpretation by a 'prophet'. A somewhat similar interpretation was given earlier by Duhm and Elliger among others. If this is so, the **watchmen** are probably heavenly beings serving Yahweh, although the view that they are prophets is not impossible. The highly imaginative character of the passage makes the problem a difficult one.

6. The thought is to be understood in the light of 49 : 16. There Deutero-Isaiah represents Yahweh as constantly reminding himself of his promise to rebuild Jerusalem. But in the interval since those words were spoken the exiles, now returned, have the impression that he has after all forgotten his promise. The oracle with which this verse begins is a further assurance by Yahweh that he has made arrangements to have himself constantly reminded of his undertaking. This thought, which seems strange to modern readers, becomes more comprehensible in the second half of the verse, where the **watchmen** or watchers (*šōmᵉrîm*) are interpreted as **You who put the LORD in remembrance** (*hammazkīrîm*). The *mazkîr* in monarchical times was a court official (2 Sam. 8 : 16; 1 Kg. 4 : 3; Isa. 36 : 3); and, while neither the meaning of the word nor the functions of the office is entirely clear, the view, based on its etymology (*zāḵar* = 'remember'), that it means 'recorder' has not been disproved. If this is so, Yahweh as a great king is here seen as having recorders among his heavenly courtiers, one of whose functions was to see that the programme of duties to which he was committed did not go by default. The prophetic comment here is then a correct interpretation of the oracle, and the two together amount to an assurance to the people that their cause is not forgotten.

The above interpretation suggests a somewhat different translation of the first words of the verse: 'Concerning the (building of) your walls, O Jerusalem, I have appointed responsible (heavenly) officials.' The word 'watchers' was used in intertestamental times of angelic beings, though with a somewhat different function. Cf. also Zech. 1 : 11 (MT 1 : 12).

7. establishes; makes: in view of the metrical irregularity it is possible that each of these verbs originally had an object, one of which has been lost. 1QIsᵃ has a longer line, but it is unlikely that its text is reliable here.

8–9. These verses, like verses 1 and 6, begin with an oracle of Yahweh, this time introduced by a most solemn oath which undergirds his words of promise. It is not clear how far the oracle extends. In verse 9 he is referred to in the third person (**the**

LORD), but the first person reappears in the final word (**my sanctuary**). It is possible that **the LORD** (*'eṯ-yhwh*) is a corruption of *'ōṯî*, 'me', due to a misunderstanding of an abbreviation. On the other hand, the not infrequent confusion in some MSS of the letters *yodh* and *waw* might suggest that **my sanctuary** (*ḳoḏšî*) is a corruption of 'his sanctuary' (*ḳoḏšô*). The suggestion of Michel that here as in the previous two passages we have an oracle of Yahweh subsequently interpreted or expanded is therefore precarious. Apart from the variations mentioned above the passage seems to be a literary unit.

8. Yahweh promises that Jewish farmers will no longer be subject to the carrying-off of their crops by foreigners as plunder or through taxation as formerly. Since Jerusalem and the surrounding countryside had been subjected to foreign oppression, whether through war, conquest, plunder, hostile neighbours, or taxation, ever since the fall of the monarchy in 587, it is not possible to identify these foreigners or to suggest a precise date for these verses. All that is stated is that in the future the Jews will be independent and self-sufficient. It should be noted that this is a much more modest expectation than that expressed in many passages in chapters 60 and 61.

9. This verse refers to the bringing of the first-born of cattle and the first-fruits of grain and wine to offer them to God at the great festivals (see Dt. 12 : 17–18; 14 : 22–27; 16 : 9–17). This was Yahweh's requirement, but it was also the spontaneous action of a loyal people. **and praise the LORD** (*wᵉhillᵉlû 'eṯ-yhwh*)**:** the use of the verb *hillēl* suggests that there may be a reference here to the bringing of such offerings to Yahweh as an 'offering of praise' (*hillûlîm*, Lev. 19 : 24; cf. also Jg. 9 : 27).

10–12. These verses appear to have no direct connexion with the preceding passage. They are regarded by some commentators as the conclusion of the whole section chapters 60–62. Their meaning is, however, far from clear; and this is probably due to the fact that they are mainly constructed out of a series of quotations and near-quotations from Deutero-Isaiah used in a new sense. It is not certain that they form a literary unit; if they do, they must be judged to be of inferior composition due at least to some extent to the inability of the author to handle his borrowed material.

10. Go through, go through the gates with its double

imperative—a characteristic of Deutero-Isaiah's style—is somewhat reminiscent of 52 : 11 where the Babylonian exiles are commanded to depart from the city. The next two lines (to **stones**), like 57 : 14 with which they are largely identical, are closely dependent on 40 : 3 both in theme and language (**prepare the way**, *pannû dereḵ*, appears in all three passages). The final line is adapted from 49 : 22. But Deutero-Isaiah's words have been given entirely new meanings. The **way** is no longer 'the way of the LORD' (40 : 3) but **the way for** (or, 'of') **the people**: no longer a road along which Yahweh will come to Jerusalem as conqueror, bringing with him the returning Babylonian exiles. It has been suggested that it is a **highway** to be prepared for the return of the Jews of the Dispersion, but this is improbable in view of the fact that these would have to return by many quite different routes. It is more probable that, as in 57 : 14, it is the 'way' of the life of devotion to Yahweh which the inhabitants of Jerusalem must lead if their desire for her prosperity is to be fulfilled. The commands to **prepare**, **build up** and **clear** this **highway** are then addressed, not as in 40 : 3 to heavenly beings but to the present inhabitants of Jerusalem. The **gates** are probably the gates of the Temple which they must enter to serve God to this end. **lift up an ensign over the peoples:** in 49 : 22 it is Yahweh who will make a signal to the peoples to bring back Zion's 'sons and daughters'. The phrase is clearly a reminiscence of that passage; but here it appears to refer to a signal to the nations that Jerusalem's triumph is accomplished. The thought is probably based on 40 : 5 where, after the building of the highway, 'the glory of the LORD shall be revealed, and all flesh shall see it together'.

11. The first line of this verse (to **the earth**) is a reminiscence of 48 : 20, where the content of the proclamation is that 'The LORD has redeemed . . . Jacob'. Here the content of the message is not specifically stated: it cannot be what immediately follows—this would be an absurdity, as Duhm pointed out. The line is rather to be taken with verse 10: what **the LORD has proclaimed to the end of the earth** is the same as the message conveyed by the **ensign over the peoples.** The remainder of the verse is almost entirely taken from 40 : 10, 11, though with significant changes. It is not Yahweh himself who **comes** but **your salvation**: the triumphant advent of Yahweh himself has been toned down. This change introduces a new and weaker meaning for the next two lines, which are virtually a quotation: **reward** and **recompense** no longer have the pregnant sense which they have in 40 : 10, but signify simply the 'reward' of prosperity which Yahweh has promised. The plur. imperative **Say** is difficult to explain. It can hardly be addressed to the same persons as the imperatives in verse 10, and is probably to be understood impersonally. The author has perhaps been influenced by the plur. imperatives in 40 : 1, 2 which introduce the passage which he is re-interpreting, and which he may have understood in an impersonal sense.

12. A distinction (though not, of course, a contrast) is made between **they** (the nation as a whole) and **you** (the city of Jerusalem). On the metaphorical employment of the idea of giving new names see on verses 2, 4. **redeemed:** perhaps a reminiscence of 51 : 10. **forsaken:** see on verse 4.

YAHWEH THE AVENGER

63 : 1–6

Almost all commentators agree that these verses form an independent unit. They are unrelated to their immediate context, although there is an undeniable literary relationship between them and 59 : 15*b*–20, and they have in common with 61 : 2 the theme of the **day of vengeance** (verse 4). They contain a remarkable number of rare or very rare words, a fact which is not entirely explained by the special character of the theme with which they deal. They are in the form of a dialogue: a bloodstained warrior returning from the direction of Edom is challenged—perhaps by a watchman or sentry—to reveal his identity. He replies in words which, though indirect and mysterious, reveal that he is Yahweh himself (verse 1). A further question concerning the reason for the red stains on his garments (verse 2) elicits a long reply (verses 3–6) in which Yahweh relates how he has intervened on behalf of his people, annihilating **the peoples** who were their enemies. This extremely dramatic scene, which has no real parallels in the *OT*, is clearly a prophetic vision which has the effect of a very powerful assurance to the Jews that their God will effectively defend and protect them. In this sense the passage conveys a message similar to that of other passages in chapters 56–66. It has been called 'apocalyptic' by some commentators, but in fact the theme of a universal divine victory over the peoples conceived as a single enemy goes little further than such passages in Deutero-Isaiah as 41 : 8–13, where, although the prophet no doubt has *one* hostile nation—the Babylonians—principally in mind, the fact that they are not specifically named confers on them something of a universal character. The passage no doubt reflects the feeling of the Jews that they had not a friend in the world and a consequent tendency to regard all foreign nations as enemies whose destruction was to be desired. But the passage entirely lacks the cosmic overtones characteristic of apocalyptic. See on 66 : 15–16.

It has frequently been remarked that while in verse 1 Yahweh comes specifically from **Edom**, verses 3 and 6 refer to a general defeat of **the peoples**. This apparent inconsistency has led to proposals to eliminate the references to Edom by emending the words **from Edom** and **from Bozrah** (see on verse 1). There is no justification for this. Edom had, because of its hostile actions towards the Jews of Palestine during the Exile, already become their enemy *par excellence* (cf. Ps. 137 : 7; Ob. 13–14; Lam. 4 : 21–22; Ezek. 25 : 12; 35 : 1–15) and it was therefore natural to use its name in a representative sense: cf. also Isa. 34. There is no reason to see here a specific reference to any historical event: the victory of Yahweh referred to here is in the future. Since Jewish hostility to Edom continued to be expressed long after the Exile, it is impossible to date the passage precisely.

1. Lagarde, followed by Duhm and others, proposed the emendation of *mēʿeḏôm*, **from Edom**, to *meʿoddām*, 'stained red', and of *mibboṣrāh*, **from Bozrah**, to *mibbōṣer*, yielding the translation 'with garments redder than (those of) one who treads grapes'. These are purely conjectural changes of the text. Rather what we have here is a play on words which is particularly effective because the name **Edom** was thought to be (and probably was) derived from the root *ʾdm* 'to be red', and was also famous for its wine production. **Bozrah** was the chief town of Edom (Jer. 49 : 13). It may be of significance that the text does not specifically refer to a victory won over Edom to the exclusion of other enemies, but speaks only of Edom as the place where the battle was fought. Some commentators have suggested that there is an allusion here to Jg. 5 : 4, where also Yahweh comes **from Edom**; but this is improbable because there he is coming *to* the battle, not from it. **marching:** MT has 'bending' or 'bowed' (*ṣō'eh*). *RSV* rightly follows most commentators in emending to *ṣō'ēḏ* on the basis of Vulg.'s *gradiens*. **announcing vindication:** *ṣᵉḏāḵāh* is here once again used in the sense of 'victory'.

2. Why is thy apparel red . . .?: better, 'Why is there red on your clothing . . .?'. Emendation of *lilᵉḇûšeḵā* by the omission of the first letter is unnecessary, and changes the meaning. The returning conqueror is not wearing red clothes, but clothes on which (*lᵉ*) there are red bloodstains.

3. In answer to the question in verse 2 Yahweh accepts the figure of the **wine press** and uses it as a metaphor: the 'grapes' are the peoples whom Yahweh has crushed in the 'wine press' of battle; the 'juice' (this is apparently the meaning of the rare word translated by **lifeblood**) is the blood of the slain, with which the 'grape-treader' has inevitably stained his clothes. The metaphor was evidently so well known (it occurs again in Lam. 1 : 15; Jl. 3 : 13 (MT 4 : 13)) that no explanation of it was needed. **alone; no one was with me:** there was no Cyrus, as in Deutero-Isaiah, to act as Yahweh's agent; on the contrary, all the peoples were arrayed against him; he was forced to take direct action himself. The alternative reading of 1QIsᵃ, 'from my people', is hardly appropriate. **I have stained:** the unusual form *'eg'altî* might be explained as an unusual spelling of the Hiphil influenced by Aramaic (so G–K §53p); but it is probably best to read the Piel *gē'altî* with 1QIsᵃ. Most commentators repoint the three previous verbs **trod**, **trampled**, and **is sprinkled** to *waw* consecutives.

4. On the literary relationship between this verse, and indeed this whole passage, and 59 : 15*b*–20 see the commentary on that passage. **day of vengeance** (*yôm nāḵām*) has an appropriateness here which it lacks there. On the other hand the phrase **my year of redemption** (*šᵉnaṯ gᵉ'ûlay*, which can also mean 'the year of my redeemed ones') is probably similar in meaning to the 'year of release' in 61 : 2 and may be associated with the law of the 'redemption' or enfranchisement (*gā'al*) of slaves and property laid down in Lev. 25. To secure this freedom for his people is the firm intention of Yahweh (**in my heart**). **has come:** it must be remembered that Yahweh is here represented as speaking after a victory which is as yet in the future. As elsewhere in chapters 56–66 there is not the same sense of urgent expectation of an imminent event as is found throughout Deutero-Isaiah.

5. This verse is clearly a variant of 59 : 16 but is in the first rather than the third person. On the relationship between the two see on 59 : 16. Here the verse is in place in that it expands the statement in verse 3 that Yahweh was forced to take action alone. As in verse 3 most commentators repoint two verbs, **I looked** and **I was appalled**, with *waw* consecutives. So also with the verbs in verse 6.

6. This verse is mainly a variant of verse 3*b*, though, as Duhm points out, such repetition is not necessarily a sign of textual corruption. **I made them drunk:** we should probably read *ʾašabbᵉrēm*, 'I smashed them' for MT's *ʾašakkᵉrēm*, with a number of MSS and with reference to Targ. **lifeblood:** the same rare word as in verse 3, but here clearly to be translated as in *RSV*.

LAMENTATION AND PRAYER

63 : 7–64 : 12 (MT 63 : 7–64 : 11)

The commentators are in agreement about both the extent and the character of this remarkable passage. It belongs to the category of psalm known as the communal lamentation, a category which embraces a wide variety of different attitudes and forms of expression, and it would not be out of place if it stood in the Psalter rather than in a prophetical book. Its four main elements, all of which are to be found in other psalms of the same type, are the account of Yahweh's acts of redemption towards his people in the past (63 : 7–14), the appeal to him for help, including references to the present pitiable state of the petitioners (63 : 15–64 : 5*a* (MT 63 : 15–64 : 4*a*)), the confession of sin (64 : 5*b*–7 (MT 64 : 4*b*–6)) and the final renewed appeal in which earlier themes are brought together (64 : 8–12 (MT 64 : 7–11)). The thought of the psalm seems to move on more than one religious level, and the view of Pauritsch that it was not all composed at one time is perhaps justified, although there is little in it which may be termed inconsistency of thought.

There is no real evidence to support the view of L. Browne (*Early Judaism*, 1929), Snaith, and others that this is a polemical psalm in which one group (the Samaritans or 'proto-Samaritans') complains about its rejection by another (the returned exiles). Like most of the compositions in chapters 56–66 it reflects a feeling of disillusionment and of abandonment by God; but apart from this the only clues to its date are the references to the ruined state of Jerusalem and the Temple, and of other cities, as a result of enemy action (63 : 18; 64 : 10–11 (MT 64 : 9–10)). There is no reason to doubt that the acts of destruction referred to are those of 587 BC; and the intensity of the emotions expressed here suggests that they had occurred within living memory (cf. Lam. 1 : 10; 2 : 7–9). On the other hand the harrowing descriptions of human misery consequent upon the Babylonian conquest so characteristic of the book of Lamentations are lacking, and the suggestions of, among others, Fohrer and Muilenburg that the psalm should be dated in the middle rather than the early years of the Exile may be right. If so it is probably the earliest part of chapters 56–66, a product of the population left in Palestine. The other period (*c.* 538–520 BC) most frequently suggested is less likely. If, as is probable, this is a liturgical composition used at gatherings for worship during the exilic period in Palestine it is not difficult to understand how it came to find its way into this collection of prophecies: it would have become familiar to the exiles on their return, and would have been adopted by them as matching the mood of their own subsequent disappointment which is reflected elsewhere in the collection. The mid-exilic period in Palestine is therefore the most probable date, though certainty on this point is not possible.

63 : 7–14. The historical survey which is also a feature of some other corporate lamentations occurs here, as in Ps. 44, at the beginning, but it is notable that Yahweh is spoken of in the third person: the prayer does not begin until verse 15. The account of Israel's election, rebellion and punishment together with subsequent reflection on these events (cf. also Ezra's prayer in Neh. 9 : 7ff.) reflects the same growing awareness of the 'theology of history' as is found in the roughly contemporary Deuteronomic History (Westermann). The purpose of the historical survey is not, as in Ps 44, to reproach Yahweh with his recent neglect of an innocent people, but to express penitence and to appeal for another chance.

7. I will recount: cf. the similar expression in Ps. 77 : 11 (MT 77 : 12). **steadfast love** (*ḥasᵉḏê*), like **praises** (*tᵉhillōṯ*) is in the plural, referring to a plurality of actions of Yahweh (cf. 55 : 3). **praises** here means 'praiseworthy deeds'. **according to** (*kᵉʿal*): see on 59 : 18. **and the great goodness** (*wᵉraḇ-ṭûḇ*): the rendering of *RSV* is a possible translation of MT and there is probably no need to emend. The phrase is the third object of **I will recount.** The omission of **to the house of Israel** is probably also not justified. **them:** i.e. the house of Israel.

8. they are my people: this is a quotation of part of the so-called 'covenant formula' of which the corresponding clause is 'I am (or, "will be") their God': cf. e.g. Lev. 26 : 12; Dt. 29 : 13; Jer. 7 : 23; Ezek. 11 : 20. The author begins his account of Yahweh's 'steadfast love' with a reference to his original election of Israel to be his people. Then in anticipation of their subsequent tragic rejection of him (verse 10) he introduces a kind of dramatic irony: Yahweh trusted them to be faithful to him. **sons:** that Israel was, by virtue of its election, Yahweh's son (or individually his **sons**) was a familiar notion. Here the thought is especially close to Isa. 1 : 2: the rebellion of sons against their father was an unthinkable impiety, yet Israel was guilty of it. **and he became their Saviour:** metre and sense require that **In all their affliction** should be transferred from verse 9 to complete this line: 'he became their Saviour in all their affliction.' The election of Israel is represented as having occurred before the great acts of salvation which began with the Exodus (so also Gen. 17 : 7–8; Exod. 6 : 2–8—both passages belonging to the Priestly strand of the Pentateuch).

9. he was afflicted, and the angel of his presence saved them: his presence (*pānāw*) is literally 'his face'. The acceptance by *RSV*, following earlier translations, of the Qere *lô* ('to him') rather than the Kethib *lō'* ('not'), together with its retention of the traditional verse-division (see on verse 8 above) creates a number of difficulties. One of these is that the phrase **the angel of his presence** would be a unique and improbable concept in *OT* times. The most plausible solution, though itself not entirely free from difficulties, is to follow LXX, accepting the verse-division proposed above and the Kethib, and repointing the phrase as *lō' ṣîr ûmal'āḵ*. This allows the whole line to be translated, 'it was no messenger or angel, but his presence which saved them'. The meaning is that Yahweh personally intervened to save his people. This concept of Yahweh's 'face' or **presence** is found in Exod. 33 : 14, 15, a passage to which this line is probably an allusion. (The word is also used of the personal presence of human beings: 2 Sam. 17 : 11.) **he lifted them up and carried them:** cf. 46 : 3.

10. Psalms 78 and 106 also recount Yahweh's acts of redemption and Israel's ungrateful response, and in similar terms: cf. especially Ps. 78 : 40; 106 : 33, 43. This verse is to be interpreted as referring in general terms to Israel's whole history of rebellion and its culmination in the disasters of the Assyrian and Babylonian conquests which are seen as due to Yahweh's deliberate instigation. **his holy Spirit** (*rûaḥ ḳoḏšô*)**:** this expression, which is repeated in verse 11 with a further reference to **the Spirit of the LORD** in verse 14, occurs in only one other place in the *OT*: Ps. 51 : 11 (MT 51 : 13). God's **holy Spirit**, dwelling within his people (verse 11), leading them through the desert to their destined home in Canaan (verse 14), but then **grieved** by their rebellion, is here personified more clearly than anywhere else in the *OT*, and is on its way to its later full development as a distinct hypostasis in late Jewish and in Christian thought.

11. he remembered: the subject is clearly the people of Israel, though it is probably not necessary to emend the verb to the plural as is proposed by some commentators. It is especially in Deuteronomy and in the Psalms that the remembering of Yahweh's past actions on behalf of his people (or, in some Psalms, of an individual) becomes a criterion of Israel's faith and conduct. To remember them continually was to remain grateful and obedient to him and to continue to receive his blessings; for such remembering the cult was the most appropriate occasion (Ps. 105 : 5). To forget them was to depart from him, and the consequences of this were disastrous (Ps. 78 : 42; 106 : 7). But to remember them again after the disasters had had their effect was to be moved to appeal for help on the basis of the nation's or individual's past experience of a gracious God (Ps. 77 : 11 (MT 77 : 12); 143 : 5); and this is what is described here. The reference is general; but it includes the present, and so gives the author the opportunity to put into the mouths of the people, in the verses which follow, an appeal for help which expresses exactly what he wants to say himself. **of Moses his servant:** Heb. has 'Moses his people'. LXX omits the phrase altogether. *RSV*, following some MSS and Pesh., has accepted the emendation of *ʿammô*, 'his people', to *ʿaḇdô*, **his servant**. An alternative solution is to put *wᵉ*, 'and', before 'his people'. It is not certain that either of these solutions is correct. The two words in MT may be a corruption of some other phrase. **the shepherds of his flock:** the plur. **shepherds** can hardly be right. Most commentators emend it to the sing. in agreement with LXX and Targ. If this is correct, it refers to **Moses**, and probably to the deliverance at the Red Sea, although a few commentators think of it as a reference to the rescue of the baby Moses from the waters of the Nile (Exod. 2 : 1–10). **brought up:** MT has 'brought *them* up' (*maʿalēm*). *NEB* retains the reading of MT, taking the particle *'ēṯ* which precedes **the shepherds** as meaning 'with'; but 1QIsª has *maʿaleh*, a reading which had been long proposed on the basis of the Versions; and *RSV* has, probably rightly, followed this. This verb is the first of a series of participles expressing God's activity in the past, concluding with **who led them** in verse 13. This construction is a characteristic of the hymn or song of praise, but is equally appropriate to poetical narrative of this kind. **in the midst of them:** MT has 'in the midst of him'. The reference is, however, to the whole people rather than to Moses alone. **his holy Spirit:** see on verse 10.

12. who caused his glorious arm to go: on Yahweh's **arm** see on 40 : 10; 51 : 9; cf. also 59 : 16; 63 : 5. The personification is very fully developed here. **who divided** (*bôḵēaʿ*)**:** a traditional word for the dividing of the Red Sea, used in Exod. 14 : 16, 21; Ps. 78 : 13. The account in Exodus also makes Moses' **hand** the instrument of the miracle.

13–14. The simile of the **horse** moving sure-footedly across the **desert** or plain adds a new feature to the miracle of the crossing of the Red Sea: the Israelites find no difficulty in negotiating the boulders and weeds which might be expected to have been found on the sea bottom. The second image, of the return of the herds to the greener pastures of **the valley** from their more arduous period of grazing on the mountain sides, is an appropriate simile for the conclusion of the story of Yahweh's miraculous guidance of Israel in the past: the giving of **rest** to them in the land of promise. This root, *nûaḥ*, is that traditionally employed in referring to that event. Some Versions seem to have regarded the verb as derived from *nāḥāh*, 'lead, guide' (perhaps reading *tanḥennû*), but the reading of MT (*teniḥennû*, **gave them rest**) is more suited to the context. The use of the verb *nûaḥ* in Exod. 33 : 14 supports this view.

63 : 15–64 : 5a (MT 63: 15–64 : 4*a*). Westermann comments at this point that it is difficult to see the structure of this psalm. The only clear evidence of structure in this section is provided by the three direct words of appeal, **Look down** (verse 15), **Return** (verse 17*b*) and **O that thou wouldst . . .** (64 : 1*a* (MT 63 : 19*b*)), dividing the passage into three sections of unequal length. Upon these 'pegs' are hung a variety of supporting arguments and statements intended to move God to help: a reproach and an appeal to the father-son relationship (verses 15–17); an appeal to the past (verses 17*b*–19); and an appeal to God's mysterious power (64 : 1–3 (MT 63 : 19*b*–64 : 2)) and his accustomed graciousness (64 : 4–5*a* (MT 64 : 3–4*a*)).

15. Look down from heaven and see: precisely the same words occur in Ps. 80 : 14 (MT 80 : 15), a communal lamentation on the same theme as this psalm. Such duplications are often to be explained as examples of a common traditional stock of phrases available to psalm-writers. The idea that Yahweh dwells in **heaven** was an ancient one; here, however, it is used to emphasize the apparent withdrawal of Yahweh from his people. The fact that the Temple was in ruins may also have brought the idea into prominence. The whole verse implies that Yahweh has become indifferent to the fate of his people: cf. Ps. 79; 83; 115, which are all corporate lamentations on a similar theme. **are withheld from me:** the Heb. is strange—literally, 'have restrained themselves to me' (*'ēlay hiṯ'appāḳû*). The singular **me** and the use of the particle *'el*, 'to', together with the non-personal subject, all suggest a corrupt text. In LXX (as also in 64 : 12 (MT 64 : 11) and 42 : 14) the subject of this verb is Yahweh. The original reading may have been something like *'al-nā' tiṯ'appāḳ*, 'do not restrain yourself', i.e. 'do not stand aloof', the previous two nouns being governed by **Where are . . .?**

16. For thou art our Father: these words are best taken with the previous phrase. The idea of God as the **Father** of Israel, the corollary to that of Israel as God's son(s), occurs in Dt. 32 : 6, where its meaning is given in terms of his 'creation' of the nation (cf. also 64 : 8 below). The meaning of the references to Abraham and Israel is much disputed. Duhm takes this as an indication of ancestor worship: appeals to Abraham and Jacob (Israel) have been made, but have failed. Schoors, following Pauritsch, sees here legal formulae of rejection and exclusion from fellowship and support: the community, whose views are represented by the psalmist, feels that the patriarchs, the mediators of God's promises, have in some way rejected their descendants and cut them off from the promises. The more usual view is that the two patriarchs are simply cited in order to emphasize a feeling of hopelessness: the great charismatic figures are long dead, and therefore unable to help. None of these views is entirely satisfactory. The one thing that is clear is that the psalmist is making a direct appeal to Yahweh as **Father** and **Redeemer** of his people which he hopes will be successful in spite of all that has happened in the past. This verse is therefore intended to broaden the appeal to God in verse 15 not to withhold his love and compassion.

17. The psalmist does not deny that the people have sinned: indeed, there is an extended confession of sin in 64 : 5*b*–7 (MT 64 : 4*b*–6). But Yahweh is regarded always in the *OT* as the initiator of all that happens in the world (cf. e.g. Am. 3 : 6): consequently even sin is regarded as within his power to permit or to hinder from occurring. This paradox of the 'hardening of the heart' finds no solution in the *OT*, but it is never held to absolve human beings of their responsibility for their actions. However, if God permits sin he is also the only source of grace; and the psalmist is therefore able, in spite of his sorrowful perplexity (**why?**) about his reasons for allowing the present state of affairs to happen, to appeal with some degree of confidence to him to **Return for the sake of thy servants**, adding a further phrase, **the tribes of thy heritage**, to remind him of the special relationship which once existed between him and his people (see on 54 : 17, and cf. 58 : 14).

18–19 (MT 18–19*a*). The description of the present situation and its cause is one of the most characteristic features of the lamentation. In communal lamentations it often takes the form of a narrative of past events: cf. especially Ps. 74 : 3–8; 79 : 1–4; Lamentations *passim*. Here the destruction of Jerusalem, especially its Temple (*miḳdāš*) is referred to.

18. *RSV* does not truly represent the order of the words in the Heb. **thy sanctuary** (*miḳdāšeḵā*) occurs not in the first half of the verse but in the second, where it is represented by **it**. The first half is almost certainly corrupt, and it is not certain that the Temple is referred to there. It may be translated either as 'For a little while a (the) people took possession of thy sanctuary (*ḳoḏšeḵā*)' or 'For a little while thy holy people (*ʿam-ḳoḏšeḵā*) possessed . . .' (there is no object). Neither of these translations is satisfactory: it can hardly be said that Solomon's Temple lasted only a short time; and the second alternative is an incomplete sentence. The majority of commentators propose emendations yielding a sense which provides a parallelism with the second half of the verse. Of these, 'Why have the wicked treated thy sanctuary with contempt?' (*lāmmāh ṣiʿarû rešāʿîm ḳoḏšeḵā*) is perhaps the most plausible.

19 (MT 19*a*). **never** (*mēʿôlām*)**:** literally, '(not) from of old'. **who are not called by thy name:** literally, 'over whom thy name was not called'. The phrase *ḳārāʾ šēm* X *ʿal* signifies ownership, and is used with reference to Israel as Yahweh's possession in Dt. 28 : 10; Jer. 14 : 9. Yahweh is thus reproached with being a king who abandons his subjects and an owner who is indifferent to the loss of his property.

64 : 1–5a (MT 63 : 19*b*–64 : 4*a*). This section (ending with **in thy ways**) is the most impassioned part of the psalm. The prayer that Yahweh would 'Look down from heaven' (63 : 15) is now eclipsed by an intense longing for him to descend in majesty and power as in the days of old at the Exodus (Exod. 19) and at the waters of Megiddo (Jg. 5) to strike terror into the hearts of Israel's enemies and to bestow his gracious presence upon his forlorn people. The psalmist uses much of the traditional language characteristic of descriptions of such 'theophanies': cf. among other passages Exod. 19 : 16–18; Jg. 5 : 4–5; Ps. 18 : 7–15 (MT 18 : 8–16); Mic. 1 : 3–4; Hab. 3 : 3–6, and see on 66 : 15–16.

64 : 1 (MT 63 : 19*b*). Yahweh is here thought of as concealed from men by a partition—perhaps of clouds—which constituted **the heavens**. He is urged to **rend** or rip aside this partition—a violent expression which goes beyond the otherwise similar thought in Ps. 18 : 9 (MT 18 : 10); Ps. 144 : 5—and **come down**. **quake** (*nāzōlleᵉlû*)**:** this is the Niphal of *zālal*. LXX, however, has 'flow down', which presupposes a different pointing: *nāzālû*, the Qal of *nāzal*. In Jg. 5 : 5, on the other hand, where the same consonants occur with **the mountains** as subject, MT has the Qal of *nāzal*, while LXX presupposes the Niphal of *zālal*. In both cases either interpretation yields reasonable sense, with the balance perhaps just in favour of **quake**.

2 (MT 1). The meaning of the first half of this verse (to **boil**) is not entirely clear, and some commentators regard it as an irrelevant and obtrusive interpolation. The rendering of *tiḇʿeh* by **causes . . . to boil** is somewhat dubious. LXX has a quite different text, though the common element **fire** perhaps suggests that both MT and LXX are corruptions of an original in which **fire**, a frequent element in theophanies, played a part.

3 (MT 2). The second half of this verse (from **thou camest down**) is in the Heb. an exact repetition of **come down . . . presence** in verse 1 and should probably be omitted as a gloss. The first half of the verse should then be taken with the previous verse and translated 'when thou dost . . .'. **terrible things** (*nôrā'ôṯ*): this stock expression for Yahweh's mighty acts (cf. Dt. 10 : 21; 2 Sam. 7 : 23; Ps. 106 : 22) would perhaps better be translated 'awesome things', since in the contexts in which it occurs the emphasis is on the benefits conferred on the Israelites rather than on the effects upon their enemies. **which we looked not for:** the psalmist gains confidence from the reflection that Yahweh's acts of salvation in the past have occurred when they were least expected.

4 (MT 3). The thought of the unexpectedness of God's grace is now translated into something like an act of praise. Unfortunately the verse is very corrupt. LXX diverges considerably from MT, and Paul, who quotes the verse in 1 C. 2 : 9, even more so. The suggestions which follow are very tentative. **From of old no one has heard** (literally, 'and from of old they did not hear'): the verb should be emended to the first person and the phrase transposed to the end of verse 3 (i.e. after **looked not for**): 'and of which from of old we had not heard'. **or perceived by the ear** (*lō' he'ezînû*, literally, 'they did not listen') should be emended with LXX to *lō' he'ezînāh 'ōzen*, 'no ear has heard', in parallelism with **no eye has seen. besides thee**, which conflicts grammatically with the third person verb **who works** (*ya'aśeh*), should be omitted. The second half of the verse (from **God**) can then be translated 'what God does for those who wait for him' (reading, with *RSV*, the plur. for MT's sing.). It should be noted that **wait** is not inconsistent with **we looked not for** in verse 3: the former verb (*ḥikkāh*) signifies patient waiting which does not necessarily expect immediate gratification, while the latter (*ḳiwwāh*) denotes eager expectancy.

5a (MT 4*a*). The ingenious suggestion of Grätz that the word *lū*, 'O that . . . !', has been omitted by haplography from the beginning of this verse (the previous verse ends with *lô*) has been adopted by many commentators. Its addition would turn this part of the verse into an appeal to God. But it makes sense as it stands as a continuation or reinforcement of the sentiment of the previous verse. The Heb. text, however, presents a number of difficulties. **Thou meetest** (*pāga'tā*): nowhere else in the *OT* does this verb unqualifiedly have the sense of 'accept, welcome' which the context seems to require. Some other verb may originally have stood here; Volz' *pāḳaḏ*, 'visit', used in just such a favourable sense in passages like Jer. 15: 15; 27: 22, is the most plausible of the suggestions which have been made. **him that joyfully works:** the Heb. *'eṯ-śāś we'ōśēh* hardly makes sense. The shorter reading of LXX ('those who work' = *'ōśê*) is to be preferred. Similarly LXX's 'remember thy ways' is preferable to **remember thee in thy ways.**

5b–7 (MT 4*b*–6). Like 63: 17 this section is part confession, part reproach. The petitioners' sin and God's hardening of their hearts which leads them to sin are inextricably mixed together.

5b (MT 4*b*). **Behold, thou:** the emphatic particle *hēn* draws attention to the difference between the present situation and that described in the previous verses. **and we sinned:** this translation would imply that God's anger drove the people to yet further sin by hardening their hearts; but this would be to read too much into the Hebrew. Another possible rendering is 'and yet we sinned' (see Driver, *Hebrew Tenses*, §74): a confession that the people deliberately sinned in spite of Yahweh's clear warning. The remainder of the verse is textually corrupt and obscures the problem rather than illuminates it. **in our sins we have been a long time** is hardly a possible translation of *bāhem 'ôlām*, and the final word *weniwwāšēa'*, most naturally rendered by 'and we shall be saved', hardly makes sense even if regarded, as in *RSV*, as a question. Volz' emendation of the whole phrase to *behē'ālemeḵā wannirša'*, '(and) when you hid yourself we behaved wickedly', has the greatest plausibility. If it could be accepted with confidence this would confirm the view that the psalmist is speaking of a hardening of hearts caused by Yahweh's anger. There is, however, a third interpretation: that of S. H. Blank (*JBL* 71 (1952), pp. 149–54), who argues that both *ḥāṭā'* and *rāša'* sometimes have the meaning of 'bear the blame' and 'stand convicted', whether justly or unjustly. According to him the psalmist is making no confession of sin but rather accusing God of unjustly condemning and punishing his people. The most important question is, therefore, whether these lines contain a confession or a reproach. In spite of the force of the arguments in favour of the latter interpretation, a consideration of the context (that is, of their relationship to the verses which follow) favours the former. Whether or not there is an element of reproach here it is difficult to deny that there is also a recognition of sin.

6 (MT 5). The further deterioration of the spiritual state of the people is now forcefully described. The term **unclean** (*ṭāmē'*) signifies primarily a ceremonial impurity which makes a person or thing totally unfit for association with God or for use in his worship. Persons who have contracted this condition may become free of it after a fixed period; but the simile of the **polluted garment**, that is, a garment stained by a woman during her menstruation (cf. Lev. 12), describes a situation which is even more serious: such an object can never become clean again (cf. Hag. 2 : 11–14) and is clearly fit only for destruction. So the psalmist complains that the situation has become so hopeless that even the virtues or **righteous deeds** (*ṣ*ᵉ*ḏāḳôṯ*) of the people have become worthless in God's eyes and abhorrent to him. Further similes describe the outcome of this separation from God. **We . . . fade:** MT's *wannāḇel*, derived from *bālal*, hardly gives the desired sense. 1QIsᵃ indicates that we should repoint as *wannibbōl*, from *nāḇēl*, 'fade, droop'. **take us away:** pointing *yiśśā'ēnû* for MT's *yiśśā'ūnû*.

7 (MT 6). Here again reproach and confession are mingled together. Spiritual apathy has resulted from God's withdrawal; but the fact of sin is not denied. **take hold:** or, 'cling to (in supplication)'. **hast delivered us:** MT's *watt*ᵉ*mûḡēnû* is derived from *mûg* = 'melt', hardly a possible translation even if a transitive sense for this verb were allowed. *RSV*, probably rightly, emends to *watt*ᵉ*magg*ᵉ*nēnû*, the Piel of *mgn*, with LXX and some other Versions.

8 (MT 7). The initial word **Yet** (*w*ᵉ*'attāh*, literally 'And now') introduces a new argument: an appeal, in a more confident mood than that of the previous verses, to God as Israel's maker not to destroy what he has made. The notion of God as Israel's **Father**, already employed in a somewhat different way in 63 : 16, is now allied to the image of the **potter** and the **clay**, an image also capable of being used in more than one way, as a comparison with 45 : 9 shows. Its use here is similar to its use in Job 10 : 9.

9 (MT 8). **exceedingly:** perhaps better, 'excessively'. **remember not iniquity for ever:** a very similar plea is made in Ps. 79 : 8.

10–11 (MT 9–10). The description of the present wretched situation in Palestine is now taken up from 63 : 18 and expanded as an introduction to the final appeal to God in verse 12.

10 (MT 9). The plur. expression **Thy holy cities** is unique; but there is no reason to emend to the sing. in imitation of LXX. Since the whole land is a holy land (Zech. 2 : 12 (MT 2 : 16)) each of its **cities** may be regarded as **holy**. The repetition of the phrase **have (has) become a wilderness** is inelegant, but calls for no emendation.

11 (MT 10). **our fathers:** this phrase does not necessarily exclude the present generation, though it does perhaps suggest that enough time has elapsed since the burning of the Temple to have made a historical perspective possible. There is probably no significance in the fact that the Temple, called 'thy sanctuary' in 63 : 18, is now called **Our . . . house:** this is merely a slight change of mood in the expression of grief.

12 (MT 11). The lamentation ends with an imploring question; cf. Lam. 5 : 22. **Wilt thou restrain thyself:** see on 63 : 15. **Wilt thou keep silent:** that is, refuse to intervene on behalf of his people, as he promised to do in 62 : 1. **sorely:** the Heb. expression has the same meaning as in verse 9, where *RSV* translates it by 'exceedingly'.

REWARDS AND PUNISHMENTS

65 : 1–25

Although at first sight verse 1 might suggest that this chapter contains Yahweh's answer to the preceding lamentation there is no connexion between the two passages. The most prominent feature of this chapter, the fact that it is addressed to a religiously divided community, is entirely absent from the preceding chapters. Chapter 66 also, although it has strong affinities with this chapter, must also be regarded as distinct from it. A more difficult question is that of the internal unity of this chapter. If we exclude verse 25, which is certainly a later addition, there is a kind of unity here: the theme of the contrast between two elements—the faithful and the apostate—within the Jewish community cannot be entirely due to editorial activity. There is also some consistency in the vocabulary, e.g. the use of the phrases **my servants** (verses 8, 13) and **my chosen** (verses 9, 22). But there are good reasons for regarding the chapter as having been composed from a number of smaller units. Verses 16*b*–23 not only have marked characteristics of their own but are also pure promise: the contrast between the fates of the two opposing groups is absent. This section was almost certainly originally quite separate, although it has now been firmly joined to the first part of the chapter by the addition of verse 24, which echoes verse 1 and forms with it a framework which binds the chapter together as a whole. It has, however, affinities with verses 1–16*a* which suggest that it was composed at a time not far removed from the date of those verses. On the question of the unity of verses 1–16*a* see further below.

There is no agreement among the commentators with regard to the date of composition. The descriptions of idolatrous cults in verses 3–5, 11 do not suggest a connexion with the similar passage 56 : 9–57 : 13. The two primary criteria for the dating of verses 1–16*a* are the identity of the two opposing groups and the nature of the idolatrous cults. On this basis a Hellenistic date has been proposed (Volz), while at the other extreme some commentators have suggested a pre-exilic date. The view that the cults in question belong exclusively to the Hellenistic period has been strongly opposed by R. de Vaux (*Von Ugarit nach Qumran*, Eissfeldt *Festschrift* (*BZAW* 77), 1958, pp. 250–65 = *Bible et Orient*, 1967, pp. 499–516). On the other hand the division of the community into two clearly defined religious groups would appear to rule out the pre-exilic period, but leaves almost unlimited scope for a dating later than that. An early post-exilic date is quite possible.

1–16a. After a statement about his readiness in the past to admit to his fellowship even those who had turned their backs on him (verses 1–2*a*), Yahweh, who is the speaker throughout, describes and condemns (referring to them in the third person) a **rebellious people** for their idolatrous practices and announces his vengeance upon them (verses 2*b*–7). But in verse 8 he makes a crucial distinction between the corrupt mass and a faithful kernel to whom (referring to them also in the third person) he promises a peaceful and blessed existence (verses 9–10). He now addresses the idolaters directly, describing their idolatrous practices a second time but in a different way and once more announcing their destruction (verses 11–12). Finally, still addressing the idolaters, he draws a detailed contrast between their fate and that of the faithful (verses 13–15), ending with further reassurances for the latter. In its present form the passage possesses a certain coherence of thought, its unity being supplied by the contrast between the idolaters and the faithful; but the repetitions and changes of the persons addressed suggest that it is composite. These difficulties are largely removed if verses 1–7, which refer exclusively to the idolaters, are taken as a distinct and original composition.

1–2a (to **people**). These verses are quoted in Rom. 10 : 20–21 by Paul, who interprets verse 1 as referring to the Gentiles who have had the gospel preached to them in contrast to the rebellious Jews of verse 2*a*. But this is not the meaning of the author, who is referring throughout to the rebellious Israelites. The Pauline interpretation was a natural one, since the two verbs **I was ready to be sought** (*nidraštî*) and **I was ready to be found** (*nimṣē'tî*) are in the Niphal, which most frequently has a simple passive sense, and are translated by passive verbs in the LXX: 'I was sought', 'I was found'. But all commentators are agreed that this is the so-called 'tolerative' use of the Niphal (G–K §51c) which *RSV* has rendered correctly. Yahweh offered himself but was rejected. **ask for me:** MT has simply 'ask' (*šā'ālû*). But 1QIs[a] and some later MSS have the suffix 'me'. **that did not call on my name:** reading Qal perfect *ḳārā'* or participle *ḳōrē'* with the Versions. MT has the same consonants but points them *ḳōrā'*, 'was (not) called', which would mean that they were not Israelites. MT's pointing shows the same tendency as Paul to regard this verse as referring to foreign peoples. But it is clear from the following verses that the reference throughout is to apostate Israelites who have ceased—at least in any real sense—to acknowledge Yahweh. **ask, find,** and **seek** frequently refer to cultic activity, but in the immediate context they probably have a general sense. **nation** (*gôy*), **people** (*'am*): these words here denote not national entities but simply groups of people. **I spread out my hands:** normally a gesture of prayer, but here clearly one of appeal. Yahweh is represented as condescending so far as to implore these people to return to him. **rebellious** (*sôrēr*): the metrical line is too short. We should add 'and disobedient' (*ûmôreh*), following LXX and Paul. 1QIs[a] has only one word, probably *môreh* (the text is not clear).

2b–5. The catalogue of sins is presented in a series of participial clauses: **who provoke**; **sacrificing**; **burning incense**; **who sit**; **who eat**; **who say**. Although the exact nature of some of the more specific accusations is not clear, these are all religious rites totally incompatible with the worship of Yahweh.

3. to my face (*'al-pānay*)**:** that is, openly. **sacrificing in gardens:** cf. 66 : 17. Such sacrifices in the open air, probably connected with fertility rites, are condemned by pre-exilic prophets: cf. Isa. 1 : 29 and references in Dt., Jer. and Ezek. to rites performed 'under every green tree' etc. **burning incense upon bricks** *m[e]ḳaṭṭ[e]rîm 'al-hall[e]ḇēnîm*)**:** although the offering of **incense** had its place in the worship of Yahweh, the Piel of *ḳṭr* is virtually always used of idolatrous worship. There is, however, no other reference in the *OT* to **bricks** in connexion with this. If **bricks** is original here the reference might be to altars made of brick, to the use of heated bricks in the preparation of incense, or to the offering of incense to the 'host of heaven' on the brick or tile roofs of houses (cf. 2 Kg. 23 : 12; Jer. 19 : 13; Zeph. 1 : 5). This last was a Babylonian custom introduced into Israel in the pre-exilic period, and there is Babylonian evidence that the incense was sometimes offered up on clay bricks (D. Conrad, *ZAW* 80 (1968), pp. 232–4; G. R. Driver, *Festschrift für W. Eilers*, 1967, p. 56). An alternative theory is that of M. Dahood (*CBQ* 22 (1960), pp. 406–8) who suggests on the basis of an inscription on an incense-altar found at Lachish that *l[e]ḇēnîm* is related to *l[e]ḇōnāh*, 'incense' and means an incense-altar.

4. who sit in tombs: probably in order to consult the dead (necromancy). This practice is attested in pre-exilic times (Isa. 8 : 19), but was strictly forbidden to Yahwists. Close contact with the dead was believed to make a person unclean. **and spend the night in secret places:** this practice, which is closely associated with the previous one, is that known as 'incubation', that is, the seeking of an oracle from a god—in this case demons or the dead—by spending the night in his presence. The sin here lies in the fact that it is not Yahweh but other supernatural beings who are consulted. **in secret places** (*bann[e]ṣûrîm*), however, is a somewhat vague expression. *NEB* repoints the word as *banniṣṣûrîm* and translates 'keeping vigil' (a word supposedly derived from *nāṣar*, 'keep watch'). M. Dahood (*CBQ* 22 (1960), pp. 408–9) proposed *bên ṣûrîm*, 'inside mountains' (i.e. in caves) on the basis of an inscription inside a Palestinian rock-tomb (LXX has 'in the caves'). **who eat swine's flesh:** the pig was an unclean animal and to eat pork was, as it still is by the Jews, regarded as abominable (Lev. 11 : 7; Dt. 14 : 8), possibly because it was associated with non-Yahwistic cults. It is referred to only here and in 66 : 17 (cf. also 66 : 3); but the fact that it is forbidden in Dt. 14 : 8 suggests that the problem existed before the post-exilic period, and this accords with what is known of the situation elsewhere in the ancient Near East (R. de Vaux, *Bible et Orient*, pp. 499–516; A. von Rohr Sauer, *BZAW* 103 (1968), pp. 201–7). The final line of this verse refers to the eating of other creatures forbidden in Lev. 11 and Dt. 14. **broth:** reading *m*ᵉ*raḳ* with Qere, 1QIsᵃ and Versions. Kethib has *p*ᵉ*raḳ*, 'fragment', which is less probable. **in their vessels:** reading *biḵ*ᵉ*lêhem* with 1QIsᵃ, Targ., and Vulg. MT has simply 'their vessels' (*k*ᵉ*lêhem*).

5. Finally the practitioners of these rites are accused of blasphemously claiming that they possess, through serving their gods, a 'holy' status equivalent to that possessed by the priests of Yahweh (cf. Lev. 21 : 6–8). But it is doubtful whether *ḳ*ᵉ*ḏaštîḵā* can mean **I am set apart from you** (see G–K §117x). Many commentators prefer to repoint the verb as Piel: *ḳiddaštîḵā*, which may be translated 'for (otherwise) I should communicate holiness to you'. This would correspond to the idea which lies behind Ezek. 44 : 19 and is implied elsewhere in the *OT* of a special 'holiness' resulting from contact with holy objects which is communicable to other persons like a contagion and dangerous to those who acquire it improperly. We must suppose that these words are imagined to be spoken by a priestly officiant of such cults to his followers. The second half of the verse (from **These are a smoke**) begins the announcement of punishment which follows the accusation, in the manner of the pre-exilic prophets. It is expressed in traditional language: cf. Jer. 17 : 4; Dt. 32 : 22.

6. it is written before me: apparently a reference to a heavenly book recording sins to be punished, a concept perhaps derived from the practice of keeping annals at royal courts in which notes about crimes yet unpunished may have had a place. The other references in the *OT* to a 'heavenly book' (Exod. 32 : 32; Ps. 69 : 28 (MT 69 : 29); Isa. 4 : 3, Mal. 3 : 16) refer to favourable rather than unfavourable bookkeeping. The apocalyptic concept of books used in evidence at the examination of individuals after death at the Last Judgment, to which the earliest reference is Dan. 7 : 10, is a later development. **I will not keep silent:** see on 62 : 1. The intervention of Yahweh signified by his breaking silence can be for either good or evil. **but I will repay** (*kî 'im-šillamtî*)**:** better, 'until I have repaid'. From this point to the end of verse 7 the text is in disorder. **yea, I will repay:** literally, 'and I will repay'. Apart from the 'and' this word is simply a repetition of the preceding word. It is lacking in LXX and other Versions, and may have been misplaced from verse 7 (see below). **into their bosom:** this phrase is virtually repeated in verse 7 and is perhaps intrusive here.

7. their iniquities and their fathers' iniquities: *RSV* here follows LXX and Syr. MT has 'your' in both cases, which can hardly be right. The phrase is the object of the first **I will repay** in verse 6. The author does not mean to imply that the earlier generations had not suffered punishment for their sins, but that there was a continuity of sin from one generation to another: the new generation had not changed its ways, and was to pay for the sinfulness which it had inherited. **together, says the LORD:** these words are also probably a later addition. The text from **I will not keep silent** in verse 6 may perhaps be reconstructed as follows:

> I will not keep silent until I have repaid
> their iniquities and their fathers' iniquities.

because . . . upon the hills: these are characteristic practices taken over from the Canaanites and attested in Israel since the pre-exilic period; cf. verse 3. **reviled me:** an accusation of blasphemy or 'high treason' against the honour of Yahweh: see on verse 5. **for their former doings:** hardly a possible translation of *pe'ullāṯām rī'šōnāh. rī'šōnāh* is probably to be taken adverbially: 'I will first measure'. If *wešillamtî* is now transferred from verse 6 to stand before **into their bosom** we obtain the following lines:

> I will first measure out their reward (*pe'ullāṯām*)
> and (then) pay it into their bosom.

bosom (*ḥêḳ*)**:** better, 'lap'. A free translation might be 'purse'. So Yahweh assures the sinners that they will receive their due in full and without fail.

8. The absolute dichotomy which runs through the whole of this chapter in its present form between the apostates within the Jewish community, doomed to destruction, and the faithful (**my servants**; **my chosen**), who are assured of the fullness of God's blessing, goes far beyond any concept of a 'remnant' in the pre-exilic literature (see W. Eichrodt, *Theology of the Old Testament* I, 1961, pp. 379*n*., 466; G. Sauer in *Wort—Gebot—Glaube*, Eichrodt *Festschrift*, 1970, pp. 277–95). It was the fruit of a more individualized understanding of faith which emerged after the destruction of Israel's national institutions in 587 BC and became a characteristic feature of post-exilic Judaism. The imagery of the finding of juice (*tîrôš*, *RSV* **wine**) in a **cluster** of grapes is somewhat obscure, but its general sense is made clear by the subsequent application of the simile. Yahweh says that he will not destroy the *whole* (*hakkōl*; *RSV* inadequately **them all**) of the community: that is, he will preserve the faithful. The imagery is evidently concerned with decisions made by the vinegrower with regard to the destruction of unproductive vines. There is no indication, as has been suggested, that the words in quotation marks are part of a vintagers' song; and to connect them with the mysterious 'Do not Destroy' which occurs in the titles to Psalms 57; 58; 59; 75 is even more hazardous. **a blessing:** perhaps in the sense of life-power or vitality given by God. See J. Pedersen, *Israel* I–II, 1926, pp. 182–3.

9. Deutero-Isaiah had seen the ancient promises made to the Patriarchs of a great and numerous people descended from them who would take possession of the land as about to be realized (54 : 1–3). In spite of the return from Babylon after the Exile that promise could not be said to have been fulfilled (see on 57 : 13). It is now renewed again, but restricted to the **chosen.** The promise of an increased population in the future is not intended to exclude the present generation from participating in the blessing (cf. the same thought in Deutero-Isaiah). The mention of **Jacob** and **Judah** shows that the restoration of the entire people of Israel to their land is envisaged as in 60 : 4–9. **my mountains:** that is, the whole land, as in 14 : 25. The land is Yahweh's: he allots it to his people. **my chosen** (*beḥîray*, plur.)**:** Deutero-Isaiah (43 : 20; 45 : 4) speaks of the whole nation as Yahweh's **chosen** (sing.); here it is faithful individuals within the nation who are so designated. The same is true of the **servants** of Yahweh: contrast 54 : 17.

10. The promise ends with an idyllic pastoral picture of undisturbed peace. **Sharon** is the coastal plain in the west; **Achor** a valley near Jericho in eastern Palestine (Jos. 7 : 24–26; 15 : 7). The mention of the two extremities is intended to embrace the whole land. **who have sought me:** a reference back to verse 1. Only those who have accepted Yahweh's appeal are entitled to be called **my people.**

11. Before announcing the destruction of the apostates Yahweh adds new specific indictments to those made in verses 2–5. **forget my holy mountain** is to be interpreted in the light of the parallel phrase **forsake the LORD:** the apostates have abandoned the worship of Yahweh for their pagan rites. The reference to the **holy mountain** does not necessarily imply that the Temple has already been rebuilt, but it does imply that those addressed are in Palestine and that the Temple site is in use for the worship of Yahweh. The practice of *lectisternia*, or preparing a meal for the gods, existed among a variety of peoples. **Fortune** (*haggaḏ*) conceals the name of the god Gad, a personification of good fortune (hence the article in Heb.), a Syrian god worshipped over a wide area including Phoenicia and Palmyra, whose name is preserved in the Palestinian place-names Baal-gad (Jos. 11 : 17; 12 : 7) and Migdal-gad (Jos. 15 : 37), a fact which implies that he was at home in pre-exilic Palestine. **Destiny** similarly conceals the name of the god Meni (Heb. *hamᵉnî*, again with the article), also a god of fate, possibly identical (though masculine) with the Arabian goddess Manât. Both may have been star-deities.

12. It is not clear in what way **sword** and **slaughter** were to overtake the apostates. This may simply be traditional language not to be taken literally. **I will destine** (*ûmānîṯî*)**:** literally, 'I will number'. The choice of the verb, similar to the name Meni, has a grim appropriateness. The last lines, from **because**, are repeated almost verbally in 66 : 4. Here they round off the section by recalling verses 1–2. The phraseology is traditional: **when I called . . . listen** has echoes in 50 : 2; Jer. 7 : 13, and **but you did what was evil in my eyes** is a characteristically Deuteronomic expression. On the meaning of **chose what I did not delight in** see on 56 : 4.

13–15. The fates of the two groups set out respectively in verses 9–10, 11–12 are now brought together in a way which suggests that verses 9–15 form a single piece. The form, a series of parallel announcements of blessing and of judgment, has a liturgical ring. This is an early example of a literary type which later came to play an important role in Jewish eschatology and continued into early Christian literature (e.g. Lk. 6 : 20–26), and in particular influenced the picture of the Last Judgment (cf. Mt. 25 : 31–46).

15. The first and last parts of this verse form a contrasting pair like those in verses 13–14. **and the Lord GOD will slay you** is intrusive and impairs the parallelism both of metre and of sense. It is probably a marginal gloss based on the actual form which the curse mentioned in the previous line might take: 'May the Lord GOD slay you as he slew X!' (cf. Jer. 29 : 22). This intrusive reference to Yahweh in the third person seems subsequently to have led, in the manuscript tradition represented by MT, to an alteration of the next line to continue the third person reference. LXX, although the intruded line is also present, has 'but my servants shall be called (pointing the verb as Niphal) by a new name'; and this is probably the original text.

The original intention of the verse was to pursue the contrast between the fates of the two groups beyond the present into the future by indicating what will happen to the **name** of each. The predictions are not, however, entirely parallel. It is not clear what is meant by the **name** of the apostates; possibly the author was thinking of their individual names. The use of a name **for a curse** is well illustrated in Jer. 29 : 22, where the lying prophets Ahab and Zedekiah are to be remembered only by the use of their name to invoke their terrible fate on others. So the terrible fate of these people will be perpetuated for ever in an exemplary way. We might at this point expect to be told that the name(s) of the other group will be similarly used for a blessing (see on verse 16*a*). Instead we are told that Yahweh's **servants** will be given the new or **different name** which, as in 62 : 2 (though not in 62 : 4) remains unspecified but signifies the beginning of a new era of blessing for them.

16a (to **shall swear by the God of truth**). It is possible though not certain that this is an addition. There is a connexion with the thought of verse 15, but the point is somewhat different. After the reference to the use of the apostates' name to make an effective curse we should not be surprised to discover here a similar statement about the use of the new name of Yahweh's servants to make an effective blessing, as is promised with regard to the name of Abraham in Gen. 22 : 18, where the families of the earth are to invoke a blessing upon themselves (the verb is the same) by asking God to bless them as he blessed him. But instead we have a reference to 'blessing oneself' (and taking oaths) by invoking *God*'s name (cf. Jer. 4 : 2). The unique phrase **the God of truth** (*'ᵉlōhê 'āmēn*; but we should in both cases perhaps read *'ōmen*, 'faithfulness' for the adverbial *'āmēn*) emphasizes that God can be relied upon to perform all that he has promised. **So that:** a dubious translation of *'ᵃšer*. The word may be a somewhat clumsy addition made in an attempt to strengthen the link with the previous verse.

16b–25. In its present state this passage is dominated by verse 17, in which Yahweh declares that he is about to **create** (*hinnᵉnî bôrē'*) **new heavens and a new earth**; and this impression of a radical cosmic transformation is strengthened by the final verse (25). But the intervening verses (18–23) have no cosmic reference: they are wholly concerned with the renewal of **Jerusalem** and its people (cf. chapters 60–62). The probability that verse 17 is not part of the original composition is strengthened by the fact that much of it is duplicated in the neighbouring verses: **For behold, I create** is an exact duplication of part of verse 18, and the second half of the verse is very similar to verse 16*b*. Westermann's suggestion that verses 17 and 25 may have been added to the passage to give it a quasi-apocalyptic tone deserves attention.

But the removal of verse 17 does not entirely solve the problems of the opening verses, since verse 16*b*, though related thematically to what follows rather than with what precedes, remains syntactically isolated. There has perhaps been some disarrangement of the lines. Westermann suggests that verse 18*a* (to **which I create**) with its command to rejoice over the creation of a new Jerusalem originally stood at the beginning.

16b. the former troubles (*haṣṣārôṯ hāri'šōnôṯ*): both this phrase and **the former things** (*hāri'šōnôṯ*) in verse 17 are based on Deutero-Isaiah and in particular on 43 : 18–19, where Yahweh urges his people to 'Remember not the former things, nor consider the things of old', and continues, 'Behold, I am doing a new thing'. In verse 18, which was probably originally the continuation of this verse, these 'former' things are contrasted with the 'new things' which Yahweh is about to **create**; but this is once more a reinterpretation of Deutero-Isaiah's thought. Whereas for him the **former things** are the great deeds which Yahweh has done in the past now to be overshadowed by even greater deeds to come, here they are the **former troubles** of God's people from 587 BC onwards which in spite of Deutero-Isaiah's promises have still not been put right. Now the promise is made again: the days are coming when past sufferings will be **forgotten** in present joy. **from my eyes:** we might expect 'from your eyes', but this is not a textual error. The meaning is that Yahweh is so intent on the immediate future that the past is for him as though it had never been.

17. See on verses 16*b*–25 above. Here **the former things** are given yet another interpretation: they stand for the whole created order which is to be replaced by a **new**. The author appears to have taken Deutero-Isaiah's statement in 51 : 6 about the ephemeral character of the **heavens** and the **earth** as a prophecy of their immediate destruction; and, taking a further clue from the use of the verb **create** (*bārā'*) in some passages in Deutero-Isaiah (e.g. 41 : 20; 42 : 5–9; 43 : 7, 15; 45 : 8) where he supposed that he was speaking of a new creation, he has concluded that there is in fact to be a completely new beginning. He emphasizes this by using language reminiscent of Gen. 1 : 1. It would however be rash to classify this brief assertion, unique though it is in the *OT*, as apocalyptic in the full sense. It entirely lacks the detailed description characteristic of the apocalyptic predictions of the end and of the new creation, and it would be better to say that it marks the beginning of a new radical theology, born of the despair of post-exilic life, which the apocalyptic writers later adopted and developed in even more critical times.

18. The tone of this and the following verses is similar to that of chapters 60–62. **for ever:** the guarantee of permanence is an essential feature of all such promises of salvation. **in that which** (*'ašer*)**:** the meaning is plain, though *'ašer*, if correct, is used in a very pregnant sense. **I create Jerusalem:** like the author of verse 17, this author also has been influenced by Deutero-Isaiah's frequent use of the verb *bārā'*. The thought may, apart from the use of this word, be compared with 62 : 7. By using it in connexion with Jerusalem he implies that the city will be more than simply a restoration of the old: when Yahweh creates it is always something quite new. But this is an extension of the meaning of the word which goes beyond even Deutero-Isaiah.

19. The second half of this verse (from **no more**) begins a description of the ideal life which will be enjoyed by the citizens of the new Jerusalem. This thought occurs also in 35 : 10; 51 : 11. This is a reversal of the situation prophesied in Jer. 7 : 34; 16 : 9; 25 : 10, prophecies which had been amply fulfilled.

20. For the Israelite long life was one of the signs of God's blessing, and early death often attributed to sin. In Gen. 6 : 3 the shortness of human life in general was also attributed to sin. A restoration of what would now be regarded as exceptional longevity would therefore be a characteristic of life in the newly created Jerusalem. This is clearly the tenor of this verse, but there are some difficulties of detailed interpretation. **an infant that lives but a few days:** literally, 'an infant of days'. The accents in MT show that the Massoretic editors did not accept this as a possible interpretation of the phrase, although their own interpretation is most improbable. Possibly a verb is missing. Another possibility, though unsupported by concrete evidence, is that *vāmîm*, 'days' is a mistake for *yāmûṯ*, 'dies': 'an infant who dies'. **the child shall die a hundred years old:** that is, death at the age of a hundred will be regarded as premature. It should be observed that there is no question, in contrast with 25 : 8, which comes from a much later period, of the abolition of death, or of life after death. To die at a ripe old age after a full and happy life was not regarded as a misfortune. What is promised here is a return to the legendary longevity of the age before the Flood recorded in Genesis. The last line of the verse is difficult. The traditional interpretation is that **the sinner** will be punished by dying young!—**a hundred years old**!—and that this is a further indication of the change in the normal lifespan. This is an interpretation dictated by desperation. Perhaps the most plausible interpretation is that which understands *ḥôṭeh* not as **sinner,** but as 'one who fails': anyone who dies without attaining the age of one hundred may be assumed to have been cursed for some fault.

21–22a (to **and another eat**)**.** See on 62 : 8. The formulation of this promise is reminiscent of the curse of Dt. 28 : 30 and is intended to be a deliberate reversal of former prophecies of woe: cf. on verse 19. It should be noted that ancient cities like Jerusalem were not 'urban' in the modern sense. It is also important to notice that the ideal life as conceived by the ancient Jews was not one of idleness but of satisfying work.

22b. like the days of a tree: a frequent image of a healthy and useful longevity. Cf. especially Ps. 92 : 12–14 (MT 92 : 13–15). **long enjoy:** literally, 'wear out' (*y*ᵉ*ḇallû*). The meaning is that they will live to make full use of the results of their labours.

23. Once more a reversal of the present state of affairs, which is regarded as under God's curse. **labour:** not, as the context might suggest in the English translation, 'be in labour', but 'toil'. There is perhaps an allusion here to 49 : 4. **calamity:** the noun *behālāh* is used exclusively (Lev. 26 : 16; Ps. 78 : 33; Jer. 15 : 8) of unexpected and unexplained, and therefore terrifying, death sent by God as a punishment. From now on no parent will suffer the experience of having his **children** snatched away in such a manner: the children will inherit the blessing conferred upon their parents. There is a similar thought in 61 : 9.

24. See the introduction to this section. The background to this promise is the complaints made in the communal lamentations and echoed both in Deutero-Isaiah (e.g. 40 : 27; 49 : 14) and elsewhere in these chapters (e.g. 58 : 3; 64 : 12) that God is indifferent to his people's cry. The faith in God's 'prevenient grace' expressed here goes beyond the assurances of verse 1 and of 58 : 9, and also beyond anything demanded of God in the communal lamentations.

25. This verse is a condensed version of 11 : 6–9. Apart from the phrase **and dust shall be the serpent's food** everything here is to be found there, with only slight verbal differences. It is generally agreed that the first part of the verse (to **like the ox**) has been taken from Isa. 11. About the priority of the last part, however (from **They shall not hurt**), there is no agreement among the commentators: some (notably Duhm) have held that originality is on the side of Isa. 65. The expression **my holy mountain**, which occurs five times in chapters 56–66 including an occurrence in verse 11 of this chapter, occurs nowhere else in Proto-Isaiah. In Isa. 11 the verse is attached to a passage about the 'messianic' king, and here also it introduces a theme—the radical transformation of nature—which is characteristic of apocalyptic into a passage which, apart from verse 17 (on which see the commentary) is entirely this-worldly. **and dust shall be the serpent's food:** it is probably useless to seek a logical link between this phrase and the rest of the verse. It impairs the metrical structure, and its allusion to the eating habits of animals seems to be its only link with the context. It is a gloss based on Gen. 3 : 14. **my holy mountain:** here this phrase appears (as in 11 : 9) to have a wider sense than in verse 11, a fact which confirms the view that, though it may not have been borrowed from 11 : 9, its authorship is different from that of the rest of the chapter.

JUDGMENT AND SALVATION
66 : 1–24

Most commentators agree that this chapter is a collection of disparate elements with a minimum of editorial links. The extreme frequency of formulae like 'Thus says Yahweh', 'says Yahweh' and other phrases which usually point to editorial and amplificatory activity invite a comparison with Zech. 14 and with the final chapters of other *OT* books which have acquired successive appendices before their final redaction. In verses 1–5, 7–14, 17, there are allusions to conflicting groups within the Jewish community which suggest an origin not far removed in time from that of chapter 65, and in the case of verses 1–2 a date near 520 BC seems certain. The remainder of the chapter is of a somewhat different character and gives expression to a fully developed eschatology, whether of judgment or of universal salvation, which goes beyond anything else in chapters 56–66 but is mainly still far removed from the apocalyptic eschatology. Only verse 24, which appears to refer to a belief in eternal torment after death, may require a date not far removed from the second century BC.

1–4. This section abounds in ambiguities and has been interpreted in many ways. The difficulties are increased by uncertainty whether, short though it is, it all comes from the same hand.

1–2. The tone of these verses is polemical at least to the extent that they express God's disapproval of a particular view of the importance and value of a temple which those addressed are preparing to build. It is now generally agreed by the commentators that the temple in question can only be that of Zerubbabel whose building was begun in 520 BC, although other views have been held, notably that it is a sectarian temple such as that built much later by the Samaritans (so e.g. Duhm). Discussion is now mainly centred on the question whether this is an absolute condemnation of temples and temple-worship as such (so Fohrer, Pauritsch) or whether it is rather a warning against the kind of teaching propounded by the prophet Haggai that salvation can only come to God's people if the temple is first built. The former view presupposes the existence at that time of a group within the Palestinian community entirely opposed to temple and sacrifice, for which there is very little if any firm evidence elsewhere in the *OT*. The latter view supposes the existence of a prophetical group not necessarily opposed to the building project but carrying on the traditions of the pre-exilic prophets in pointing out that God's requirements of humility and obedience to his spiritual laws are more important than, and must be at the heart of, outward observances (Muilenburg, Westermann, Schoors; J. D. Smart, *ExpT* 46 (1934–5), pp. 420–4). That this is the correct interpretation is supported by the fact that these verses find distinct echoes in cultic psalms (especially Pss. 50; 113) and in the Deuteronomic prayer of Solomon at the dedication of the first Temple (1 Kg. 8 : 27).

1. Heaven is my throne: the phrase occurs also in Ps. 11 : 4 (cf. Ps. 103 : 19), where Yahweh's simultaneous presence 'in his holy temple' is also affirmed in the same breath. **and the earth is my footstool:** elsewhere (1 Chr. 28 : 2; Ps. 99 : 5; 132 : 7; Lam. 2 : 1) Yahweh's **footstool** is the Ark, or Zion, or the Temple. The concept is deliberately broadened here to stress Yahweh's transcendence. **what** (twice): the phrase *'ê-zeh* usually means 'where?'; LXX, however, has 'what kind of . . . ?'. The sense is not affected, except for those commentators who hold that the reference is to a schismatic temple to be built elsewhere than in Jerusalem. **my rest:** the word (*m^enûḥāh*) is used of the Temple in Ps. 132 : 8, 14; 1 Chr. 28 : 2.

2. All these things: the reference is not clear, but probably heaven and earth are meant. The author is concerned to point out the absurdity of any tendency to regard Yahweh as capable of being confined to a building made for him by men. **are mine:** *RSV* probably rightly accepts the emendation of MT's *wayyih^eyû*, 'and they came to be', to *w^elî hāyû* or the like, following LXX and other Versions. A similar thought occurs in Ps. 50 : 8–15. The connexion between the reference to the **humble and contrite**

in spirit and what precedes can be seen more clearly in the similar passage in Ps. 113 : 5–7. The same ideal is expressed in 57 : 15. **to whom I will look:** or better, 'at whom I will look in favour'. **and trembles at my word:** this expression is found elsewhere only in Ezr. 9 : 4; 10 : 3, where it refers to the Law, though here it might well refer to the prophetic rather than the priestly word. But it was probably in the post-exilic period that it came to be a fixed expression describing the loyal Jew.

3. The larger part of this verse (to **blesses an idol**) consists —after one textual emendation has been made, on which see below—of eight participial clauses: literally, 'slaughtering an ox, killing a man, sacrificing a lamb', etc. These are arranged in pairs, the first of each pair referring to a legitimate sacrificial action and the second to a heathen one forbidden and abominable to a Jew. The clauses are simply set side by side with no connecting particles (*RSV*'s **like** is not represented in the Heb.), and the syntactical relationship between the two members of each pair is ambiguous. *RSV* assumes that each pair is a nominal sentence expressing identity between the two members: 'a man who slaughters an ox *is* (i.e. is performing an action in every way comparable to) one who kills a man'. The point would then be that sacrifice of every kind is wrong, that the entire sacrificial system of Israel has from the very beginning been an offence against Yahweh (so Duhm, Fohrer, Pauritsch). Grammatically, however, it is equally legitimate to understand it as meaning that the same person is performing both actions: 'the person who slaughters an ox is the same as the one who kills a man'. The passage would then be an accusation of syncretism (so Volz, Muilenburg, Snaith, Bonnard, Schoors). The latter opinion is the more probable: nowhere else in the *OT* is the sacrificial system attacked in such extreme terms as would be the case if the former interpretation were accepted. But if the charge is one of syncretism there is no obvious connexion between the thought and that of verses 1–2, and verses 3–4 may be a quite separate oracle of judgment. **him who kills a man:** the expression is general, but in the context a reference to human sacrifice must be assumed: cf. 57 : 5. **him who breaks a dog's neck:** presumably a reference to the sacrifice of dogs. There is no other reference in the *OT* to such sacrifices, but there is some evidence of the practice among the Carthaginians, which suggests the possibility that it was practised also in Phoenicia or Canaan. The **dog**, which was regarded as unclean, may have been one of the 'abominable things' referred to together with swine's flesh in 65 : 4. **him who offers swine's blood:** MT lacks **who offers**, but a participle is demanded by the otherwise regular structure of the piece. Volz suggested the substitution of *ḥōmēḏ*, 'enjoys', for MT's *dam*, blood—'him who enjoys pork' (cf. 65 : 4). **he who makes a memorial offering** (*mazkîr*)**:** a reference to the offering of the *'azkārāh* (perhaps 'token offering') prescribed in Lev. 2 : 2, 16; 6 : 15 (MT 6 : 8) and elsewhere in Leviticus. See G. R. Driver, *JSS* 1 (1956), pp. 99–100. **blesses:** that is, worships. The remainder of the verse emphasizes that such syncretism is without excuse, and prepares for the announcement of judgment.

4. I also will choose: this is very emphatic. God will reply to these people, who have arbitrarily **chosen their own ways** (verse 3), by exercising his own free choice of punishment for them. **affliction** (*ta'alûlîm*)**:** perhaps better, 'confusion' or 'disorder'. **bring their fears upon them:** that is, make their worst fears to be realized. The remainder of the verse is virtually identical with 65 : 12*b*.

5. This is an isolated oracle. Apart from the phrase **you who tremble at his word** which recalls verse 2 but is probably a purely superficial link which perhaps accounts for the editorial juxtaposition of the two passages, it bears no relation to its context. The situation is similar to that of chapter 65 in that there are two opposing parties within the Jewish community (note the words **Your brethren**), one of which is here identified with the true believers; but there is nothing to indicate that the other party is idolatrous, or indeed what is the cause of the quarrel. The language is strongly polemical, and it is quite possible that both parties would have laid claim to the epithets at the beginning of the verse. The taunt **Let the LORD . . .** does not necessarily indicate a blasphemous attitude on the part of the speakers but rather implies that when the time for seeing Yahweh's glory comes (cf. verse 19) it will be they and not their adversaries who will rejoice. Nor is there any indication—though this is not excluded —of a persecution of a minority by the official religious leaders: there is no evidence that the verb *niddāh*, **cast . . . out**, had already acquired the later technical sense of 'excommunicate'. The situation *may* be the same as that of 56 : 9–12, but this is not certain. **be glorified:** MT has the Qal (*yiḵbaḏ*), but the Niphal *yikkāḇēḏ* is to be preferred: cf. the Versions.

6. This verse may owe its present position to an editor who understood **his enemies** to refer to the Jewish opponents of Yahweh's word mentioned in verse 5. But the style suggests that this is the beginning of a prophecy of divine judgment against the nations which originally found its immediate continuation in verses 15–16 (cf. 13 : 4; Jl 3 : 9–16). If this is so these three verses now constitute a framework to verses 7–14, which are of a quite different character. Verses 7–14 are entirely concerned with the restoration of the fortunes of Jerusalem, and their only reference to the nations (verse 12), far from prophesying their destruction in a final cataclysm, looks forward, like chapters 60 and 61, to their continuously bringing their wealth to enrich the holy city. Westermann's suggestion that the purpose of this editorial tailoring was to give verses 7–14 a quasi-apocalyptic flavouring which was originally alien to them has much to be said for it (cf. on 65 : 17). **Hark, an uproar:** as in 13 : 4, where the same phrase is used in the Heb., the prophet in imagination hears the sounds of battle proceeding from the city and the Temple. This probably refers to Yahweh's going out from city and Temple to wreak vengeance on external enemies (cf. Jl 3 : 16; Mic. 1 : 2–3), though a different view has been put forward by J. D. Smart (*ExpT* 46 (1934–5), pp. 422–3). It should be noted that the verse presupposes the existence of the Temple.

7–14. These verses possess a certain unity of theme: that of Mother Zion and her unexpectedly born children. The influence of Deutero-Isaiah is particularly marked here. The frequent changes of style and form perhaps indicate that the piece was not composed in a single moment of inspiration. In particular, verses 12–14 read like a separate oracle of salvation which covers again in a somewhat different way what has already been expressed in verses 7–9.

7–8. The image of Zion as a mother, used to express the promise of the return of the dispersed Jews to their homeland and of the future prosperity of a well-populated Palestine, has been taken from Deutero-Isaiah (49 : 18–23; 54 : 1–3). But though the thought is similar the image has been used in a quite different way. Whereas Deutero-Isaiah's picture is the curious one of a bewildered mother surprised by the appearance of numerous sons of whose birth she had not been aware, here she is depicted in the moment of giving birth to them. Behind the imagery lies an implied promise that the return of the dispersed Jews to their homeland will take place not gradually but immediately and in a single moment. The questions in verse 8 represent a sceptical attitude towards that promise, which it is the purpose of the oracle to dispel. Ordinary birth cannot take place without a preliminary period of labour; but Yahweh can dispense with this. The point is clear, but the argument, which is an attempt to prove the possibility of one kind of miracle by comparing it with something else equally miraculous, is hardly cogent. The argument from Yahweh's omnipotence would have been equally convincing (or unconvincing) without the imagery of birth. That it is in fact used indicates the extent to which the author saw himself as an interpreter of his illustrious predecessor, an allusion to whose prophecies would add weight to his own even though it did nothing to strengthen the argument itself.

7. Before she was in labour she gave birth: only three words in the Heb. But it is probably a mistake to assume that some words have dropped out and to expand to 'Before the woman was in labour she gave birth to a son', so avoiding the mystery of the unknown **she** and providing an exact parallel to the following line. The lapidary character of MT suggests that the author has used as his starting-point a proverbial expression of surprise or incredulity at the unexpected. **was delivered of:** literally, 'let slip out'. This is not a normal word denoting birth, though it is used in 34 : 15 of the laying of eggs. It has been chosen to draw attention to the facility of the birth. Cf. the English word 'drop', used of animal birth.

8. Shall a land be born (*hᵃyûḥal 'ereṣ*)**:** the verb is masc., the noun fem. This is the impersonal passive construction (G–K §121a): 'Shall there be born a land . . . ?'. No emendation is necessary. **as soon as Zion was in labour:** the apparent contradiction with verse 7 is simply poetic licence.

9. Shall I (*ha'ᵃnî*); **shall I** (*'im-'ᵃnî*)**:** a strong emphasis on Yahweh's control of events. This verse sets the seal on the assertions of verses 7–8 with a divine assurance that he will not go back on his promise but will bring to a successful conclusion the process of gestation which he has secretly set in motion.

10–11. These verses presuppose the message of verses 7–9 that through the return of the dispersed Jews a populous nation is to be **born** full-grown **in one moment**. They are addressed to these new 'sons' of Zion and the present inhabitants of Jerusalem, who together make up the total of **all you who love her**. At present they can also be described as **all you who mourn over her**; but they are urged to **Rejoice with Jerusalem**, their mother: as in the 'eschatological songs of praise', there is an anticipation of the promised event. The theme of the change from mourning to joy (cf. 60 : 20; 61; 65 : 18–19) is ultimately derived from Deutero-Isaiah (e.g. 49 : 13; 51 : 11; 54 : 1).

11. The thought of Zion as the mother of her children leads, though somewhat incongruously, to one of her roles as nursing-mother. As in 60 : 16 the ultimate source of the thought is probably 49 : 23, but the idea is now used in a different way. The metaphor is one which was used in a variety of ways in the ancient Near East. **her consoling breasts:** literally, 'the breast of her consolations'. *tanḥûmîm*, 'consolation', is from the same root as the characteristically Deutero-Isaian verb *niḥam*, 'to comfort'; cf. also 61 : 2; 66 : 13. **abundance:** the rare noun *zîz* probably means 'nipple', and *kāḇôḏ* (**glory**) here, as in 61 : 6 (where *RSV* translates it by 'riches') means 'wealth' or 'abundance'. The whole phrase therefore means something like 'from her rich supply of milk'.

12–14. Formally the first word of this section (*kî*, **For**) introduces the reason justifying the call to rejoice in verse 10. But the section is a mosaic of quotations and near-quotations from Deutero-Isaiah and elsewhere and seems to be a commentary on verses 7–11 rather than their continuation.

12. prosperity: Heb. *šālôm*. This is a reference to 48 : 18, where Yahweh tells the people that if they had obeyed him 'your peace (*šālôm*) would have been like a river'. This state of blessedness, forfeited in the past through sin, is now at last to become a reality. **the wealth of the nations** (*keḇôḏ gôyīm*)**:** cf. similar phrases in 61 : 6. The idea of the **river** and **stream** flowing into Jerusalem is perhaps inspired by the language of 60 : 5, though the phrase **an overflowing stream** (*naḥal šôṭēp̱*) itself comes from Proto-Isaiah (30 : 28). The present author has given it a radical re-interpretation, turning it from an expression of wrath into one of blessing. **and you shall suck** (*wînaḳtem*)**:** this makes poor sense in the context. The great majority of commentators emend it to *w^eyōnaḳtāh*, 'her sucklings' (the sing. having a collective sense), making it the subject of the verbs which follow: 'and your sucklings (i.e. babies) shall be carried . . . and dandled'. (LXX has 'their children', which is probably based on the pointing of the Heb. as *w^eyōnaḳtām*.) The two verbs would then have to be emended from second person plur. to third person sing. The alternative proposed by Volz, which is to omit *wînaḳtem* altogether as an intrusive variant of *tîn^eḳû*, **that you may suck**, in verse 11, deserves some consideration. **upon her hip** (*ʿal-ṣaḏ*): in 60 : 4 the same expression is translated in *RSV* by 'in her arms'. The author has borrowed the phrase **shall be carried upon her hip** from 60 : 4, which is itself a paraphrase of 49 : 22; but unlike the author of 60 : 4 this author has ignored its original reference to the role of the nations or their kings as attendants upon Zion's children and has applied it to the role of the mother in caring for her own children.

13. The theme of Yahweh's comforting his people (or specifically, Zion, 51 : 3) is of course taken from Deutero-Isaiah. The abrupt change from the idea of Jerusalem tending her children (verse 12*b*) to that of Yahweh playing the role of **mother** is probably to be explained by the influence of 49 : 13–15 which, if read as a single piece, presents Yahweh successively as comforter of Zion and as the one who loves her even more than a human mother. **As one:** Heb. has *k^e'îš*, 'As a man'. It is not certain whether *'îš* can mean 'male child': the precise meaning of Eve's words in Gen. 4 : 1 are disputed (cf. also the use of *geḇer*, 'man' in Job 3 : 3). If this interpretation is not possible we must conclude that the author is speaking of a mother's comfort of a grown-up son: *RSV*'s translation simply avoids the issue. **you shall be comforted in Jerusalem:** some commentators omit this somewhat weak line as a gloss.

14. The first part of this verse (to **rejoice**) is an echo of 60 : 5*a*. **your bones shall flourish like the grass:** on the image of vegetation see on 44 : 4; 58 : 11. The state of various parts of the body was held to be symptomatic of mental and spiritual, as well as physical, health; with regard to the **bones** see, e.g. Ps. 6 : 2 (MT 6 : 3); 109 : 18; Job 21 : 24; Prov. 15 : 30. The second part of the verse (from **and it shall be known**) is perhaps a transitional passage linking this section with the next. *RSV* hardly represents the Heb., which would be better rendered 'and the hand (i.e. the power) of Yahweh will make itself felt among his servants, and his indignation among his enemies'. **his indignation:** Heb. has 'and he will show indignation' (*wᵉzāʿam*), but the slight emendation to *wᵉzaʿᵃmô* improves the sentence and is probably justified.

15–16. These verses were originally the continuation of verse 6 (on which see the commentary), and the opening words **For behold** form the connecting link. This is a brief example of what is generally called the 'theophany of judgment'. The *OT* contains many descriptions of a 'theophany' or appearance of Yahweh accompanied by various awe-inspiring signs of his cosmic power. The question of the origin of this tradition is a complicated one, and it is not certain whether all the examples have a common origin: both the purpose of the appearances and the accompanying phenomena vary greatly. It is probably significant that some of the passages which most closely resemble this one are found in the book of Isaiah: 13 : 3–16; 29 : 6; 30 : 27–28; 34. In all of these **fire** is an important element as it is here. This passage goes beyond the other two theophanic passages in Trito-Isaiah (63 : 1–6; 64 : 1–3) in that the expected appearance of Yahweh is judgment not against a group of people or a single nation but against **all flesh**, that is the whole world. This feature indicates a relatively late date, although the passage is too short for a precise conclusion to be drawn.

15. and his chariots like the stormwind: exactly the same phrase occurs in Jer. 4 : 13 where it depicts the arrival of a Babylonian army. The image is presumably derived from the clouds of dust raised by advancing chariots. However, the figure of Yahweh riding the skies, sometimes in a chariot, is a feature of other theophanies (cf. Ps. 18 : 10; 68 : 17 (MT 68 : 18); Hab. 3 : 8) and is associated with the idea of Yahweh as the storm-god. **to render his anger** (*lᵉhāšîḇ . . . ʾappô*)**:** that is, to express it in an act of well-deserved punishment.

16. execute judgment: the use of the Niphal here is somewhat anomalous, and variants in 1QIsᵃ and LXX suggest that the original text may have read 'come to judge all the earth'. **and by his sword** (*ûḇᵉḥarbô*)**:** cf. 34 : 5–6. But the context really requires a verb. The proposal to repoint the consonants as two words, *ûḇāḥar bô*, 'and will test with it', is ingenious but open to more than one objection. **and those slain by the LORD shall be many:** another theophanic figure: cf. Jer. 25 : 33; Zeph. 2 : 12.

17. This condemnation of practitioners of heathen rites can hardly have been the original continuation of the announcement of worldwide judgment in the previous verses. It is clearly directed against the Jewish apostates in Palestine; and its references to rites performed in **gardens, eating swine's flesh** and other unclean creatures, and special attention to achieving a state of sanctification leave no doubt that it belongs to the same strand of prophecy. However, it is an isolated fragment. Attempts to fit it into the early part of this chapter (66 : 3–5) on the assumption that it has been accidentally misplaced are not really convincing. **following one in the midst** (*'aḥar 'eḥāḏ battāweḵ*, if Kethib is followed; Qere has the fem. *'aḥaṯ*): no satisfactory explanation has been found for this expression. Volz' view that **following** is used in the sense of obedience or imitation, and that the phrase refers to 'the mystagogue of the Eleusinian mysteries or the *pater patrum* of the worshippers of Mithras who initiated the members of the community into all the secrets', which would necessitate a very late date for the passage and so fits his theories about chapters 56–66 in general, has not found general acceptance. It is more probable that this is a rite similar to that described in Ezek. 8 : 7–11, where also there was a single leader standing **in the midst** of the group of worshippers (*b^e^ṯôḵām*). If so, this is a rite practised before the Exile which had survived in Palestine. If the reading of the Qere (*'aḥaṯ*), which is also that of 1QIs^a^ and a number of MSS, is correct, we must think of a priestess: there is no reason to suppose that the statue of a goddess is meant. **the abomination** (*haššeḳeṣ*): this word is used in Lev. 7 : 21; 11 : 10–45) of the uncleanness of certain animals which the Israelites were forbidden to eat. It is interesting that its only other occurrences in the *OT* are here and in Ezek. 8 : 10 which has been referred to above. There is no need to emend it to *šereṣ*, a generic term for small unclean animals. **mice** (*'aḵbār*): classified as unclean in Lev. 11 : 29. It has been suggested that small creatures such as **mice** may have been among the 'abominable things . . . in their vessels' of 65 : 4. We have no knowledge of this kind of rite.

18–24. This final section of the book has an eschatological character throughout, but is not all of one piece. At least verses 18–21 appear to be in prose.

18–21. Although there are some difficulties in the interpretation of these verses they basically form a single unit, with some interpolations.

18. For I know their works and their thoughts, and I am coming: *RSV* has followed Pesh. in adding **I know.** The Heb. is unintelligible: 'And I their works and their thoughts it (fem.) is coming . . .'. Most commentators agree that **their works and their thoughts** is an intrusion from a nearby verse, but the various attempts to fit it back, with or without a supposedly lost verb, into verse 16 after **all flesh** (Volz, *BHS*), or at the end of verse 17 as the subject of **shall come to an end** (many commentators following Duhm) or at the beginning of verse 17 (Torrey) all fall far short of conviction. It may be a gloss or part of a gloss. With its omission the whole of this section (verses 18–21) is seen to have a very positive, universalistic character quite different from the oracle of judgment in verses 15–16. The thought behind this verse is that of the assembly of the **nations** to Jerusalem to worship Yahweh which is also found in 2 : 2–3; but the most remarkable feature is the way in which language usually reserved for speaking of Israel is here extended to the nations. The verb **to gather** is regularly used in promises of the restoration of the scattered Israelites to their land (e.g. Ps. 106 : 47; Jer. 23 : 3; often in Ezek.), to which they are, in some passages, to be conducted by foreigners occupying an entirely inferior status (e.g. Isa. 11 : 12; 43 : 5). But here the nations will come in their own right to **see my glory**. The interpretation of this phrase is more difficult. There is a sense in which Yahweh's glory may be seen by the whole world without thereby conferring any privilege on those who see it (e.g. 35 : 2; 40 : 5); but in the context here **glory** almost certainly has the more restricted and intensive sense illustrated by Ezek. 11 : 22–23; 44 : 4, where it signifies Yahweh's presence in the Temple. In this sense to **see** Yahweh's **glory** is to be on an equal footing with Israel. But the tone here is quite different from that of Ezekiel, where immediately after the vision of the return of the glory to the Temple (44 : 4) it is stated with great emphasis that it was precisely the admission of foreigners to it which had profaned it in the past (44 : 7). **am coming:** the fem. *bā'āh* must be a mistake for a masc. form, probably the masc. participle *bā'*.

19. and I will set a sign among them: these words conclude the sentence begun in verse 18. The nature of the sign (*'ôṯ*) is not clear. The word has a wide range of meanings; but it is often used of something which God gives as an enduring reminder of his presence or activity, and it is probably within this field that we should place its use here. However, the text gives no hint which would permit a more precise interpretation. **from them:** that is, representatives from among the nations mentioned in verse 18. Since they are to be sent to **the nations** (*haggôyīm*, the same word as in verse 18) it would seem that the author intended to make a distinction between two groups of nations: those who live nearest to Palestine will be drawn to worship Yahweh first, and from among them will be sent messengers to the more remote peoples who have never heard of Yahweh. This writer did not count clarity of expression among his virtues. **survivors** (*pᵉlêṭîm*): this word is puzzling, since it refers properly to those who have survived a catastrophe; but there is no reference in this passage to a divine judgment or other catastrophe. The most probable explanation is that of G. Rinaldi (*Mémorial Gélin*, 1961, pp. 109–18) who argues that the words *pᵉlêṭāh, pᵉlêṭîm, pᵉlîṭîm* became in the post-exilic period technical terms for the post-exilic Jewish community which had survived the judgment of 587 and were therefore assured of the eschatological hope (cf. 37 : 32; 4 : 2). Those foreigners who attached themselves to the Jews as fellow-worshippers of Yahweh (cf. 56 : 6) could therefore also be referred to as *pᵉlêṭîm*, almost in the sense of 'those who are saved'. (Cf. also Duhm, Volz.) This may be a re-interpretation of 45 : 20. The list of exotic names of distant peoples and places, like 'China and Peru', may well be secondary. It is drawn from Ezek. 27 : 10–13 and 38 : 2, and although the author himself may have had little idea of their geographical location, they are all probably genuine names. On **Tarshish** see on 60 : 9. **Put:** this is the reading of LXX and is preferable to the Heb. 'Pul', which is unknown. **Put** and **Lud** occur together in Ezek. 27 : 10; 30 : 5. **Put** is in Africa, probably either Somaliland or Libya. It is not certain whether **Lud** is Lydia in western Asia Minor or, like Put, in Africa (cf. Gen. 10 : 13). **who draw the bow** (*mōšᵉḵê ḳešeṯ*): this descriptive phrase is somewhat out of place, and is probably a corruption of two further proper names. The first of these is almost certainly Meshech (so LXX), which is mentioned with **Tubal** and **Javan** in Ezek. 27 : 13. Both Meshech and Tubal are attested in cuneiform inscriptions and in Herodotus as peoples living south-east of the Black Sea. It has been conjectured that the second corrupted name is Rosh, which supposedly occurs also in Ezek. 38 : 2, but is unidentified. **Javan** is the Greeks, specifically the Ionian colonists of the west coast of Asia Minor and the neighbouring islands.

20. The acceptance of the converted Gentiles on the same footing as Jews does not release them from the task of assuring the return of the scattered Jews to their homeland (cf. 43 : 5; 60 : 4, 9), without which the work of restoration would not be complete. But in the performance of their task their status is quite different from that envisaged by Deutero-Isaiah and chapter 60. They are compared to the vessel in which Israelites brought their *minḥāh* (**offering**; **cereal offering**) to the Temple to offer it to Yahweh. The dispersed Israelites (**your brethren**) are the offering which they bring. As can be seen from the Priestly Code, everything connected with sacrifices had to be ceremonially **clean.** These Gentiles are therefore compared to **a clean vessel** (*keli ṭāhôr*). This is a striking reversal of the general attitude towards foreigners, who were regarded as *ipso facto ṭāmē'*, 'unclean' (the exact opposite of *ṭāhôr*, **clean**): cf. 52 : 1, 11. The attitude taken here is strikingly similar to that of 56: 6–7 except that here the conversion of *all* the nations is envisaged. **upon horses . . . upon dromedaries:** these phrases, evidently intended to emphasize still further the remoteness and variety of countries from which these caravans will set out (cf. 60 : 4–9) makes the sentence extremely clumsy and is probably a gloss. It is noteworthy that transport by sea is not mentioned (contrast 60 : 9), perhaps because this author shared the traditional Jewish dislike for the sea. **in litters** (*baṣṣabbîm*)**:** or, possibly, 'covered wagons'. Cf. the use of the word in Num. 7 : 3. **upon dromedaries** (*bakkirkārôṯ*)**:** this word occurs only here and its meaning is uncertain.

21. There is no agreement among the commentators about the meaning of this verse. Grammatically **some of them** (*mēhem*) could refer either to the nations or to the Israelites whom they accompany to Jerusalem. But if this verse is an original part of the passage and not a later addition the former seems the most probable interpretation since the whole emphasis is upon them. There is also some difficulty in interpreting the verse of Israelites, since those returning from dispersion would already be divided by heredity into laymen, priests, and Levites, although the latter would have been unable fully to perform their functions up to their return. There would be no need for Yahweh to **take** them, that is, select or appoint them. We should therefore accept this verse as a radical reversal of the traditional attitude towards foreigners, going even beyond 56 : 6–7. **for priests and for Levites:** MT has 'for priests, for Levites' (*lakkōhanîm lalewiyyîm*): but some MSS add **and**, and this reading is supported by some of the Versions. Whichever is the original reading it is improbable that the author intended to speak of a single class of 'levitical priests' as in Deuteronomy; had this been so he would have written *lakkōhanîm hallewiyyîm* (Delitzsch). He recognized a distinction between the two, but may have omitted the copula because the two together formed a single sacred ministry distinct from the laity (on the construction see C. Brockelmann, *Hebräische Syntax*, §128).

22. In spite of the connecting particle *kî*, **For**, it is not certain that this verse was originally the continuation of verse 21. It is more poetical in form, and there is an abrupt change to the second person. Since the previous verses refer to two groups, the Jews and the converted heathen, it is not certain which is now addressed. In favour of the view that it refers to the latter it may be urged that **so shall your descendants and your name remain** is reminiscent of 56 : 5, which, though not addressed to proselytes, occurs in a passage (56 : 1–8) which is of a distinctly liberal character. The alternative theory, which is the more widely held, is that this is a promise to the Jews that although they will now share their privileges with others, they will preserve their identity and continue to be in the centre of the scheme of salvation. This may be so, although the comparison which is often made with Jer. 31 : 35–36; 33 : 25–26 does little to confirm this view, since the method of argument is quite different. Whereas in the passages from Jeremiah the authors support their statements by making comparisons with the undisputed realities of the existing order, here the author merely compares one unfulfilled promise with another (drawn from 65 : 17).

23. In the Heb. this verse begins with 'And it shall be (that)' (*wehāyāh*), an expression whose use elsewhere suggests that what follows is a subsequent addition. Probably the purpose of the verse was to fill out the promise of verse 18 with more precise detail. This has the effect of making it even clearer that the promise could only be fulfilled in a world quite different from the present one. In view of the impossibility of monthly and even weekly pilgrimages of the whole of humanity to Jerusalem, it was argued by Duhm that **all flesh** (*kol-bāśār*) here refers only to the Jews, and, more precisely, only to Jews living in or near Jerusalem. This argument is based on the view that this phrase sometimes means 'everyone' in a rather imprecise sense which is determined by the extent of the group of people referred to in the immediate context. But it is not certain that the passages which are cited in defence of this argument (principally Ps. 65 : 2 (MT 65 : 3); Jl 2 : 28 (MT 3 : 1); Ezek. 21 : 4 (MT 21 : 9)) need be interpreted in this way, and in view of the use of the phrase elsewhere in the book of Isaiah and especially in this chapter (verses 16, 24) and of the style of this verse, which has something of the character of a legal formulation, Duhm's theory must be rejected. (See A. R. Hulst, *Oudtestamentische Studiën* 12 (1958), pp. 28–68.) **From new moon to new moon:** that is, every month at the time of the new moon. Similarly **from sabbath to sabbath** means every week on the sabbath day. Both of these occasions had been observed from ancient times. Their rites as they had developed by the time of the redaction of the Priestly Code are described together in Num. 28 : 9–15.

24. This verse, though composed in such a way as to give the appearance of being the continuation of verse 23, was probably composed to form the conclusion of the book of Isaiah as a whole. The phrase **that have rebelled against me** (*happōšᵉʿîm bî*) recalls 'but they have rebelled against me' (*wᵉhēm pāšᵉʿû bî*) in the very first oracle of the book (1 : 2). If this is the case it is evident that the author was possessed by a polemical passion which made him determined that the book should not end on a universalistic note. (The synagogue later reacted in a very different way, ordering that at public readings of the book verse 23 should be repeated after verse 24 so that the final words should be words of comfort.) The verse is clearly intended as a direct contrast with verse 23. The regular worship at Jerusalem is always to be followed by a procession from the Temple (**And they shall go forth**) to look with satisfaction (*rā'āh bᵉ*) at the dead bodies of those who have not repented of their rebellion against God and for whom there has been no forgiveness. **for their worm shall not die, their fire shall not be quenched:** this is probably an early description of eternal punishment: though dead, the rebels will continue to suffer for ever. Sir 7 : 17, Jdt. 16 : 17, and Mk 9 : 48 took their inspiration from here, and the imagery also became a feature of the apocalyptic literature. The place envisaged is the Valley of Hinnom (from which is derived the *NT* Gehenna) at the foot of Mount Zion, which had acquired a gruesome reputation from the fact that human sacrifice was offered there during the period of the monarchy (2 Kg. 23 : 10; Jer. 7 : 31; 32 : 35). According to rabbinic sources it later became the city's rubbish dump, and unclean corpses to which proper burial was denied were also deposited there to be burned or to be left to decompose. It is no doubt this scene which inspired the double image of ever-burning fires and continuous decomposition.

INDEX OF AUTHORS

(See also Select Bibliography)

GENERAL INDEX

Elam, 22
Elephantine Papyri, 142
Eleusinian mysteries, 288
Elijah, 124, 177, 240
Elisha, 240
El(s), 55, 203
Enuma Eliš, 54
Ephah, 232
eschatological hymn (song) of praise, 77, 102, 106, 134, 166, 245, 285
eschatology, 30–1, 42, 77, 274, 279, 288, 290
Ethiopia, 83, 109
eunuchs, 198
Euphrates, 87
Eve, 286
Exile, Babylonian, *passim*
Exodus, 31, 34, 50, 52, 59, 78, 79, 89, 104, 126, 130, 134, 141, 150, 159, 168, 230, 257, 259, 262
Exodus, book of, 183, 259
Ezekiel, 23, 24, 25, 29, 72, 92, 128, 129, 130, 142, 148, 164, 175, 183, 187, 203, 209, 235, 269, 289
Ezra, 197, 256

fasting, 212, 213, 214, 215, 216, 218
Flood, 186, 187, 277
form-criticism, 25–6, 27, 43
former things, 68, 76, 77, 88, 116, 126, 127, 128, 275, 276
funeral-song, 118

Gad, 273
Genesis, book of, 186, 187, 277
Gerichtsrede, 30
gō'ēl, 65, 82
Greeks, 291
Gudea, 144

Hagar, 146
Haggai, 280
Haggai, book of, 230
Hasmoneans, 38
Hazor, 95
heavenly bodies, 37, 57, 125
heavenly book, 270–1
heavenly council, 33, 48, 71
Heilsankündigung, 66
Heilsorakel, 62–3, 66
Hephzibah, 248
Herodotus, 105, 290
highway, miraculous, 31, 50, 208, 251
Hinnom, 203, 294
ḥippāzôn, 168
Horace, 101
Hosea, 23, 25, 148, 212
hymns of praise, 29, 34, 56, 74, 77, 87, 102, 103, 106, 133–4, 142, 166, 167, 184, 259

idolatry, 36, 55–6, 62, 96, 98, 99, 100, 102, 110, 113, 114, 115, 126, 128, 200, 202, 203, 204, 206, 207, 208, 209, 224, 267–8
incubation, 269–70
India, 23
Isaiah, 20, 23, 26, 35, 48, 60, 65, 151, 166
Israel, *passim*

Jachin, 237
Jacob, 93, 184, 260
Javan, 290, 291
Jehu, 147
Jeremiah, 23, 24, 25, 33, 35, 71, 112, 136, 148, 151, 175, 176, 187, 203, 269, 292
Jericho, 273
Jerusalem, *passim*
Jeshurun, 94
Job, book of, 222
John the Baptist, 155
Josiah, 203
Jubilee, 241
Judah, *passim*
judgment in the gate, 60

Kedar, 78, 233
ḳînāh-metre, 119
ḳiḇᵉlayim, 49–50

Lachish, 269
Lagash, 144